Lawyering Skills and the Legal Process

Lawyering Skills and the Legal Process

Caroline Maughan

Senior Lecturer in Law, University of the West of England

Julian Webb

Principal Lecturer in Law, Head of the Graduate School of Law,
University of the West of England

with illustrations by

Ron Tocknell

Butterworths
London, Dublin, Edinburgh
1995

United Kingdom	Butterworths, a Division of Reed Elsevier (UK) Ltd, Halsbury House, 35 Chancery Lane, LONDON WC2A 1EL and 4 Hill Street, EDINBURGH EH2 3JZ
Australia	Butterworths, SYDNEY, MELBOURNE, BRISBANE, ADELAIDE, PERTH, CANBERRA and HOBART
Canada	Butterworths Canada Ltd, TORONTO and VANCOUVER
Ireland	Butterworth (Ireland) Ltd, DUBLIN
Malaysia	Malayan Law Journal Sdn Bhd, KUALA LUMPUR
New Zealand	Butterworths of New Zealand Ltd, WELLINGTON and AUCKLAND
Puerto Rico	Butterworth of Puerto Rico, Inc, SAN JUAN
Singapore	Reed Elsevier (Singapore) Pte Ltd, SINGAPORE
South Africa	Butterworths Publishers (Pty) Ltd, DURBAN
USA	Butterworth Legal Publishers, CARLSBAD, California and SALEM, New Hampshire

A CIP Catalogue record for this book is available from the British Library.

ISBN   0 406 04466 X

Typeset by B & J Whitcombe, Nr Diss, Norfolk, IP22 2LP
Printed in England by Clays Ltd, St Ives Plc

Preface

Most academic law courses do not go beyond the study of law in the abstract. In other words, they deal with problems, not people. Lawyers in practice, on the other hand, cannot separate the problem from the person. They have to develop a broad range of skills to deal with all sorts of issues, both legal and non-legal. Technical knowledge of law and procedure alone will not enable the professional lawyer to do this competently.

This book is an attempt to bridge the gap between academic and practical law. Its purpose is not to turn you the reader into a practitioner, but to enable you to experience and reflect critically on the problems and uncertainties of 'real' law, from the point of view of both lawyers and their clients. It is reflection and critique which we believe distinguishes our 'academic' approach from the more functional emphasis of the vocational courses, though we share with the vocational courses (and any undergraduate skills-based course for that matter) a belief that learning has to be grounded in *doing*. Skills are not acquired passively, but actively by experimentation. Please do not skip the Introduction which follows, as we talk quite extensively there about the assumptions and expectations about learning which we make.

The materials in this book are based on our teaching of second and third year LLB students at the University of the West of England. Though we have written the book primarily for students at these stages in their legal education, we envisage that aspects of the book will be applicable to students on a range of undergraduate skills and clinical modules from first to final year. More optimistically, we would like to think that it could be useful on professional courses for students who want to think beyond the technical aspects of skills acquisition.

We welcome (constructive!) criticism and evaluation, and would be pleased to hear from any students or teachers who want to tell us about their experiences in using this book, or to suggest ways in which we could improve upon it.

Caroline Maughan

Julian Webb

August 1995

Acknowledgments

We have been assisted in putting this book together by an embarrassingly large number of people, some of whom would quite likely prefer to remain anonymous. We won't let them.

Our greatest debt is to Mike Maughan who has had an input into virtually everything we have written.

A large number of colleagues across the country have helped, either by allowing us to plunder their ideas or by reading chunks of our text. In this category we wish to thank Ed Cape, Steve Dinning, Domenica Fazio, John Flood, Philip Jones, Marcus Keppel Palmer, Maurice Moore, Donald Nicolson, Margaret Rogers, Leslie Sheinman, Avrom Sherr and Hilary Sommerlad. A special 'thank you' is also owed to Diana Tribe, whose own work was instrumental in getting us started, and many of whose ideas we borrowed shamelessly when setting up the Legal Process course at UWE.

More formally, we must acknowledge the following for allowing us to reproduce copyright material: the *Guardian* for permission to reproduce the article by Francis Wheen in Chapter 7; British Telecommunications plc and Hilary Jordan, (the author of their Plain English Conditions for Telephone Service) for permission to reprint the old and new versions of the Conditions in Chapter 8 and the Appendix respectively.

Finally, our thanks to Ron Tocknell who has illustrated our ideas so brilliantly.

Contents

Contents

3 Problem-solving: (i) the practical dimensions 35

Introduction

If this book has a single theme it is that being a skilled lawyer means much more than acquiring the capacity to manipulate legal rules. It means having the ability to deal with people and their problems as a competent, ethical and socially responsible lawyer.[1] We feel that this requires that skills are developed in a reflective and critical environment, through a combination of what we call 'skills' and 'process' learning.

The main skills we explore are the classic lawyering or DRAIN skills – Drafting (and its underlying writing skills), Research (which we widen into a concept we call problem-solving), Advocacy, Interviewing and Negotiation. You will be expected to develop those skills by practising, by analysing your practice, and then practising some more. At this level we hope you will gain some real insights into the 'what' and the 'how' of law in action.

The 'process' dimension takes us more deeply into the 'why' of lawyering. We shall ask you to draw on your experiences of the course and to reflect on our discussions of the practice of law, together with psychological, sociological, linguistic and management research which sheds light on what really happens in the law office and the courtroom. Through this, we hope you will be able to stand back from the skills and think about lawyering as something that is socially and culturally constructed. The lawyer plays an important role as a 'gatekeeper to legal institutions and facilitator of a wide range of personal and economic transactions'.[2] How we choose to play that role, and with what consequences for ourselves and our clients are two of the most central questions about law in society. It seems extraordinary to us that legal education frequently fails to address either of them in any depth, if at all. We hope that thinking about the lawyer's role will help you determine how you will deploy the skills at your disposal.

1   Cf G S Laser 'Educating for Professional Competence in the Twenty-First Century: Educational Reform at Chicago–Kent College of Law' (1993) 68 *Chicago–Kent Law Review* 243. We discuss this notion of lawyering further in Chapter 1.
2   W Felsteiner, R Abel & A Sarat 'The Emergence and Transformation of Disputes: Naming, Blaming, Claiming' (1981) 15 *Law & Society Review* 631 at 645; also J McCahery & S Picciotto 'Creative Lawyering and Business Regulation' in Y Dezalay & D Sugarman *Professional Competition and Professional Power: Lawyers, Accountants and the Social Construction of Markets*, Routledge, London & New York 1995, p 238 at 240–1.

The aims of this book

These are:
- To encourage you to develop –
    (1) a range of practical legal skills:
        -   case preparation and management;
        -   legal research;
        -   client interviewing and counselling;
        -   writing and drafting;
        -   negotiating;
        -   advocacy.
    (2) a range of general intellectual and interpersonal skills:
        -   problem-solving;
        -   oral communication;
        -   written communication;
        -   team working;
        -   reflection and conceptualisation;
        -   self-assessment;
        -   peer evaluation.
- To increase your capacity for independent and reflective learning.
- To encourage a critical awareness of
    -   the impact of legal procedures on the lawyer and other participants in the legal process;
    -   the importance of a client-centred approach to legal practice;
    -   the conflicts of interest (and self-interest) that arise in legal practice.

How to use this book[1]

Tutors can use it either as a course workbook, or as a flexible resource from which to select and adapt materials. We developed most of what this book contains in the context of an LLB course we call 'Legal Process'. This is a skills based programme constructed around simulated case studies in the civil and criminal law. We team-teach our materials in a series of three-hour workshops, running across a full academic year. We do not teach everything in the book every year. To work through all these materials in this way would certainly take us more than one academic year! With some care it is possible to pick and choose materials rather than follow everything to the letter. Many of the exercises can be undertaken by students working outside formal class contact. We suspect the materials as presented might also lend themselves well to a series of more discrete skills modules (eg on interviewing, trial advocacy, etc), though we have not used them in this way.

We have stuck with a fairly standard structure for each chapter. The format is as follows.

---

1 We have also produced a short *Teachers' Guide* to accompany this text. It is available from the authors, though regrettably we have to charge the cost of postage.

1. Introductory material

Each chapter begins with a brief summary of its contents, followed by a list of broad learning objectives.

2. Presentation of information

This is accompanied by discussion exercises and skills building exercises.

Most materials for the exercises are either incorporated into the text, or in the Appendix. However, in some situations (Exercises 3.7, 5.5, 6.6, 7.5, 9.7 and 10.23) we want students to discover the purpose of the exercise for themselves. Providing instructions in the text would give the game away, so we have incorporated these, with additional materials and commentary, in the *Teachers' Guide*.[1] Teachers might also like to note that there are two exercises which require the use of questionnaire materials from outside this book. Exercise 2.8 relies on the learning styles questionnaire which is produced as part of Honey & Mumford's *Manual of Learning Styles*. Users of the *Manual* can copy the questionnaire for training purposes. Exercise 9.2 relies on a questionnaire published in Johnson & Johnson's *Joining Together* (1991) pp 305–6. The original is rather longer and more detailed then we really need, so we adapt it for our own purposes.

1 This is available from the authors, though regrettably we have to charge for postage.

3. Consolidation and further reflection

At the end of every chapter there is a sequence of exercises:
(a) Concepts. This exercise checks that students have understood the information in the chapter.
(b) Review. This allows students to reflect on and discuss important issues covered in the chapter. Tutors may prefer students to do these exercises after doing some further reading.
(c) Further skills building exercises, where appropriate.
(d) Learning points. In chapters 1, 7, 9 and 10 we have introduced an additional exercise to help students focus on their own needs and abilities in specific skills situations, and to explore how they will adapt certain theoretical constructs for their own use.

Chapters 1 and 2 set out the learning theories this book is based on. We take the view that enabling students to understand the learning process is fundamental to what we are trying to do. If you intend to follow our programme, rather than just use this as a secondary resource book, these chapters must be covered first. Apart from that, we leave issues of coverage to you.[1]

We thought long and hard before adopting footnotes. They are unusual in (English) skills books, particularly in the quantity we have. In the end we felt that they were necessary given the more academic dimensions of our task, and would be less distracting than endnotes or Harvard referencing. We have not distinguished in footnotes between materials tutors might need to follow up more than students, or vice versa. The further reading section at the end of each chapter is designed more with students in mind.

1　We discuss our organising principles and the underlying aims and rationale of each chapter more fully in the *Teachers' Guide*.

How to learn from this book

We base our learning methodology on the experiential learning cycle devised by David Kolb and the methods of reflective practice developed by Donald Schön (see Chapter 2). Learning is based around a large number of practical exercises. By doing these exercises students observe and analyse their own behaviour, thoughts and feelings and those of their fellow-students. This process of reflection enables them to identify what worked well, what did not, and why. They can then experiment with new forms of behaviour at the next opportunity.

This methodology will be unfamiliar to some law teachers,[1] and probably to many law students. It may therefore involve you in a reappraisal of your attitudes to learning and your perceptions of tutor and student roles in the learning process. We therefore hope it will be helpful if we address a number of issues involved in this type of learning.

1　Some accessible discussion of learning methodologies can be found in the following collections: K Raaheim, J Wankowski & J Radford *Helping Students to Learn*, SRHE/Open University Press, Milton Keynes 1991; R Barnett (ed) *Learning to Effect*, SRHE/Open University Press, Milton Keynes 1992; N Gold, K Mackie & W Twining (eds) *Learning Lawyers' Skills*, Butterworths, London 1988; J Webb & C Maughan (eds) *Teaching Lawyers' Skills*, Butterworths, London 1996 (forthcoming).

Do I have to join in?

TO STUDENTS:

Yes, this is essential! Because you are 'learning by doing', you will take a much more active role in class than you may be used to. You will participate actively in the practical exercises, often by role playing. You will give and receive feedback both on your own performances and the performances of other members of the class. Your tutor may video exercises to help you review your performance.

Active learning also means taking responsibility for your learning. This book and your tutor provide much of the learning content, but you are in charge of the process. This means you will analyse your behaviour, thoughts and feelings, experiment actively to change your behaviour, and challenge your personal values and attitudes. We strongly advise that you record your learning process in your own personal learning diary, which (we suggest) need not be read by your tutor unless you think that would help you to learn.

TO TUTORS:

If you are new to skills teaching, the process will be as much a challenge for you as it is for the students. Active learning for students does not mean that teachers can become passive! Preparing for and running skills workshops can be exhausting. At times we ask you to role play, so you will have to learn the role and then act it out. While groups are doing practical exercises, you will probably want to circulate and listen in, to check that your students have got the hang of what they are supposed to be doing. You will also want to note down points to raise in the feedback sessions. You will find you spend a great deal of time summarising on boards, flipcharts and overhead transparencies, sticking flipchart pages on walls, or providing the materials for your groups to do all these things. And don't forget the video! This is an incomparable part of feedback. When we first set up the course we used to spend probably too much time trying to review videos in class. We still use them for demonstration purposes, but have found that it is far more effective to let the students take the videos of their performance away with them for either individual or small group analysis.

Keeping to time can be a major problem. It is important to devote plenty of time to feedback, so as to enable students to reflect on and conceptualise their experiences in the workshops. You may set aside what you think is sufficient time, but find you exceed it, because you do not want to cut off valuable feedback. This still happens to us. We have yet to find any easy solution which does not involve us imposing a strict, and sometimes quite arbitrary, time limit.

Will my tutor tell me everything?

No, definitely not!

TO STUDENTS:

Taking more control over your learning means that your relationship with your tutor may be different from the one you are used to. Your tutor's job is to set up conditions and situations in which you can experiment and improve your skills. Your tutor will want to become redundant as soon as possible, by enabling you to evaluate for yourselves the success or otherwise of your performance.

You will spend a good deal of your time working in groups. This method of working may be new to you. It involves a number of skills. You will have to work out how to allocate responsibility for tasks within the group, and find ways of handling any problems which arise between members of your team.

TO TUTORS:

We can all find it difficult to break long-established habits of didacticism. However, telling students how to perform the skill will not enable them to learn it. Similarly, feedback should not consist of the tutor telling the student how they should have performed. To develop the skill of critical self-assessment, students need to evaluate their own performance before anyone else does it for them. After all, they are the people who are going to have to deal with the problem next time, not you.

How do I reflect on and evaluate my experiences?

Through feedback and your learning diary.

1. FEEDBACK

We think feedback has two functions: (a) it should encourage the performer to reflect on their performance; (b) it should support that reflection and reinforce good practice.

(a) We suggest the following feedback sequence should always be used:

    (i) Start with the student who has performed the exercise. So, for example, in a practice client interview, the 'lawyer' feeds back first.

    (ii) The 'client' responds with views on her feelings and perception on the process.

    (iii) Anyone else actively involved in the exercise.

    (iv) Observers (the student's group or the whole class).

    (v) The tutor.

If you are to encourage reflection you need to start by questioning the performer on their behaviour, and their thoughts and feelings about the performance. We start feedback by using a very general, open, question to get a response from the performer. We then use the performer's responses to focus on specifics. By your questioning you should try to get the performer to recognise their own strengths and weaknesses, without you telling them. Don't give them advice at this stage. For example:

Observer: How do you think the interview went?

Lawyer: OK. I didn't do as well as I hoped: he seemed a rather difficult client.

Observer: What made him 'difficult'? Was there anything in particular which gave you that feeling?

Lawyer: I don't think I established a rapport with him.

Observer: So what could you have done to improve rapport?

Lawyer: Perhaps if I'd made fewer notes, and looked at him more, responded a little more openly, that would have helped.

(b) If you are going to give advice then address specific aspects of performance rather than just giving a general 'I think Jo could have summarised the facts better'. What aspects of recapping could be improved upon, and how? Be prepared to share experiences in this kind of feedback.

Remember, whether you are asking questions, or giving advice, or reflecting on your performance: feedback needs to be focused, constructive and honest. Performers and observers should try and avoid feedback that sinks to the level of banality. Observers should not offer destructive or 'negative' feedback. It can damage a performer's confidence, and encourages them to be defensive, rather than open, about their practice.

2. THE LEARNING DIARY

To students:

You should make an entry in your learning diary after you have had a few hours to think about your behaviour, thoughts and feelings during the exercise and the feedback session immediately afterwards. Wherever possible, however, you should make contemporaneous notes about your performance, your feelings and the feedback you gave and received. Use these to help construct your learning diary entries. Try and avoid writing up entries purely from memory – it can be misleading.

To tutors:

If you adopt our methodology learning diaries play an important part. We recognise that there is a long-standing debate over whether tutors should even review, never mind assess, student diaries. For what it is worth, our position is that review is useful, but should be a consensual aspect of the course rather than a formal requirement. The student diaries are personal and may include much confidential material. We suggest you don't include them in your assessment of students for that reason. There is also a problem of determining what you would be assessing: the student's performance, their reflection and evaluation of it, or their ability to write an experiential learning diary?

You may also find it useful to keep a diary to record your own learning, particularly if you are not experienced skills tutors. We have found it both a salutary experience, and a hard discipline to maintain.

Will I enjoy it?

We hope so. Our own experience is that learning skills can be stressful, frustrating, infuriating . . . and more fun than you ever thought studying could be – but only if you are prepared to get involved and make it work!

The descent into the swamp

1 Descent into the swamp

In this chapter we explore the concepts of legal professional knowledge and the art of lawyering. To resolve the problems of uncertainty, uniqueness and value conflict which are the reality of legal practice (the 'swamp'), legal practitioners use their artistry: a combination of tacit knowledge, technical knowledge of the law, and practical skills. The aim of this book is to help you to develop your artistry before you hit the swamp.

Objectives

To:
- Identify and discuss the separation of theory and practice in traditional legal education.
- Examine and evaluate definitions of legal professional knowledge and recognise the importance of tacit knowledge.
- Examine the nature of 'artistry' in legal practice and its use in non-routine problem solving.
- Consider the lawyer's social responsibility.
- Enable students to discover and reflect on concepts and principles introduced in this chapter.

A dinosaur snack?

In Stephen Spielberg's film *Jurassic Park* a lawyer abandons two children threatened by a tyrannosaurus rex to dash to the lavatory. The dinosaur demolishes the hut housing the lavatory, picks up the lawyer sitting on it, tosses him about playfully and eats him. The audience is delighted; he has got what he deserves.

The public's perception of lawyers as 'dishonest, arrogant, greedy, venal, amoral, ruthless buckets of toxic slime'[1] is reflected in the present plethora of anti-lawyer jokes. It is a perception which is a matter of concern to many of the professionals themselves. In *Educating the Reflective Practitioner*[2] Donald Schön offers this proposition: that within the last twenty years or so we have come to face a public crisis of confidence in professional knowledge, which has challenged the legitimacy and status of the professions and has led to a similar crisis of confidence in professional education. Schön is writing about professional knowledge and education generally in the USA, but his argument may help to explain the relatively low esteem in which the legal profession is held[3] and the dissatisfaction voiced against our system of legal education.[4] The dialogue in the following exercise should help you to enter the debate.

1   James D Gordon III 'How Not To Succeed in Law School' (1991) 100 *Yale Law Journal* 1679 at p 1680.
2   Jossey-Bass, San Francisco 1987.
3   See, for example, sources cited later in this chapter and in Chapter 5.
4   For example, the Lord Chancellor's Advisory Committee on Legal Education and Conduct has recently criticised the present subject-based approach of much law teaching for leading:

> students, and perhaps some teachers, to see the aim of the process as being one of *training*, through mastery of a body of knowledge (often at low levels of rigour), rather than of *education*, understanding the discipline of law and its associated intellectual and social processes. (*Review of Legal Education: Consultation Paper – The Initial Stage*, ACLEC, London, June 1994, para 3.5.)

> Similarly see W Twining *Blackstone's Tower: The English Law School*, Sweet & Maxwell, London 1994, pp 163–4.

Exercise 1.1   Is there a crisis of confidence in legal professional knowledge?

Imagine that this dialogue takes place in a seminar on the above title (based on some advance reading).

NELSON: *(self-consciously)* I suppose we really ought to start by trying to define what we mean by professional knowledge.

BENAZIR: Boring!

BILL: Maybe definitions are boring, but if we don't define our terms, how can we be sure of interpreting the question properly? At least that's what our tutors always tell us!

BENAZIR: OK, but is there really anything to define? Surely what we mean by knowledge is pretty obvious? Knowledge is knowledge about law and procedures; the kinds of things that people go to lawyers about.

HILARY: So, what you're implying is that if there is a crisis it's because the public have caught us out and found out that a lot of lawyers don't really know the rules and how to use them? Come off it, I don't believe things are that bad, or that simple.

BENAZIR: I'm not sure that does have to follow from what I said, but maybe it isn't so far from the truth either. Look at some of these people who have been wrongly convicted because of mistakes by their original defence lawyers, like Stefan Kiszco and Stephen Miller.[1]

BILL: Right, and just look at the amount of stuff written about the lack of good client relations. Sherr's work on interpersonal skills is one example.[2] Then there are the statistics on complaints. In 1987, for example, out of 13,852 complaints to the SCB, nearly 4,000 were about shoddy work or poor service, and over 3,300 more concerned delay or failure to answer clients' correspondence[3] – and the number of complaints generally has been rising since then.[4] Is *that* evidence of professional conduct?

NELSON: Yes, but Hilary has got a point. Surely what we're seeing is a far more fundamental distrust of lawyers which goes beyond doubts about their technical competence . . .

HILARY: That's what I was getting at. I don't have anything to support this, but it seems to me that we just aren't thought of as an *ethical* profession any more. There always seem to be things in the papers about fraudulent lawyers, and all the fuss about discrimination in training and recruitment lately.[5]

BORIS: There's also still a problem of class perception. The majority of law students and practising lawyers are middle class[6] and see themselves as a professional élite. Large sections of the general public are bound to see them as remote and unapproachable – there are studies that support that view.[7]

HILARY: Remote and unapproachable? Isn't that a rather old-fashioned view of lawyers and their clients? Don't forget that a lot of solicitors' private clients are also going to be from the same sort of better-off background, especially with the decline in legal aid work. And what about all the international, corporate and commercial work? Isn't that still the big money-spinner, despite the slump in the City?

NELSON: This is starting to get a bit more complicated. I have to agree with Bill, but maybe Hilary's right as well, though it's hard to support or deny her argument. There doesn't seem to be the same level of research on City lawyers today that there was surrounding the growth of legal aid practice and law centres in the 1970s, so there isn't the same kind of information about corporate lawyers and their clients . . .

BORIS: I think there's also another reason for suggesting the profession is in crisis. Larson[8] made the point in the 1970s that professionalisation is about creating your own market. It's about developing a sphere of autonomy where the lawyer is the expert, and everyone who wants advice on particular matters has to consult a lawyer. It's a mystification process, disguising, as Dickens said, that 'the one great principle of the English Law is to make business for itself'.[9] But people are starting to see through that one now. The government has wiped out the solicitors' conveyancing monopoly; incredibly the Bar's monopoly over advocacy has gone the same way. It's becoming far more obvious that professionalism is about holding on to power – and money.

BENAZIR: Thank you, Karl Marx!

BORIS: Who?

3

NELSON: So what's your answer, Boris? Do we kill all the lawyers?
BORIS: If only we could – there might be a few more jobs for us, then! Seriously, though, if there is an answer maybe it does lie in the way we define professional knowledge, and what it is that a lawyer needs to be competent. If the public doesn't like our professional image and all the other things we have talked about, then perhaps we need to think about being a good lawyer in terms that are wider than simply being 'good at doing law' in the sense that Benazir meant. The only trouble with that is I'm not sure I want to save the legal profession!
HILARY: You have raised a real issue there, but so far it seems to me that virtually everybody is assuming that it's simply us, the lawyers, who are to blame. It's always us who are playing the con tricks. But haven't *we* also been conned? Aren't we being constantly trained into an image of a profession that doesn't really exist? And don't we tend to assume that we will have the capacity to cope with the job, because that's what we have been trained for? I'm not convinced. At best, we seem to have been indoctrinated with the *idea* of law, but not prepared for the law as a business – and that is what is out there.

I'm not sure I've put this very well, but something I read the other day put me onto this . . . here we are. Sells reports a whole series of studies in the States showing lawyers to be suffering all sorts of psychological stress; one third of all attorneys suffer from depression or abuse alcohol, or do drugs . . . many lawyers report strong feelings of social alienation . . . over sixty per cent of lawyers would not recommend law as a career to their children, and so on.[10]

When I first read this I thought, yeah, but that's America. Then I remembered this thing in *The Lawyer*, which said that the alcohol-related mortality rate in the *English* legal profession was notably above the occupational average – so here we have the President of the Law Society going public on his concern that we're turning into a bunch of alcoholics[11] – I mean, what next? Maybe things aren't as different as we would like to think.
JOHN: I'm not sure I accept your particular example, Hilary, but I think the general idea of a crisis within the profession is a fair one. Our self-image is important. The idea of a lawyer as an ethical professional person is a strong ideal. One reason I want to be a lawyer is because I *do* think I can help people, and I don't care if that sounds corny.
BILL: Come on, get to the point!
JOHN: I am . . . Economic pressures, like competition for conveyancing, like the squeezing of the legal aid budget, are forcing us to be businesspeople first and lawyers second. Dirks has made my point for me when he says that 'efficiency

	and effective costing can best be judged by the number of clients that the firm can *produce* in the working day'.[12] But I want to work with people, not products.
BORIS:	I told you, you should have stayed on the buses!
HILARY:	Leave John alone, he's all right. I've got to thinking along the same lines. Maybe part of the problem is that our idea of being a good lawyer is too narrow: at the academic level it's too intellectual and problem-focused; at the practitioner level it's becoming too efficiency-driven. We *have* forgotten that doing law is about people and their search for justice, and perhaps, when we stop and think about it, we can't handle that any more than the public can.
BENAZIR	Slow down, Hilary, I don't see how that helps us with this idea of professional knowledge . . .

Now answer the following questions.

(a) *What is the evidence put forward by the participants for the view that there is a crisis in the legal profession?*

(b) *On the evidence cited, is it a crisis of professional image or professional knowledge?*

(c) *Is Hilary right to say we have been 'conned'? If so, why? If not, why not?*

(d) *Despite what Benazir says, is there a link between Hilary's views and our notions of professional knowledge?*

1   Kiszco was released 16 years after his conviction for the murder of a young girl. It was discovered that available forensic evidence, which would have shown conclusively that he could not have been the killer, had not been produced at the trial. Miller was one of the Cardiff Three. His conviction for murder was quashed once it became apparent that his confession had been extracted by oppressive questioning. The Court of Appeal in Miller's case was particularly critical of the duty solicitor's failure to intervene during police questioning to protect his client – see *R v Paris, Abdullahi and Miller* (1992) 97 Cr App Rep 99.

2   A Sherr 'Lawyers and Clients: The First Meeting' (1986) 49 *Modern Law Review* 323.

3   *First Annual Report*, Solicitors Complaints Bureau, London 1988.

4   In 1993 the total number of complaints received by the SCB was 19,582 – a 15% increase on 1992. 80% of those complaints concerned inadequate professional service: see *Annual Report 1993*, Solicitors Complaints Bureau, Leamington Spa.

5   For statistical data see D Halpern *Entry Into The Legal Professions*, Research Study No 15, The Law Society, London 1994 pp 78–80.

6   A number of studies suggest that the expansion of legal education since the early 1980s has made little difference to the class composition of law school. Cf P McDonald 'The Class of 81' (1982) 9 *Journal of Law & Society* 267; A Sherr and J Webb 'Law Students, the External Market and Socialisation' (1989) 16 *Journal of Law & Society* 225; D Halpern, op cit, pp 21–2.

7   A Byles & P Morris *Unmet Need: The case of the neighbourhood law centre*, RKP, London 1977; J Jenkins, E Skordaki & C Willis *Public Use and Perception of Solicitors' Services*, Research Study No 1, The Law Society, London 1989. We discuss the latter survey in Chapter 5.

8   *The Rise of Professionalism: A Sociological Analysis*, University of California Press, Berkeley 1977.

9   *Bleak House*, Penguin, Harmondsworth 1971, p 58.

10 See B Sells *The Soul of the Law*, Element Books, Shaftsbury & Rockport, Ma 1994, p 17.

11 *The Lawyer*, 2 August 1994, p 1.

12 J Dirks *Making Legal Aid Pay and Franchising Development*, Sweet & Maxwell, London 1994, p 5.

Exercise 1.2   Redefining knowledge

Boris suggests we rethink our notions of professional knowledge. To stimulate your thoughts on this, imagine you are watching a highly competent advocate cross-examining a witness in the Crown court.

(a) *List the skills and characteristics she is displaying.*
     No doubt your list will include a number of items in addition to excellent knowledge of the relevant law.
(b) *Now consider which items on your list, in your view:*
     (i)   *you can learn from books;*
     (ii) *you can learn on the law degree;*
     (iii) *you can learn on the Legal Practice, or Bar vocational course; and*
     (iv) *which items cannot be taught at all.*

Where the action isn't

This exercise should have helped you discover and define other kinds of knowledge the lawyer needs for successful practice besides technical knowledge of the law. Yet it is this that forms the bulk of most law school curricula. Wesley-Smith points out the dangers of relying on 'knowing the law' as preparation for legal practice:

> Mere acquisition of legal knowledge in law school is of little value to a practitioner because that knowledge (a) can only be a tiny part of the whole (b) can be understood only superficially (c) is easily forgotten or only partially or inaccurately remembered (d) is rarely needed in practice in the form in which it is learned (e) is likely to be quickly outmoded and thus dangerous to rely on and (f) is of little use where new problems arise to be solved.[1]

According to this view, therefore, legal knowledge is of little use in professional problem-solving. Is this true?

1 P Wesley-Smith 'Neither a Trade Nor a Solemn Jugglery: Law as Liberal Education' in R Wacks (ed) *The Future of Legal Education and the Legal Profession in Hong Kong*, 1989, cited in J Macfarlane 'Look Before You Leap: Knowledge and Learning in Legal Skills Education' (1992) 19 *Journal of Law and Society* 293 at p 299.

Exercise 1.3   What's the problem?

Here is a 'problem' question from a first year Contract Law course. Read it and answer the questions that follow.

> Webb Ltd writes to Maughan Ltd: 'We are in the market for 70,000 Flibber bricks at not more than 15p per brick, inclusive of delivery, which must be within 28 days of contract date. Agreement to be on our standard terms.'
> On 1 April Maughan Ltd, which has never dealt with Webb Ltd before,

writes back: 'We have bricks – our price 14p'.

Webb Ltd receives Maughan's note on 2 April and replies: 'Please send bricks' with an accompanying order form which contains their usual terms of business, including the period of delivery as specified in their original letter.

Maughan Ltd sends a confirmation of order form on 5 April which has their usual terms of business on the back. One of these clauses gives Maughan the right unilaterally to change the date of delivery. This letter is unread and filed.

Advise Webb Ltd on their legal position in the following alternative circumstances:

(a) On 10 May Maughan Ltd delivers the required number of bricks and Webb accepts them but then decides to sue for the lateness of delivery.

(b) On 10 May Maughan delivers the required number of bricks but Webb refuses to accept them.

(c) The facts are as in (b) above, but the two companies have contracted many times before.

1. *What are the legal issues you need to determine for your client? (Be brief!)*
2. *Once you have 'solved the problem', will your client go away satisfied? Why/why not?*
3. *What else might the client want to know?*
4. *What things do you need to know about your client in order to represent his interests adequately?*
5. *How would your advice differ if you gave it*
   (a) from the court's point of view, and
   (b) from the client's point of view?

If this were an examination question you would do well to concentrate on Question 1 and ignore the others. In professional practice, however, ALL the questions are relevant.

This is not to say that the knowledge of principles and rules learned at university is without value. It forms part of what is known as the *social knowledge* of the legal profession. That is to say, it represents the body of knowledge that a lawyer needs to share with other members of her profession. It is valuable because it enables the law student or novice practitioner to sort things into categories. *Ah yes! This is a battle of the forms problem: has a contract been made at all, and if so, on whose terms?*

It marks a starting point for the professional to get to grips with any case she takes on. (If this starting point has eluded you because you have forgotten your contract law, please re-read the Wesley-Smith quotation on page 6.)

The danger lies in the assumption that many academic and practising lawyers make, that this social knowledge plus a few 'bolt-on' skills, such as client interviewing and negotiation, is all that needs to be learned. The exercise that you have just done should have demonstrated to you that each case you deal with has an element of routine law about it, but also has aspects which are unique, and which are not taught in the traditional law syllabus, and are not to be found on the library shelves.

Where the action is

Schön has referred to this social knowledge learned at university as the 'high ground' but maintains that the real practice of any profession takes place 'in the swamp'. By this he means that the everyday cases that come before a practitioner, such as that in Exercise 1.3, have an element of the routine about them, but are never as clear-cut as a law school problem might lead us to believe. What are your client's best interests in the situation? How can you assist her to identify and articulate them? What kind of timescale is involved? How much will it all cost? Are you getting the whole story? None of these 'swampy' factors are broached by the law school problem, nor are they susceptible to a technical, high ground solution. Nevertheless, all of them, and many others, are relevant in every case you undertake.

Karl Mackie, too, makes this point when he argues that in professional practice knowledge of the rules is only one of a number of factors involved in making a 'legal' judgment:

> . . . in many other cases, possibly a majority, such a simple analysis is misleading in that it fails to acknowledge the often problematic nature of law, of the behavioural alternatives available within the terms of the law, and the problems of proof, evidence and enforcement in the application of legal rules to behaviour. Legal rules are generally abstract 'essence' statements which are designed to apply to a range of diverse fact-situations by way of prohibition or of mandatory guidance. The problematic nature of legal rules is particularly clear in modern regulatory controls over detailed business practices, although it is also at the heart of the common law. Thus, unfair dismissals are in most instances assessed in terms of whether the company acted 'reasonably' 'in all the circumstances'; what does this standard on its own really tell anyone about guiding behaviour in practice? Similarly ambiguous criteria can be found in many other areas of law from negligence to health and safety legislation or rules regarding certain exclusion clauses in consumer contracts. Added to this core element of obscurity in many legal provisions is the uncertain nature of factual evidence and the interpretation of that evidence in court – what facts are available to support the evidence for one's interpretation of the legal rule? Can they be used in court? What evidence will be put forward by the other party? Will particular aspects of the situation carry special weight with the judicial forum? Will an issue be presented adequately by counsel? And so on. Finally, the enforcement of a law may be erratic, uncertain or unlikely.[1]

On the high ground your legal judgment is circumscribed. The law school academics decide on the nature and constraints of the problem being attempted. These are usually carefully thought out to raise specific points of legal principle for you to grapple with. In the swampy lowlands, on the other hand, you are the one who will have to define the problem for yourself and for your client. How many aspiring lawyers are taught to do that?

> [T]he problems of real world practice do not present themselves to practitioners as well-formed structures. Indeed, they tend not to present themselves as problems at all but as messy, indeterminate situations.[2]

Consider, for example, this comment by Laurence Lee, the solicitor defending eleven-year-old Jon Venables in the James Bulger murder:

> I knew I would have to try to get to the bottom of what went on. I developed a plan. I would go and visit him every week at the home where he was being kept and took along a computer game . . . That's the only way I could ever really take instructions from him . . . It doesn't appear in any textbook, this sort of situation.[3]

The indeterminacy here was not 'legal', but situational. It was not a question of knowing and applying the law, but far more fundamentally, of working out how to get through to the client in the first place.

Schön argues that the high ground problems, although of interest technically, are unimportant to the individual and society at large. The problems of greatest human concern lie in the swamp:

> The practitioner must choose. Shall he remain on the high ground where he can solve relatively unimportant problems according to prevailing standards of rigor, or shall he descend to the swamp of important problems and non-rigorous inquiry?[4]

Some, however, might argue that Schön undervalues high ground technical competence. Without it, would the novice practitioner be able to distinguish what is and what is not routine and unimportant?

1   K Mackie *Lawyers in Business*, Macmillan, London & Basingstoke 1989, pp 95–6.
2   Schön *Educating the Reflective Practitioner*, Jossey-Bass, San Francisco 1987, p 4.
3   *The Guardian*, 25 November 1993, p 2.
4   Ibid, p 3.

The skills of lawyering

How, then, do professionals deal with the indeterminate zone that is the swamp? What other kinds of knowledge besides 'knowing' the law do they use?

Go back now to the list of skills needed for advocacy which you made in Exercise 1.2. Here are some which you might have identified:

COMMUNICATION SKILLS
– listening;
– putting questions which the witness (and the jury) understand;
– the ability to speak clearly;
– using body language appropriate to the jury, judge, witness;
– conveying to the jury your response to a witness's answers through selective summarising, tone of voice, follow-up questions.

ORGANISATIONAL SKILLS
– case preparation and management.

COGNITIVE SKILLS
– assessing a situation;

- reacting quickly and appropriately (thinking on one's feet);
- sorting out the important/relevant from the unimportant/irrelevant ('seeing the wood from the trees').

This practical kind of knowledge is *knowing how*, rather than *knowing what*. It is not learned from books or lectures, but acquired through experience. No manual, for example, could ever teach you to drive. Reading a book does not put you into the position where you have to process as much data as you need to process when you drive. You need to experience the whole act of driving in order to learn how to do it and to improve. This is normally achieved with the aid of an instructor who talks you through performance of the various activities until you are able to carry them out without consciously thinking about them. It is not surprising that this takes time when you consider the amount of data that a driver has to process when driving. He not only has to operate the mechanical functions of the car, but also has to be aware of and respond to the changing environment in which he is driving and at the same time remember and act according to the rules of the road.

Knowing in action

The ability to perform activities automatically, without having consciously to think about what you are doing is known as *tacit*, or *personal* knowledge. Schön calls it *knowing in action*. When you perform the skill you observe a set of rules, but because you do not know what the rules are, you are unable to state them explicitly:

> If I know how to ride a bicycle or how to swim, this does not mean that I can tell how I manage to keep my balance on a bicycle or keep afloat when swimming. I may not have the slightest idea of how I do this or even an entirely wrong or grossly imperfect idea of it, and yet go on cycling or swimming merrily. Nor can it be said that I know how to ride a bicycle or swim and yet do *not* know how to co-ordinate the complex pattern of muscular acts by which I do my cycling or swimming. I both know how to carry out these performances as a whole and also know how to carry out the elementary acts which constitute them, though I cannot tell what these acts are. This is due to the fact that I am only subsidiarily aware of these things, and our subsidiary awareness of a thing *may not suffice to make it identifiable*.[1]

Let's take this concept of knowing in action a little further.

1 M Polanyi *Knowing and Being*, Routledge & Kegan Paul, London 1969, pp 141–2.

Exercise 1.4 When you were a child . . .

All human beings possess the capacity for language. All learn to speak, unless they are prevented from doing so by malfunctioning organs of hearing or speech, or extreme social deprivation. Consider the following questions.

(a) How old were you when you began to speak?
(b) Did someone give you lists of rules to use to help you to speak?

(c)   Did you have formal lessons in the language?
(d)   What kind of knowledge did you use (and still do use) to enable you to produce speech?

As a young child you had the ability to produce utterances spontaneously which you had never heard before, using rules you had not only never been taught, but the existence of which you were unaware. This creative, dynamic power of humans to produce language is probably the most vivid illustration of tacit knowledge in operation because it demonstrates the innate capacity we all have to make and develop rules and theories. You will hear young children make grammatical mistakes in their speech, such as 'He *goed*' for he *went*, or 'I *brang*' for I *brought*. They are experimenting with the past tense rules of English. In the first example the child assumes that *goed* follows the normal rule: add *-ed* to the verb to form the past tense, as in *look-ed, walk-ed*. In the second example she is clearly aware there are exceptions to this rule, but applies the incorrect one, assuming perhaps that *bring* is like *sing*, which has past tense *sang*. The child is very unlikely to have heard these forms from adults, so cannot be said to be copying what she's heard.

The art of lawyering

The kind of improvisation illustrated above is what lawyers do when confronted by the uncertain and unique situations of practice. They search through their repertoire of knowledge and experience, and select, adapt or invent strategies which they try out in the situation. The way the professional integrates her legal knowledge, practical know-how and tacit knowledge to produce competent performance of her tasks forms what Schön calls 'the *art* of practice'. What do we mean by this?

The art of practice reflects a capacity for holistic learning. Artistry is built upon your technical knowledge of law and procedure, your experience of practice and your ability, intuitively, to respond effectively to a new situation. It is not just standardised, textbook, knowledge. Just as you go on to be your own driver, driving quite differently from when you took your test, the professional develops her own highly personalised legal artistry.[1]

The word 'artistry' is potentially misleading, because it can suggest that only some people are capable of developing it; the 'brilliant' advocate, the charismatic politician, the talent shown by Ryan Giggs bursting down the left flank. The example of language learning above should dispel this suggestion. Everyone is capable of developing artistry. It is merely an extension of what we all do already in the swamp of everyday life: we use our *knowing in action* to make perceptions, decisions and judgments spontaneously in unpredictable situations. For example, think of the ways in which parents have to alter their responses to their children's behaviour as the children grow up.

Laser illustrates how the lawyer uses her artistry in situations of uncertainty:

The ways in which the lawyer frames to herself each separate uncertainty in the case and the way in which she balances all of the uncertainties in framing the overall problem or problems of the case to herself are also functions of her artistry. There is artistry in strategising, given the uncertainty of a client's or adversary's case. The lawyer must decide whether the client should admit the weaknesses in her case as a preemptive strike or ignore them in the hope that the other party will not identify them. The lawyer must decide whether to resolve a particular factual uncertainty with or without the aid of discovery. If she chooses discovery, she must implement a discovery plan deciding which discovery devices should she use, and in what order. With a legal uncertainty, such as the likelihood of prevailing on a motion for summary judgment, deciding whether to bring the motion and how to present the issue to the client are also functions of the lawyer's artistry.

There is often much uncertainty in deciding whether to settle or go to trial; some law firms bring in a different team of lawyers to negotiate, for fear that their litigators would resolve the uncertainty in favor of going to trial for the unacceptable reason that litigators like to try cases. There is artistry in evaluating the uncertainty present at trial – for example whether the case is being well received by the judge and jury. Finally, there is artistry in considering the uncertainties of an appeal. The art of lawyering in the face of uncertainty involves the way in which the lawyer selects and formulates the issues, organises them, and chooses the strategy for the case.[2]

The quote from Laser focuses on a particular aspect of artistry: the need to make practical decisions for which the law school leaves you relatively unprepared. This, however, is only one kind of 'swamp' problem anticipated by Schön. A solution may be difficult to determine because a problem forces you – the lawyer – to confront some kind of moral or ethical dilemma. To be a competent practitioner thus requires not only practical artistry, but the ability to develop your own sense of ethics and social responsibility, and to make decisions consistent with those values. This is the issue we now turn to.

1   In their research on the skills needed by trainee solicitors Kim Economides and Jeff Smallcombe provide us with a good example of developing artistry. They identify a composite problem-solving skill which they term 'break-in'. This is the ability to 'get inside' a new subject or problem. It involves the capacity to absorb information quickly and to interpret it accurately and efficiently. Clearly, it is not the kind of skill that is 'taught' in academic training, nor is it one that all trainees in their research had developed, either at all or to the same degree. This suggests that it is an art: a more developed kind of performance than mere technical competence. See Economides & Smallcombe *Preparatory Skills Training for Trainee Solicitors*, Research Study No 7, Law Society, London 1991, p 23.
2   G Laser 'Educating for Professional Competence in the Twenty-First Century: Educational Reform at Chicago-Kent College of Law' (1992) 68 *Chicago-Kent Law Review* 243 at pp 253–4.

The values of lawyering

Exercise 1.5   High ideals

Would you like to help the less fortunate?
Would you like to see liberty and justice for all?
Do you want to vindicate the rights of the oppressed?

If so you should join the Peace Corps. The last thing you should do is attend law school.[1]

In your groups, discuss which professional values you think are fundamental to legal practice.

If you agree with James D Gordon III that promoting justice, equality and morality is the lawyer's social responsibility, you might have listed:
● Striving to ensure that legal services are available to those who cannot afford to pay for them.
● Striving to rid the profession of discrimination on the basis of gender, race, age, sexual orientation, disability.
● Striving to ensure that legal institutions do justice.

Other possibilities are:
● Achieving and maintaining high standards of competence in your dealings with clients.
● Improving the profession. This might entail assisting with the preparation and training of new lawyers.
● The pursuit of financial goals, to underpin the other fundamental values of ensuring a high quality legal service.
● Maintaining the status of the profession in society.

When you have reflected on and discussed these issues, move on to the following exercise.

1 James D Gordon III 'How Not To Succeed in Law School' (1991) 100 *Yale Law Journal* 1679.

Exercise 1.6   Swampy situations?

In small groups, imagine you are discussing the following cases with colleagues in practice. What decisions would you make in each case?

(a) You are members of a small environmental law department in a firm of solicitors. A major chemicals company approaches you to take on its environmental casework. You know that the company has a poor environmental record, and anticipate that it will enlist you not only to defend it in court, but also to advise on pollution control avoidance. At the same time, the company has indicated that if you take on the job, it would be willing to transfer all its other external legal work to your firm. This would give a major boost to your department, and greatly increase its status in the firm (and possibly your own prospects of a partnership).

1. Would you take on the client?
2. Why/why not?

(b) You are an expert in housing law at the Bar. A client and his family are referred to you after they have been evicted from their home by the local council. The details of the case reveal that the grounds for the eviction is the family's persistent racial harassment of their next-door neighbours.

1. *Would you take the case?*
2. *Why/why not?*

We are now back in the swamp. You may find that, when working in a professional environment, notions of social responsibility, personal values and interpretations of the professional code of conduct are in conflict. Even if it's not an internal conflict for you,[1] your superiors or your colleagues may take a different ethical stance on the problem, and these differences may need to be resolved. In the second situation, you might feel that professional ethics (the cab rank rule) require that you take the case, and the reasons for this may well accord with your notion of professional/social responsibility. In one or both of the above situations, however, you – or your colleagues – may find it *morally* unacceptable to act for the clients. Has law school prepared you for this kind of dilemma?

Similarly, what if your objection is not moral, but simply a profound dislike of the client? Technical knowledge alone won't help you here. Again, as with all the unique and unpredictable messes of the swamp, the practitioner needs to use her artistry to resolve such dilemmas.

1   We discuss this in more detail in Chapters 2 and 3.

Learning the art of lawyering

Traditionally, lawyers have acquired the basic values of legal practice and the art of lawyering after graduating, in the swamp of legal practice. It is knowledge picked up as they go along, gained largely from their own experience and that of fellow-professionals. Whether they develop artistry or not is therefore a matter of chance; unfortunately, not all develop it to the same degree.

It is this hit and miss process that has led many to believe that artistry cannot be taught. However, if legal education treats the 'high ground' as isolated from the swampy lowlands, then it is hardly surprising that the novice practitioner flounders. The social knowledge acquired in law school in no way equips her to practise competently.[1] Moreover, the belief that it does must retard the development of artistry, which as we have seen is a holistic learning process, involving the combining of various kinds of knowledge and experience.

The purpose of this book is to provide a framework in which you can begin to develop artistry *before* you enter the swamp. We attempt to put in place a setting in which you can become what Schön calls *reflective practitioners*. You will encounter problems and perform tasks which, as far as possible, simulate the swampy lowlands of practice, containing elements of uniqueness, uncertainty and value conflict.

1   Some teachers of law argue that this is not its purpose, but that might come as a bit of a surprise to some of their students.

Exercise 1.7   Concepts[1]

In this chapter we have discussed a number of concepts. We list the main ones below. The procedure for learning these concepts is as follows:

1. *Divide into pairs.*
2. *Each pair is to*
   (a) *define each concept, noting the page on which it is discussed, and*
   (b) *make sure that both members of the pair understand the meaning of each concept.*
3. *Combine into groups of four. Compare the answers of the two pairs. If there is disagreement, look up the concept and clarify it until all agree on the definition and understand it.*

high ground	*swamp*
knowing in action	*holistic learning*
social knowledge	*personal/tacit knowledge*
legal artistry	*reflective practitioner*

Exercise 1.8   Review questions

1. *How do you think the skill of problem solving differs from the art of problem solving?*
2. *In the light of the discussion so far, how would you define legal professional competence?*
3. (a) *Divide into pairs.*
   (b) *Draw up a list of the competences you think a lawyer in practice should have.*
   (c) *Compare your list with the list in the Marre Committee's Report.*[2]
   (d) *Is there anything you would add to your list or Marre's list? If so, what?*

1 This exercise is taken from D W Johnson & F P Johnson *Joining Together*, Prentice-Hall, Englewood Cliffs, NJ 1991
2 *A Time for Change: Report of the Committee on the Future of the Legal Profession*, General Council of the Bar/The Law Society, London, July 1988, para 12.21.

Exercise 1.9   Learning points

In this chapter we have tried to get you thinking about the philosophy behind this book.

What, if anything, have you learned from this discussion:
(a) *about legal education generally?*
(b) *about your legal education?*
(c) *about yourself?*

If it helps, first make a brief summary of the discussion.

Further reading

Legal Education and Professional Development – An Educational Continuum (The MacCrate Report), American Bar Association, Chicago 1992.

D Schön *Educating the Reflective Practitioner*, Jossey-Bass, San Francisco 1987, Ch 1.

C Stanley 'Training for the Hierarchy? Reflections on the British Experience of Legal Education' (1989) 22 *Law Teacher* 78.

J Macfarlane 'Look Before You Leap: Knowledge and Learning in Legal Skills Education' (1992) 19 *Journal of Law and Society* 293.

C Menkel-Meadow 'Narrowing the Gap by Narrowing the Field: What's Missing from the MacCrate Report – Of Skills, Legal Science and Being a Human Being' (1994) 69 *Washington Law Review* 593.

W Twining *Blackstone's Tower: The English Law School*, Sweet & Maxwell, London 1994.

2 Learning to live in the swamp

This chapter introduces you to the concept of experiential learning. This demands that you take charge of your own learning and practise critical self-assessment. We will ask you to record your learning in a personal journal and to make an assessment of your preferred learning style. Experiential learning processes enable you to develop a flexible repertoire of responses and techniques which you will continuously refine through new experiences and reflection. This is how you acquire artistry.

Objectives

To:
- Examine Schön's concept of reflection.
- Outline behaviourist and cognitive learning theories.
- Explain the principles and techniques of experiential learning.
- Enable you to discover and apply these principles and techniques.
- Examine the concept of discrepant reasoning.
- Discuss and assess techniques for self-assessment, in particular the learning diary and learning styles questionnaire.

What is reflection?

In Chapter 1 we made the following points:
- All aspiring lawyers can learn the art of lawyering.
- It is a form of holistic learning.
- It integrates *knowing* and *doing*.
- 'High ground' learning separates knowing and doing.
- 'High ground' learning alone will not enable competent practice.
- Artistry means using your *knowing in action*.

However, in the examples we gave – swimming, riding a bike, producing speech – it was clear that it is not possible to describe the processes involved in the performance of these skills because we are not aware of what is going on. Likewise, ask an experienced advocate why she put a particular question in cross-examination, and she may find it difficult to give you a rational explanation. 'Intuition', or 'Just a hunch', she might reply. Our *knowing in action* is spontaneous, and we rely on it to get us through the routine tasks of the day, which for an experienced advocate will include cross-examining a witness in court.

"Actually, now you mention it . . . that's a damn good question"

But what happens when we are faced with a situation which is not routine?

Exercise 2.1   To smoke or not to smoke?

Students divide into pairs. One plays the role of the Boss (Jane/John). One plays the role of the Smoker (Paul/Pauline).

Allow the players 15–20 minutes to prepare their roles. The interview should last 10–15 minutes. Each pair then feeds back to the group.

FEEDBACK

(a)   *Ask both role players:*
      What was the outcome? Did the interview go as you had planned? Did you get what you wanted? If not, why not?
      What were the key stages in the interview? How were you feeling at each key stage? What was going through your mind?
(b)   *Ask the boss:*
      Where, if at all, did you find it difficult to go on/lose control of the interview? How did you feel when this happened? How did you handle it?

The process of reflection you have just gone through in this exercise should have brought your tacit knowledge to the surface and articulated it. What you were doing in the situation was what we all do in unpredictable situations: frame the problem, and improvise to find a solution – during the action, on the spot. Donald Schön calls this type of analysis *Reflection in Action*. Reflection after the event, in this case during feedback, he calls *Reflection on Action*. In both situations you hold a 'reflective conversation' with yourself, a kind of internal dialogue.

Let's try this in a 'legal' situation.

Exercise 2.2   An unexpected visit

BACKGROUND

A student plays the role of the lawyer, Jo(e) Evans. The tutor plays the role of the client, Mr/Ms Cross.

The interview takes place in the firm's reception area and should last 10–15 minutes.

Allow the players 10 minutes to prepare their roles.

FEEDBACK

(a) *As the lawyer, describe your thoughts and feelings at the following points in the scenario:*
   (i)   *When the receptionist asks you to come down.*
   (ii) *When the abuse is hurled at you.*

To show you more clearly how the process of reflection can work, here is one possible reflective conversation on Exercise 2.2:

Problem framing:	Oh no! Something's wrong, and no one's here to deal with it. I'm going to have to. Can I stall?
Reflection:	What can I do? I haven't been in this situation before. I could get the file and look through it. That might help me spot the problem and give me time to get my thoughts together.
Problem framing:	*(file not found)* I'll have to see them. See what the problem is. Here goes. Try not to look stupid. Try to keep cool and be helpful.
Problem framing:	They're having a go at me. Why? I hate them. It's not my fault.
Reflection:	I feel really upset. But it's not me, there must be a reason. Nobody behaves like this without a reason, surely. Stay calm and polite. Find out the reason.
Problem framing:	Ah! Now it's getting through. They've got a genuine worry, but I still don't know what to do about it. I can't solve their problem, because I don't know their case. I can't give them a more general idea of what might happen, because I don't know this area of law.
	Why won't they stop shouting at me? I don't like it. What can I do about it? How dare they behave like this? It's uncivilised. I want to be rude back. That would be a way of getting rid of them. It worked that time when that gang of idiots kept pestering us in the pub.
Reflection:	I've got to calm things down and give them some sort of answer. Obviously I can't deal with it.

19

Problem framing: The best thing would be to get hold of Mary Carmichael. I can't do that off my own bat. I'll go and see one of the senior partners. They'll have to do it.

(b)   On reflection, are you happy with the way you dealt with the situation?
(c)   If the situation were to be repeated, what might you do differently?

Experiential learning and the learning cycle

By the time you have answered (c) above, you have gone through several processes of reflection and experimentation which enable you to use your tacit knowledge to solve a problem. Reflection *in* action allows you to improvise on the spot. Reflection *on* action provides you with a description of the process, which you will then add to your repertoire for use in the future.

Although the term 'reflective practitioner' was coined by Schön, the notion that reflection is an essential part of personal and professional development has a long history in educational theory.

Modern theories about learning fall into two broad categories, with several variants or developments of each. The first group of theories comes under the general title of *behaviourism*. Broadly, this approach says that learning takes place by the learner responding to external stimuli, and altering behaviour according to the type of reinforcement that the stimulus provides. Burning your hand in a fire, for example, would lead you to alter your behaviour so that you avoided contact between fire and your body. This kind of stimulus is known as *negative reinforcement*. There also exists the notion of *positive reinforcement*. This is where a certain kind of behaviour elicits a reward which encourages the learner to emulate that behaviour in order to get more of the reward.[1]

The second approach is the cognitive[2] one which says that human beings not only respond to their environment but actively seek out experience from their surroundings in order to make sense of the world around them. This making sense takes the form of the learner formulating and memorising rules of how to respond, and how to behave autonomously. Child language acquisition, which we discussed in Chapter 1, is a good example. This approach stresses the importance of the personal, subjective interpretation of your past experience, so that your learning is dependent on the integration of experience with reflection, of theory with practice.

Johnson and Johnson use the term *action theories* to denote the rules made in this way:

> All humans need to become competent in taking action and simultaneously reflecting on their action to learn from it. Integrating thought with action requires that we plan our behaviour, engage in it, and then reflect on how effective we were. When we learn a pattern of behavior that deals effectively with a recurrent situation, we tend to repeat it over and over until it functions automatically. Such habitual behavioral patterns are based on theories of action. An *action theory* is a theory as to what actions are needed to achieve a desired consequence in a given situation. All theories have an 'if . . . then . . .' form. An action theory states that in a given situation if we do x, then y will result. Our theories of action are

normative. They state what we ought to do if we wish to achieve certain results. Examples of action theories can be found in almost everything we do. If we smile and say hello, then others will return our smile and greeting. If we apologise, then the other person will excuse us. If we steal, then we will be punished. If a person shoves us, then we should shove back. All our behavior is based on theories that connect our actions with certain consequences. In essence we build an action theory. As our behavior becomes habitual and automatic our action theories become tacit (we are not able to put them into words). When our behavior becomes ineffective, we become aware of our action theories and modify them.

As children we are taught action theories by parents and other socialising agents. As we grow older we learn how to modify our action theories and develop new ones. We learn to try and anticipate what actions will lead to what consequences, to try out and experiment with new behaviors, to experience the consequences, and then to reflect on our experiences to determine whether our action theory is valid or needs modification.[3]

The authors go on to define the cognitive-based theory of *experiential learning*:

. . . *Experiential learning* may be defined as generating an action theory from your own experiences and then continually modifying it to improve your effectiveness. The purpose of experiential learning is to affect the learner in three ways: (1) the learner's cognitive structures are altered, (2) the learner's attitudes are modified, and (3) the learner's repertoire of behavioral skills is expanded. These three elements are interconnected and change as a whole, not as separate parts.[4]

The experiential approach is characterised by a model of learning known as the *learning cycle*:[5]

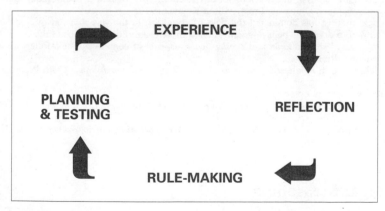

Learning is a sequential four-stage process:

EXPERIENCE   You experience an event, or problem. It unsettles you, excites you, perplexes you.

REFLECTION   In order to make sense of it, you examine and analyse both the experience and your feelings and attitudes towards it.

RULE-MAKING   Out of this reflection come new meaning and perspectives,

21

new ideas about how things work. You formulate rules (action theories) about what constitutes appropriate behaviour in similar situations.

PLANNING AND TESTING   These rules provide the basis for experimentation. At the next opportunity you modify your behaviour, in order to test whether your new action theories will give you the outcome you would prefer.

These action theories then become the basis of future behaviour, and so the cycle begins again. When an appropriate event next occurs, you put your plan into action and continue through the cycle, refining your behaviour and revising your action theories in the light of your reflection, until you are satisfied.

The notion of the learning cycle is a very powerful one, because it suggests that pursuit of knowledge for its own sake is insufficient for learning, as is a merely leisurely appraisal of your strengths and weaknesses. Learning and self-development will only take place if there is a challenging, stringent assessment of your own behaviour, thoughts and feelings.

Moreover, experience alone does not constitute learning, because it will not generate any action theories. As Aldous Huxley said:

> . . . experience is not what happens to a man; it is what a man does with what happens to him.[6]

Those of you who drive can probably think of other drivers you have encountered on the road (or narrowly missed) who have not had 20 years' driving experience, but one year's experience 20 times over. Unless we analyse it, we may fail to understand our own behaviour and its impact.

1   A brief and basic explanation of the theories of Pavlov and Skinner can be found in L Mullins *Management and Organisational Behaviour*, Pitman, London 1993, pp 117–21. More detailed description and analysis of behaviourism can be found in J Medcof & J Roth (eds) *Approaches to Psychology*, Open University Press, Milton Keynes 1979.
2   No single theorist has dominated the field of cognition in the way that Pavlov and Skinner have tended to dominate behaviourism. Indeed there is a multiplicity of cognitive approaches. We emphasise here the *social* and *developmental* aspects of cognition. For a fuller discussion see Medcof & Roth, op cit.
3   D W Johnson & F R Johnson *Joining Together: Group Theory and Group Skills*, Prentice Hall, New Jersey 1991, pp 39–40.
4   Johnson & Johnson, op cit, p 40.
5   See D A Kolb *Experiential Learning: Experience as the Source of Learning and Development*, Prentice Hall, New Jersey 1984.
6   *Texts and Pretexts* (1932), in T Augarde (ed) *Oxford Dictionary of Modern Quotations*, Oxford University Press, Oxford 1991, p 109.

Discrepant reasoning

Exercise 2.3   The discrepant solicitor?[1]

Alex, a solicitor, has been working for a large city firm for ten years. Bridget is her principal. Alex has recently been performing well below standard, not for the first time. She has a reputation for 'sloppy' client care: she is late with correspondence, and a couple of clients have complained about arrogance. Also, over the last quarter, she has been submitting fewer billable hours than the firm would expect. Bridget has been assigned to talk to Alex, in order to help her improve performance. Bridget's view is that the firm wants to keep Alex in the job, but that this is the final warning. If there is no improvement, unpleasant but appropriate action will have to be taken.

The following is a transcript of some of the things Bridget said to Alex. These statements represent the whole range of meaning that Bridget communicated to Alex.

> 'Alex, your performance is not up to standard and, what's more, you seem to be carrying a chip on your shoulder. It seems to me that this has affected your performance in a number of ways. I have heard words like *sloppy*, *uncommitted*, *disinterested* used by others in describing your recent performance. Our people cannot have those characteristics.
>
> Let's discuss your feelings about your performance, Alex. I know that you want to talk about the injustices you feel have been perpetrated against you in the past. The problem is that I am not familiar with the specifics of those problems. I don't want to spend a lot of time discussing things that happened several years ago. Nothing constructive will come of it. It's behind us. I want to talk about you today, and about your future in the firm.'

(a)   Write an analysis and critique of the way Bridget dealt with the problem.
(b)   What recommendations would you give to Bridget to make her performance more effective?

You are a colleague of Bridget's. Imagine that Bridget comes to you and asks: 'How well do you think I dealt with Alex?' What would you tell her? You are to assume that Bridget's purpose in coming to you is to learn.

(c)   You have ten minutes' preparation time. Make a note of what you will say to Bridget. Note down any thoughts or feelings which, for whatever reason, you will not communicate to her.
(d)   In pairs, take turns at role playing the conversation between Bridget and her colleague.
(e)   Feed back to each other and the group.

Self-development is not just a question of formulating new rules or action theories to shape future behaviour. It also involves modifying or even eliminating old ideas and attitudes which have outlived their usefulness. This is not easy, since many of our attitudes and beliefs stem from our cultural backgrounds and our value systems as well as our past experience. They are deeply ingrained and powerful. They may therefore continue to shape our behaviour even though we are prepared to accept and try out new ideas.

Argyris and Schön[2] describe two kinds of action theories:

- *Espoused theories*, which are what we say we believe in. In other words, we use these to justify our behaviour. Here is a familiar scenario: 'the tutors are always telling us how important it is in exams to answer the question rather than write all we know about the subject. I ignore that at my peril, because if I write all I know about the subject, I'll lose marks for irrelevance.'
- *Theories-in-use*, which are implicit in what we actually do, and so are usually tacit. They often conflict with our espoused theory. If we take our example further, the speaker, going against her espoused theory, writes

everything she knows about the subject in the exam. She may be unaware of this, or if she realises she has done so, cannot explain her behaviour.

1   Adapted from C Argyris *Reasoning, Learning and Action*, Jossey-Bass, San Francisco 1989, pp 28–9, and D Schön *Educating the Reflective Practitioner*, Jossey-Bass, San Francisco 1987, pp 260–1.
2   *Theory in Practice: Increasing Professional Effectiveness*, Jossey-Bass, San Francisco 1974, and *Organisational Learning*, Addison-Wesley, Reading, Mass 1978.

Exercise 2.4   Write all I know about . . .

In your groups, consider which values and assumptions you think underpin this particular theory-in-use.

In your reflective conversations, then, you deconstruct your theories-in-use to learn about and challenge the values and assumptions that shape your behaviour, and other people's. Argyris and Schön call this *double loop* learning. On the other hand, failure to confront the validity or otherwise of your theories-in-use restricts your learning to *single loop*; you are defensive about your actions and this closes your mind to new ideas and change. As Argyris says:

> Individuals or organisations who achieve their intentions or correct an error without reexamining their underlying values may be said to be single loop learning.[1]

Furthermore:

> We strive to organise our individual and organisational lives by decomposing them into single loop problems because these are easier to solve and to monitor.[2]

As we saw in Chapter 1, the swamp is crawling with double loop issues. Imagine, for example, that a client goes to see a solicitor about a divorce. She wants to take her husband 'to the cleaner's' and stop him seeing the children. This particular lawyer, on the basis of his experience and reflection, firmly believes that disputes like this have better outcomes if resolved through mediation. This is his espoused theory. His client, on the other hand, is adopting an adversarial position. The lawyer's suggestion that she consider mediation therefore falls on deaf ears. She is looking for confrontation.

How is the lawyer going to resolve the conflict between his espoused theory and what the client wants him to do?

If the lawyer decides to go along with the client's wishes, how might he justify going against his espoused theory?

His internal conversation might go something like this: 'Let's look at this coolly, objectively and rationally. The client isn't interested in a mutually acceptable compromise. This is a win-lose situation. My duty is to do what the client wants. My own feelings about it are immaterial. Moreover, if I insist too strongly on getting my own way, she'll probably get herself another lawyer and the firm will lose the business. Anyway, who knows, she's probably right about her situation. A fight may well be the best thing in this instance.'

1   C Argyris *Reasoning, Learning and Action*, Jossey-Bass, San Francisco 1989, pp xi–xii.
2   Ibid, p xii.

Distancing and disconnectedness

Studies done by Argyris and Schön[1] give us information on how discrepant reasoning works. They distinguish two reasoning processes: *distancing* and *disconnectedness*.

DISTANCING means that, consciously or unconsciously, we find reasons not to follow our espoused theory. In our example, the lawyer uses three typical ways of distancing himself from responsibility for following his espoused theory:

1. He objectifies the issue: 'Let's look at this objectively and rationally . . . My own feelings are immaterial.'
   Although his espoused theory is based on his experience, reflection and personal value system about acceptable outcomes, he is trying to persuade himself that there is an objective reality about the situation which can be arrived at through a depersonalised reasoning process.
2. He claims to follow a 'greater good' argument by saying that there are commercial imperatives which overshadow his personal beliefs and preferences: '. . . she'll probably get herself another lawyer and the firm will lose the business'.
3. He seeks refuge in the safety of professional ethics. In denying the validity of his own feelings about the matter he is falling back on the principle that a lawyer has a duty to do what the client wishes, provided that this is not illegal or unethical: '. . . My duty is to do what the client wants.'

This use of the norms and values of a group or organisation to which we belong, in order to avoid following our espoused theory, is common in the distancing process.

Alternatively, we may make a deliberate decision not to follow our espoused theory: 'My career is more important to me than rocking the boat'; or 'I've got such a heavy caseload that I haven't got the time or energy to justify recommending mediation to the client or justifying it to the senior partner.'

DISCONNECTEDNESS occurs where you are unsure or unconfident about your own reasoning processes. In our example the lawyer's final remark in his internal conversation appeared to doubt the universal validity of his espoused theory: '. . . she's probably right about her situation'. Often a person's disconnectedness may arise from their unwillingness to challenge the norms and values of a group, membership of which is valued by the individual.[2] This is particularly likely to be the case with members of a profession like law which has powerful socialisation processes. The traditions, ethics and prestige of the profession all combine to discourage individuals from challenging its norms and values. The long-standing resistance of many barristers and judges to fusion is a good example.

You may also find it difficult or impossible to reason in a frame-breaking way because you are not sure what theory you espouse: 'I'm not altogether happy with this system, but it's been operating for 20 years, so there must be some good in it.' Or you might keep changing your mind about it: 'Normally I would say we should stick to the rule, but in this case I'm prepared to make an exception.'

We fall prey to these processes of distancing and disconnectedness fairly frequently. We are not usually aware that they are happening because they are such automatic responses to difficult or threatening situations. However, not identifying and analysing them inhibits double loop learning and so prevents us developing our artistry.

1   See above, Exercise 2.3, note 1.
2   K Lewin, *Resolving Social Conflicts: Selected Papers on Group Dynamics* (1948), cited in Johnson & Johnson, *Joining Together: Group Theory and Group Skills*, Prentice Hall, New Jersey 1991, pp 83–7.

Summary

To summarise the discussion on experiential learning so far:
- Having experiences does not constitute learning.
- Learning is a cyclical process which continues through life.
- The process involves double looping: questioning not only your behaviour, but your values and attitudes too.
- You need to train yourself to recognise when you are distancing or disconnecting yourself from your espoused theories.

The learning diary

Exercise 2.5   Re-cycling

Either: *think back to your reflective conversation in Exercise 2.1*
or: *reflect on some other event/problem/dilemma which is on your mind.*
Then write your reflective conversation in circle form.

This more detailed model might help you:

EXPERIENCE

An event/problem

PLANNING AND TESTING

When a similar event
occurs, I'm going to do . . .
(something different)

REFLECTION

What am I doing?
What did I do?
What was I thinking?
How did I feel?
What would I like to
have done?

RULE-MAKING

Was what I did satisfactory?
If so, why? If not, why not?

Do I need to change my
behaviour/thoughts/feelings?
How?

From the discussions and feedback on these exercises you will doubtless have noticed that some reflections, action theories and feelings may be shared by a number of the group. You will find that the process of sharing in group work and group feedback and discussion will assist your own learning process.

However, you will also have discovered much that is personal to you. Your learning circle for Exercise 2.5, for example, will be quite different from those of your fellow-students. The purpose of Exercise 2.5 is to introduce you to the device of the learning diary, or personal learning log, where you record your reflective conversations with yourself and, if helpful, those with others. This is, of course, your reflection-on-action, and you need to record it as soon as possible after the event.

To guide you into the habit of keeping a log, Honey and Mumford recommend a simple procedure for carrying out steps 2, 3 and 4 of the circle.[1] We summarise it as follows:

2 *Reviewing the experience* Start by thinking back over the experience and selecting a part of it that was significant for you. Write a detailed account of what happened. Don't at this stage put any effort into deciding what you learned.
3 *Concluding from the experience* List the conclusions you have reached as a result of the experience. These are your personal learning points. Don't limit the number and don't worry about the practicality or quality of the points.
4 *Planning the next steps* Decide which learning points you want to use in the future and work out an action plan which covers:
    what you are going to do;
    when you are going to do it.
Spell out your action plan as precisely as possible so that
(a) you are clear what you have to do, and
(b) it is realistic.

Not only is it essential to get into the recording habit quickly, it is also important to keep in mind its purpose. Remember, careful analysis of your behaviour and attitudes during an event won't enable learning to take place. You need to complete the cycle. This means bringing your action theories to the surface, recognising discrepant reasoning, and experimenting with and modifying your behaviour, thoughts and attitudes.

To give you ideas on the sort of material that is usefully entered in learning logs, here is an example.

EXPERIENCE

Today was my assessed negotiation on the civil case.

Up until the day before there really was little to negotiate on, as we had all been caught short over the time. There was much more to do than we appreciated. We were at a pre-action stage but our client did not want to go to court. It was quite interesting thinking about all this later in the week, as on Wednesday morning the settlement between Michael Jackson and a young boy was announced with both sides maintaining their positions. This is what I had wanted to achieve: a settlement with no admission of liability.

My strategy was to avoid an in-depth discussion on liability. I assumed that the other side would readily admit fault and was taken by surprise by how strongly Andy argued about this.

I did plan to start by denying liability but then to concede this quite readily in return for the same from Andy and then discuss quantum.

I was well-prepared for this, as we felt the sum they wanted was realistic and quite near to our own estimation. I had looked at comparators in Kemp & Kemp and was quite happy that the amount we both had in mind was reasonable. How could we go wrong? Easily! I did not foresee what happened and found myself unable to steer the conversation round to what I wanted to discuss. Andy took the lead.

REFLECTION

I should not have made *any assumptions*. We were both extremely (unbelievably) nervous and I wonder if that was why Andy talked and talked? Did nerves make him seem adversarial?

I had to interrupt him as I was feeling increasingly lost and uncomfortable. I remember thinking: he hasn't heard the sound of my voice yet! I almost felt superfluous as I couldn't respond at all. He was listing things outside my agenda. This wasn't what I wanted.

If I had been discussing this with Andy as myself, a student, I would probably have admitted that the evidence was inconclusive and going to court would be an expensive gamble, so how much would be reasonable? I should have done this.

I wish I had decided that if the negotiation didn't move my way, after say 10 minutes, then I should have simply changed the tone completely and effectively stopped the messing about and asked about quantum, simply and directly.

We wasted so much time on the evidence that I felt threatened, in that Andy really wanted to hammer home the question of fault. I wasn't brave enough to leave it to one side. It was difficult to counteract his pugnaciousness. I didn't know how to. It's obvious that much comes with experience. Why was I afraid?

I could have regained the initiative and softened the tone if I had done this. We were suspicious of each other. The atmosphere was not open and trusting. Despite myself I was drawn into a stereotypical confrontation.

RULE-MAKING

I was well prepared on the facts and quantum but my strategy failed. I should not have assumed anything and should been willing to change my plan as the negotiation went on.

I was unable to isolate the real issue and my opening position was not the best. I was in a reactive position and failed to diffuse the atmosphere.

PLANNING AND TESTING

I must not be put off by a negotiator who appears competitive. Although I felt totally flattened I could have turned the discussion by being honest and not reacting to this style in a defensive manner. After all, if a fight was what he wanted then no strategy of mine would achieve a fair settlement or any settlement at all.

Next time I would either interject sooner, or allow the negotiator to run out of steam, ignore (more or less) what was said and start again. I played the game this time. I must not allow myself to be intimidated and must try to stay calm and relaxed.

It was fascinating that Andy also said he felt trapped into a situation he didn't want to be in. It was almost as if we were both in a corner and too proud to come out.

I would certainly handle a negotiation differently and remember that this means agreement – a problem solved! I must re-read the manual on this.

1   P Honey & A Mumford *Using Your Learning Styles*, Honey, Maidenhead 1986, p 26.

Exercise 2.6   More re-cycling

The following diary entry was made after a workshop on fact analysis. This took place in the second week of a Legal Skills and Process course, when the students had just started to work together in small groups.

In your groups, consider these questions:
1. *What is the event or problem which concerns this author?*
2. *Under which heading is this problem identified?*
3. *Is the section headed 'Rule-making' relevant to the author's reflections on the problem?*
4. *What does the author plan to do at the next opportunity?*
5. *If you were recording this event, what would you do that is different? Why?*

EXPERIENCE

We were asked to construct a plausible diagram of an inadequately described road traffic accident as a group effort.

RULE-MAKING

A group task which demonstrated that without a clear common view of the goal much effort is wasted in negotiation. It also demonstrated that without adequate information it is impossible to choose between alternative or multiple scenarios, except by the exercise of assumptions/prejudices which are necessarily idiosyncratic and not always consciously recognised.

REFLECTION

No surprises or enlightenment here but a good opportunity for challenging one's own abilities and self-image. The necessity of working in a group highlights my own lack of patience and a need for restraint when dealing with others. I must accent the positive aspects of each group member and praise their efforts. Survival in the profession, especially during articles, will depend upon co-operation and mutual respect; I must take advantage of the opportunity to practise 'social interaction' and accord each member the respect they feel they deserve.

I can easily mess this up! J (my partner) describes me as having the 'personality of a bulldozer' and I must resist the temptation to push the group in the direction I have chosen. I must practise encouraging and motivating them as individuals through skilled negotiating rather than bullying tactics.

ACTION

Speak softly and leave the big stick behind. Learn to value others and their contributions. Learn to trust others to perform their tasks while giving them what help they ask for.

Do not dominate, do inspire.

We should point out that your learning diary, like all diaries, is confidential. We do not make a habit of analysing your entries in public or asking other students to do so. However, you might find it helpful to discuss an entry with a tutor or another group member if you are not sure that your recording method is enabling you to learn. The purpose of Exercise 2.6 is to show you there are more and less effective ways of recording and to give you an idea of the possible pitfalls.

Student/teacher roles and relationships

By now some of you may be wondering what you have let yourselves in for, choosing a course where it appears you are required to 'let it all hang out', often in public. And you haven't even had a go at client interviewing yet. What is going on? Is all this 'touchy feely' stuff really necessary?

Exercise 2.7   Re-learning

You should now be in a position to reflect on the experiential learning method as we have used it so far in this book.

What comparisons can you make between this method and the more usual method you have experienced in your legal studies? To help stimulate your thoughts, here are some pertinent questions:
- *Is learning active or passive?*
- *What is the relationship between teacher and student?*
- *Who controls the learning process?*
- *What is assessed?*

This type of learning is very different from what most of you are used to. In your law studies the content is usually determined by your tutors and delivered in a formal way, through lectures and seminars. The emphasis is normally on the *outcome* of the teaching provided, ie you are assessed by 'answers' given in assignments and exams. Formal instruction of this kind is so familiar that most of us are comfortable with it. We know what is expected of both teacher and students.

Experiential learning, however, is more concerned with the *process* of learning: hence its emphasis on the analysis of behaviour, thoughts and feelings. It is not only important to practise performing the skill, it is just as important to know what you are feeling when doing it. This can be quite discomfiting, even threatening, for some of us at first, because we naturally feel inhibited in front of people we don't know very well.

It would be so easy if we could pick up skills by sitting there quietly, absorbing information and saying nothing, while the teacher or fellow-students do the talking and make fools of themselves role-playing. Or perhaps we could 'mug up' from a textbook like this one and miss a workshop or two. However, as we have said, you learn a skill by doing it. This means practising and experimenting actively. Others will observe and perhaps comment on your mistakes. Losing some of your self-esteem can be painful.

Furthermore, your tutor is not the expert in control that you are used to, with more or less right answers that you can depend on. Much of what your law lecturer tells you will be new information. In skills-based learning, however, she will be helping you develop and transfer skills you already have to a different context. For example, you may know nothing about the Companies Acts at the start of your company law course. However, all of you know how to ask questions, and spend a good deal of your time asking questions. What you probably won't yet know is how to use your questioning skills effectively in client interviewing, legal negotiation and advocacy.

The skills tutor's task is to design situations in which reflective practice can take place. In this sense she has control of the content, like the law lecturer. However, much of the rest is left up to you. This can be disconcerting at first. We won't give you a set of rules on how to conduct a negotiation, for example. We can help you develop guidelines on how to structure a negotiation, but the context is so unpredictable and open-ended that your guideline could inhibit your reflection in action if you suddenly find yourself in the swamp.

Likewise, we won't tell you afterwards how you should have conducted the negotiation. This is the subject of your reflection, where you discover what works for you and make your own rules through your own learning cycle. You are therefore in control of your learning, whereas our task is to provide the opportunity for you to test, reflect and share your experience with us and the group. This is more valuable than going through the process on your own.

What kind of learner am I?

What formal courses do not take into account is that people have a variety of learning styles. We are all able to use different strategies at different times in the process of learning. Some of you will consider yourselves good at exams, for example, while others will be happier talking in seminars. Most of us have one or two preferred styles, and find difficulty in adapting to ways of learning we find uncomfortable.

Honey and Mumford[1] have identified four styles:
- Activist
- Pragmatist
- Reflector
- Theorist.

Any attempt at self-development must begin with a self-assessment. This should take the form not only of an assessment of needs in relation to *what* should be learnt, but must also take into account *how* it should be learnt in the light of what you know about your own learning style and your other personal strengths and weaknesses.

1   P Honey and A Mumford *The Manual of Learning Styles*, Honey, Maidenhead 1992. David
    Kolb also describes four learning styles: diverger, converger, assimilator, accommodator, op
    cit, pp 61–98.

Exercise 2.8   The learning styles questionnaire

(a)   *Complete Honey and Mumford's questionnaire and plot your answers on the
      graph provided.*
(b)   *Read Honey & Mumford's* Learning Styles – General Descriptions.[1] *How
      accurately do you think the questionnaire results describe your learning style
      preferences?*
(c)   *Exchange your results with a friend and discuss the extent to which your self-
      assessment corresponds with their assessment of your learning style preferences.*
(d)   *What do you think are the strengths and weaknesses of each style?*
(e)   *Which type(s) of learner(s) learn(s) most or least from the following learning
      activities?*
      –   *taking part in games and role-playing exercises;*
      –   *listening to lectures;*
      –   *working in groups;*
      –   *working alone;*
      –   *activities emphasising feelings and emotions;*
      –   *lots of examples to illustrate how things are done;*
      –   *open-ended exercises, such as client interviewing;*
      –   *preparing answers to questions for a seminar;*
      –   *preparing a number of drafts for an essay;*
      –   *being offered systems, theories, checklists;*
      –   *being 'pitchforked' into an activity with no apparent purpose;*
      –   *practising techniques and getting feedback;*
      –   *giving a seminar presentation;*
      –   *brainstorming.*
(d)   *Do you think that your legal education is geared towards a particular learning
      style?*

Exercise 2.8 should have helped you not only to identify your own habits,
likes and dislikes and the reasons for them, but also to draw some more general conclusions:
(a)   the four learning styles correspond to points on the learning circle;
(b)   we tend to prefer a style we are familiar with;
(c)   no one learning style is better than any other;
(d)   some types of learning involve activities appropriate to more than one
      style;
(e)   other types of learning are heavily dominated by one type of activity, so
      that only those learners with the corresponding style will benefit from it.
Identifying learning preferences may not resolve all our learning problems,
but should at least encourage reflection. Most of our students have found it
helpful to discover *why* they don't enjoy or learn from particular learning
activities. Moreover, the questionnaire can provide the starting-point for you
to aim to become an all-round learner, so that all four styles are within your
repertoire. If you are a Theorist/Reflector, for example, you now know you
will need to develop Activist/Pragmatist styles to help you come to terms with

experiential learning techniques.

Look again at the questionnaire items you crossed. These are pointers to what you will need to think about. For instance, if you crossed Question 15: 'I take care over the interpretation of data available to me and avoid jumping to conclusions', you will probably conclude that this is not an advantageous position to adopt when collecting and analysing the facts of your client's industrial accident!

It might help to divide your crossed items into strong and less strong disagreements:
−   this is me most of the time;
−   this is me in some situations, not in others, etc.
Do you tend to jump to conclusions when answering a problem question in an exam as well? Are you prone to making value judgments? If so, what kind, and in what situations?

Careful reflection and analysis will help you develop strategies for improving on your weak points, and pinpoint opportunities for trying them out: at the next seminar on problem analysis, for example. There is plenty of material for your learning diary here.

1   See Honey and Mumford, 1992, op cit.

Exercise 2.9   Concepts

In this chapter we have discussed a number of concepts. We list the main ones below. The procedure for learning these concepts is as follows:

1. *Divide into pairs.*
2. *Each pair is to:*
   (a) *define each concept, noting the page on which it is defined and discussed, and*
   (b) *make sure that both members of the pair understand the meaning of each concept.*
3. *Combine into groups of four. Compare the answers of the two pairs. If there is disagreement, look up the concept and clarify it until all agree on the definition and understand it.*

reflection in action	*reflection on action*
tacit knowledge	*action theory*
espoused theory	*theory-in-use*
discrepant reasoning	
double loop learning	*single loop learning*

Exercise 2.10   Review questions

1   FORMAL AND INFORMAL LEARNING

In your groups, consider:
(a) *What do the following scenarios have in common?*
   −   *a child falling off a bike;*
   −   *an employee receiving instruction on how to work new equipment;*
   −   *a law student listening to a lecture;*

> – *a pupil barrister watching a judge sum up to the jury;*
> – *a young soccer fan watching a match for the first time.*[1]

(b)   *What don't they have in common?*

(c)   *What are the main features of*
  (i)   *formal, and*
  (ii) *informal learning?*

(d)   *It is said that learning is a social process. What does this mean?*

(e)   *What are attitudes, and what purpose do they serve?*

2   EXPERIENTIAL LEARNING

Divide into pairs. Each member of the pair should:

(a)   *briefly describe the characteristics of experiential learning, and then*

(b)   *explain these to her partner, so that she understands them. Illustrate with examples if it will help.*

3   THERE'S A HOLE IN MY BUCKET

In your groups, discuss this statement:

> *Trainers too often assume that learners are empty buckets waiting to be filled up by the training method the trainer favours. The fact that the buckets are different sizes, and/or leak and/or are upside down is conveniently overlooked.*[2]

4   WHEN DID YOU LAST DOUBLE LOOP?

(a)   *Think back to the last time you analysed a legal problem in a seminar. Did you use single or double loop thinking processes?*

(b)   *Do you think judges should use double loop thinking when deciding cases? If so, why? If not, why not?*

5   WHAT HAVE YOU LEARNT FROM THIS CHAPTER THAT IS NEW TO YOU?

1   Adapted from L Mullins, *Management and Organisational Behaviour*, Pitman, London 1993, p 115.
2   P Honey & A Mumford, 1992, op cit, p 1.

Further reading

J Dewey *Experience and Education*, Macmillan, London 1963.

P Honey and A Mumford *Using Your Learning Styles*, Honey, Maidenhead 1986.

P Honey and A Mumford *The Manual of Learning Styles*, Honey, Maidenhead 1992.

D Schön *Educating the Reflective Practitioner* Jossey-Bass, San Francisco 1987, Chapters 2, 10.

3 Problem-solving: (i) the practical dimensions

> This chapter identifies the basic principles of problem-solving and suggests a sophisticated model that you can follow in your own practice. It takes you through the steps of information gathering, theory development, evaluation and implementation, and basic library research. It offers a number of techniques which you can adopt to help in the presentation and understanding of legal and factual material. It also seeks, at various points, to locate problem-solving in both its practice and 'human' contexts.

Objectives

To:
- Outline a structured model for professional problem-solving.
- Enable you to enhance your fact analysis and management skills.
- Encourage you to adopt a creative and reflective approach to problem-solving.
- Introduce you to advanced case management techniques, including the use of outlines and simplified charting.
- Introduce you to the library techniques and resources of practical legal research.
- Introduce the participatory dimension of lawyer–client problem-solving.

Introduction

Problem-solving, it has been said, provides a unifying theme between legal education and legal practice.[1] In this chapter and the chapter following we present a three-dimensional model of legal problem-solving. At the centre of this model are the information management and analytical skills, which constitute the 'practical dimensions' with which this chapter is concerned. We propose a problem-solving technique to assist with these. However, these technical aspects are themselves bounded by both a business and an ethical dimension, which, as we shall find out in Chapter 4, may pull your decision-making in quite contradictory directions.

1 S Nathanson 'Problem Solving in Professional Legal Education' (1989) 7 *Journal of Professional Legal Education* 121.

Problem-solving and legal education

Exercise 3.1   The art and the skill

To start you off we want you to think about two things.

(a)   *What kind of problem-solving do you do in law school?*
(b)   *How do you think this compares with the problem-solving you would do in practice?*

Note down brief answers to each of these questions. We shall offer some pointers of our own in the remainder of this section.

We hope that you spotted straight away the links between these questions and the material in Chapter 1.[1] Thus, you have probably emphasised some or all of the following:

● Much academic law treats facts as unproblematic – whereas, in practice, most matters turn primarily on issues of fact rather than law.[2]
● Indeterminacy in most law school problems is tightly controlled – the parameters of the problem are defined by the subject-matter of the course.
● The focus on appellate decision-making – which is relatively rarely invoked in the routine world of practice.
● Professional problem-solving takes place within a practice framework that is shaped by a variety of commercial and professional pressures which do not exist in the law school.

In sum, if you have thought through the implications of artistry, you may have worked back to a position which recognises, as Laser[3] notes, that legal practice is surrounded by many different kinds of uncertainty. Much of this uncertainty derives from the fact that, as practitioners, we have to make *choices* which have to be constructed, in Schön's terms, *in action* and cannot necessarily be determined from technical-rational knowledge. Indeed, we go so far as to suggest that uncertainty and ambiguity are an inevitable feature of much lawyering.[4] Consequently, we need to develop the research and problem-solving skills that are capable of dealing with that environment.

1   In particular Exercises 1.3 and 1.8.1.
2   See W Twining 'Taking Facts Seriously' (1984) 34 *Journal of Legal Education* 22.
3   G Laser 'Educating for Professional Competence in the Twenty-First Century: Educational Reform at Chicago–Kent College of Law' (1992) 68 *Chicago–Kent Law Review* 243 at pp 253–4, cited in Chapter 1, above.
4   If this sounds dangerously like transposing an academic 'hard cases' view of law to practice, that is not what is intended, as should be apparent as we progress through both this and the following chapter.

The practical dimension – an overview[1]

Legal practice may involve a particular species of problem-solving, but, of course, we engage in other kinds of problem-solving throughout our daily lives. Problem-solving is such a common activity that we tend not to think of much of it in those terms – it is a key feature of our tacit knowledge. The downside to that is that its very tacitness shields it from examination – we tend to act without deep reflection, and many (most?) of us treat our professional problem-solving in much the same way. So, perhaps, if we start by thinking about how we deal with everyday problems, that will help us focus on how we deal with problems in the professional sphere as well.

1   The model we present in this chapter is primarily litigation orientated. Some of the techniques discussed can be used in non-contentious matters, though it is our view that most of the case management techniques discussed in the published literature tend to support litigious far better than non-litigious work.

Exercise 3.2   Problems, problems, problems

In pairs:
(a)   *Each describe an ordinary, everyday, problem you have had to deal with recently (eg, losing your wallet, the car breaking down on the way to college, etc). Try to imagine yourself back into the situation and describe the steps you took to deal with it.*
(b)   *Now, together, review your examples to see if you can identify common steps or stages in your problem-solving processes.*
(c)   *Imagine you had to describe your method of problem-solving to someone who had never had to solve a problem before. See if you can identify a number of general rules or principles that will take them through the process.*

It so happened that, as we were working on this chapter, Caroline had a little incident, which, with a large amount of artistic licence, Julian has developed into the following illustration of Exercise 3.2.

Imagine, if you will, a hot spring day. You have just returned home from the supermarket with a car full of shopping. You switch off the ignition. You go to unlock the front door, return for the remaining bags of shopping, come back to lock the car . . . and find your child has locked it for you, leaving the key in the ignition. The following internal conversation takes place: 'Oh dear, (or words to that effect) no key. I need to go out this afternoon: what am I going to do? Let's just check the windows . . . no, we closed them all. The boot's closed too, and that's self-locking, so there's no way through there. Why do they design cars so you can't get into them? (Kicks car – discrepant reasoning – does not feel any better.) OK, so what are my options? I can sit and wait for a miracle, or I can do something useful. There is a spare key – but Mike's got that with him. I could phone him to see if he's coming home early; alternatively there's the AA, or I suppose I could try the local garage. Perhaps that's not such a good idea. The garage will probably charge me nearly the value of the car to come out here, and we haven't got a Home Start, so the AA won't help either. Looks like it's Mike or nothing . . .'

We have simplified this a little. Often we do not reason things through in quite such a rational or linear fashion, but the processes are still there. In this internal conversation our 'guinea pig' takes the problem through a number of sequential steps. First, *she identifies the situation as a problem* (need to go out – car locked – key in car). She then *assesses the situation* and starts to look for possible solutions (no obvious way in – no spare key to hand – what do I do?).

Now she begins to *identify possible solutions* (AA – garage – Mike) and to *evaluate* each of them, until she finds the solution which she thinks is most likely to work.

You may have used different labels, perhaps even slightly different phasing in your description of problem-solving, but we would anticipate that the ideas are broadly the same. If they are not, stop and reflect on the differences and try to see how and why they have arisen.

Now consider the following:

Mr and Mrs Xenos come to see you for advice. They run a highly successful business as roofing contractors.

Five years ago, a close relative's accountant suggested a tax-saving scheme to them. They were to invest money in a stud farm. Most of the money invested was to be borrowed from a bank. The interest payments to service the borrowing would be tax deductible – hence the tax saving. The scheme was promoted by a public company in which the accountant had a financial interest, though this was not disclosed at the time. They borrowed the money, secured by collateral mortgages on their personal property.

Three years ago, the building industry went into recession. Mr and Mrs Xenos's income from the business fell sharply. At the same time interest rates on the loan rose. They were unable to keep up the payments. The promoter of the investment scheme offered to take over and reschedule the loan. Mr and Mrs Xenos agreed thankfully, particularly as the new loan would be at a lower rate of interest than the old. This loan, like the previous one, was to be secured on their home. The loan agreement is 50 pages long and was drawn up professionally.

Shortly afterwards, your clients fell into arrears again. They sought, unsuccessfully, to get more time to pay and were sued. The case has been settled, on relatively favourable terms, reducing the interest rate and extending the time for repayment of both the arrears and the principal. Mr and Mrs Xenos are still worried that they might have to sell their home to meet the repayments. They have been told by a friend that you are an excellent negotiator, and want you to try to obtain even better terms for repayment.[1]

1   Adapted from a real case used by Margot Costanzo *Problem Solving*, Cavendish, London 1995, pp 96–8.

Exercise 3.3   The accountant, the roofer, his partner and their loan

Using Exercise 3.2 as a guide, list the general principles you think you would apply in solving legal problems, like the Xenos case.

(You might find it helpful again to start by thinking about the specific steps you would take in that case, and then using those as the basis for abstracting your general principles.)

Now compare your list with the following statements, paraphrased from the MacCrate Report.[1] These offer quite detailed descriptions of the steps involved in legal problem-solving. Are there any genuine differences between your list and the Report's? Are those differences due to an oversight (yours or the Report's?), or a reflection of the specific needs of the Xenos case, or both?

- Identifying and diagnosing the problem, including noting the client's situation, goals, supposed and preferred courses of action, financial resources and the timescale for resolution.
- Generating alternative solutions and strategies, noting limitations of the analysis by identifying assumptions, gaps and assertions of little evidential value.
- Developing a plan of action by listing possibilities, ranking them and settling upon (the best) one.
- Implementing the plan, including assessing whether (you) are the appropriate person to do so.
- Keeping the planning process open to new information.

Spelt out like this, perhaps professional problem-solving does not look quite as fearsome a prospect as you thought. A lot of those items are things we would say, intuitively, are important, and we would probably expect that, equally intuitively, we would take the necessary steps. It is at this point, however, that a lack of experience and established methodology can start to let us down, because the scale and complexity of 'swampy' legal problems is something that we are not readily equipped to handle. This argument starts from a psychological premise, termed the principle of 'bounded' or 'limited' rationality.[2] One of us has previously described the problem thus:

> In common with other professional decision-makers we face a basic psychological problem in dealing with (clients' problems). We possess information given by the client about the problem. We also possess certain professional knowledge. But we all suffer from certain limits in our ability to *use* those sets of information. This is primarily because, so psychologists tell us, we have a relatively limited working memory, by comparison with our long-term memory. This lack of memory capacity restricts our information-processing capabilities. It means that we cannot work efficiently, in a relatively short time span, with all we know about a problem. So we develop strategies to deal with this shortcoming. We process the information we receive serially, a piece at a time; we use that data selectively to construct a simplified model of the problem, and then we match that model with our own mental representations of legal problems – a sort of 'pigeon-holing' process. In this way we are able to produce an initial formulation and 'diagnosis' of the problem.
>
> For an experienced professional these processes seem instinctive, but they are techniques we all develop from experience – essentially they are well-developed coping strategies.[3]

But coping strategies need first to be acquired! What we suggest is that a substantial first step is to try to adopt this 'instinctive' approach as a conscious, reflective, methodology. To do so, you need first to recognise that problem-solving involves a four stage reasoning process.

1. GATHERING THE INFORMATION First we have to obtain factual information by whatever methods are appropriate – interview, letter, etc. Once we

have the basic story, information gathering continues in order to refine and (hopefully) strengthen the case.

2. GENERATING WORKING HYPOTHESES   We then retrieve possible legal formulations of the problem from memory. To do this we use basic cues (key words or concepts) generated by the problem to access the knowledge we keep in long-term memory. Where necessary we use research skills to assist in problem formulation.

3. INTERPRETING THE INFORMATION   Judge your information against your hypotheses to see if it confirms, denies, or is irrelevant to each particular hypothesis. Use this process to identify (and help fill) gaps in the evidence and to begin to construct the story you will use in the case.

4. EVALUATING YOUR HYPOTHESES   Assess your data by weighing up the pros and cons for each alternative problem formulation and then choose whichever hypothesis (if any) gives the best fit.[4]

It is this final hypothesis which forms the basis of whatever plan of action we implement for a specific case. Now, let's use these phases as a framework for exploring problem-solving technique.

1   American Bar Association *Legal Education and Professional Development – An Educational Continuum*, ABA, Chicago 1992.
2   A Newell & H Simon *Human Problem Solving*, Prentice-Hall, Englewood Cliffs, NJ 1972.
3   J Webb 'Legal Research and Problem-Solving' in P A Jones et al *Lawyers' Skills*, 2nd Edition, Blackstone Press, London 1994, at p 5.
4   Costanzo, in *Problem Solving*, Cavendish, London 1995, also adopts a four stage model, involving what she terms 'situation appraisal', 'problem analysis', 'solution analysis' and 'implementation analysis'. While our models have a number of clear similarities, the phrasing is rather different.

Exercise 3.4   Using the model

Assuming the information given in the Xenos's case is all that you have, see if you can use the above model:
(a)   *to generate a number of working hypotheses about the case;*
(b)   *to determine what additional information you may need;*
(c)   *to begin to assess, on the facts, which hypothesis gives the best fit.*

We will return to your answers at various points in the chapter.

Gathering information

Your first step is to obtain sufficient information to open a file on the matter and to give your client initial advice and assistance.

This phase of the process is therefore about getting the facts. Facts are, of course, central to the legal process. A client's legal problems do not arise in the abstract, but out of a constructed set of circumstances which constitute the facts of the case. Your ability as a lawyer will largely be measured by your ability first to obtain and then to organise and use the relevant information underpinning your client's case. We begin by looking at the processes and problems of fact investigation. We will then consider information management separately.

The processes of fact finding

The initial fact-finding context tends to depend on whether you are a solicitor or barrister. For a solicitor, the first means of acquiring information about a case will be the client interview; for a barrister, it tends to be the solicitor's brief to counsel, though this will be supplemented by opportunities for case conference with the client. Despite this difference in context, it means that your initial, and often most important information resource, is your client.

As a case develops you will frequently encounter, or be required to find, a diversity of other sources – mostly human and documentary, though inanimate objects other than documents can also be significant. Potentially the specific categories are almost limitless, but in most cases your initial sources are going to fall into one or other of five sets:

- your client;
- other participants in the case (eg witnesses);
- your colleagues;
- your 'opponent';
- evidence from the site where the event (road accident, assault, accident at work, etc) took place.[1]

Nevertheless, it is possible, as a starting point, to propose a simple typology of *information categories*. The one we have adopted is litigation orientated, and based on the tripartite categorisation of evidence as oral, documentary and real.[2]

1 In the jargon this is sometimes referred to as the 'locus in quo'.
2 For a definition of these terms, see P Murphy *A Practical Approach to Evidence*, 4th Edition, Blackstone Press, London 1992, pp 7–8.

Exercise 3.5   Information sources

Note down some common information sources under each of the following categories (there is no catch, this is intended to be just a simple brainstorming task):
(a)   Oral evidence;
(b)   Documentary evidence;
(c)   Real evidence.

Specific examples you might have come up with could include the oral testimony of various kinds of lay and expert witnesses; real or documentary evidence may come from the police in a variety of civil or criminal proceedings (eg a road traffic accident report which may be obtained either once they have decided not to prosecute, or once criminal proceedings have been completed). Opponents can also be very useful, albeit rather more reluctant, sources of documentary information. This is especially true of civil cases, where the intelligent use of pleadings can produce valuable information.[1] Disclosure of aspects of your evidence may also sometimes force the other side into disclosing evidence in rebuttal.

In addition to thinking about the sources of information you could use, you also need to consider what you want from those sources. It is useful to devise your own checklists to help you determine your information needs, and to act as an aide-memoire in interviews.[2] Much of the information you will be obtaining is reasonably standard across most areas of contentious and non-contentious work.

1   Especially the notice to admit facts (RSC Ord 27, CCR Ord 20), interrogatories, and requests for further and better particulars – see S Sime *A Practical Approach to Civil Procedure*, Blackstone Press, London 1994, pp 98, 244–50, 304–6.
2   Many practitioner texts also offer model checklists. The quality of these is sometimes variable, but they can be, at the least, a useful starting point. A number of basic checklists are reproduced in H Brayne & R Grimes *Professional Skills for Lawyers: A Student's Guide*, Butterworths, London 1994, pp 148–69.

Exercise 3.6   An interviewing checklist

Individually, building on the discussion of information sources so far, construct a basic checklist that you could use in taking instructions on any contentious civil matter. Try and think about ease of use and the ordering of information, as well as the contents.

Then:
(a)   In fours, swap your checklist with your neighbour. Identify any significant differences you find.
(b)   In pairs, discuss your respective models and the assumptions that underpin them.
(c)   In fours, pool your collective reflection and re-draft a single checklist for the group.

Although there may be some specific differences, any checklist you devise is likely to incorporate most elements in the seven information categories listed in Figure 3.1: cross-check your draft against them.[1]

1   Adapted from A Sherr 'Lawyers and Clients: The First Meeting' (1986) 49 *Modern Law Review* 323.

Problems in fact finding

Binder and Bergman have made the point that 'ferreting out evidence may not be the most publicised or romanticised aspect of litigation. But in the main, it is what litigators "actually do".'[1] They might well have added 'and a difficult and sometimes frustrating task it is, too'. What makes it so? Before reading any further, identify what you would expect to be the main problems involved in fact finding.

We suggest there are at least three substantial areas of difficulty.[2]

First, you may simply be *missing important information*. Evidence may be lost or destroyed; a witness may die, or remain untraced. The great danger here is that because the evidence is missing, the gap may not be spotted.[3] An analogy is often drawn in this context between the tasks of the lawyer and the historian.[4] The historian's task is to reconstruct the past; you could argue that the same is true of the lawyer: both have to 'play with the teasing gap separating a lived event and its subsequent narration'.[5] But the analogy is not perfect. The

Figure 3.1 The seven information categories

Personal information

eg, name, address, phone numbers, family ties, work, age, nationality, income, health may all be relevant – though not necessarily in all cases.

Other parties (if known)

Personal details; solicitor instructed (if any); connection with the client (if any).

Witnesses (if relevant)

Basic personal details (though often the client will not know them – must be followed up by the solicitor at a later date); witness to what and for whom? Connections with the client.

Events

Dates; times; place(s); persons involved; the cause of events; chronology; persons affected; property affected; precipitating incident to visiting the solicitor.

What the client wants

Identify the main problem; desired outcome; difficulties in achieving outcome; persons to be affected by outcome.

Previous advice and assistance

Anyone else consulted? Details of consultant; the advice given; action taken by consultant and by client; effects of any action taken.

Existing legal proceedings

Nature of the proceedings; parties; stage of process; past/future hearing dates.

---

historian has perhaps a greater degree of freedom in conducting the search; she is (we hope) less likely to be blocked by another historian refusing her access to a critical document. She is almost certainly better trained to spot the gaps in the first place.

Second, your evidence may be tainted by *unreliability*.

---

1   D Binder and P Bergman *Fact Investigation: From Hypothesis to Proof*, West Publ, St Paul, Minn 1984, p 3.

2   Other problems of *fact analysis* will be considered later in the chapter.
3   There is psychological support for this tendency; see eg D Kahneman, P Slovic and A Tversky *Judgment under Uncertainty: Heuristics and biases*, Cambridge University Press, Cambridge 1982, p 470.
4   See eg Binder & Bergman, op cit, p 4.
5   The phrase is an historian's – see Simon Schama's *Dead Certainties (Unwarranted Speculations)*, Granta Books, London 1991, p 320.

Exercise 3.7   The emperor's new clothes?

Follow your tutor's instructions.

Exercise 3.8   The doctor's dilemma[1]

(a)   *Form two groups. Group A will be given a copy of Note A; group B, a copy of Note B (both in the Appendix of this book).*
(b)   *Every member of each group must select their preferred option from the information given, without discussion with their colleagues.*
(c)   *When everyone has completed the task, the tutor will write up the two options given to groups A & B and take a straw poll of the responses.*
(d)   *How do you explain the variations you have found?*

Both of these exercises are intended to help us recognise the inherent unreliability of much of the information we receive. In Exercise 3.7 the problem is largely self-explanatory, which saves us from giving the game away here! In Exercise 3.8, the problem is more subtle and, perhaps, offers a conclusion that is counter-intuitive. We tend to assume that professional decision-makers will act rationally, and one feature of this assumption is the expectation that if people are presented with the same options, they will come up with the same outcomes.[2] The particular violation of invariance in Exercise 3.8 is termed a 'framing effect', ie the way a problem is framed influences the choices individuals make. In the legal process framing is likely to be important in a number of contexts: can you identify any?

It can arise in lawyer–client interviewing, where, for example, the client has already identified a legal frame for the problem. In the Xenos's case, for example, your clients have presented the facts to you on the assumption that they have an obligation, and all you can do is negotiate a further rescheduling of the loan. You have to be careful, therefore, because if you adopt their frame, you may overlook possibilities that the loan may be voidable, or that they might obtain compensation, say, from the accountant. Similarly, the way in which expert evidence is constructed by different experts will often disclose the use of different problem frames.[3]

In all these contexts, you need to guard against a naïve approach to the information you obtain. Reports may be ambiguous; witnesses may lie; they will often recall details of events inaccurately, or not at all;[4] they may even be led into giving unreliable answers by your own questioning.[5]

Thirdly, your evidence or, more specifically, your assessment of it may be coloured by *assumptions* or *prejudgment*.

1   Based on A Tversky & D Kahneman 'The framing of decisions and the psychology of choice' (1981) 211 *Science* 453.

2   This is termed *invariance* of decision-making – A Garnham & J Oakhill *Thinking and Reasoning*, Blackwell, Oxford & Cambridge, Ma 1994, pp 186–9.
3   Brian Wynne's discussion of how the Abbeystead methane explosion in 1983 (which killed 16 people) was reconstructed through expert knowledge discloses a number of examples of framing problems: see 'Establishing the rules of laws: constructing expert authority' in R Smith & B Wynne (eds) *Expert Evidence: Interpreting Science in the Law*, Routledge, London & New York 1989, p 23 at pp 39–43.
4   See eg S Lloyd-Bostock *Law in Practice*, Routledge/British Psychological Society, London 1988, pp 3–23.
5   See further the discussion of questioning styles in Chapter 6.

Exercise 3.9   The surgeon's story

Read the following:

> A father and son have been out for a day's drive in the country. As they are returning home, their car is hit by an oncoming vehicle which swerves into their path on a tight bend. The father is killed outright and the son is seriously injured. He is rushed to hospital for emergency treatment. A surgery team, led by one of the hospital's top orthopaedic surgeons, is standing by. As he is wheeled into the operating theatre, the surgeon turns around, sees his face and exclaims: 'It's my son!'

Who is the surgeon?

At its crudest, prejudgment can involve overt or tacit prejudice – lawyers are not immune from racism or sexism, for example, which may influence their attitude to a client's 'story'.

However, as Blake points out,[1] prejudgment goes beyond this, to include our (natural) inclination to assess a case in the light of our own values or experience. One feature of this is the tendency to look for analogies between a present case and similar cases that you have worked on in the past. In part, that is a positive activity which enables you to apply things you may have learned from the earlier cases to the new one. It only becomes negative if you start to assume that factual similarities will exist without actually looking to see if that is the case. To give a very simplistic example, do not assume that every client who comes in to discuss her marital problems actually wants a divorce!

There are few simple methods of avoiding these sorts of problems. Clearly, you have to be aware of their existence and allow for that in your analysis of facts. This may not be as easy as it sounds. Problem-solvers can easily fall into the trap of misplaced confidence. Jury research, for example, suggests that extrinsic factors such as the advocate's choice of order in which evidence is presented can influence not just the jury's decision, but its confidence in the rightness of that decision.[2] Evidence similarly indicates that most professionals are not sufficiently reflective on past mistakes to use them to improve the quality of present judgment.[3] You need to think clearly about the attitudes and assumptions you bring to the task; good quality planning and a degree of caution will help, as will the capacity to think creatively about a situation.

1   *A Practical Approach to Legal Advice and Drafting*, 4th Edition, Blackstone Press, London 1993, p 82.

2   N Pennington & R Hastie 'Explanation-based Decision Making; Effects of Memory Structure on Judgment' (1988) 14 *Journal of Experimental Psychology: Learning, Memory, and Cognition* 521. We discuss this research further in Chapter 10.
3   See Kahneman et al *Judgment under Uncertainty: Heuristics and biases*, Cambridge University Press, Cambridge 1982, p 431.

Managing information

Most legal work, whether it is contentious or non-contentious, requires effective information and time management. We shall concentrate on some specialised litigation management tools later in this chapter, but, for the moment, we will just consider some basic techniques you can apply to any task in hand. These techniques all have one thing in common: they rely on visual presentation techniques (to a greater or lesser extent) to clarify the tasks/data you are trying to manage. We have organised this section under three headings: representing the problem; representing the time-line, and representing decisions.

REPRESENTING THE PROBLEM

One of your first tasks is to try and obtain an overview of the problem and to identify different solutions. In any one problem you will have to make sense of your factual data: how do the facts relate one to the other? You will have to identify the legal significance of particular facts; you will have to consider how to use those facts to meet your client's objectives. A technique called *mind mapping*[1] can assist with all of these elements. Mind mapping works by using non-linear and diagrammatic means of representing a problem. Linear models can restrict our capacity for making associations between ideas or actions. By avoiding traditional linear modes of representation, mind maps increase our capacity to handle problems creatively.

There are few 'rules' to mind mapping. With a mind map you always start at the centre of a sheet of paper with a representation – a statement or picture – of the concept or problem you are working on. From the centre you radiate outwards, setting out the links and associations your central concept/problem has raised. We include an example of a mind map in the solution to exercise Exercise 3.11, though please do not work through it until you have done that exercise. You can use different colour pens, pictograms, or just words to describe the interrelationship between your ideas and information. Because no two people structure information, or make associations, in identical ways, no two mind maps of a problem will look exactly the same.

Another technique you can use is *flow charting*. A flow chart, unlike a mind map, works on a linear basis. It enables you to identify from your start point what stages you have to take the problem through, and where alternative consequences/problem formulations can arise. Though you can use it for fact analysis also, flow charting can be particularly helpful in working through legal – especially legislative – material because of the broadly deductive structure that such regulations adopt. If you analyse, say, a section or part of an Act which establishes liability for something, it tends to take the following form:

If [condition a] and [condition b] apply,
then [outcome a];
otherwise [outcome b].

In a flow chart, this can be represented very simply, as shown in Figure 3.2. By working out the structure of the legal rules in this way it becomes far easier to see how your client's (or opponent's) actions need to be translated to fit the legal criteria you are trying to use.

1   See T Buzan *Use your Head*, BBC Books, London 1989.

Figure 3.2   A simple flow chart

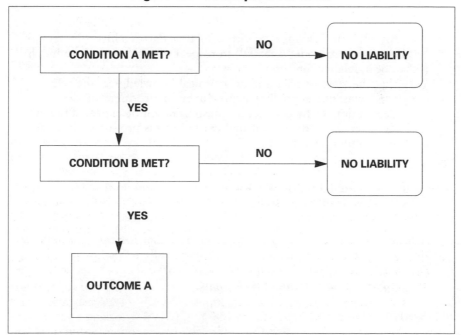

Exercise 3.10   A statute flow chart

Consider the following provisions from the Consumer Protection Act 1987.

SECTION 2

(1)   Subject to the following provisions of this Part, where any damage is caused wholly or partly by a defect in a product, every person to whom subsection (2) below applies shall be liable for the damage.

(2)   This subsection applies to –

    (a)   the producer of the product;

    (b)   any person who, by putting his name on the product or using a trade mark or other distinguishing mark in relation to the product, has held himself out to be the producer of the product;

    (c)   any person who has imported the product into a member State from a place outside the member States in order, in the course of any business of his, to supply it to another.

SECTION 3

(1)   Subject to the following provisions of this section, there is a defect in a product for the purposes of this Part if the safety of the product is not such as persons generally are entitled to expect; and for those purposes 'safety', in relation to a product, shall include safety with respect to products comprised in that product and safety in the context of risks of damage to property, as well as in the context of risks of death or personal injury.

SECTION 4

(1)   In any civil proceedings by virtue of this Part against any person ('the person proceeded against') in respect of a defect in a product it shall be a defence for him to show–

   (a)   that the state of scientific or technical knowledge at the relevant time was not such that a producer of products of the same description as the product in question might be expected to have discovered the defect if it had existed in his products while they were under his control;

SECTION 5

(1)   Subject to the following provisions of this section, in this Part 'damage' means death or personal injury or any loss of or damage to any property (including land).

(a)   *Assume your client is the producer of a product who is being sued under the Act. He might be able to rely on the development risks defence.*

(b)   *Design a flow chart which shows what the plaintiff will have to prove to establish liability in a case to which the Act applies.*

REPRESENTING TIME-LINES

Much legal work involves building a chronology, of events and of tasks. Litigators need to construct a clear picture of the events in a case. This must come out of their information gathering, and should underpin the process of story construction necessary for the trial.[1] Listing all the events chronologically is a useful way of obtaining an overview of the time-lines in a case.

Moreover, most legal work requires careful time management, whether cases are contentious or not. Litigators face deadlines for pleadings, limitation periods etc; conveyancers have specific tasks to complete by exchange of contracts and more tasks to be finalised before completion, and so on. One of the most fundamental mistakes a lawyer can make is to miss a deadline. Use a combination of checklists and diary entries to try and avoid this.

For example, you can place a task checklist, indicating what steps should be completed by a given date, in the front of a client's file. This helps you review the file quickly and easily. Tasks can be checked off as they are completed, so you can see immediately where you are with a case, and what needs to be done next. Because in practice (and often in clinic as well) you will have several cases running consecutively, key dates should also be recorded in your diary, as a further safeguard.

Figure 3.3

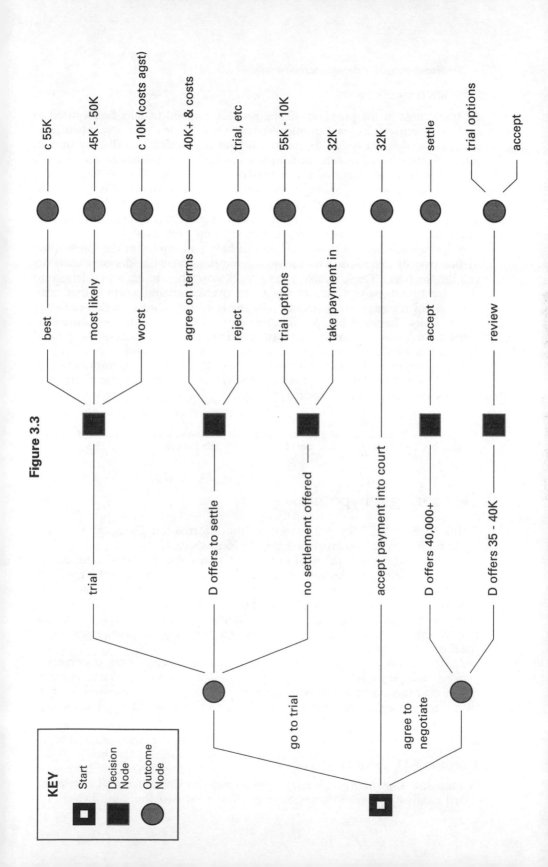

REPRESENTING DECISIONS

At some stage in the problem-solving process you will usually be required to make decisions, or at least to offer alternatives to your client – eg whether to accept a settlement or go to court; whether to continue or discontinue an arbitration; whether to remain within a contractual relationship, or rescind. Such decisions often turn on a variety of complex factors. For example, in any choice between settling or litigating, you will have to consider a range of possible outcomes – ie the possibility that you lose; the possibility that the court awards less than the other side offers; the possible effect of costs on the level of damages even if you do win more than is on the table now.

A specialised form of flow charting can help you represent the alternatives in this type of situation. The method involves using what decision theorists call *decision trees*.[2] These enable you to break down big decision problems into their constituent parts, based on the alternative *actions* and *outcomes* that exist. The system recognises that most problems need to be solved in a sequential order. Thus, action *A* has possible outcomes *O1* and *O2*; if you chose outcome *O1* that decision may have further alternative consequences *B1*, *B2* and *B3*, each of which may, in turn, have different outcomes, and so on. You can probably begin to see how you might chart the options diagrammatically. Using Moore and Thomas's conventions, we include an illustrative negotiation decision tree to help you (Figure 3.3).

1   See the 'outline' technique discussed below.
2   We have adapted a particular method used by P G Moore & H Thomas *The Anatomy of Decisions*, 2nd Edition, Penguin Books, Harmondsworth 1988, p 44ff.

Generating a hypothesis

Think back to Exercise 3.3. Based on the information given, what sort of story did you try to construct to argue the Xenos's case?

There could be a number of options. Perhaps the more legalistic among you would begin with the loan agreement – to see if there are technical flaws. This is a possibility though, with a professionally constructed contract of this complexity, it could be a lengthy and possibly fruitless task. What about the circumstances of the agreement? There might be faults in the loan's execution, or the advice your clients received at the time: might these prove a more positive avenue to pursue?

Although you might not realise it, what you have been doing is starting to generate a hypothesis, or (as here) hypotheses about the case. You have established the initial factual framework of the case, so now your attention shifts to using those facts to construct *legally* acceptable explanations of what happened. Let's try a more technical example.

Exercise 3.11   Malice aforethought?[1]

A man and a woman, who are in the living room of the man's house, are heard arguing by a neighbour. Shortly afterwards two shots are heard. The

Figure 3.4

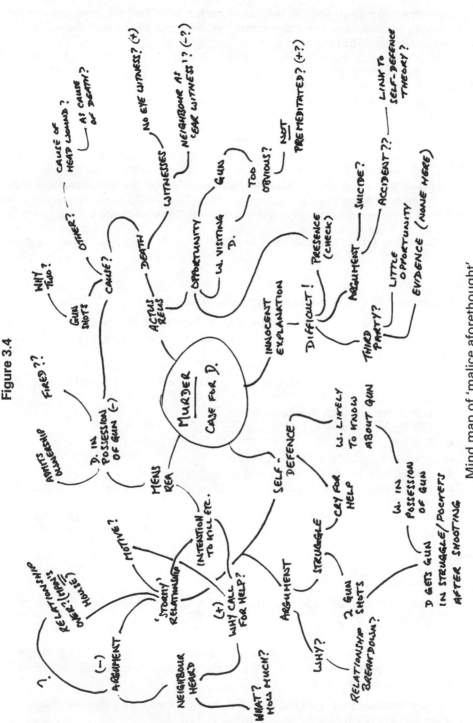

Mind map of 'malice aforethought'

man shouts for help, and the neighbour rushes in to find the man nursing the woman, who has a severe head wound. A doctor is called and the woman is taken to hospital but she later dies.

You have evidence that a handgun was found in the man's pocket shortly after the incident by a policeman investigating what happened. The man admits that he has owned the gun for several years. You also have evidence that the man and woman had been living together for several years, but their relationship had not been happy recently.

Assuming the man is charged with murder:
(a) *In pairs, construct an explanation which might establish the man's innocence of the charge. (You could mind map this – cf our example, Figure 3.4.)*
(b) *Test your theory on another pair. How credible is it? Are there significant gaps you have missed?*
(c) *What elements of the story require further investigation by the defence?*

1   Taken from Inns of Court School of Law *Evidence and Casework Skills*, Blackstone Press, London 1994/95, p 264.

Exercise 3.12   'Elementary, my dear Watson . . .'

Now, on the basis of your experience with Exercise 3.11, construct a general checklist of the questions you would ask yourself to test a hypothesis you have constructed.

We suggest you need to consider the following when constructing a working hypothesis:
● Is it consistent with the facts I have?
● Is it consistent with my client's objectives?
● Is it believable?
● Are there significant gaps in the story?
● Is it an argument, ethically, that I can advance?
● If it is accepted, what will be the legal outcome (eg, what remedy would I obtain)?
At this stage, there are two principles of problem-solving you must keep in mind.

Be creative!

Do not underestimate the opportunities for creativity here. As one solicitor has put it:

There are two kinds of lawyer: the 'fixed paradigm' type and the creative sort. The former treats the law as a rigid set of 'cans' and 'cannots', while the latter treats it as an art form, skilfully manipulating its rich pattern to evolve a solution.[1]

Often a worthwhile hypothesis can only be developed with the aid of creative thinking. Try the following techniques.

LOOK FOR REMOTE ASSOCIATIONS

The defining characteristic of creativity is often said to be the capacity to link ideas that had not previously been associated[2] – eg Stephens's success for his client lay in his capacity to see that malicious falsehood might be resurrected, and could be brought within the legal aid eligibility criteria, even though defamation could not. Techniques like mind mapping can help in creating such associations, by giving you an overview of the problem. Another useful technique is 'brainstorming'.

Many of you will be familiar with this method, which is intended to increase the flow of creative ideas around a reasonably well defined problem. The aim in a brainstorming session is to produce as many solutions as possible without regard, initially, to their viability. This suspension of judgment is essential to promoting the free flow of ideas. Only once you have brainstormed the problem, do you begin to assess the solutions proposed. Brainstorming can be undertaken as an individual or group task – both are effective.[3] In the legal context, consider the possibility of brainstorming not just with colleagues, but also with your client – as Binder and Bergman point out,[4] although you have the legal expertise, there will be many situations where the client's experience of the subject matter of the action will be greater than yours.

GO WITH YOUR INTUITION

Intuition is not always right, but in today's rational world there is a great temptation to throw this particular baby out with the bathwater. Intuition can be a useful creative tool. Many of us have had what you might call the '*Eureka!* experience', where a solution has come to us in an unexpected way, or where we 'sense' a solution without having worked out how we got there. To be sure, such intuitive conclusions need to be tested and validated subsequently, but they are often worth following up.

USE EXPANSIONARY THINKING[5]

There are a variety of expansionary techniques. Ones that strike us as particularly useful are the methods of
- *reversing* (look at the problem from the other side's perspective);
- *rearranging* (choose a different starting point in the chronology of a case; start with your desired outcome and work back to your objectives, etc).

USE LATERAL THINKING

It is important to be able to use this as well as *logical* thinking. The idea of lateral thinking has been popularised by Edward de Bono.[6] Its essence is the rejection of standard – what de Bono terms vertical – methods for problem-solving. Lateral thinkers are those who tend to deploy fresh, often visual or spatial, perspectives on a problem. Activists, in Honey & Mumford's terms,[7] are meant to be good lateral thinkers. We will take one of the classic examples, which some of you may know.

1   Mark Stephens in *Law Society's Gazette*, 25 November 1992, p 14. Stephens's particular piece of ingenuity was to rediscover the long-dormant action of malicious falsehood, which

enabled his client to sidestep the rules preventing individuals from obtaining legal aid to pursue actions for defamation.

2   A Koestler *The Act of Creation*, Hutchinson, London 1964.
3   Though small groups are generally more effective than large. Brainstorming is also of interest to us because it was initially devised, intuitively, as a management tool. Its general efficacy has since been validated by a number of research studies – see Garnham & Oakhill, *Thinking and Reasoning*, Blackwell, Oxford & Cambridge, Ma 1994, pp 287–9.
4   *Fact Investigation: From Hypothesis to Proof*, West Publ, St Paul, Minn 1984, p 205.
5   See Costanzo *Problem Solving*, Cavendish, London 1995, pp 61–2.
6   *The Five-Day Course in Thinking*, Allen Lane, London 1968.
7   See Chapter 2, above.

Exercise 3.13   Matchmaker

Take six matches. Without breaking them, use them to construct four equilateral triangles.

Vertical thinkers really struggle with this one (we know!). Lateral thinkers succeed by avoiding the false assumption that the problem can be solved in two dimensions. In fact, it requires the construction of a tetrahedron – a three dimensional figure.

Clearly tricks with matchsticks are not likely to impress clients or fellow professionals, or at least not for long, but lateral thinking does have a place in legal practice. A widely quoted example from fiction is Portia's ploy from Shakespeare's *The Merchant of Venice*.[1] When Shylock tries to enforce the contract entitling him to a pound of the merchant Antonio's flesh, Portia responds:

PORTIA:	A pound of that same merchant's flesh is thine;
	The court awards it, and the law doth give it.
SHYLOCK:	Most rightful judge!
PORTIA:	And you must cut this flesh from off his breast; The law
	allows it, and the court awards it.
SHYLOCK:	Most learned judge! A sentence: come, prepare.
PORTIA:	Tarry a little: there is something else.
	This bond doth give thee here no jot of blood;
	The words expressly are, a pound of flesh:
	Take then thy bond, take thou thy pound of flesh;
	But in the cutting it, if thou dost shed
	One drop of Christian blood, thy lands and goods
	Are, by the laws of Venice, confiscate
	Unto the state of Venice.

Having said all this, we have to acknowledge that it is much easier to say 'be creative' than to produce meaningful advice on how to go about it. This is something teachers and psychologists have been struggling with for many years now.[2]

1   Act IV, scene 1.
2   See eg Garnham & Oakhill *Thinking and Reasoning*, Blackwell, Oxford & Cambridge, Ma 1994, chs 13 and 15.

But remember your limitations

Exercise 3.11 emphasises that, at this stage, you are constructing only a working hypothesis. It is nothing more than a plausible explanation as to what may have happened and its legal consequences. You must never lose sight of this limitation. You are concerned with theory not *proof*. The whole purpose of developing an hypothesis (or hypotheses) is to provide you with something tangible which can then be used to assist further information-gathering and evaluation. In short, it gives you a sense of direction, and prepares you for the time when you are ready to develop a final theory of the case.

Interpreting your information

Having established your initial hypothesis/es, your task is to use it/them to inform further information gathering and thence to develop a coherent story or theme of the case. This is, in essence, an interpretative process. The importance of the story is emphasised by Anderson and Twining:

> . . . many trial lawyers and decision theorists believe that juries (and other fact finders) make 'holistic' judgments – they are persuaded by stories. In this view, juries choose between two stories presented by the contending lawyers (or adopt a variant of their own) and decide the case accordingly. The central tenet here is that the jury bases its decision on a story-as-a-whole, and rarely recalls any significant number of the individuated propositions that specific items of evidence were offered to prove . . .[1]

At this stage you start to advance beyond your working hypothesis, to construct a *theory of the case*. This is not as abstract as it sounds. Brayne and Grimes explain it with their characteristic clarity:

> In summary you are saying: taking this legal framework, at least for now, the relevant facts fit like this – the way I make the facts and the law fit is my current theory of the case.[2]

Developing a theory involves two main elements:
- creating a legal theory of the case;
- creating a factual theory of the case.

1 T Anderson & W Twining *Analysis of Evidence*, Butterworths, London 1991, p 168. We develop this idea of story construction in later chapters, especially Chapter 10.
2 *Professional Skills for Lawyers: A Student's Guide*, Butterworths, London 1994, p 183.

The legal theory of the case[1]

By developing a 'legal theory' we mean the construction of an argument for a specific legal action, ie a claim for breach of contract, negligent misrepresentation, etc. The creation of a legal theory requires three things:
- identifying a legal right from the facts;
- identifying the legal source of that right;[2]

● identifying the appropriate cause of action accruing from that right, eg an action for damages, an application for an injunction, etc.

1   See Anderson & Twining *Analysis of Evidence*, Butterworths, London 1991, pp 124, 165–6; J Webb, 'Legal Research and Problem-Solving' in P A Jones et al *Lawyers' Skills*, 2nd Edition, Blackstone Press, London 1994, p 4 at p 13.
2   That is, the specific common law or statutory rules – which may involve you in an element of library-based research.

Exercise 3.14   After the accountant

So, for example, in the Xenos's case, you might have decided that your best bet would be to pursue the conflict of interest against the accountant who initially advised your clients.

As a small piece of research, see if you can identify: (a) the precise legal right, (b) its source and (c) the cause of action that would enable you to do so.

The factual theory of the case

This is the participants' part of your story. It is your explanation of what happened, why and how, as told through your client and witnesses. It must fit together as a 'story' – a coherent whole, and it must also link into the legal framework, so as to 'activate'[1] your legal theory.

In the earliest stages of analysis you should not worry too much about evidential requirements. Your first aim is to try and build up as full a picture of what happened as you can – regardless of the relevance or admissibility of that information. However, by the interpretation stage you should begin to process that information more critically, both on logical and, increasingly, on evidential grounds.

Most practitioners apply broadly *logical* criteria spontaneously to the information in their possession.[2] Information is assessed according to whether it tends to confirm or deny a hypothesis, or is neutral.

While there are no equivalent studies in law, studies of medical decision-making indicate that mistakes at this stage are made more because of failure to *use* the information in your possession appropriately, rather than as a result of faulty information gathering.[3] This places the onus on your organisational skills. Techniques like mind-mapping may help you to sort out the relationship between various bits of information, and between law and fact, but these are not sufficient by themselves. A useful technique, which forms the basis of Binder and Bergman's[4] work, is to summarise your case through a series of interlocking 'outlines'. These can subsequently form the basis of a 'trial notebook' if the case proceeds to court.[5] We only have the space to summarise the system here. If you wish to pursue the technique more fully, you should read Binder & Bergman for yourself.

The purpose of an outline is twofold. First, it is a means of marshalling your existing information into both narrative and evidentially useful forms. Second, it is a mechanism for determining what additional information you require. Binder and Bergman[6] draw a distinction between two types of outline – *story* and *evidentiary outlines*. Their method in fact involves five such outlines:

(a) the story outline;
(b) outline of client's existing affirmative evidence;
(c) outline of opponent's existing affirmative evidence;
(d) outline of client's potential affirmative evidence;
(e) outline of client's potential rebuttal evidence.

These should be developed more or less contemporaneously, and together will provide you with a reasonably thorough and complete representation of the case.

The story outline provides you with an overview of the case. In it you should present the events leading up to the case in a chronological order. You should try to represent both sides' versions of events (they will usually agree on more of the story than they dispute) and identify inconsistencies in those versions which need to be explained. Gaps in the facts which are of importance and need to be filled can also be listed separately. The outline thus breaks down into three columns:

GAPS	EVENTS	INCONSISTENCIES

In putting together a story outline, begin with the events column, as this will provide the core of your case. It should focus only on the specific facts which constitute the parties' explanation of what happened. For simplicity's sake, you should save the fine detail for the evidentiary outlines.

The evidentiary outlines each marshal the evidence, according to its proponent and its purpose. Each outline is structured so that the evidence is listed under the substantive legal element it supports. In respect of each outline of existing affirmative evidence, you can also list your opponent's rebutting evidence in a parallel column to its equivalent affirmative evidence.[7] Thus, assuming you are the plaintiff in a simple contract dispute, your affirmative outline might contain the following:[8]

AFFIRMATIVE EVIDENCE	EVIDENCE IN REBUTTAL
Agreement	
Jack agreed to lend Jill £500, repayable on 1 April 199X.	Jack agreed to lend Jill £500, with no stipulation as to date of repayment.
Performance	
Jack gave £500 to Jill.	Admitted.
Breach	
Jill failed to repay the loan on or before 1 April 199X.	Jill paid £100 on 30 March 199X.

In addition to the items of evidence, you could also note the source (eg, 'oral evidence – Jack', etc) under each respective item. This system can thus provide useful narrative support for the charting method which is discussed below.

In assessing the *evidential* strength of your case, your first problem is getting used to the terminology used and understanding what it really means in practice.

1 D Binder and P Bergman *Fact Investigation: From Hypothesis to Proof*, West Publ, St Paul, Minn 1984, p 169.
2 The labels applied to these techniques are relatively insignificant, we think, but if you feel that you would find an introductory discussion of the forms of reasoning helpful, see J Holland & J Webb *Learning Legal Rules*, 2nd Edition, Blackstone Press, London 1993, pp 217–26.
3 A Elstein & G Bordage 'Psychology of Clinical Reasoning' in J Dowie & A Elstein *Professional judgment: A reader in clinical decision making*, Cambridge University Press, Cambridge 1988, p 109 at pp 114–15.
4 Binder and Bergman, op cit.
5 See further Chapter 10.
6 See Binder and Bergman, op cit, pp 39–42 for a summary of their system.
7 An alternative model is also discussed in Chapter 10.
8 Damage is excluded here because it does not require evidence other than that admitted as proof of performance; you could list the amount alleged again under the heading 'Damage' if you thought you might otherwise overlook it, or where the other side takes issue with the quantum, rather than traverses by a bare denial.

Exercise 3.15 Learning the language

Below are three sets of evidential antonyms.

Fact – Inference

Fact in Issue – Evidentiary Fact

Direct Evidence – Indirect Evidence

In respect of each pair:
(a) find a technical definition for each term;
(b) give a specific example of the difference between each item within each pair.

The relationship between facts and inferences is critical to the process of proof. The link between a fact in issue and an evidentiary fact is made by *inference*. We infer (assume, if you prefer) from the proof of an evidentiary fact that the fact in issue *should*[1] be taken as proven. Technically, then, an inference is the means whereby one can draw a conclusion about one fact from another piece of evidence. An inference is not the same as proof, however, because it is based on a premise – a generalisation[2] that something is true; and some premises are more or less debatable than others. For example, to quote from Binder and Bergman:

> . . . assume a litigant with the words 'rinse cycle' impressed in her head introduces evidence that a washing machine was pushed out of a window. The premise which may support an inference that the washing machine fell toward the ground is something like, 'Objects pushed into the air are affected by gravity'.[3]

As they point out, inferences at this level are virtually indisputable (unless presumably the defence could adduce evidence that the plaintiff was living on the moon at the time) but, most often, cases have to be constructed out of chains of inference, based upon generalisations having varying degrees of cogency.

Let's try this in a less abstract context.

1 We cannot logically say *is* proven, precisely because inferring involves some degree of value-judgment.
2 See further Anderson & Twining, *Analysis of Evidence*, Butterworths, London 1991, pp 66–9. On the links between generalisation and story structure in court, see Pennington & Hastie 'Explanation-based decision making; Effects of memory structure on judgment' (1988) 14 *Journal of Experimental Psychology: Learning, Memory, and Cognition* 521.
3 Binder and Bergman, op cit, p 83

Exercise 3.16 Moriarty's a murderer

Moriarty is accused of murdering Holmes. The only evidence in the case is as follows: Holmes was strangled two days ago. Scratches are apparent on Moriarty's arm; they are no more than three days old. Traces of blood and skin were found under the deceased's fingernails. Moriarty could not account for his movements at the time of the killing.

(a) Identify:
    (i)   the evidentiary facts, and
    (ii) the fact(s) in issue they would go to prove.
(b) Construct the necessary chains of inference between the evidentiary facts and the fact in issue.

Suppose your chain of inferences looks something like Figure 3.5 (though perhaps not as pretty).

In this example the evidentiary facts obviously go to one fact in issue: the *actus reus* – the killing. You have insufficient evidence of the mental element (though the scratches could be consistent with an intention to kill, etc – otherwise why didn't Moriarty let go at that point?). Note too how the overall chain of inference may be drawn from an amalgam of evidence. There is absolutely no reason why you cannot draw a chain of inferences from a single evidentiary fact, but it may be more speculative than one that is supported at various points. Moreover, as a rule of thumb, the longer the chain of inferences between an evidentiary fact and the fact in issue, the weaker the probative link between the two. Remember always that your aim is to determine whether your evidence is sufficient, both in terms of its relevance to the legal issues, and in terms of its *weight* – ie its sufficiency to persuade the trier of fact that you have satisfied whatever burden of proof you bear. At this point interpretation tends to blend imperceptibly into the process of . . .

Evaluating your hypothesis

Your ultimate aim in a case must be to establish a single hypothesis, or, at worst, a set of reasonable alternatives that will hold up in court. This means that, once you feel you have sufficient additional information, you should

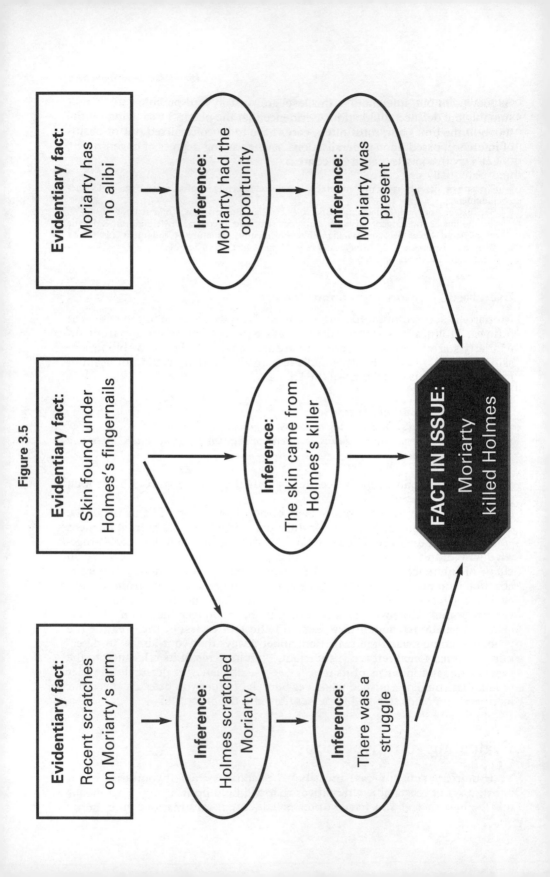

Figure 3.5

Evidentiary fact: Moriarty has no alibi

Inference: Moriarty had the opportunity

Inference: Moriarty was present

Evidentiary fact: Skin found under Holmes's fingernails

Inference: The skin came from Holmes's killer

Evidentiary fact: Recent scratches on Moriarty's arm

Inference: Holmes scratched Moriarty

Inference: There was a struggle

FACT IN ISSUE: Moriarty killed Holmes

begin to evaluate your hypothesis/hypotheses. This is unlikely to be a one-off exercise, as it will usually be desirable to evaluate your case analysis at various points. The most appropriate points for review, particularly in non-contentious work, tend to differ according to the nature of the transaction. In (civil) contentious work, most litigators would suggest that there are three potentially critical review points. These are, first, just before the first pleadings are filed; the second is just prior to discovery; and the third is just before the trial itself; but there are no hard and fast rules. In criminal work you will often not have the luxury of such extensive opportunities for review.

The actual process of evaluation is simply a balancing exercise. You look at the data you have; you consider your hypotheses and choose the best fit simply by adding up the pros and cons for each alternative.

Exercise 3.17   Xenos case – your evaluation[1]

Your clients are now seeking recovery of the full £150,000. Assume that your research and inquiries in this case highlight two possible causes of action: one against the promoter of the scheme for breaches of the Companies Acts, which require the issuing of a prospectus to potential investors in the scheme; the other against the accountant for breaches of his fiduciary duty.

Your checks have disclosed that the promoter's company is solvent but, if it comes to trial, you anticipate they will fight your interpretation of the law. You know the accountant is running scared, but you are not sure why. He might be prepared to agree a quick settlement, but only for a substantially lower sum. You wonder if there might be a problem with his professional indemnity insurance, which could leave you chasing a 'man of straw'. There is a professional indemnity fund, but it is notoriously slow at investigating and paying claims. Your clients are also rather more reluctant to pursue the accountant, because of their relative's role in making the introduction. You now have to decide, with your clients, who to issue proceedings against.

Note down:
(a)   what you would advise your clients to do;
(b)   what particular factors you have taken into consideration in giving that advice.

In evaluating any case, we suggest you need to take account of four things:
● the information in your possession;
● the inferential strength of your explanations;
● the external (legal, ethical, procedural, financial or personal) constraints on a course of action;
● your objectives.

1   Adapted (very freely) from Costanzo *Problem Solving*, Cavendish, London 1995, p 174.

The information in your possession

In evaluating each hypothesis you must, of course, contrast it with the known (or alleged) facts. Try considering the following questions:
–   Is the hypothesis consistent with the facts as presented by my client?

- Is there any evidence known to me which is inconsistent with this account?
- If so, can that inconsistent evidence be accommodated by the hypothesis, or must it be challenged/explained away?
- If that is so, do I have the evidence to mount a successful challenge?
- Is any of the evidence that I need likely to be inadmissible?[1]

In any legal proceedings you must be conscious, as we have said, of the 'weight' of your evidence. This requires you to treat the evidence for your case with a healthy degree of scepticism. That does not mean, of course, that you need to subject your client or witnesses to the 'Spanish Inquisition', but it does mean that you should attempt some process of verification. Try and subject all important evidence to your own critical analysis. Do not simply assume that, if it is your evidence, it is correct. Even if there are no glaring gaps or inconsistencies, think about the parts of the story that may require testing or substantiating. Now try the following example.

1   You need to assess the possibility that certain evidence may be disallowed because it offends an exclusionary rule of evidence (eg hearsay).

Exercise 3.18   Poisoning the American ambassador

Some years ago a news story appeared in *The New York Times* under the headline 'Clare Luce's Illness is Traced to Arsenic Dust in Rome Villa'.

The article stated that Mrs Luce, then the American Ambassador to Italy, had in the summer of 1954 started to suffer anaemia and extreme fatigue. These symptoms had disappeared when she left her post in Rome, but recurred as soon as she returned to it. Hospital tests disclosed that she was suffering from arsenic poisoning. This had created a scare that an attempt was being made to poison her. However, Mrs Luce had now announced that the source of the poisoning had been traced to paint on the ceiling of her flat in Rome. Minute flakes of the paint were dislodged by people walking through a laundry located above the flat, and were thus inhaled as a part of the ordinary airborne dust. The article credited detection work by the Central Intelligence Agency with finding the problem, and announced that steps were being taken to remove the danger.

What elements of that story do you think need to be verified? Why?

The inferential strength of your case

In so far as your hypothesis is built on inference rather than fact, you should make some assessment of the inferential strength of your hypothesis. Do remember what we have said: no inference is logically conclusive and may be viewed as more or less strong or weak. Problems can arise because the evidence forces us to make a large number of inferences about the facts, and there is a danger therefore that we lose sight of the distinction between fact and inference in the process.[1]

1   Cf the discussion in *Voelker v Combined Insurance Co of America* (1954) 73 So 2d 403 – see Exercise 3.24, below.

Exercise 3.19   Moriarty rides again?

Look again, critically, at the links in the Moriarty chain and compare them with your own analysis. Does it convince? If so, why? If not, why not? Consider the following questions.

–   *Are you satisfied that the inferences logically follow the evidentiary facts, or are any based on a false premise?*
–   *How convincingly do they lead to the fact in issue? Is this a strong or a weak chain?*
–   *What evidence would you need to make it stronger?*

We do not guarantee that these are always the only questions you need to ask when assessing the inferences you draw, but they are a start.

External constraints on your course of action

Your choice of solution will also depend upon your ability to recognise external constraints on any course of action. The illegality of certain activities; the constraints of professional ethics; rules governing the disclosure of evidence, etc, will all influence your proposed solution to the case. Of all these elements, however, it is often the personal constraints that are the most difficult.

It is often said, quite rightly, that lawyers are not trained social workers and should not play a part for which they are unqualified. Nevertheless, as a lawyer you will be seen by clients as a trained problem solver, and given the traumatic contexts in which many private and commercial clients come into contact with lawyers, it will almost certainly be impossible to avoid responding to their 'non-legal' needs also. The legal aspects of a client's problem cannot be considered in isolation, and this reality must inform your relations with the client, your problem-solving strategy, and your advice.

For example, there is little point in recommending a client to take a course of action which they cannot cope with either financially or emotionally, and in such cases your advice will have to go beyond that which is strictly 'legal'.

The Xenos's case offers a good example. Your clients are seeking a substantial settlement – £150,000, presumably plus at least a proportion of their costs. Their bottom line[1] will clearly depend on the seriousness of their financial difficulties. They will need your assessment of risk.[2] If they go to court, how likely is it that they will win? If they win, what are the chances of an order for costs: how much of the costs will be met in that case?[3] You may have to advise them also that the higher their bottom line figure, the harder it may be to establish an early settlement. All this in a context where your clients are likely to have a substantial emotional commitment – remember, it is their home that is on the line.

Dealing with this aspect of the work is not easy, not least because it can seem to go against much of our training, as Ben Sells points out:

> The simple fact is that there appears to be something about law school that disconnects people from the life they had before law school. When I talk to experienced lawyers who spend a lot of time teaching new lawyers the ropes, they very often tell me how hard it is to get new lawyers to look at a problem in non-legal terms. It's as if new lawyers are unable to

connect their law school training with the vast range of experience they acquired before law school. Somehow legal training usurps this experience . . . At its worst, the 'life begins at law school' syndrome encourages an arrogant and aristocratic attitude that assumes a legal response to life always is superior to non-legal responses.[4]

While you should try to avoid the blinkered approach Sells identifies,[5] you must remain conscious of your own limits and recognise that a stage may be reached where it would be appropriate to advise a client to obtain other forms of professional advice or assistance.

1   That is, the minimum for which they can afford to settle.
2   The difficulty is that such an assessment is, ultimately, wholly intuitive. You have no other basis than your own (or your counsel's) experience to depend on – see Costanzo *Problem Solving*, Cavendish, London 1995, pp 174–80.
3   On the general principles applying to costs in civil cases, see Sime *A Practical Approach to Civil Procedure*, Blackstone Press, London 1994, pp 440–2.
4   *The Soul of the Law*, Element Books, Rockport, Ma & Shaftesbury 1994, pp 47–8.
5   Cf the discussion of the lawyer's counselling role in Chapter 6, below.

Your objectives

In evaluating your hypothesis you need to take account of your *objectives* in the case. Consider the following questions.
● Does your proposed hypothesis provide your client with the most appropriate remedy for her needs?
● Does the case require urgent action? Does the proposed solution deliver in time?
● Do you have the expertise to see the matter through?
Any solution you propose must ultimately be matched against your client's objectives. It is your first obligation to identify your client's aims and find the legal remedy, or other outcome, that provides the best potential solution. This can often be the point at which you can exercise some of the creativity we talked about earlier. Try not to be pigeon-holed by an unduly prescriptive view of the options. The victim of an assault does not really care whether compensation is obtained via a claim in tort, a compensation order from a criminal court, or an award of the Criminal Injuries Compensation Board. Her concerns are more likely to be variations on the theme of 'How can I get the most compensation for the least cost or inconvenience and in the shortest time?'

If there is a lack of congruence between your solution and the client's objectives, you must consider whether to drop that particular hypothesis. If in all other respects that hypothesis constitutes the best fit, it is probably time to suggest to the client that his or her objectives may not be achievable, and to obtain further instructions.

From evaluation to implementation

Once you have a theory you feel reasonably happy with, you must implement it. Implementation is simply *converting theory into action*. You must now take the necessary procedural steps to move your case along (you will almost certainly have already sent a letter before action by this stage; you may even have commenced proceedings, or issued a defence).

In these final stages there are various devices you can use to make sure you are on top of the case:

- Use *action checklists* to keep track of the tasks to be undertaken – identify who has to do what, by when.
- Maintain a regular system of *case review* to keep a check on progress and to ensure your theory continues to offer the best fit. *This is absolutely critical.*
- Use *Murphy's law analysis.*[1] Murphy's law states that, in any conceivable situation, if something can go wrong, it will. Anticipate Murphy's law by checking for weak points; try and devise alternative courses of action for if, or when, the worst happens.

Before we move on to consider how we can best organise the information which informs our final theory of the case, let's try and consolidate what we have done so far.

1   Costanzo *Problem Solving*, Cavendish, London 1995, p 204.

Summary so far

ANALYSE THE SITUATION
- Identify the problem (broadly).
- Gather the information you need.

ESTABLISH YOUR WORKING HYPOTHESES

DEVELOP A THEORY OF THE CASE; IDENTIFY:
- a legal right;
- the source of the right;
- a cause of action;
- what needs to be proved;
- your evidence;
and so construct your story.

EVALUATE YOUR THEORY

IMPLEMENT AN ACTION PLAN

REVIEW! REVIEW!! REVIEW!!!

And remember, throughout this process, aim to be a *creative* not a complacent problem solver.

Presenting the case

One of the greatest problems of information management lies in presenting your factual material in a manner that is easily comprehensible, and that makes the law/fact/evidence linkages apparent. The volume of evidence may itself greatly limit the lawyer's ability to absorb that information.

There are several fact management techniques that are open to you; we have already touched on some of the narrative ones (notably the outline method). If the opportunity arises we would encourage you to experiment with a variety of such techniques. For our present purposes, however, we will focus on one technique only, what we shall call 'simplified charting'. We begin with an exercise.

Exercise 3.20   Another contract case

Here is another contract 'problem'. Read it and answer the questions that follow.

> Webb Ltd writes to Maughan Ltd: 'We require 30,000 2mm widgets by Friday week (17/X/9X). Can you provide? Please fax confirmation urgently.'
>
> Maughan Ltd replies: 'Have widgets on our standard terms, can deliver from stock – price £15,000.'
>
> Webb Ltd confirms its acceptance by telephone on 15/X/9X.
>
> Friday arrives and 30,000 widgets are duly delivered to Webb Ltd by one of Maughan Ltd's drivers. The driver checks the load off the lorry, and gets Webb Ltd's Stock Control Manager to sign the delivery note. Maughan Ltd's standard terms appear on the back. Clause 4 states: 'All goods to be paid for in full within 10 working days of delivery or by the end of the calendar month in which the goods are delivered, whichever period shall be the longer.'
>
> The Manager keeps the top copy, the driver takes the carbon.
>
> Webb Ltd does not pay by 30/X/9X. One month later (on 31/X/9X) Maughan Ltd writes to Webb Ltd demanding immediate payment. Webb Ltd does not reply.
>
> Maughan Ltd seeks your advice.

In small groups, identify and write down:
(a)   What legal right and cause of action should Maughan Ltd pursue?
(b)   What are the facts Maughan Ltd must prove to succeed in their case?
(c)   What evidence have they supporting their case?

How did you get on? Are you satisfied that your method enabled you to identify the facts that need to be proved *and* enabled you to establish clearly what evidence supports which fact? Looking at your notes, is it *immediately apparent* how facts and evidence are linked? If it is, well done. Do you think your method could work as well with a fraud case running to 3,000 pages of documentary evidence and over a dozen key witnesses?

This is where charting comes in. Charting techniques are intended to provide a graphic representation of the law and evidence relevant to a case. The basis for our system of simplified charting is material developed originally for the Law Society of Upper Canada, though it has now been adopted in much of the Common Law world. The chief strength of this system is its capacity

Figure 3.6 The charting structure

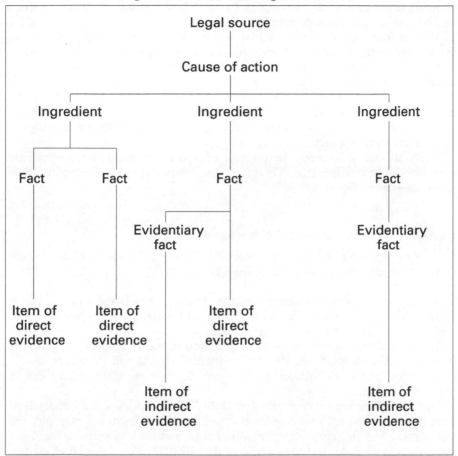

for representing the legal and fact analysis conjunctively.

In litigious work, this system operates by representing the legal and fact analysis of a case on five separate levels:

Level 1: the source of the client's/Crown's right;

Level 2: the cause of action or charge;

Level 3: the ingredients of the cause or charge;

Level 4: the propositions of fact;

Level 5: items of evidence.

Levels one, two and three represent the kind of research you are already well familiar with.

At levels one and two you determine from the facts whether a legal right/ remedy exists, identify the formal source of the right (eg Common Law negligence, etc) and translate that into a specific cause of action and jurisdiction (Action for damages for negligence in the County Court). At this stage, you will also identify the appropriate plaintiff/defendant.

At level three you must establish more precisely the particular elements or ingredients of the action or offence (eg, in negligence, duty, breach, causation and remoteness of damage). This is essential if you are to establish what needs to be proved or admitted.

Levels four and five will probably take most of you into newer territory. At level four you are identifying the necessary facts to prove each ingredient while, at level five, you will identify the specific evidence you will bring to prove each level four fact.

The relationship between these various levels is represented diagrammatically rather like a family tree. This gives you a very clear visual representation of the case, as in Figure 3.6.

Exercise 3.21   Maughan v Webb – again

In your groups, using the charting technique, construct a diagrammatic representation of the issues, facts and evidence in Exercise 3.20.[1]

This makes it a relatively simple system, though the charting can become quite complex if one takes account of two additional elements we have not considered so far, but shown in Figure 3.3.

The first of these arises out of the distinction between issuance and evidentiary facts discussed above. Proof of evidentiary facts will introduce a new element into the chart between levels 4 and 5. This can change the form of the chart in a number of ways.

The second element reflects the desirability of attempting a chart analysis of your opponent's case. This enables you to note facts which, for example, are not admitted or are traversed by the other side, and thereby helps to highlight the points in dispute, and the nature of that dispute. For the sake of clarity, the analysis of an opponent's evidence is best done on a separate chart rather than superimposed on the chart of your own evidence, though the two could technically be presented in parallel on the same sheet of paper – provided the issues are not too complex, you have a sufficiently large piece of paper, and a good supply of different coloured pens!

1   When you have done so, compare your chart with the example in J Webb, 'Legal Research and Problem-Solving' in P A Jones et al *Lawyers' Skills*, 2nd Edition, Blackstone Press, London 1994, p 4 at p 15.

Practical legal research

In a practice context, the term 'research' is most often used to refer to both factual and library-based research.[1] Here, for our present purposes, we use it to mean library research only.

We do not intend to dwell at length on legal research techniques, as there are a number of other texts which cover that territory admirably.[2] However, there are a couple of basic points and techniques we ought to address.

1 This is the sense, for example, in which the term is used in the Legal Aid Board's transaction criteria for franchisees – see A Sherr, R Moorhead & A Paterson *Transaction Criteria*, HMSO, London 1992.
2 Notably V Tunkel *Legal Research*, Blackstone Press, London 1993; Brayne & Grimes *Professional Skills for Lawyers: A Student's Guide*, Butterworths, London 1994.

The professional context

As Morison and Leith point out, both solicitors and barristers 'work in a hostile environment which is not conducive to carrying out detailed research'.[1] This view is supported by empirical work which suggests that, by academic standards, practitioners make relatively infrequent use of both primary (statutes, law reports, etc) and secondary sources (texts and journals).[2] What is it that makes this environment hostile?

THE COST OF RESEARCH TO THE CLIENT

There is considerable anecdotal (and therefore, admittedly, unsubstantiated) evidence that lawyers have helped create a market environment which makes it difficult to charge clients the true cost of research time and resources.[3] If extensive research is required it may be delegated to trainees (and passed on to the client at no or low cost) or disguised by seeking counsel's opinion. Perhaps in part we have been caught out by the mythology of our own professional omniscience – clients do not expect to pay for the time it takes us to look up the law.

THE COST OF RESEARCH TO THE FIRM/CHAMBERS

Practitioner texts and primary sources are expensive. Smaller firms and chambers may take the view that they do not have the resources to invest in extensive library materials. One of the more striking findings in the Bristol survey was that one in ten of the solicitors surveyed did not use their firm's library when they needed access to library resources[4] – the most obvious inference being that the library was not adequate for their needs. Start-up cost has been a major disincentive to practitioners acquiring computerised information retrieval systems, with the result that these are very much the preserve of the largest firms and chambers.[5]

LIMITED ACCESS

Practitioners obviously do not have equal access to research resources, not just for the resource reasons already considered, but because of geographical constraints and a lack of library networks within the field. There is thus considerable disparity of access to legal information services, particularly outside the major centres of population.[6]

TIME CONSTRAINTS

For most practitioners, time is limited and cases are many. Lawyers are therefore obliged to prioritise tasks, and research, certainly that which is not essential to a given case, is likely to be a low priority:

> Time's short during the week – trying to get time off and time to work –
> and basically if you have a briefcase full of paperwork you try to turn it
> round as quickly as you can. You don't have a whole lot of opportunity
> to go to the library and study the journals as you want to or in a way that
> is not related to specific cases.[7]

THE CONSTRUCTION OF LEGAL PROBLEMS

Morison and Leith also make the valuable point that arguments about the
meaning of law are made relatively uncommon in this practice environment.
Disputes about the law may be sidestepped by the lawyers progressing the
case on a shared assumption of what the law *is*. This is one way in which disputes become focused on factual issues, and it is often the most efficient
method of dealing with cases in terms of time and cost. Most run of the mill
cases thus rely on the practitioners' day-to-day background knowledge of law,
not on their capacity to do research.

Nevertheless, you would be hard-pressed to find experienced practitioners
arguing that lawyers do not need good research skills. Indeed, one outcome of
the reforms to English vocational training in the late '80s and early '90s has
been an increased emphasis on the acquisition of research and casework skills.
So, why this apparent contradiction?

First, there is the obvious point that cases will arise where you cannot rely
on your background knowledge. The law changes and needs to be re-learned;
cases which will be fought on points of law do arise.

Second, research skills and resources are seen as a quality of service issue.
Appropriate library holdings are required of Legal Aid franchisees, and of
any firm seeking compliance with the Law Society's *Practice Management
Standards*.[8]

Third, rightly or wrongly, there appears to be some feeling within the profession that the research element in legal work is becoming more important.[9]
Again, this seems to reflect a variety of pressures. For example, the rapid
internationalisation of many areas of practice makes updating far more important – and problematic; similarly, large commercial clients will often bring
with them specific expectations and needs for specialist research.

1   *The Barrister's World*, Open University Press, Milton Keynes 1992, p 88.
2   J Webb *Legal Research and Information Systems: Research Resources and Needs in the Bristol
    Legal Profession*, Faculty of Law Working Paper No 1, University of the West of England,
    Bristol January 1994, pp 15–17.
3   This is an over-generalisation. In many civil areas, such intellectual property, tax and licens-
    ing clients do seem more readily to accept the need for extensive legal research, and, of
    course, usually have the resources to pay for it.
4   Webb, op cit, p 18.
5   See eg G Chambers 'IT in Practice' *Law Society's Gazette*, 11 December 1991; J Webb
    'Legal Research and Information Systems: the impact of information retrieval systems on
    provincial legal practice' (1993) 2 *Law, Computers & Artificial Intelligence* 203.
6   LAWLIP Steering Group *LAWLIP: A Library and Information Plan for Law*, John Rees,
    London 1993, pp 12–13.
7   Barrister quoted by Morison & Leith, op cit, p 92.
8   Law Society *Practice Management Standards*, The Law Society, London 1993, para E3.
9   See LAWLIP, op cit, p 13.

Doing practical legal research

Practical legal research differs from academic legal research in three key ways. First, it tends to start from an unfocused problem. As we have seen, *you* have to provide the focus by your problem analysis. Second, it also differs in that the range of justiciable issues may be wider: a case may throw up disputes about substantive law, evidence, procedure or an amalgam of these. Lastly, the sources you will be expected to refer to are often different. Practitioner texts, precedent and form books take the place of most of the academic texts you are familiar with.

The actual process of research can be broken down into four phases:[1]

- Analysis of the problem.
- Initial review of the subject matter.
- Search of primary and secondary sources.
- Updating the research.

1 ANALYSIS OF THE PROBLEM

This inevitably starts with your fact analysis. A client comes to you with a problem, and your first technical task is to translate[2] that problem into something which has legal significance and meaning. In the Xenos's case, for example, you are translating their fear about repossession of their home into a dispute grounded in contract or company law. This translation exercise is essential before you can begin meaningful research.

For research purposes, your analysis needs to focus on keyword searching. Keywords are the important terms you have identified/translated from your client's story. These keywords may be based on either the specific facts of the case, or on any legal concepts which you have identified as relevant. We therefore call the techniques you use 'key-fact' and 'key-concept' searching.

If you have little idea of the law involved, you will be forced to rely on key-fact searching. In trying to identify appropriate key-facts, you can use the acronym '*PEPT*'[3] – ie *Parties, Events, Places* and *Things* – as a guide to what might be important. Thus:

Parties Do the persons involved belong to a particular class – employees; minors; lessors or lessees, etc? Are they in a legally significant relationship – eg, as husband and wife; mortgagor/mortgagee; consumer/ supplier; director/shareholder?

Events What key event, or events, created the problem – eg, selling shares; conveying a house, unloading a ship, etc?

Places How important is the place (and/or timing) of the event? For example, did an accident take place at your client's place of work, during or out of normal working hours?

Things Does the case involve a specific object (a will, letter, gold ring) which might be significant to the legal issue?

Key-facts can be used directly in literature or case searches. However, in most cases you will also be able to identify relevant legal concepts, so that it is possible to integrate key-fact and key-concept searching to provide a more precise search strategy.

Once you have translated the problem into a specific legal category or categories, you can use those terms for key-concept searching. This is a form of search strategy you will certainly be familiar with – you are simply using subject or topic labels (eg 'contract', 'specific performance', 'Anton Piller') to find information in indexes and books.

Key concepts can be established by thinking about four things:
1. the cause of action or crime charged;
2. any defence available;
3. in civil cases, the remedy sought;
4. the stage you are at in the legal process (eg pre-trial review).

2   INITIAL REVIEW OF THE SUBJECT MATTER

Your second stage will be to review the subject. How far this is necessary obviously depends on your familiarity with the area and the complexity of the problem, but some element of review reading will often be necessary to help establish your working hypotheses. More specifically, in research terms, the purposes of review reading may be one or more of the following:
● To familiarise yourself with the legal principles.
● To enable you to refine and/or extend your keyword search.
● To find references to primary sources which will form the basis of a further search.
● To find references to additional secondary sources so as to extend your review.

3   SEARCH OF PRIMARY AND SECONDARY SOURCES

Once you have reviewed the area, you can begin the in-depth research necessary to solve the legal dimension of the problem. This is the third, search, phase. Both primary and secondary legal materials may be necessary at this stage. The Bristol survey suggested that, as we would expect, barristers refer more frequently to primary sources than solicitors. But primary sources are clearly important to practitioners in both halves of the profession. Of the 474 lawyers surveyed, virtually all the barristers surveyed used both law reports and statutes more than once a month, while, among solicitors, over 70% referred to statutory material and nearly 50% to law reports more than once a month. Half the barristers surveyed also used statutory instruments with a similar frequency.[4] Both search and updating methods in respect of primary sources are therefore essential skills for practitioners.

Secondary sources are also important at both review and search phases. For the trainee, this means becoming familiar with a whole new set of texts. Key practitioner sources include the following:
● Legal Encyclopaedias, eg
    – *Halsbury's Laws*;
    – *Halsbury's Statutes*;
    – *Halsbury's Statutory Instruments*;
    – *Encyclopaedia of Forms & Precedents*;
    – *Atkin's Court Forms*;
    – Specialist (subject-specific) encyclopaedias.
● The Court Practice books, eg
    – *Supreme Court Practice* (the 'White Book');
    – *The County Court Practice* (the 'Green Book');
    – *Archbold's Criminal Pleading, Evidence and Practice*;

– *Blackstone's Criminal Practice*;
– *Stone's Justices' Manual*.
● Drafting texts, eg
– Melville *The Draftsman's Handbook*;
– *Kelly's Draftsman*;
– Specialist precedent books in each subject.

4   UPDATING THE RESEARCH

Whether you are relying on primary or secondary sources, it is vital that your research is as up to date as you can make it. If you are still unsure how to update primary sources, use the techniques described in Tunkel, Brayne & Grimes, or Webb. Note that many of the standard practitioner texts are published in loose-leaf format, and are regularly amended by the issue of new updates. Other texts may be supported by a noter-up, or supplement. You should always check these, if they are available, and note the date of publication.

In practice, it is vital that you maintain a record of your research, as part of the client's file. This not only assists you in keeping the research up to date, but enables anyone else working on the file to see what has been done. You will find a specimen checklist for legal research at the end of this chapter.[5]

Finally, we will close this section with some practical research exercises.

1   M Price, H Bitner & S Bysiewicz *Effective Legal Research*, 4th Edition, Little Brown, Boston 1979
2   We discuss the role of the lawyer as translator further in Chapters 5 and 6.
3   See Webb 'Legal Research and Problem-Solving' in Jones (ed) *Lawyers' Skills*, Blackstone Press, London 1994, p 29.
4   See Webb *Legal Research and Information Systems*, Faculty of Law Working Paper No 1, UWE Bristol, January 1994, pp 14–16.
5   Taken from Webb, op cit (see note 3), pp 45–7.

Exercise 3.22   Practical legal research exercises

Below are three research problems. In respect of each of them:

(a)   Complete a record of your research, noting sources used for review, search and updating functions.

(b)   Draft a note of your findings, giving an answer to the problem identified in each brief.

1.   Andrea is a full-time childminder. She is also expecting her first child. One of the children she looks after has just been diagnosed as having rubella. It is possible others might also be infectious. Andrea is uncertain whether she has had rubella, or been vaccinated against it. Her doctor has therefore advised her to refrain from work until tests have been completed to ascertain her immunity (or otherwise). Andrea now wishes to know whether she can claim sickness benefit for that period.

Assume for the purposes of this question that Andrea meets the necessary contribution conditions for sickness benefit and that the days in question fall before 1 April 1995.

2.   A new Act of Parliament (fictitious) makes it an offence for any person in a public place to cause a disturbance, provided that the disturbance is of

'significant proportion or degree'. There is no definition of that phrase within the Act. You are consulted by a client who has been charged with the offence after shouting, briefly, across a road to some friends on the other side.[1]

Advise.

3. Your client Jennifer has a son, Peter, at Dotheboys Hall, an independent school. Peter was caned by the French teacher for an incident in class. Jennifer had made it clear to the head teacher, when Peter joined the school, that she was unhappy with caning for relatively minor infringements (which she feels this particular incident was). The head teacher had assured her that teachers were restrained in their use of the cane. Jennifer feels that the school has broken its word, and seeks your advice on any legal action she could take.

---

1   This example is loosely adapted from Inns of Court School of Law *Evidence and Casework Skills*, Blackstone Press, London 1994/95, p 226.

Problem-solving and people-working

So far we have tended to treat problem-solving largely as a technical domain. We have not really placed much emphasis on the fact that, behind your problem there is a person – your client.

Does that matter? Isn't it your job to solve your client's problem? Doesn't this mean that your primary task is to relieve your client of their problem, and present them with a solution (and a bill) when it is all over?

Well, we think that it is not as simple as that. For reasons that we will develop in Chapters 4 and 6, we would argue that the lawyer–client relationship is far more *participatory* than that – lawyers work with clients as well as for them. For this reason we would define lawyers (perhaps somewhat idealistically) as 'people-workers' as well as problem-solvers, who:

> . . . through the communication of information and sharing of insights, attempt to help the client help himself. They can be differentiated from those professions who use knowledge to help the client but do not share it with them . . .[1]

The notion of people-working raises very important questions about the way we deploy our knowledge and skills. The quote from Bennett and Hokenstad gives some indications of the kind of answers a participatory approach implies, and, for the moment we will leave it at that. However, we would ask you, before you leave this chapter, to reflect on the techniques we have discussed and to think about the stages in the process where you think it generally would be (a) advisable and (b) essential to involve your client in decision making.

---

1   W S Bennett & M C Hokenstad 'Full-time People Workers and Conceptions of the "Professional"' in P Halmos (ed) *Professionalisation and Social Change*, Sociological Review Monograph No 20, Keele University, 1973, p 21 at p 23.

Exercise 3.23 Concepts

(a) *Produce your own definition for each of the following technical terms used in this chapter.*

(b) *In small groups, compare your answers and, where there are differences, try to agree a common understanding of the term.*

admissibility	framing effect
affirmative evidence	inference
bounded rationality	invariance
brainstorming	lateral thinking
expansionary thinking	people-working
evidence in rebuttal	proof
evidentiary fact	

Exercise 3.24 Review questions

1 GUESSING GAMES?

Read the judgment of Justice Hobson in *Voelker v Combined Insurance Co* (1954) 73 So 2d 403, then answer the following questions.

(a) *What was the single item of evidence in the case on which all further inference was based?*

(b) *What was the central fact in issue?*

(c) *Identify the various links in the chain which the court found necessary to determine that fact in issue. Which of these were based on direct evidence and which were inferential?*

(d) *Can the statement 'Voelker had been in a car accident' be reduced to a series of inferences?*

(e) *Does the court's rule succeed in preventing verdicts 'based upon speculation'? Why/why not?*

2 PEACE TRAIN COMING

Read the newspaper story in Anderson & Twining, pp 285–7, as if it were an opening statement by counsel for the plaintiff. Then answer the following questions.[1]

(a) *Assume that an action is brought by the family of Donna Ulrich against the Ford Motor Co. From the standpoint of plaintiff's counsel:*

　　(i) *who are the witnesses and what other evidence would you call to support this statement of facts?*

　　(ii) *Are there any assertions in the statement that are insupportable by evidentiary facts? Identify them.*

(b) *Assume that you also have expert testimony which supports the assertion that Ford's engineers knew that, for an additional $25 on the manufacturing cost per vehicle, the company could have reduced the probability that the fuel tank would explode in such a collision from 1 in 10 to 1 in 50. National regulatory standards did not require the design features that would have had that effect. Invent additional facts that seem plausible inferences accordingly.*

(c)   Assuming the following legal principles govern liability, chart the case using five-level analysis.

Manufacturer's liability requires that:

(i)   The vehicle or its components were defectively designed, manufactured or assembled, and

(a)   the manufacturer knew or should have known of the defect, and

(b)   the defect was correctable at reasonable cost, and

(c)   correction of the defect would have significantly reduced the probability that injury or death would occur.

(ii) But for the specific defect in design (etc), injury or death would not have occurred.

1   Adapted from Anderson & Twining *Analysis of Evidence*, Butterworths, London 1991, pp 287–8.

Further reading

T Anderson & W Twining *Analysis of Evidence*, Butterworths, London 1991.

D Binder & P Bergman *Fact Investigation: From Hypothesis to Proof*, West Publishing, St Paul, Minn 1984.

H Brayne & R Grimes *Professional Skills for Lawyers: A Student's Guide*, Butterworths, London 1994.

M Costanzo *Problem Solving*, Cavendish, London 1994.

V Tunkel *Legal Research*, Blackstone Press, London 1993.

Legal research checklist

Background information
Researcher . . . .
Memorandum for . . . .
Commenced . . . . . . Completed . . . .

Strategy
Material facts . . . .
. . . .
. . . .
Legal issue . . . .
. . . .
Keywords:
Fact . . . .
Concept . . . .

Database search?   YES/NO

Encyclopaedias and digests
. . . *Halsbury's Laws*
. . . *Halsbury's Statutes*
. . . *Halsbury's Statutory Instruments*

. . . *The Digest*
. . . Other loose-leaf
. . . .
. . . . (name)
. . . *Words and Phrases*

Checked:
. . . Cumulative supplement
. . . Noter-up
Updated to: . . . .

Checked:
. . . Supplement
. . . Service
. . . . (dates)

Other secondary sources
Books:
Name . . . . Date published . . . . . .
Name . . . . Date published . . . . . .
Name . . . . Date published . . . . . .
Name . . . . Date published . . . . . .
Journals:
Legal Journals Index checked?   YES/NO
Current Law checked? . . . yearbook . . . monthly parts

Primary sources

Legislation
. . . HMSO copy
. . . *Current Law Statutes*

Case law
. . . *Law Reports*/WLR etc
. . . Specialist series

... *Statutes in Force*   ... Daily law reports
... *Halsbury's Statutes*
... Other source
. . . .
. . . . (name)
... SI/SR & O
Updated by:
... *Is It In Force?*   ... Case citator
... Statute citator   ... *Current Law* (monthly)
... *Current Law monthly parts*   ... *Law Reports Index*
... *Halsbury's Statutes* (noter-up)   ... *Daily Law Reports Index*
... HMSO *Daily List*
... Journal source
Checked to: . . . . (latest dates)

European law
General
... *Encyclopaedia of European Community Law*
... *Common Market Reporter*
... *Halsbury's Laws*
... *Official Journal*
... Other source
. . . .
. . . . (name)

Legislation   *Case law*
... *Official Journal*   ... *Common Market Law Reports*
... *Halsbury's Statutes*   ... *European Court Reports*
... *Encyclopaedia of European*   ... Other law report
       Community Law   . . . . (name)
... *Common Market Reporter*
Supplement or service checked?
. . . . (latest date)

Updated by: *To date:*
... *Official Journal*   . . . .
... *EC Brief*   . . . .
... *Halsbury's Laws of England noter-up*   . . . .
... *Halsbury's Statutes noter-up*   . . . .
... *Current Law*   . . . .
... *European Current Law*   . . . .

Forms and precedents; court practice
Title   *Supplement or service date or date*
                                                          of publication (if not updated)

... *Encyclopaedia of Forms and Precedents*   . . . .
... *Atkin's Encyclopaedia of Court Forms*   . . . .
... *Longman's County Court Precedents*   . . . .

. . . Other precedent books:
Title . . . .
Title . . . .
Title . . . .
. . . Journal precedent (ref:)   . . . .
. . . Database search   (ref:)
. . . White Book   . . . .
. . . Green Book   . . . .
. . . Stone   . . . .
. . . Archbold   . . . .
. . . *Blackstone's Criminal Practice*   . . . .
. . . Other
. . . .
. . . . (names)   . . . .

Summary of research findings

Advice (if appropriate)

'Problem-solving is a multi-dimensional task'

4 Problem-solving: (ii) the business and ethical dimensions

In this chapter we expand our model of problem-solving to take account of the 'business' and 'ethical' dimensions of legal problems. We start by considering some of the threats and opportunities created by the drive for a more business-like approach to legal practice. In the second part of the chapter we build on that to explore, first, the ethical dimension introduced by the professional codes of conduct. We then encourage you to consider whether the standards imposed by the codes are enough, or whether a genuinely ethical standard of legal practice needs to be based on other internal or external criteria.

Objectives

To:

- Enable you to recognise the value conflicts created by a rapidly changing professional environment.
- Introduce you to the main ethical responsibilities laid down by professional codes of conduct.
- Encourage you to analyse and reflect on the ethical basis of legal practice.
- Provide you with a basis to evaluate your own sense of ethics and its relationship to professional problem-framing and problem-solving.

Introduction

Donald Schön's analysis recognises the significance of value conflicts in professional problem-solving.[1] Problem-solving refuses to remain simply a technical skill – where you can resolve cases just by looking up the right books, using your checklists and flow charts and applying the rules and procedures required. To be sure, some basis of factual and legal analysis and argument must form the root of all legal problem-solving.[2] But you cannot stop there. The messy part of legal practice is sorting out the frames and contexts within which problems are presented and resolved. This means determining whether you can afford to take on a particular case, or adopt a particular strategy; trying to assess whether a client's objectives, or your choice of strategy, set you an ethical dilemma, or trying to re-frame the problem once an ethical dilemma arises. It is these dilemmas that make problem-solving a multi-dimensional task.

For simplicity's sake, we have organised this chapter somewhat artificially to distinguish two sets of values in the modern legal profession: those that emphasise (i) law as a business, and (ii) law as an ethical profession. These sets are not wholly separate in real life, and certainly not always in opposition to each other.

1   See eg *The Reflective Practitioner*, Basic Books, New York 1983, pp 14–15; 41–3.
2   See eg the analysis by Paul Bergman 'Is that a fact? Argument in problem-solving negotiations' (1994) 1 *International Journal of the Legal Profession* 81.

The business dimension

Just for a change we start by getting you to do some of the work.

Exercise 4.1   The law business

Read each of the following quotes. What do they tell you about law as a business?

1.   The practice must be managed as a business. Each client . . . is merely the raw material, and the finished product is a completed file. It is imperative that the cost of completing the work is reduced to a minimum in order to achieve maximum profit . . . This exercise is not an economy drive; it is a radical reconstruction of the traditional working practices of the firm.[1]

2.   What does it mean to be a professional? Providing a service basically whatever the cost, even if you have to bear the cost – or part of it – yourself . . . the most important thing is standards and service . . . Now the most important thing is being paid for the job . . . We're being inexorably pushed towards being hyper-commercial . . . As a result, were I to repeat my life I wouldn't be a lawyer . . . it's becoming a trade not a profession.[2]

3.   Michael Shapiro practised predominantly in the real estate area and worked mainly for Segal Partners [a firm of property developers]. His mentor in Tischmann [the law firm in which he worked] was Robert Levi who brought Segal Partners to the firm. As this client was one of the firm's largest, Levi exercised considerable authority in the firm and indeed headed the firm's policy committee which managed the firm's internal affairs . . . Segal Partners' principals dealt primarily with Levi, but in individual matters the work was assigned to a middle-ranking partner, such as Shapiro, who would shepherd the deal through the various intermediate stages. As much as a partner like Shapiro was in charge of a matter, he could never forget he was at best only a second in command . . . His relationship with the client, therefore, would always contain an irresolvable tension for him. That is, if the professional is granted the mantle of expert, how is that expertise to be exercised authoritatively when the professional is placed in an ambiguous position vis-à-vis the client?[3]

We suggest that these quotes represent three key 'business' aspects of modern legal practice through which value conflicts may emerge. These aspects we term: the routinisation of legal work; challenges to the professional self-image of the lawyer; and the 'politics' of the law firm.[4]

1   J Dirks *Making Legal Aid Pay*, Waterlows, London 1989, p 7.
2   Solicitor in private practice quoted by Hilary Sommerlad 'Some Implications of Professional Restructuring in the Justice Community', paper delivered at the Socio-Legal Studies Association Annual Conference, University of Leeds, March 1995.
3   J Flood 'Doing Business: The Management of Uncertainty in Lawyers' Work' (1991) 25 *Law & Society Review* 41 at 49–50.
4   The relative lack of detailed research in the UK on some of these issues has forced us, in what follows, to argue from analogy and anecdote, and to hypothesise rather more than we would like. We have tried, so far as possible, without making the whole section too long and too cumbersome, to indicate what is speculation and what is grounded in research.

The routinisation of legal work

One of the clearest trends in recent years has been the increased pressure to routinise legal work. By this we mean the tendency to create systems for the resolution of 'straightforward' legal problems. Routinisation has been encouraged by a variety of commercial pressures both to keep down the costs of legal services, and to maintain or improve their quality. Routinisation is reflected in a number of trends.

First, there is standardisation. This emerges in both the increased automation of practice by using specialist database systems – eg for producing precedents, or for the virtual management of standard files, such as simple conveyancing and debt-collection transactions, and by the restructuring of much day-to-day work into simplified transactional stages, many of which can be undertaken by unadmitted staff. Routinisation aids profitability by increasing the throughput of chargeable work, and often means that unit costs can be kept down by increasing the number of tasks that can be performed by support staff or paralegals.

Second, we have seen experiments in streamlining case management and service delivery. The 'hub and spoke' model piloted by the major legal aid firm, Deacon Goldrein Green, was a prime example in which litigation expertise was concentrated at a central office, with most client contact and client care functions being provided by the various branch offices of the firm[1] – a kind of production-line 'Taylorist' or 'Fordist'[2] approach to legal services. Bureaucratisation is a related phenomenon. Consumer demand for higher standards of service has been translated into an emphasis on accreditation and management.[3] Schemes such as the British Standards Institute BS 5750 and, arguably, the new legal aid franchises, tend to equate quality of service with the visibility of and adherence to management systems, rather than trying to measure the intrinsic quality of the advice. The efficacy of such measures is hotly debated;[4] as one article has put it, there is concern that such bureaucratisation might simply result in 'Kentucky Fried Law'.[5]

The effects of routinisation are the subject of much debate. On the positive side, it is argued that it should release admitted staff from mundane practical tasks, so that they can concentrate more fully on those cases which require a lawyer's expertise. We have some doubts. Our main concern is simply that, by definition, routinisation does not work well in conditions of uncertainty. This can lead to a number of results.

First, commercial pressures may be such as to encourage practitioners to cut corners and try to make the exceptional more like the routine. Certainly, the financial return for the extra effort that exceptional cases require is often relatively low – particularly in situations where contingent or conditional fee schemes are in place.[6] This may encourage lawyers to pressure for early settlement or adopt other labour-saving devices which protect their profit margins.[7] To draw an analogy with America, there is the risk that firms will

> . . . slop through with quickie work, or as one lawyer put it, make good guesses as to the level of malpractice at which they should operate in any given situation.[8]

Second, we suspect there is a danger that bureaucratisation in particular may distract fee-earners' attention from client-centred to management tasks: if you want an analogy, ask a university teacher about the bureaucratisation of higher education! The reorganisation of the National Health Service probably provides an even better example.

Third, it follows that, from a client's perspective, uncertainty becomes expensive. This can be seen best in the development of corporate and commercial practice. Though aspects of 'big city' practice can be as routinised as other types of work, 'swamp' problems are more likely to abound in that environment. Quite simply, corporate clients may be the only ones who can afford the costs of complex litigation, especially where firms use a fees 'mark-up' to inflate their hourly rate to reflect the technicality of the issues involved.[9] As one study has argued:

> . . . the discovery of a unique issue is likely to be a function of the amount of time that lawyers devote to a case, and thus of the amount of money that the client spends on lawyers. If the stakes are high, the problems can become very complex; if the client lacks money, his problems are likely to be routine.[10]

Uncertainty can thus be seen as not just an intrinsic characteristic of legal work, but something that is actively created out of a problem by the lawyer – if resources and other factors allow.

In sum, it means that routinisation can limit the organisation's capacity for experimentation and innovation. Standardisation and bureaucratisation can be *de-skilling*.[11] And there is undoubtedly a certain irony in the legal profession's discovery of the Fordist mode of production at a time when many professions are stressing the importance of developing a multi-functional, flexible ('Post-Fordist') workforce.[12] While routinisation may improve the efficiency with which a firm can deliver normal services, it may prevent it from being able to identify, let alone provide quality services in, non-standard cases.

1   See J Dirks *Making Legal Aid Pay*, Waterlows, London 1989, p 85ff.
2   See eg D Harvey *The Condition of Postmodernity*, Blackwell, Cambridge, Ma & Oxford 1989, pp 125–6 for a brief discussion of these terms.

3   See eg R Chaplin & N Morgan 'How do you evaluate a Quality Service?' *Legal Business*, November 1991, p 45; also R Bowles 'The Structure of the Legal Profession in England and Wales' (1994) 10 *Oxford Review of Economic Policy* 18 at 21–2; J Watkins & L Drury 'The pressures on professional life in the 1990s' (1994) 1 *International Journal of the Legal Profession* 369 at 373–7.

4   See eg the special issue on Competence and Quality Issues in the Legal Profession, (1994) 1 *International Journal of the Legal Profession* 131–250.

5   S Webster 'Kentucky Fried Law' *Solicitors Journal*, 5 February 1993, p 86.

6   See D E Rosenthal *Lawyer and Client: Who's in Charge?* Russell Sage Foundation, New York 1974, pp 106–16; H S Gravelle & M Waterson 'No Win, No Fee: Some Economics of Contingent Legal Fees' (1993) 103 *Economic Journal* 1205.

7   Cf Rosenthal, op cit.

8   G Hazard *Ethics in the Practice of Law*, Yale University Press, New Haven & London 1978, pp 152–3.

9   This practice is allowed under conditional fee arrangements authorised under the Courts and Legal Services Act 1990.

10 J P Heinz & E O Laumann 'The Legal Profession: Client Interests, Professional Roles, and Social Hierarchies' (1978) 76 *Michigan Law Review* 1111 at 1117.

11 Such criticisms of the Deacon Goldrein Green experiment emerged after the firm collapsed spectacularly in 1994 – see J Bezzano 'Paying for Legal Aid' *Legal Action*, January 1995, p 9.

12 Watkins & Drury, op cit, pp 380–1.

The challenges to professional self-image

As the second quote in our series indicates, the notion of 'being a professional' is ideologically highly loaded. Although Schön might argue that the craft dimension of legal *knowledge* no longer prevails, the craft *image* of legal *practice* remains a powerful one, stressing as it does the skilled handiwork and practical application of the lawyer's tasks.[1] What are the characteristics of legal craftsmanship? You might like to try drawing up your own list before considering ours.

We suggest that, as a minimum, the idea of legal practice as a craft implies the following:

● the provision of a personalised and independent service;[2]
● outcomes that are the result of highly skilled production processes;
● practitioners who are ethically responsible;
● a service that is not just profit driven.[3]

This offers an undoubtedly idealised picture of practice. Many would add that the craft image also implies an environment that is resistant to changes in the mode of production, and there, ultimately, it is said, lies the problem. Lawyers are constantly being urged to be more 'business-like' – a phrase which tends to mean 'commercial' or profit-driven. But what are the implications of this in terms of professional image?

First, it raises questions about the 'collegiality' or competitiveness of lawyers. The traditional image of the profession is of a group that is socially homogeneous, and whose practice is grounded in a chivalric tradition – the *Noblesse Oblige* tradition of the Bar. It is this that creates the sense of law as an honourable calling for gentlemen of substance who do not need to demean themselves by worrying about profit.[4] Of course this has long been open to challenge, and there is evidence that the professions generally have outgrown their traditional roles and values.[5]

The contradictions between professional collegiality and competitive survival are becoming ever more apparent. As Allaker and Shapland note, both within and between professions:

> . . . current socio-economic climates have produced an increasingly complex and competitive market where professions are being forced to become 'service providers'. Professions are thus under economic pressure to offer both low costs and an extended range of services.[6]

One result of this competitiveness may be to increase the potential for intra-professional 'turf wars' between groups. This is a subject which has barely been researched, but when reports in the press include disclosures of one senior litigator faxing a copy of an opponent's letter back to him with the message 'the kind of crap to be expected from you' scrawled across it,[7] or when barristers attempt to bar solicitor-advocates from the court robing room,[8] it is tempting to suggest that collegiality is the most probable victim.

Second, a business orientation clearly has both economic and ethical implications for the profession, some of which will contradict the craft image. Does it mean that more and more lawyers will refuse to serve as duty solicitors because it is not economically worthwhile?[9] Will criminal defence lawyers push even more legally aided defendants to plead guilty in the magistrates' court because of the impact of standard fees?[10] Does it matter if large commercial practices only undertake *pro bono* (no-fee) work because 'it's a nice positive marketing image'[11] rather than a professional responsibility? Such decisions would certainly fit uncomfortably with the traditional conception of the lawyer's role, whereby

> . . . membership [of the profession] entails an ethical obligation to temper one's selfish pursuit of economic success by adhering to standards of conduct that could not be enforced either by legal fiat or the discipline of the market.[12]

It follows that the clash here between the new entrepreneurialism and the traditional service ethic will also create individual crises of self-image for practitioners; studies such as Sommerlad's offer strong qualitative support for such a view.

1   See eg K N Llewellyn 'The Crafts of Law Re-Valued' in *Jurisprudence: Realism in Theory and Practice*, University of Chicago Press, Chicago 1962, p 316ff; also W Twining 'The Idea of Juristic Method: A Tribute to Karl Llewellyn' (1993) 48 *University of Miami Law Review* 119 at 147–51.

2   T J Johnson *Professions and Power*, Macmillan, London & Basingstoke 1972, p 23.

3   Ibid. Cf the Marre Committee's conclusion that

> . . . because lawyers have overriding duties to the rule of law, to their clients, and to the court, commercial considerations cannot be paramount when considering the future supply of legal services.

– *A Time for Change: Report of the Committee on the Future of the Legal Profession*, General Council of the Bar/The Law Society, London 1988, para 6.10.

4   See J H Baker *An Introduction to English Legal History*, 3rd Edition, Butterworths, London 1990, p 187; cf D Luban 'The Noblesse Oblige Tradition in the Practice of Law' (1988) 41 *Vanderbilt Law Review* 717.

5   See eg the discussion in P Atkinson 'The Reproduction of the Professional Community' in R Dingwall & P Lewis *The Sociology of the Professions: Lawyers, Doctors and Others*, Macmillan/SSRC, London & Basingstoke p 224 at 227; also Johnson, op cit, pp 53–4.

6   *Organising UK Professions: Continuity and Change*, Research Study No 16, The Law Society, London 1994, p 65.
7   *The Lawyer*, 13 December 1994, p 3.
8   *The Times*, 6 December 1994, p 37.
9   Cf Sommerlad 'Some Implications of Professional Restructuring in the Justice Community', paper delivered at the Socio-Legal Studies Association Annual Conference, University of Leeds, March 1995.
10 See M McConville, A Sanders & R Leng *The Case for the Prosecution: Police Suspects and the Construction of Criminality*, Routledge, London & New York 1991, pp 167–70 for a review of the recent literature on guilty pleas. The regulations on standard fees are contained in Part III, Sch 1, Legal Aid in Criminal and Care Proceedings (Costs) Regulations 1989; see the commentary in Legal Aid Board *Legal Aid Handbook 1994*, Sweet & Maxwell, London pp 149–52.
11 City partner quoted by Fiona Bawden, 'The needy and the greedy', *The Guardian*, 14 March 1995.
12 Per O'Connor J *Shapero v Kentucky Bar Association* (1988) 486 US 466 at 488.

The politics of the firm

In law firms, as in other types of business, there is often an added organisational dimension to decision-making processes. In the working environment you are not a free agent. This lack of control is, in legal practice, often disguised by the apparent independence of the individual practitioner. You have your own cases, often your own support staff. You appear to be in control, but you are not. Why?

Theoretically, this situation can be explained by reference to notions of *organisational choice*.[1] Organisational choices are not necessarily determined by individual preferences and actions, but by a complex interaction of internal and external events and personalities. These changing contexts of organisational decision-making can lead to outcomes which are not really intended, or desired, by the individual decision-maker. To put it bluntly, in practice your choices will be influenced by factors like your status in the firm, and the commercial imperatives of that firm; the relative needs and statuses of your clients; the influence of different personalities and power-dimensions in the firm's management – and so on.

As the third of our quotes, from John Flood's study, shows, the organisational dimension can be problematic. A lawyer can become caught between two constituencies, her superior in the firm and her client, with the result that she is forced to engage in sometimes quite difficult negotiations of status and power across her professional relationships.

1   See J G March & J P Olsen 'The Uncertainty of the Past: Organisational Learning under Ambiguity' (1975) 3 *European Journal of Political Research* 147–71.

From business to ethics

In this brief overview of the modern working environment we have attempted to show how the business dimension can complicate professional decision-making in a number of ways. In so doing we have consciously emphasised the negative at the expense of the positive aspects of modern practice – which do exist! The fact remains, however, that, over the last twenty years, virtually all parts of the profession have faced some major transitions – in working practices, client expectations, their own expectations.

The curious thing is that, against this backdrop, the sense of what it is to be a lawyer has come under question time and again, and that is, fundamentally, a question of role and ethics. Yet, at an intellectual level, there has been virtually no discussion of the ethical basis of English legal practice.

The ethical dimension

. . . There is no way of avoiding th[e] ultimate responsibility of law to ethics. Every final determination of the general end of law, the standard of legal criticism (whether this be labelled 'justice', 'natural law', 'the protection of natural rights' or 'the organisation of social interests'), must reduce to the general form, 'The law ought to bring about as much good as it can.'[1]

For us, the subject of ethics is of central importance to legal education and legal practice. First, we adopt David Luban's phrase, that 'for practical purposes, the lawyers are the law'. Think about what he means by this. Second, we argue that a lack of ethical awareness restricts our ability to achieve a critical understanding of the legal process, and our capacity for reflective practice.

We begin by establishing some basic themes.

1   F Cohen *The Ethical Basis of Legal Criticism* (1959) in W R Bishin & C D Stone *Law, Language and Ethics*, Foundation Press, Mineola, NY 1972, pp 32–3.

Exercise 4.2   Define your terms

Working individually, write down brief answers to each of the following questions.

1. *What does the term 'ethics' mean to you?*
2. *Do you think lawyer's ethics differ from 'ordinary' ethics? If so, how do they differ?*
3. *Would you expect ethical conflicts to be rare or commonplace in legal practice?*
4. *Do you think use of the terms 'Code of Professional Conduct' and 'Code of Professional Ethics' indicates significant differences in the content or purpose of the respective documents? Can you give an example of the kind of difference you have in mind?*
5. *Can you give at least one example from your legal education (other than this course) where you have had to consider the ethical dimension of lawyering (focus on your formal education here, rather than experiences in work placements and the like).*

Now, if possible, compare your answers to those of other members of your group. What do you find?

We shall come back to your answers at the end of these materials.

Having got you to think about these issues in the abstract, have a go at Exercise 4.3. This exercise is based around a genuine trial of 1743 – the case of *Annesley v Anglesea*.[1] This extraordinary case arose out of the Earl of Anglesea's attempts to gain the estate of Lord Altham, contrary to the rights of the legitimate heir, Altham's only child, and Anglesea's own nephew, James Annesley.

Anglesea had already 'acquired' the property after Lord Altham's death by kidnapping James (then aged 12) and shipping him to America, where he was sold into slavery. Thirteen years later, James escaped and returned to England, where he commenced proceedings to recover his inheritance.

Anglesea attempted to thwart him again. He instructed his lawyer, James Giffard, to prosecute Annesley for murder after he (Annesley) had accidentally shot and killed a man. Giffard was privy to Lord Anglesea's reasons for pursuing the action, which, if it had succeeded, would have disentitled Annesley as a convicted felon. However, the prosecution failed. James's suit proceeded, and Giffard became a key witness for Annesley, who sought to show that his uncle's repeated attempts to get rid of him were, in effect, evidence that he was the true heir.

Counsel for Anglesea were thus forced into the interesting position of having to impugn in cross-examination the testimony of Giffard, their client's former lawyer, and to question his honour for following that same client's instructions! This is where we come in . . .

1   (1743) 17 How St Trials 1139. The use of these materials follows D Luban *Lawyers and Justice: An Ethical Study*, Princeton University Press, Princeton, NJ 1988, pp 3–10.

Exercise 4.3   Faust and the Devil?

Read the following extract from the cross-examination of Giffard,[1] and then consider the questions following.

[Note that *A* = Anglesea's lawyer (who is not named in the transcript) and *G* = Giffard].

A	Pray now, when my lord Anglesea said to you, that he did not care if it cost him £10,000 to get the plaintiff hanged, did you understand that it was his resolution to destroy him if you could?
G	I did, Sir.
A	Did you advise my lord Anglesea not to carry on that prosecution?
G	I did not advise him not to carry it on; I did not presume to advise him . . .
A	Did you approve or disapprove of his expressions and design altogether?
G	I cannot say that I did either.
A	Did not you go on as effectually after, with the prosecution, as you could?
G	I did, to be sure, Sir. Indeed, I advised my lord Anglesea not to appear upon the trial.

A	When my lord Anglesea said, that he would not care if it cost him £10,000 so he could get the plaintiff hanged, did you apprehend from thence, that he would be willing to go to that expense in the prosecution?
G	I did.
A	Did you suppose from thence that he would dispose of £10,000 in any shape to bring about the death of the plaintiff?
G	I did.
A	Did you not apprehend that to be a most wicked crime?
G	I did.
A	If so, how could you, who set yourself out as a man of business, engage in that project, without making any objection to it?
G	I may as well ask you, how you came to be engaged for the defendant in this suit . . .
A	Did you not apprehend it to be a bad purpose to lay out money to compass the death of another man?
G	I do not know but I did. But I was not to undertake that bad purpose. If there was any dirty work, I was not concerned in it.
A	If you did believe this, I ask you, how came you to engage in this prosecution without objection?
G	I make a distinction between carrying on a prosecution and compassing the death of a man.
A	How came you to make that distinction?
G	I may as well ask, how the counsel came to plead this cause?
A	Did you ever mention to any of your counsel, that my lord made that declaration?
G	I did not.
A	If you had told any of them that my lord made that declaration, would they have appeared for you?
G	I can't tell whether they would or not.
A	Do you believe any honest man would?
G	Yes, I believe they would, or else I would not have carried it on, Sir. And I do assure, it is the only cause I was concerned in at the Old Bailey in my life, and shall be the last.

1. *What, if any, is the moral principle underpinning the argument presented by Lord Anglesea's counsel?*
2. *What, if any, is the moral principle underpinning Giffard's responses?*
3. *Should, in Faust's words 'Striving with all my power is precisely what I promise' be sufficient justification for a lawyer's activities? What, if anything, does it overlook?*

What we have presented you with in this case is the classic ethical dichotomy between one's duty to the client, and the possibility of any wider duty to promote 'justice', or whatever you may wish to call it. With this dichotomy in mind, we shall now take you through some materials and exercises to help you evaluate your views on legal ethics and their role in legal practice.

It is fair to say that ethics is a huge issue in its own right, and in a text of this sort we can only scratch the surface. We shall do this in two stages. First, we shall explore, fairly uncritically, the main ethical dimensions of the professional codes governing English lawyers. We shall then deepen the discussion to look at how the codes and other, more abstract, ethical principles might inform our sense of professional responsibility.

1 Adapted from the report at 1248–50.

The nature of professional ethics

One of the commonly ascribed features of any profession is its operation as a self-regulating body. These processes of self-regulation normally develop through the channel of a code of professional ethics, administered by some body within, or closely connected to, the profession itself.[1] This pretty accurately describes the model of regulation adopted by the English legal profession.[2]

Codes of professional conduct are laid down by both Law Society and Bar for the regulation of the profession. The term *conduct* usefully highlights a very basic point about the nature of these professional rules, which is that they are not wholly concerned with the *moral* regulation of the profession. They also serve to define professional boundaries and autonomy, and can greatly influence the range of economic activities undertaken by the profession.

For example, s 66 of the Courts and Legal Services Act 1990 both enables solicitors to form partnerships with non-solicitors, and (indirectly) confirms that there is no Common Law rule restricting barristers from so doing. Nevertheless, rules of conduct regulating the private practice Bar continue to prevent barristers from forming such relationships.

Structurally, professional conduct rules tend to reflect the Common Law tradition by providing 'general normative principles, which are made cumulatively more precise and more complex by decisions in particular cases adjudicated in courts'.[3] There are three particular limitations created by this approach (at least, in the context of the English system of professional regulation).

First, the Codes have grown substantially and reactively in response to political and/or economic pressures on the profession.[4] As a result, we have codes of conduct which have been accurately described as 'a ragbag of things that have been important at some time or another'.[5]

Second, given the way in which they are structured, the Codes are rather incoherent, when viewed as a whole, and open to much interpretation and assessment. This will mean that one of your primary tasks is to work out ethical priorities from among conflicting obligations. For example, the obligation of loyalty to the client potentially conflicts with two other aspects of the lawyer's professional responsibility: namely, her duty to other lawyers and her duty to the court. You may have to make decisions on where your primary obligation lies 'off the cuff' with little opportunity for advice or reflection.

Third, the Codes are incomplete. Many specific ethical rules are grounded in substantive or procedural rules of law. Sometimes the relationship between the legal rules and the Codes is 'explicit', in the sense that ethical rules within the Codes have a foundation in the substantive law. This is true of much of the ethical prescription surrounding client confidentiality. But this is not always the case. Sometimes it is simply that the law itself has a substantial impact on conduct/ethics, but that impact is not reflected in the contents of the Codes.

Legal rules governing advocacy and on professional negligence tend to fall into this category. Let us take a specific example. In *White v Jones*[6] the House of Lords has ruled that a solicitor who delayed so long in preparing a will that the client died before signing, was liable in negligence to the disappointed beneficiaries. In conduct terms this case is important because it not only stresses the need to process client instructions in a timely manner, but effectively extends the lawyer's duty to the client to those third parties who might foreseeably suffer loss through the solicitor's inactivity. The point is that you cannot gauge your standards of conduct purely by the code.

1   For a more academic discussion of this process see eg W E Moore with G W Rosenblum *The Professions: roles and rules*, Russell Sage Foundation, New York 1970 at pp 116–20; for a descriptive piece on the development of the American Codes see J F Backof & C L Martin 'Historical Perspectives: Development of the Codes of Ethics in the Legal, Medical and Accounting Professions' (1991) 10 *Journal of Business Ethics* 99. There is no equivalent history of the English codes.
2   On self-regulation, see *Wood v The Law Society* The Times, 2 March 1995, which indicated that an aggrieved client had no action in negligence against the Law Society for its failure to exercise its investigative and disciplinary powers more expeditiously.
3   Moore with Rosenblum, op cit, p 119; see also G Hazard 'The Future of Legal Ethics' (1991) 100 *Yale Law Journal* 1239. The legalisation of professional ethics is less advanced in the UK than in America, but conduct rules here are increasingly framed by legislation (eg the Financial Services Act 1986; Courts and Legal Services Act 1990) rather than just the internal standards of the profession.
4   For example, the first modern Practice Rules passed in the late 1920s/early 1930s arose out of growing public concern at solicitors' embezzling client funds. The profession decided to impose its own rules before the government imposed statutory controls. Our thanks to Leslie Sheinman for this information, which is based on on-going, and currently unpublished, research.
5   Law Society interviewee cited by J Allaker & J Shapland in *Organising UK Professions: Continuity and Change*, Research Study No 16, The Law Society, London 1994, p 32.
6   [1995] 2 WLR 187.

The 'ethical' dimensions of the codes of conduct

Hazard has argued that the ethical rules of the legal profession enforce certain 'core values', which he calls the duties of 'loyalty, confidentiality, and candour to the court'.[1] In this section we use these core values as a means of organising the central ethical duties laid down by the Law Society and Bar. These are not only relevant to your later career (if you enter practice), but if you are presently involved in any form of clinical work, they will constitute the minimum professional standards to which you will be expected to aspire. We would add that we have also been somewhat selective in the principles we have chosen to address. There are other provisions in the Codes which have an ethical dimension. We confine ourselves to what we see as the key provisions.

References in this section to paragraphs in the *LSG* or *CCB* relate to the Law Society's *Guide to the Professional Conduct of Solicitors*[2] and the *Code of Conduct for the Bar of England and Wales*[3] respectively.

DUTIES TO THE (LAY) CLIENT

Loyalty to the client is a paramount professional responsibility. Lord Brougham spelt out the principle in his famous defence of Queen Caroline, the consort of George IV, who was tried for adultery before the House of Lords:

> An advocate, by the sacred duty which he owes his client, knows in the discharge of that office but one person in the world, that client and none other. To save that client by all expedient means, to protect that client at all hazards and costs, to all others, and amongst others to himself, is the highest and most unquestioned of his duties; and he must not regard the alarm, the suffering, the torment, the destruction which he may bring upon any other.[4]

The essence of that statement is echoed in the *CCB*, which states:

> A practising barrister . . . must promote and protect fearlessly and by all proper and lawful means his lay client's best interests (para 203(a)).

Beyond this general principle, different duties are borne by solicitors and barristers, because of the different nature of their professional relationships. A practitioner at the Bar has two clients: the solicitor who instructs her[5] (the professional client) and the lay client on whose behalf she acts. As between the lay and professional client, the barrister's first duty is to the interests of the lay client (*CCB* 203). Beyond this, the main duties to the client are as follows:

- A solicitor cannot refuse to take instructions on the grounds of race or ethnic or national origin, and must not discriminate in her dealings with clients or other practitioners on the basis of race or gender (see *LSG* 7.01). Barristers are obliged, subject to specific exceptions, to act for any person on whose behalf they are instructed – the 'cab-rank rule' (*CCB* 209). Additionally they are required by *CCB* 204 not to treat any person less favourably than other such persons on grounds of race, sex, ethnicity, religion or political persuasion.
- A lawyer is bound to carry out the client's instructions diligently and with reasonable care and skill (*LSG* 12.11; *CCB* 601).
- The lawyer's duty to the client extends only in so far as it is consistent with other rules of conduct, or the rules of law. If a client persists with instructions which are contrary to either, the solicitor can terminate the retainer (*LSG* 12.02). Similar provisions govern the practising Bar – see *CCB* 504–505.
- A solicitor must keep the client properly informed of matters relevant to her affairs (*LSG* 12.15).[6]
- The lawyer has a duty to act promptly in dealing with the client's affairs (*LSG* 17.01; *CCB* 601).

The overall effects of such duties are complex. On the one hand, it can be argued that they help maintain a client-centred ethic within the profession, but, on the other, it is suggested they can encourage a 'hired gun' mentality amongst lawyers – ie that lawyers are prone to carry their partisanship too far, and to disregard the impact of their actions on third parties.[7] How damaging a hired gun approach is remains a moot point among legal ethicists. While it may lead to excesses, the point has equally been made that many of the pressures facing the practitioner today create a tendency to be the obverse of the hired gun: to be indifferent to and insufficiently zealous in defending client interests, in which case the principle of partisanship may serve as a necessary corrective.[8]

The efficacy of particular aspects of the duty to the client is also debatable. The classic example here is the famous cab-rank principle. One purpose of the cab-rank is to prevent the barrister's over-identification with a particular cause or group. Some of the more radical members of the Bar reject that ideology.[9] As one barrister has argued:

> When the rules say you can't associate with your client: you don't feel; you are just there to defend. You are a barrister . . . That's the rules of etiquette – that you fight fearlessly but you don't get involved. Now that's wrong because if there's a riot in Bristol or in Brixton between black people and the police, now, if you don't get involved you are a *straight* barrister . . . You can't effectively defend them because you must appreciate the issues and you must be bold enough. As far as my profession will allow me, I associate with them.[10]

Even within less radical sections of the Bar, it is known that certain counsel will only take cases which are very strictly within their expertise as they define it – for example, those barristers who will only defend criminal cases, or those who will not defend sex offenders. Formally, there is usually no breach of the cab-rank rule involved, because solicitors know not to instruct those counsel in certain kinds of cases. But doesn't that make a nonsense of the principles? Once you allow conscience to play a part in such decisions, where do you draw the line?

Another, less obvious, example arises out of the duty to keep the client informed. What exactly does that mean? There are certainly two possible readings. One is to treat it simply as an aspect of client care: an obligation to keep the client up to date by telling them what is happening. A second reading suggests that this obligation should be considered in the light of the lawyer's duty to carry out a client's instructions. The implication is, then, that the client should be kept informed, so that she can instruct her lawyer appropriately. Even so, that does not necessarily mean that the client becomes an *active* participant in decision-making in the way we discussed at the end of Chapter 3. A lawyer may inform and instruct by telling rather than asking.

Take, for example, the following illustration used by Rosenthal.[11] Assume you are the plaintiff in a personal injury action. Your lawyer has been negotiating on your behalf, but has not really discussed the value of the claim with you. What if your lawyer says to you, 'The other side are offering £2,000; I think it fair. If you want it, sign this release.'

Your lawyer is satisfying the obligation to obtain and carry out instructions, but on what basis is the client instructing? Consent is hardly informed,[12] and most of us would say that such advice is inadequate, but is it in breach of the Code?

DUTIES TO THE COURT

All lawyers are officers of the court[13] and are under a variety of duties because of that status. However, ethically, there is really only one overriding principle – the duty of candour. That is, that a lawyer must never deceive or mislead the court (*LSG* 22.01; *CCB* 202). This, it is said legitimises the profession's affiliation with the judiciary.[14]

For many commentators the lawyer's duty to the court is seen as the fundamental duty;[15] to fail in the promotion of the administration of justice is thus the ultimate in unethical behaviour – as Beyleveld and Brownsword put it 'the failure to observe the role-morality is a failure to play the role'.[16] But what does that mean? Much could be read into the duty beyond what is explicitly stated in the Codes. We know it is a breach of the Codes for a lawyer to continue to act in the knowledge that a client has committed perjury (see *LSG* 22.08; *CCB* 504(e) & (f)). But what constitutes 'knowledge' of perjury? Moreover, just how far should the advocate play *amicus curiae* against the interest of her client? Is advancing a shaky or spurious argument contrary to your duty? Is using time-wasting tactics to try and wear your opponent's client down? Is intimidating a witness to such an extent that she contradicts her own (truthful) testimony, so that your client is acquitted? Should a belief in zealous advocacy allow you to play a game with 'justice'?

The duty to the court has been spelt out in various terms by the judiciary, so let us see if the judges help us. Lord Reid has expressed the duty as follows:

> Every counsel has a duty to his client fearlessly to raise every issue, every argument, and ask every question, however distasteful, which he thinks will help his client's case. But as an officer of the court concerned in the administration of justice, he has an overriding duty to the court, to the standards of his profession, and to the public, which may and often does lead to a conflict with his client's wishes or with what the client thinks are his personal interests. Counsel must not mislead the court, he must not lend himself to casting aspersions on the other party or witnesses for which there is no sufficient basis in the information in his possession, he must not withhold authorities or documents which may tell against his clients but which the law or the standards of his profession require him to produce.[17]

This is stirring stuff, but what does it mean? Does it mean, for example, that if you are prosecutor in a criminal trial (so, in a sense, your only client is the state) you can act in as partisan a fashion as you would for an individual client – just so long as you do not actively mislead? If so, what does that imply about the state's role in the administration of justice? When is there a 'sufficient basis' for 'casting aspersions on the other party'? Let's look at one particular case where both these issues arise.

In 1990, Sara Thornton was convicted of the murder of her alcoholic husband, Malcolm, after stabbing him as he lay on their sofa in a drunken stupor.

As is so often the case, the evidence was contradictory and confusing. Thornton had a long history of violence against Sara and her 10-year-old daughter Louise. When drunk he gave way to violent and possessive rages. But Sara too had a reputation for a violent temper and a history suggesting mental instability. The jury rejected her plea of diminished responsibility and convicted on a 10–2 majority. Her subsequent appeal, on the basis that the defence of provocation should also have been put before the court, was rejected by the Court of Appeal.[18]

The prosecution was led by Brian Escott-Cox QC. The prosecution's main theory of the case appears to have been that Sara killed Malcolm for his money – but, as Judge J pointed out to the jury in his summing-up, this was unproven; there appeared to be precious little money left, as Malcolm had almost literally drunk the family into substantial debts. Why did the jury convict, then? Of course, we cannot know for sure, but one can only assume that, despite the lack of apparent motive, the majority were convinced that she was more bad than mad (a dubious binary opposition in itself, but the only options the jury were presented with). Sara was not a good witness, which would not have helped. There was some evidence of premeditation. The defence was not as rigorous as it might have been; one or two significant items of prosecution evidence were not adequately challenged. Certain testimony, on the levels of violence Sara had faced, was not presented at the time.[19]

However, the 'trump card' may well have been the prosecution's decision to attack Sara's character. Sara was strong-willed and argumentative. She had a reputation for liking male company, she drank quite heavily, dressed provocatively and, most heinous of all, often did not wear knickers. Cross-examination on these issues clearly served to create an image of a promiscuous and difficult woman to live with.[20] (Though there was no suggestion – and indeed no evidence – that Sara had engaged in any extra-marital affair). But to what purpose? It did not fit with the prosecution's mercenary motive. At best its admission served purely to damage her character, and hence the weight of her testimony. At worst it seems to support an (unspoken) argument that Malcolm's jealousy was justified, and to explain his violence as a means of controlling a headstrong, wanton wife. What do you think of the probity of such a line of questioning? Are these appropriate inferences for counsel to encourage a jury to draw? Would you say that such an approach was *ethical*?

DUTIES TO OTHER LAWYERS AND TO THE PUBLIC

Loyalty in the ethical context encompasses not only loyalty to the client, but also loyalty to the legal profession. The potential for conflict is obvious, and the lawyer's duty to other lawyers therefore tends to be defined as secondary to her duty to her client. The lawyer's duties in this context are also surrounded by an extensive professional etiquette, much of which remains unwritten.

The main principles are as follows:
● All lawyers have a professional duty to act towards other practitioners in good faith consistent with the overriding duty to the client (*LSG* 20.01; *CCB* 203(c)).

- A solicitor should not communicate with anyone who, to their knowledge, has retained another solicitor to act in the relevant matter, except with that other's consent (*LSG* 20.02).
- When instructing counsel a solicitor must ensure, so far as is practicable, that adequate instructions are sent in good time (*LSG* 21.03).
- Where counsel has been instructed to appear in proceedings the solicitor, or their representative, must normally attend the barrister in court (*LSG* 21.05 and 22.03). Barristers similarly are instructed that they may not normally appear without the professional client, except by agreement, and provided the interests of the client are not prejudiced (*CCB* 608).[21]
- Except in Legal Aid cases, a solicitor is personally liable for payment of counsel's fees (*LSG* 18.06). This rule operates as a matter of professional conduct, not contract.[22]

The duty of good faith outlined above is by far and away the most open-textured and problematic of these principles. It implies some fairly idealised professional standards, and is closely associated with the standards implicit in a lawyer's status as an officer of the court.

The lawyer's duty to the public at large is an even more amorphous concept. In many instances it may come into play only indirectly as part of the lawyer's more specific responsibilities – eg in the lawyer's duty to the court (as per Lord Reid, above), or duty of confidentiality, or in principles such as the cab-rank rule governing the Bar. Certainly it is difficult to suggest that the lawyer's duty to the public carries any generally enforceable obligation.

CONFIDENTIALITY AND PRIVILEGE

The rules on confidentiality are really a sub-branch of the lawyer's duty to the client, but one that is so important as to justify separate consideration. The main principles can be summarised as follows.

- A lawyer is under an obligation to keep *confidential to the firm or chambers* the affairs of a client (*LSG* 16.01; *CCB* 603). The obligation is not purely personal: the rules permit necessary disclosure to colleagues and staff, though, of course, they are equally bound to keep the confidence.[23]
- The duty endures until the client expressly permits disclosure or otherwise waives confidentiality (*LSG* 16.03; *CCB* 603). If there is no waiver, the duty of confidentiality extends beyond the client's death.
- A lawyer must not make any profit (personally or for another client or third party) out of confidential information given by a client (*LSG* 16.06; *CCB* 603) – eg profiting personally on a share transaction by virtue of 'insider' knowledge obtained from the client matter.

Legal privilege protects communications between lawyers and clients from disclosure in legal proceedings.[24] It is therefore distinct from the lawyer's duty of confidentiality, though it too exists to protect the client from unwanted disclosure of her affairs. Like confidentiality, privilege extends beyond the death of the client.[25] It may be waived by the client, expressly or by implication,[26] but never by the lawyer, even if the lawyer is the creator of the relevant document.

CONFLICT OF INTERESTS

The basic principle here appears a very simple one: a lawyer must not act in a matter for two or more clients if there is a conflict, or a real risk of a conflict, between their interests (see *LSG* 12.06, 15.01 and 15.03; *CCB* 501(e) and 504), or in any situation where her own interests conflict with the client's (*LSG* 12.06 and 15.05; *CCB* 501(e)). The principles governing conflict of interests are thus a sub-set of the lawyer's duty to the client (present and past).

Determining their practical scope is sometimes less than easy. This is because of the wide range of contexts in which conflicts can arise. Thus:

(a)   The Bar must guard not only against conflict of interest between lay clients, but also conflicts that may arise between the lay and the professional client. In the latter case, a barrister is obliged to advise the lay client to instruct another solicitor (*CCB* 605).

(b)   The principle generally covers solicitors' firms, not just individuals, and may catch former as well as 'live' clients. With larger firms, therefore, it can sometimes be difficult to keep track of conflicts.

(c)   Firms that merge may be caught acting for both sides in a particular matter. Generally, in this scenario, the firm should cease to act for one or both parties. But, in certain non-contentious matters, it is legitimate for the retained solicitors to continue to act until the present transaction is concluded, provided they use a 'Chinese Wall'. That is, they must only communicate formally about the matter, and behave as if they were still working for separate firms.[27]

(d)   Individual solicitors who move firms may subsequently be approached to act against a former client. For that individual, this would create a conflict of interest. However, contrary to the general principle that conflicts taint the firm, not just the person, it *is* permissible for a different member of the same firm, who does not have knowledge of the other party, to take on the case.

(e)   Whether or not a conflict exists may largely depend on the matter, not just the client. The critical question is often whether you have knowledge that you have acquired while acting for one person, that would be damaging to that former client if you accepted instructions to take some action against her. As Silverman points out,[28] you may have here a conflict between two duties: your duty to do your best for your present client (which in the case of a solicitor includes the express duty to disclose all useful information to your present client – *LSG* 16.07) and your duty to preserve the confidentiality of your former client (eg *LSG* 16.03). The conflict rule thus saves you from having to choose between those principles.

PROFESSIONAL MISCONDUCT

Cases of misconduct are dealt with by the professional disciplinary bodies, who have various sanctions, from disbarring counsel, or striking the solicitor off the Roll, down to suspensions, fines and warnings.

The courts also have some inherent disciplinary powers in respect of abuses of process. Practitioners may be held in contempt of court, under either civil[29] or criminal[30] jurisdictions. Exceptionally, the courts may also make solicitors personally liable for the costs of their clients or of a third party where those costs have been incurred as a result of misconduct or improper conduct.[31]

There is no single definition of professional misconduct in use, and those definitions which do exist are very general. The *CCB*, for example, defines it as behaviour that is

> ... dishonest or ... discreditable ... or prejudicial to the administration of justice ... or likely to diminish public confidence in the legal profession ... (para 201).[32]

In general:

- Criminal conduct is always misconduct; whether the misdemeanour arose in the lawyer's professional or private life is not generally significant.
- Breaches of the codes, of practice rules, or account rules are invariably treated as misconduct (see *LSG* 12.13; *CCB* 802.1).
- Negligence per se is more problematic. At Common Law, a solicitor is required to exercise a reasonable degree of care and skill within the scope of her retainer, and this standard is reflected in the code of conduct, as we have seen, and this sets the limits for the solicitor's duty of care. The Bar's liability for negligence, by comparison, is more heavily circumscribed by case law.[33] On both sides of the profession negligence tends not to be treated as misconduct for disciplinary purposes, unless there are particular circumstances which make it especially culpable.

Professional misconduct with respect to other members of the profession can also be problematic territory. Nowhere is this more apparent than in relation to sex and race discrimination. The handling of these sensitive issues clearly indicates the limits of a purely reactive and regulatory approach to professional ethics. Discrimination and harassment are clearly professional misconduct, yet proven allegations of sexual harassment of colleagues, by Mr John Young over a period of nearly 20 years, resulted in no real disciplinary action by the Law Society. Indeed the whole saga was effectively covered up until Young was 'outed' by one of his victims as he sought election to the Presidency of the Law Society in 1995.[34] In this context it should also be noted that the *Shapland Report* for the Bar,[35] which tracked 822 Bar students into practice, has come up with the finding that 40% of the women surveyed had experienced sexual harassment at work. This gives a worrying indication of the possible scale of the problem, yet disciplinary action seems rare.[36]

THE SCOPE AND FUNCTION OF THE CODES OF CONDUCT

From the explanation so far it should be apparent that the codes of conduct not only serve to identify basic standards of professional behaviour, but also offer some principles for the hierarchical ranking of the lawyer's obligations. The codes also perform a number of other functions, which are not always complementary. On the positive side, Hazard has thus argued that legal professional ethics defend a narrative of 'due process', defining the lawyer's work as protecting the liberty and property of private parties.[37] They may also serve to fetter the lawyer's discretion and to better enforce the values implicit in the legal system. But equally it may be argued that they can serve to protect and define the sectional interests of the persons governed by the code – in which case people might question whether they really are 'ethical' at all.[38] In the same vein, the codes of the profession have been described as 'little more than systems for competition control'.[39]

Certainly, they remain something of a blunt instrument and do not always prevent – nor necessarily resolve – value conflicts in professional life. In reality, the parameters of professional conduct are determined not just by the Codes, but by the system and values of education and training, licensing requirements, market pressures and competition, and perhaps by more subtle, individualised, pressures applied by clients, superiors and others in the system.[40] This can be illustrated by a couple of examples. We have worked the reasoning through for you, but have ultimately left you to come up with your own answers.

1   G Hazard 'The Future of Legal Ethics' (1991) 100 *Yale Law Journal* 1239 at p 1246.
2   6th Edition, The Law Society, London 1993.
3   General Council of the Bar of England and Wales, London 1990, as amended to 1 October 1993.
4   Cited in D L Rhode 'An Adversarial Exchange on Adversarial Ethics: Text, Subtext, and Context' (1991) 41 *Journal of Legal Education* 29 at p 29; for an analysis of the extent to which Brougham's plea for partisanship was a purely rhetorical device, see ibid pp 35–6.
5   Barristers have been able, since 1991, to take instructions directly from a lay client, subject to the Direct Professional Access Rules. Direct access remains the exception rather than the rule, however.
6   Also Rule 15, Solicitors' Practice Rules 1990.
7   See eg D Luban 'The Adversary System Excuse' in Luban (ed) *The Good Lawyer: Lawyers' Roles and Lawyers' Ethics*, Rowman & Allanheld, Totowa, NJ 1983 at p 83.
8   T Schneyer 'Some Sympathy for the Hired Gun' (1991) 41 *Journal of Legal Education* 11 at 23.
9   Equally, there are those associated with the radical Bar, such as Helena Kennedy QC, who staunchly support the cab rank as a means of protecting access to legal advice.
10 From S Scheingold 'The contradictions of radical law practice' in M Cain & C B Harrington *Lawyers in a Postmodern World*, Open University Press, Buckingham 1994, p 265 at 268.
11 D E Rosenthal *Lawyer and Client: Who's in Charge?* Russell Sage Foundation, New York 1974, p 158.
12 Rosenthal defines informed consent thus:

> The professional should be obligated to disclose to the client the relevant open choices involved in responding to his particular problem. This could include the alternatives involved in identifying the problem, the alternatives for dealing with it, the professional's experience in employing those alternatives and their anticipated difficulties and benefits. No action should be taken with respect to any of these choices until the client, aware of them, has given his consent.

> – op cit, p 155. See also M Spiegel 'Lawyering and Client Decisionmaking: Informed Consent and the Legal Profession' (1979) 128 *University of Pennsylvania Law Review* 41.
13 'Court' here is interpreted widely to include tribunals and inquiries, though generally not arbitrations – these are not within the definition of 'court proceedings' in s 20, Solicitors Act 1974.
14 Hazard, op cit (1991), p 1246.
15 See also Annex 22C of the *LSG*, which, in its discussion of the *Bridgwood* case [1988] *Law Society's Gazette*, 9 November, p 53, illustrates the tremendous difficulties in balancing the duty to the court and the duty to the client.
16 *Law As A Moral Judgment*, Sweet & Maxwell, London 1986, p 408; for their answer to the question which follows see pp 406–9.
17 *Rondel v Worsley* [1969] 1 AC 191 at 227–8. Cf the partial immunity from negligence claims enjoyed by solicitor advocates which is similarly explained by the superior duty of the advocate to the court – see per Lord Wilberforce in *Saif Ali v Sidney Mitchell* [1980] AC 198 at 215. Silverman argues that this prioritisation is an implied term of the solicitor's retainer – *Handbook of Professional Conduct for Solicitors*, 2nd Edition, Butterworths, London 1992, p 68.

18 *R v Thornton* [1992] 1 All ER 306. The case has attracted considerable public interest – see eg J Nadel *Sara Thornton: The Story of a Woman Who Killed*, Victor Gollancz, London 1993; H Kingsley & G Tibballs *No Way Out: Battered Women Who Killed*, Headline, London 1994.

19 As this book was entering its final stages, Sara Thornton's case was referred back to the Court of Appeal by the Home Secretary on the basis of new testimony on this issue – see *The Times*, 5 May 1995, p 1.

20 Images that are repeated in the Court of Appeal's judgment in 1992 – see the analysis by D Nicolson 'Telling Tales: Gender Discrimination, Gender Construction and Battered Women who Kill' in (1995) III *Feminist Legal Studies* (forthcoming).

21 If the professional client fails to attend a barrister may, if there is no other alternative, conduct the case alone – *CCB* 609.

22 Though see now s 61, Courts and Legal Services Act 1990.

23 Though, in a solicitor's firm, it may be advisable, as part of your client care policy, to explain to clients the occasional need for disclosure to co-professionals. The *CCB* also normally requires the prior consent of the lay client to any disclosure.

24 The precise scope of the privilege is a complex issue, turning on both technical rules and a number of public policy exceptions – see eg A Keane *The Modern Law of Evidence*, 3rd Edition, Butterworths, London 1994, pp 453–69. Note that privilege cannot simply be claimed because documents have become part of the lawyer/client relationship.

25 *Bullivant v Attorney General of Victoria* [1901] AC 196.

26 *Lillicrap v Nalder & Son* [1993] 1 All ER 724.

27 Though see generally the doubts expressed about Chinese walls in *Re a firm of solicitors* [1992] 1 All ER 353.

28 Silverman, op cit, p 47.

29 For example, where a solicitor fails to comply with a personal undertaking given to the court – *Re Keely, Son & Verden* [1901] 1 Ch 467.

30 Where a lawyer has victimised or interfered with a witness, for example – *A-G v Butterworth* [1963] 1 QB 696.

31 RSC Ord 62, r 11; the scope of this principle has been made more difficult to determine by conflicting case law which seeks to differentiate the principles applying in civil from criminal cases – see *Gupta v Comer* [1991] 1 All ER 289; *Holden & Co v Crown Prosecution Service* [1990] 2 QB 261; *Sinclair-Jones v Kay* [1989] 1 WLR 114.

32 Cf Rule 1, Solicitors Practice Rules 1990 which contains the equivalent general principle of conduct. It is even less specific.

33 *Rondel v Worsley* [1969], above.

34 See editorials in the *New Law Journal*, 14 April 1995; 5 May 1995; also Mr Young's statement reported in the *Law Society Gazette*, 26 April 1995, pp 3 & 14.

35 See the discussion in B Hewson 'A recent problem' *New Law Journal*, 5 May 1995, p 626.

36 Hewson, op cit.

37 Hazard, op cit, (1991), p 1246.

38 Andrew Ashworth, for example, argues that a principle is not really ethical if it lacks impartiality – ie if it benefits one particular person or group over another – *The Criminal Process: An Evaluative Study*, Oxford University Press, Oxford 1994, p 51.

39 A Sherr 'Editorial – Come of Age' (1994) 1 *International Journal of the Legal Profession* 3 at 10.

40 See eg A Abbott *The System of Professions: The Division of Expert Labor*, University of Chicago Press, Chicago 1988 and G Hazard *Ethics in the Practice of Law*, Yale University Press, New Haven & London 1978, respectively.

Exercise 4.4 Conflicts in the codes (1)

EXAMPLE 1

Conflicts often arise between your duty to the client and duty to the court. The classic example is where you suspect a client is lying, say, for example, by offering a defence to a criminal charge which is concocted. It is your duty not to mislead the court, but it is also your duty to follow your client's instructions. What do you do?

The problem, here, as is so often the case, is one of degree in interpreting whether or not there is a conflict of duties within the code. There is no obligation on you, the lawyer, to find the 'truth' – whatever that is. But at the same time you cannot, ethically, ignore facts that point to fabrication. At some point, the code tells you, your duty to the court supersedes your duty to the client. The crucial issue will be whether your hunch that the client is lying is actually based on supposition or fact. A point will be reached where you should challenge your client, advise him to drop that defence, and perhaps change his plea. If he refuses, you must consider whether you can properly continue to act for him. But no one can say objectively when that point is reached, and your relationship with the client may well make it harder for you to gauge it for yourself.

EXAMPLE 2

You are a barrister who has been approached to act for a pharmaceutical company that is being sued for congenital injuries caused to unborn children by one of its products. The action is based on a statute that imposes strict liability, and the company has no defence on the facts. Its only possible defence to the action is a technical one, based on expiration of the limitation period. The point is a difficult one, turning on the issue of when the link between the product and the defect was discoverable. On the facts you believe the defence has a good chance of success. To your knowledge, more than 3,000 individual claims depend on the outcome of this case. Do you accept?

This is a different order of problem from the first one. You might feel that there is no ethical dilemma. You can resolve the problem by reference to the ethics of the profession alone – on the basis that (i) everyone is entitled to representation; and (ii) the defence is, legally, unobjectionable. The cab-rank principle apparently obliges you to act, and there can be no objection based on the codes of conduct to a case based purely on a technical defence. However, it might be that your decision depends more on how you relate the internal ethics of the profession to your own sense of professional responsibility. In 1836, for example, the American lawyer, David Hoffman, included in his personal statement of ethics the following:

> I will never plead the Statute of Limitations, when based on the mere efflux of time, for if my client is conscious he owes the debt, and has no other defence than the legal bar, he shall never make me a partner in his knavery.[1]

The question then becomes: can you, in good conscience, defend that client on that defence? But if your answer is no, how would you decline, ethically?

Have a go at the next one by yourselves.

1 'Resolutions of Professional Deportment', Resolution XII, in *A Course of Legal Studies*, J Neal, Baltimore 1836. Hoffman's position on this and a number of other points was rejected by the first ABA code drafted in 1908 – see J F Backof & C L Martin 'Historical Perspectives: Development of the Codes of Ethics in the Legal, Medical and Accounting Professions' (1991) 10 *Journal of Business Ethics* 100.

Exercise 4.5   Conflicts in the codes (2)

Your firm has been instructed by Jane Austen to bring an action for unlawful sex discrimination against her employers Gradgrind & Co. Gradgrind & Co indicate their intention to defend the action, and you commence proceedings. You are then approached by two other employees of Gradgrind, Emily Brontë and Elizabeth Gaskell, who also allege that they are victims of discrimination. You take instructions from them, and it rapidly becomes apparent both that Ms Brontë is an in-house lawyer with Gradgrind's, and that she has been working on the Austen case – that is why she approached you. You do not ask her to divulge any information about the case, nor does she volunteer any.

In small groups: discuss the ethical implications arising from these events. What should your firm do?[1]

1   Cf the American case on which this exercise is based: *Hull v Celanese Corporation* (1975) 513 F.2d 568, excerpted in D Schrader *Ethics and the Practice of Law*, Prentice Hall, Englewood Cliffs, NJ 1988, pp 268–71. Our thanks to Richard Bean for bringing it to our attention.

Ethical lawyering – how far can you go?

What we have presented so far are (professionally speaking) the broadly accepted minima. But, as the dilemmas above show, the open texture of the rules of conduct does mean that you cannot always just check the rules. Even if you can, what is there to say that you are obliged to determine your behaviour solely by reference to those rules?

Ultimately, problems of value conflict must be resolved by some choice of moral principle by you – the actor in the specific case. But what principle – your professional ethics, the law, your own morals? How far can we determine professional conduct by reference to a personal or public morality that goes beyond – or may even appear to contradict – the ethical rules of the profession? How far are professional ethics a matter of regulation or of 'virtue':[1] the capacity to have the courage or character to 'do the right thing' (assuming we can identify what the right thing is)? To address these points we will have to digress occasionally into some of the underlying metaphysics that inform the ethics debate and which must influence our capacity for rationalising any ethical position we adopt. We have tried to keep this aspect of the discussion reasonably straightforward, though much of the literature we refer to is more sophisticated than this account suggests.

We have also simplified and objectified the problem by giving you a choice of four key principles for resolving value conflict. These are not the only principles you might consider, and are by no means mutually exclusive but, in many cases, experience suggests your choice of action is likely to be determined ultimately by one or other of these considerations.

1   See B Jennings 'The Regulation of Virtue: Cross-Currents in Professional Ethics' (1991) 10 *Journal of Business Ethics* 561 at 564–6.

Exercise 4.6   The four pillars of wisdom?

Below are four basic principles by which you might resolve a value conflict.

- My professional responsibility is defined by my client.
- My professional responsibility is defined by the code of conduct.
- My professional responsibility is defined by the law.
- My professional responsibility is defined by my own standards of ethical behaviour.

Consider what these might involve and how you could use them to resolve the follow-ing problem:[1]

Ed is a law student working in clinic. You are a colleague in the same team as Ed. A maintenance case you have been working on has been listed before the family court this morning. Ed is appearing for the former wife on an applica-tion by her ex-husband to reduce the support payments. The hearing has been delayed because the husband's lawyer has failed to obtain a file which should have been sent down from the clerk's office. Under the local rules, it is the responsibility of the applicant in such a case to obtain the file. It is mid-way through Friday morning, and the judge will not postpone the hearing for long. If the file is not found, the hearing will have to be re-listed, thereby pre-serving the status quo for some weeks if not months.

The opposing lawyer is in a dilemma, as she needs urgently to contact her office about another case. Ed agrees to see if he can obtain the file for her.

When you question Ed on his motives, he says that, yes, he could see that he might be acting against the interests of his client, but he had felt caught between his client and the opposing lawyer. Previously, he had got into a fight over the case with that lawyer, and he didn't think that had helped him or his client. She had asked him if he would get the file, and to help her out this time seemed the right thing to do.

(a)   If you were in Ed's position which of those principles (ie any one, or possibly more than one of them) would you have used to resolve the dilemma?
(b)   How would you have reacted on the basis of that/those principle(s)?

We shall now work through the implications of those principles and their impact on our possible definition of ethical lawyering by asking a series of questions.

1   Adapted from a real clinic episode described by Steven Hartwell in 'Moral Development, Ethical Conduct and Clinical Education' (1990) 35 *New York Law School Law Review* 131 at 132–3.

What if my professional responsibility clashes with my personal ethics?

This is perhaps both the least and the most difficult of our questions. Taking the point in abstract for a moment, how do you resolve such a conflict?

Exercise 4.7   Resolution 1

Make a note of:
(a) Which standpoint you would tend to favour: the professional or the personal.
(b) How you would justify, morally, your standpoint.

Do not continue reading until you have completed these tasks.

Of course, there is no absolute answer to this dilemma. So far as your reasoning goes, let us consider how ethicists would defend the possible positions you might adopt.

There is, both within the professions and amongst ethicists, a 'separatist thesis'[1] which emphasises the moral autonomy or independence of the professional role. Separatism is not an argument for amoral professionalism. But it does argue that ends, which may not be morally justified on their own or as a part of 'ordinary ethics' may be justified by the profession's own criteria of value. On this basis one could argue that there should be no real clash between personal and professional ethics, since the latter can operate within a sphere that is morally autonomous. Our professional responsibility is, thus, in practice, defined by the ethical code and the underlying legal rules within which we are normally expected to operate, and that is it. For example, you can therefore argue that it is fine to represent a client belonging to, eg, an extremist political group advocating, say, class war or racist violence, so long as that client does not require you to do anything illegal or contrary to the Code. Your personal repugnance at what your client stands for does not come into the equation. This is an attractive argument at one level, since it does prevent each of us behaving like a kind of moral police, and creating a situation where unpopular causes can get no representation.

On the other hand, this emphasis on role morality as we have described it can be challenged on a number of bases.

First we might ask: what do we mean by 'role morality'? If all it encompasses is an ethics that is defined purely according to the actor's conformity with a set of rules – the code of conduct – then we have a very narrow role-determined ethics. It will actually discourage actors from questioning their (or their profession's) underlying framing of the role. In assessing the characteristics of the good lawyer, a narrow role morality merely encourages us to look at the way tasks are executed. It does not generally require us to question more deeply whether the basic activities expected of a lawyer are good or bad. To question at this deeper level goes beyond role morality in the accepted sense.

If we take this argument to its logical conclusion, one might argue that it is only by leaving role morality behind that we enter truly ethical terrain – in which case the question posed in Exercise 4.7 should be treated as creating a false dichotomy: no genuinely ethical conflicts could be resolved purely by role-compliance.[2]

Second, it can also be argued that a narrow role morality is wrong, because it enables people too easily to sidestep moral problems, with the result that the hard cases (in ethical terms) simply slip through the net. Luban explains this in the following terms:

> [One] difficulty with 'my station and its duties' is a worry about what 'my station and its duties' means in the context of modern bureaucratic

organisations. The structure of bureaucratic institutions . . . lends itself to divided responsibility. Those who make the rules, those who give the orders, and those who carry out the orders each have some basis for claiming that they are not at fault for any wrong that results . . .

When moral agency divides along lines of institutional authority, it seems to me that every agent in the institution will wind up abdicating moral responsibility, which 'falls between the players,' so that even in a morally justifiable system, unattributable wrong will be done. I am not speaking only of global horrors, but also, on a smaller scale, of the evictions and lay-offs and terminated payments that, of course, no one intended and that are not the responsibility of the people who drafted the documents or carried out the judgments.[3]

You may have spotted here an interesting parallel between Luban's view of the psychology of organisations and Argyris and Schön's fears about 'distancing', which we discussed in Chapter 2.

Lastly, even if we do not accept a highly positivistic (ie rule-based) definition of role morality then, as Gewirth concludes, the separatist thesis is still (arguably) mistaken because it disregards the extent to which professional rules and their modes of operation in turn conform to general principles of morality. The reality is, in Gewirth's view, that the actual degree of separatism is highly limited by the amount of common ground that exists between common and role morality.

But if we accept that Luban's approach is correct, the difficulty then becomes one of determining what constitutes the ordinary or common morality which will inform your behaviour![4] At this point you might like to go away and do something a little easier, like alligator wrestling. Alternatively, you could persevere with the next exercise.

1   A Gewirth, 'Professional Ethics: The Separatist Thesis' (1986) 96 *Ethics* 282–300.
2   See eg S R Salbu 'Law and Conformity, Ethics and Conflict: The Trouble with Law-Based Conceptions of Ethics' (1992) 68 *Indiana Law Journal* 101.
3   D Luban *Lawyers and Justice: An Ethical Study*, Princeton University Press, Princeton, NJ 1988, pp 121–4.
4   For differing conceptions of this term see, eg, Gewirth, ibid and as applied in Beyleveld & Brownsword *Law As A Moral Judgment*, Sweet & Maxwell, London 1986. Also B Freedman, 'A Meta-Ethics for Professional Responsibility' (1978) 89 *Ethics* 1, and Luban op cit.

Exercise 4.8   Common morality or lawyer's morality

Consider the following examples:

1. You are a solicitor. During an initial interview with a client who is seeking your advice about a neighbour dispute, your client describes the neighbours he is complaining about as 'wogs' and 'Pakis'. You suspect that his complaint is, in part, racially motivated, but it is clear that there is also an underlying legal problem over property boundaries.

What do you do?

2. You are a barrister; you have been approached to act for a 19-year-old client who is accused of rape. Your potential client acknowledges that

intercourse took place and admits that 'things got a bit out of hand, but she wanted it rough'. He intends to base his defence on consent. The complainant is aged 16. She received bruises to her face and arms, a broken rib, and some internal bruising also. On the evidence of your client, she has a reputation for 'sleeping around'. She has never had sexual intercourse with your client, but he claims that there have been instances of what might politely be called 'heavy petting' on a couple of previous occasions, at parties. There is no evidence of a steady relationship. You anticipate that it will be necessary to cross-examine the complainant on her sexual history as part of your client's defence – if you take the case.

Do you accept instructions?

(a) *In each case consider your answer (i) from the perspective of the codes of conduct; (ii) from the perspective of 'common morality'.*
(b) *If possible, contrast your answers with those of other members in the group. What conclusions can you draw from this about the scope of role and common morality?*

How far are we, as lawyers, obliged to prevent our clients from engaging in illegal behaviour?

This raises the spectre of the lawyer as a kind of 'gatekeeper'[1] whose function it is to prevent or disclose misconduct by clients. How realistic an image is this, do you think?

1 The term is used in this way by R Kraakman 'Gatekeepers: the anatomy of a third party enforcement strategy' (1986) 2 *Journal of Law, Economics and Organisation* 53.

Exercise 4.9 Resolution 2

1. *Write down:*
   (a) *an example of illegal behaviour you would not be prepared to condone in a client;*
   (b) *an example of illegal behaviour (if any) that you would condone.*
2. *In each case, how do you justify your standpoint?*

The boundaries here are difficult to draw with any certainty.

In litigation, one can argue that, in part, the duty of candour defines our responsibilities though, as we have seen, problems can still arise, eg in assessing when our knowledge or complicity is such that our duty to the court outweighs any contrary duty to the client.

But that does not give us an answer where our client's behaviour merely raises the spectre of criminality – or possibly only civil liability. Is our duty in such a case only to warn the client of the risks, or could there be situations where we must act as 'whistleblower'?

The case of the Ford Pinto and the exploding fuel tank, which we looked at in Exercise 3.24, raises a problem of this type. Let us now consider that problem from an ethical perspective.[1]

Evidence leaked to the newspapers in 1979 showed that Ford engineers had known, on the basis of crash-test data, since at least 1970 that the fuel tank on a Pinto would rupture on impact at very low speeds – as little as 21 mph. On the basis of a cost–benefit analysis, however, Ford executives had decided that it was not worthwhile re-tooling the production line to modify the fuel tank design or location. The data from the cost–benefit analysis and the crash-tests were known to corporate counsel in Ford. How far counsel warned Ford of the legal consequences, or whether counsel made any attempts to follow company procedure to get the car withdrawn or modified, is unclear. What is known is that neither a Ford lawyer, nor an engineer, nor an executive saw fit to go public on the dangers of the Pinto.

Did counsel have any particular ethical grounds for *not* revealing the risks? Rather than use the American Bar Association's Code, let us use the Law Society's, and turn this (partially) into a research question. This exercise also illustrates how the ethical dimension may influence, and need to be built into your practical problem-solving.

1   See further D Luban *Lawyers and Justice: An Ethical Study*, Princeton University Press, Princeton, NJ 1988, pp 206–34.

Exercise 4.10   The whistleblower's defence?

(a)   *What is the primary basis in the LSG for saying that the lawyer would have no right to disclose such information?*

(b)   *What criminal offence might the facts in the Pinto case disclose?*

(c)   *Is there a relevant exception to the ethical duty in (a) which might apply in the Pinto case, therefore?*

(d)   *What if the facts only disclose a civil wrong?*

(e)   *Should the fact that we are looking at the responsibilities of in-house lawyers make any difference to the principle?*

(f)   *Would your answer to (e) differ if considering counsel's duty*
   – *in 1970?*
   – *in 1976 after 13 cases of exploding petrol tanks causing death or injury had been reported to the company?*
   – *in 1981 after a civil court awarded over £3 million to a teenager burned in a Pinto accident?*[1]

In his analysis of the lessons of the Pinto case, Luban concludes:

What about the duty of confidentiality? . . . [I]t has an independent moral basis: a person should, other things being equal, respect the confidences of others, even without a special policy reason for doing so . . . [C]ommon morality may require a lawyer to keep confidences that she would rather not keep – but that is because a non-lawyer would also be required to keep those confidences. The professional role grants no special privileges and immunities.

And in whistleblowing contexts such as the Pinto example, other things are not equal. Since 'who pays the whistler calls the tune' cannot be accepted as a moral principle, our conclusion must be . . . [that] the duty of confidentiality must be weighed against the considerations in our baseline morality, and it can count no more heavily in that balance than it would for non-lawyers . . .

. . . 'You know how to whistle, don't you? just put your lips together and blow.'[2]

- Do you agree with Luban? Why/why not?
- If you were arguing from a separatist ethic, how would you respond to this argument?

You might like to consider the rather more pragmatic view taken by one of Karl Mackie's lawyer respondents:

Am I a lawyer working for the company or a law enforcement agency? With a private client, after all, there is no need to drop the client if you know of an unethical practice. You just don't become embroiled in that specific issue.[3]

In non-contentious matters our duty to the court is rather more remote, so is there an equivalent ethical duty of candour within the codes of conduct? (See if you can identify one.) Now consider the following example.

1 *Grimshaw v Ford* (1981) 119 Cal App 3d 757.
2 D Luban *Lawyers and Justice: An Ethical Study*, Princeton University Press, Princeton, NJ 1988, pp 233–4.
3 *Lawyers in Business and the Law Business*, Macmillan, London & Basingstoke 1989, p 180.

Exercise 4.11   Mind your backs?

You are acting as a legal adviser to C Ltd who are planning to refloat themselves as a public company by an offer of shares on the stock exchange. You are asked by the underwriters of the issue to provide a legal opinion on the transaction. You are aware that the (draft) prospectus misrepresents the capital value of the company to its advantage. Both you and C Ltd could face prosecution if the true situation is discovered.

What do you do?

In this scenario your decision may be made harder – or easier – (depending on your views, and your degree of exposure) by the fact that, as is sometimes the case, the client's illegality may become your illegality. The question is, are you then motivated to act by simply the desire to protect your back, rather than some ethical principle? Does that in turn mean that your reaction to client illegalities is not measured by their potential impact on the client or some third party, but on whether your own back is likely to be exposed? How will you react where there is no personal risk attached?

How far are we, as lawyers, obliged to support or enforce laws which are morally repugnant to us?

Most of us would accept that, within a liberal democracy, some linkage between legal rules and societal conceptions of moral or ethical behaviour should exist. We could go so far as to say that it is reasonable to expect that the law is based on ethical principles. As Cohen notes:

> . . . ethics is the study of the meaning and application of judgments of good, bad, right, wrong, etc, and every final valuation of law involves an ethical judgment.[1]

In this way, what we might call a sense of 'system ethics'[2] could be seen to underlie all questions about how legal processes operate.[3] These system ethics are generally reflected in the overarching principles of the legal system, eg in notions such as the right to a fair trial, and other fundamental human rights. Arguably, the professional code of ethics should not be inconsistent with such fundamental principles – should they? The difficulty here is a patently obvious one: the 'system ethics' underpinning any legal system are notoriously difficult to identify with any degree of certainty. The following is an example.

Exercise 4.12   System ethics v professional ethics

Consider the following questions.

(a)   How would you define the 'right to a fair trial'?

Defence and Prosecution both tout around for expert forensic witnesses to support their respective theories of the case. They each find their experts. D's expert is an established and respected figure, but a very poor witness. P's expert looks and sounds highly plausible, but is on the margins of his field and is widely regarded as a crank by his peers. D is convicted chiefly on the forensic evidence.

(b) (i)   Has the prosecutor done anything which is inconsistent with her professional ethics?
(ii)   Has D had a fair trial?

There are also areas where the relationship between law and ethics is problematic, because the legal rules are themselves based on no obvious ethical principle (beyond a notion of blind obedience), or are based on practices or principles which, to some of us (at least), might be dubious, or fundamentally wrong. Let us take a short example.

---

1   In *The Ethical Basis of Legal Criticism* (1959) in W R Bishin & C D Stone *Law, Language and Ethics*, Foundation Press, Mineola, NY 1972, p 32.
2   We use this phrase as shorthand for the ethical principles and values which the law and the legal system ought to be built on.
3   See eg A Ashworth *The Criminal Process: An Evaluative Study*, Oxford University Press, Oxford 1994, for a discussion of the (lack of) system ethics underlying the English criminal process.

Exercise 4.13   The poll tax refusniks

When the Community Charge ('Poll Tax') was introduced it met with considerable political and social opposition from certain quarters, including some members of the legal profession. Give your views on the following questions.

(a) Should the Law Society have viewed non-payment by a practitioner as mis-
    conduct?
(b) Should the Law Society have viewed non-payment by a student as rendering
    them unfit for membership?
Justify your views.

The underlying question thus becomes: how far are we, as lawyers, obliged to
obey the law simply because it *is* the law? For lawyers, this can create a
tremendous dilemma. We are all aware that law is often arbitrary and political
in its operation; we are aware of how easily it can be manipulated, even on the
day-to-day basis of legal practice: think about how much of the good corporate or tax or even welfare lawyer's work is actually about law *avoidance*. But
once we start to question the 'rightness' of specific laws, are we not starting to
challenge our own legitimacy?

The danger of such reasoning is that it demands our acceptance of what is
often termed 'legalism':

> [Legalism] is the ethical attitude that holds moral conduct to be a matter
> of rule following, and moral relationships to consist of duties and rights
> determined by rules . . .
> . . . the main thrust of legalistic ideology is toward orderliness, and for-
> malism can readily reinforce an inherent preference for authority. The
> ease with which Germany's lawyers accepted 'Adolf Légalité's' preten-
> sions to legitimacy, the support they gave Nazism until its radical
> anti-legalistic tendencies revealed themselves (and even after), more than
> justify de Tocqueville's and Weber's suspicions. It cannot be repeated
> often enough that procedurally 'correct' repression is perfectly compati-
> ble with legalism. That is the cost of conservative adaptability.[1]

We might legitimately argue that the rise of Nazism is a pretty extreme example of the dangers of legalism, and one that was dependent on a complex
interplay of social and political conditions.

Nevertheless, outside of such extreme cases, it is still possible to construct a
moral argument against a principle of general, or blind, obedience to law.
How might we do this? Well, we could argue that to do otherwise is to assume
either that laws are morally infallible, or that we ordinarily have an obligation
to obey the law, even if, in extreme cases (such as the Nazi scenario) it is not a
moral absolute. The claim of moral infallibility is probably self-defeating: we
either argue ourselves into an acceptance of legalism, or into a position of
accepting that law is a moral non-absolute (in which case we arrive at the second case we have stated). You may say this second ground is much harder to
refute – after all, isn't it precisely the ground that many people *do* use to justify obedience to the law? You might be right, but once we accept the second
position we are accepting that the law *is* morally fallible, and any *general* obligation to obey the law must, by definition almost, become difficult to sustain
once we begin to admit exceptions. Obedience to the law defined in this way
starts to look increasingly like a political choice rather than a moral one.
David Lyons seems to point us in that direction when he says:

> Viewed abstractly it may be puzzling that the idea of a general obligation
> to obey the law enjoys such widespread credence. Viewed in its social

context, however, its prevalence may be less puzzling. For the idea is primarily endorsed by those who see themselves as beneficiaries of the
system, and for whom the idea represents a moral commitment to abide
by the law even when it is not in *their* personal interest to do so. In this
respect, the idea reflects a deliberately conscientious attitude. But it does
not seem to reflect a great deal of moral sensitivity, for it totally disregards the position of those who are not beneficiaries of the system. It
corresponds to the attitudes of those who speak of 'universal suffrage'
and 'democracy' when they exclude both blacks and women. It is morally
myopic.[2]

It is interesting, against this background, to speculate on English law's perception of the relationship between law and ethics by looking at the approach
the Court of Appeal took in *X Ltd v Morgan-Grampian*.[3]

In this exceptional case Mr Goodwin, a journalist, was refused the right to
appeal against an injunction ordering him to disclose the source of confidential information he had obtained and published. His refusal had been based
on a direct promise to his source, and, more generally, on the National Union
of Journalists' code of conduct, which requires protection of journalists'
sources.

While the Court recognised that a conflict could arise between the law and
what it called a 'moral imperative', the Master of the Rolls, Lord Donaldson,
resolved the problem quite simply by defining the law as paramount.
Goodwin's promise to his source was thus treated as having little or no moral,
and certainly no legal, authority, while his reliance on professional ethics was
also insufficient, since the Court felt that there was 'more honour and morality in conforming to the . . . laws of the land rather than to the private
self-imposed rule of the profession . . .'[4] Goodwin's attempt to be allowed to
resolve the conflict between law and ethics for himself was thus redefined as
an attack on the authority of law, and of the courts:

> The administration of justice in a parliamentary democracy depends in
> the last analysis on a general acceptance of the authority of the Courts as
> representing society as a whole. No challenge to that authority can be
> ignored.[5]

Is that the only rational approach the Court could have adopted? What does it
tell us about the Court's view of the relationship between law and ethics?
Consider the following comments on the case:

> The argument of the Court [in *Morgan-Grampian*] resembles a well-
> known philosophical gambit associated with Hegelian metaphysics.
> Society, the 'real', and law, the 'normative' are presented as coeval or
> homologous through a succession of substitutions. Society speaks through
> Parliament, Parliament speaks through law, the law speaks through the
> courts, the courts define morality and individuals must accept their defini-
> tion. And as society is the all-inclusive figure of reality, the law too is
> actual and total . . . [I]t brings together and unifies legality and ethics, is
> and ought, the subject and his moral duty. There is no outside the law, as
> law and reality are co-extensive . . .'[6]

Of course, this kind of philosophising may not be a lot of help in the professional context, where any significant (whatever that is) disobedience of the law is very likely to leave you facing disciplinary proceedings. Does that mean that, as a lawyer, you have less freedom of conscience than other private citizens?

1   J N Shklar *Legalism*, Harvard University Press, Cambridge, Ma 1964, pp 1, 17.
2   *Ethics and the Rule of Law*, Cambridge University Press, Cambridge 1984, p 213.
3   [1990] 1 All ER 616.
4   Ibid, at 624.
5   Ibid, at 625.
6   C Douzinas & R Warrington, 'A Well-Founded Fear of Justice: Law and Ethics in Post-modernity' (1991) II *Law and Critique* 115 at 141–2.

Exercise 4.14   Resolution 3

How would you deal with a conflict between the law and your personal ethics?

Consider the following hypotheticals.

1   Suppose that Parliament passes the Sedition Act 1995, which makes it an indictable offence (a) for any person to criticise the duly elected Government and (b) makes it a summary offence for any person to fail to inform the police of any criticism made of the Government by any person in their hearing. Both offences are strict liability. There is no statutory exclusion of lawyer–client communications.
   You agree to act for a client who is charged with the indictable offence. During the initial interview:
   (i)   your client repeats the criticism which led to his being charged;
   (ii) he further criticises the Government for passing the Sedition Act.

(a)   What do you do?

2.   The Government introduces a new income tax band at a rate of 65% on higher earnings. Soon after it comes in you are offered some training work by a friend who runs a company specialising in continuing education courses for solicitors. The work would have netted you about £2,000 pa under the old tax regime, but you will lose a further slice of that because the gross amount is enough to push you into the new tax bracket. On this basis you doubt whether it is financially worth your while to take the extra work on. Your friend desperately wants your expertise. He therefore suggests that, as your spouse is currently taking a career break, he should falsify his accounts and pay the money to your spouse. Since the gross is less than your spouse's personal allowance you will pay no tax on the sum at all. Your spouse is amenable to the idea.

(b)   What do you do?
(c)   Would your answer to the second of these hypotheticals be different from the standpoint of (i) your role morality as a legal practitioner; (ii) your role morality as a private citizen?

As you may have noticed, the questions we have posed have become increasingly demanding as you work through this section. Sometimes you may have become frustrated by the questions we have asked. You may have felt academically under-equipped to deal with them. In a way that does not matter. Practice does not necessarily require an academic response to ethical problems; we think it does require a reflective response, and that is what we have tried to encourage here.

So, in a final attempt to close the loop, have a go at the next exercise, before we set you off on another loop of your own, by introducing a totally different model of ethics for your consideration!

Exercise 4.15   I'm reviewing the situation

Here are the four statements we presented you with earlier. Having worked through the materials in this section, see if you can define your own parameters of professional responsibility by defining the limits you would impose on each of the following criteria as principles governing your professional behaviour.

Write out your answers in your learning diary for future reference – and amendment?

- My professional responsibility is defined by my client.
- My professional responsibility is defined by the code of conduct.
- My professional responsibility is defined by the law.
- My professional responsibility is defined by my own standards of ethical behaviour.

Should we rethink legal ethics?

We have so far talked about ethical dilemmas within the framework established by the codes of conduct. We have suggested a number of specific ways in which that framework might be deemed problematic; we have touched on, but not really discussed, the conceptual bases of possible ethical frameworks beyond the codes. We now need to remedy that defect. Let us briefly set the scene by first addressing yet another ethical conundrum.

Exercise 4.16   In Xanadu . . .

The lawyers in Xanadu appear to be having as rough a time of it as the rest of us. Public confidence in the profession has declined; there are significant problems of access to justice, and lawyers are being attacked for their lack of altruism.

At a Council meeting of the Xanadu Bar Association, a proposal is put forward that the Code of Professional Conduct should be amended to incorporate a professional obligation on all practitioners to undertake a minimum of 35 billable hours of pro bono work per year.[1]

The debate rages on issues of cost, public relations value, the equity or iniquity of imposing a fixed minimum obligation, and so on. No one raises the ethical arguments until . . .

(a) *Two volunteers come forward – one to present the ethical case for mandatory pro bono, the other to oppose it.*
(b) *As a group, review the arguments you have just heard. Are there other ethical grounds or positions you would have adopted? What assumptions did the speakers make about their role morality? What other value judgments underpinned their arguments?*

The Xanadu debate is, of course, a piece of fiction; after all, we have no evidence that there are any lawyers in paradise! But we hope the discussion was still instructive. We suspect that, whatever the arguments, the starting points of the two sides probably had a great deal in common. We would guess that both volunteers will have adopted a position building on at least one or other of the following overlapping principles:

- Legalism;
- Individualism;
- Universalism.

Each of these 'isms' commonly underpins legal argumentation about ethics (and even ethical arguments about law). *Legalism* is most frequently used to describe the prescriptive approach to ethics criticised by Judith Shklar in which moral conduct is determined by a rule-following which excludes the deeper questioning of the lawyer's role.[2] *Individualism* denotes the assumption of a liberal political or philosophical position. This is used to construct moral arguments that are premised on individual rights and autonomy, agency, and market competition. *Universalism* is often closely allied to both the legalistic and individualistic positions, and as such has been fundamental in forming modern conceptions of ethics. As Bauman notes:

> The legislator's coercive practices (or intentions) of uniformisation supplied the 'epistemological ground' on which philosophers could build their models of universal human nature: while the philosophers' success in 'naturalising' the legislators' cultural (or, rather, administrative) artifice helped represent the legally constructed model of the state-subject as the embodiment and epitome of human destiny.[3]

Although that particular trinity has tended to dominate the debate for many years, the terrain on which our conceptions of professional ethics stand has been steadily shifting. At the root of this shift has been a growing disillusionment with our modern condition. Now, whether or not we think that these are defining features of modernity or characteristics of an amoral postmodernism, theorists from a variety of perspectives tend to agree on the following features of our present situation:[4]

- Social practices are characterised by atomistic and often alienated conceptions of the individual as something outside society – atomistic in that it has arguably become, in Freeman's phrase an '"I do my thing, you do yours" world';[5] and alienated not least because our self-perception has become atomistic and over-rationalised.

● Systems of governance – both political and commercial – are technocratic and managerial (cf our critique of managerialism, above).
● There is an increasing sense of relativism – ie that it is difficult, if not undesirable, or absurd even, to try and construct absolute standards of the good and the right.

The search for a new ethics in this context has become the search for an ethics that is sensitive to 'community', 'otherness', 'difference' or any one of a hundred different buzzwords that the theorists are passing around, but which seem to suggest:

> . . . principles that make a pluralistic society possible: a common acceptance of the value of diversity and choice; a sensitivity to the power relations that hinder and inhibit the fulfilment of individual needs; and above all, an avoidance of the proselytising zeal of those who believe they have the key to the good life.[6]

So, by way of conclusion, we will discuss, fairly briefly, an alternative formulation for professional ethics, based on an 'ethics of care'.

1   The debate in Xanadu mirrors similar debates in England and the United States – see eg G Bindman 'Debtors to our profession' *New Law Journal*, 17 December 1993, p 1789; S Bretz, 'Why Mandatory Pro Bono is a Bad Idea' (1990) 3 *Georgetown Journal of Legal Ethics* 623.
2   J N Shklar *Legalism*, Harvard University Press, Cambridge, Ma 1964. Neil MacCormick adopts a more favourable view in which he stresses that '[l]egalism is the morality of filtering through positive law all claims to official justification' – 'The Ethics of Legalism' (1989) 2 *Ratio Juris* 184 at 186.
3   Z Bauman *Postmodern Ethics*, Blackwell, Oxford & Cambridge, Ma 1993, p 8.
4   Notably Z Bauman, op cit; S Benhabib *Situating the Self: Gender Community and Post-modernism in Contemporary Ethics*, Polity Press, Cambridge 1992; C Douzinas & R Warrington *Justice Miscarried: Ethics, Aesthetics and the Law*, Harvester Wheatsheaf, Hemel Hempstead 1994; D Harvey *The Condition of Postmodernity*, Blackwell, Cambridge, Ma & Oxford 1989; A MacIntyre *After Virtue*, University of Notre Dame Press, Notre Dame, Ind 1981.
5   M Freeman *Rewriting the Self: History, Memory, Narrative*, Routledge, London & New York 1993, p 197.
6   J Weeks *Against Nature: Essays on history, sexuality and identity*, Rivers Oram Press, London 1991, p 155.

The foundations of an ethics of care

The notion of an ethics of care has developed out of the moral development theories of Carol Gilligan.[1] In her work Gilligan distinguishes between an ethics of justice, or of rights, and an ethics of care. This dichotomy requires some explanation.

By an ethics of justice, Gilligan is referring to a perspective which presumes moral judgment is normally premised on generalised principles of equality. This is exemplified by the work of the developmental psychologist, Lawrence Kohlberg:

> . . . moral judgments involve role-taking the viewpoint of the others conceived as subjects and co-ordinating these viewpoints . . . A moral situation in disequilibrium is one in which there are unresolved, conflicting claims. A resolution of the situation is one in which each is 'given his

due' according to some principle of justice that can be recognised as fair by all the conflicting parties involved.[2]

This is, essentially, the idealised view of legal as well as moral decision-making. In a legal dispute, say, the fact that both parties agree to abide by an arbitrator's decision is a simple illustration of the justice model. Both parties have agreed the procedure and, even though one will lose and one will win in the arbitration, the outcome is 'fair'.

Kohlberg thereby emphasises any motivation to act morally which is based on the fact that 'as a rational person, one has seen the validity of principles and has become committed to them'.[3] This capacity to appreciate the universality of standards is, for Kohlberg, the highest stage of moral development.

Kohlberg's stress on universalism and the 'generalised other'[4] is controversial. Both Benhabib and Gilligan take the justice model to task for excluding individual circumstances and narrative histories from moral problems. Benhabib thus talks of the absence of the 'concrete' as opposed to 'generalised' other.[5]

The ethic of care is premised on the differences in moral reasoning discovered by Gilligan's researches into the moral development of women.[6] She suggests that women's moral problem-solving is characterised by a greater sense of empathy and a concern for resolving real as opposed to hypothetical dilemmas.[7] This is not to say that women are incapable of meta-ethical thought, but rather that they assess situations by reference to what Gilligan terms 'the violence inherent in the dilemma itself', which is seen to compromise the justice of any of its possible resolutions'.[8] Thus, principles of what Gilligan terms 'nonviolence'[9] – that no one should be hurt – serve as a significant ethical criterion in a concrete situation.

Although it is an ethics which places the accommodation or mediation of relationships at its centre, Gilligan does not thereby raise the ethics of care above an ethic of justice, or of rights as it is also called. Rather, she suggests that a fully developed capacity for moral reasoning would recognise the need for a dialogue between principles of fairness and care – a dialogue between what Gilligan terms 'male' and 'female voice'.[10]

1   *In a Different Voice*, Harvard University Press, Cambridge Ma & London 1982.
2   L Kohlberg *Essays on Moral Development, Vol 1: The Philosophy of Moral Development* Harper & Row, San Francisco 1981, p 194.
3   Kohlberg, op cit, p 421.
4   That is, a frame of reference by which moral dilemmas are resolved in respect of an abstract person, rather than in the context of a real, individualised, set of human motivations. An example of the abstract approach is the legal criterion of the reasonable man. The use of such criteria defines what is sometimes called a 'meta-ethical' position.
5   S Benhabib *Situating the Self: Gender Community and Postmodernism in Contemporary Ethics*, Polity Press, Cambridge 1992, p 148ff.
6   Kohlberg's work, in common with that of most developmental psychologists, has been with male subjects. In correspondence with Gilligan, Kohlberg has stated that he did not include girls in his study of moral development in adolescence because their responses did not fit his schema! See C Gilligan 'Getting Civilised' (1994) 63 *Fordham Law Review* 17 at 17.
7   See eg Gilligan, op cit (1982), p 69.
8   Ibid, p 101.
9   Ibid, p 174.

10   On Gilligan's development of the male voice/female voice metonym, see ibid, pp 24–35.
     How far differences in moral development are gendered and thence whether an ethics of
     care is a specifically female ethic remains a moot point. Although Gilligan rejects the notion
     that men cannot develop an ethic of care, her data indicates that the justice/care distinction
     does tend to follow gender lines. This raises the highly problematic question of whether
     forms and styles of legal practice might themselves be – or become – gender-differentiated.
     Cf the thoughtful critique of this position by Naomi Cahn 'Styles of Lawyering' (1992) 43
     Hastings Law Journal 1039.

Applying the ethics of care to law

Despite (or because of?) its lack of direct law and ethics content, Gilligan's work has been hugely influential on American legal scholarship.[1] That influence has been felt most deeply in the field of feminist jurisprudence, and from there it has inevitably crossed over into discussions of legal ethics and of training for professional responsibility.[2] The ethics of care undoubtedly raises some interesting possibilities for re-evaluating professional ethics, though much of the American literature to date has been stronger on the rhetoric than the substance of a legal ethic of care.

We identify three key elements to applying a legal ethic of care. These are:
- making connections;
- obtaining consent;
- seeking resolution.

The idea of *connection* is a powerful aspect of the ethic of care, and contrasts with the traditional view of the lawyer as

> . . . an autonomous creature, connected by contract to her client, but otherwise detached from her client's perspectives and from the effects of her client's actions on the surrounding community.[3]

It describes a variety of attributes: the ability to see oneself within a network of relationships, with other lawyers and clients, and with the wider community;[4] the capacity to understand the feelings and experiences of others within those relationships;[5] the ability to talk to those others without 'violence'.

Obtaining consent is, perhaps, a special part of that connectedness. We suggest that there is a clear link between what we have already termed participatory approaches to lawyering and the ethic of care. The ethic of care demands that professional relationships are built on mutual trust and shared knowledge.[6] This would suggest that lawyer–client relations demand a significant element of 'informed consent'. Clients cannot be expected to make decisions in the absence of knowledge of the alternative courses of action available, the consequences of those alternatives, their relative costs, and the levels of uncertainty that operate within them.[7]

Seeking resolution as an ethical aim sits rather uncomfortably with the adversarialism we associate with conventional approaches to lawyering. So, if an ethic of care implies a move away from adversarialism, what would 'caring litigation' look like?

First, it would involve a greater emphasis on negotiation, on mediation and on other alternatives to trial-based dispute resolution.[8] Within this framework there would also be less emphasis on entrenched, positional, bargaining and a greater focus on creative and 'win–win' problem-solving.[9] Even within disputes that go to court, we might envisage a difference. Cases would be conducted on the basis of 'good faith'[10] principles. These would suggest a need for: (a) more dialogue and fuller disclosure between parties; (b) respect for the interests of other parties, resulting in avoidance of trial and pre-trial adversarial tactics, and (c) less intimidatory advocacy when in court.

1   In researching this book we discovered, via LEXIS, over 700 American law review articles citing *In A Different Voice*.
2   Some interesting examples include S Ellmann 'The Ethic of Care as an Ethic for Lawyers' (1993) 81 *Georgetown Law Journal* 2665; C Menkel-Meadow 'Portia in a Different Voice: Speculations on a Women's Lawyering Process' (1986) 1 *Berkeley Women's Law Journal* 39; P Spiegelman 'Integrating Doctrine, Theory and Practice in the Law School Curriculum' (1988) 38 *Journal of Legal Education* 243; Symposium on 'Theoretics of Practice: The Integration of Progressive Thought and Action' in (1992) *Hastings Law Journal*, vol 43, no 2; K C Worden 'Overshooting the Target: A Feminist Deconstruction of Legal Education' (1985) 34 *American University Law Review* 1141.
3   Cahn 'Styles of Lawyering' (1992) 43 *Hastings Law Journal* 1039, p 1063.
4   In Gilligan's terms 'we cannot know apart from relationship' – 'Getting Civilised' (1994) 63 *Fordham Law Review* 17, p 23.
5   We develop this further in Chapter 6.
6   Gilligan thus emphasises 'decision-making . . . [through] . . . open conversation and discussion, op cit (1994), p 29.
7   Cf Spiegel 'Lawyering and Client Decisionmaking: Informed Consent and the Legal Profession' (1979) 128 *University of Pennsylvania Law Review* 41, p 134. The notion of informed consent has evolved from medical jurisprudence. It is far more highly developed in the United States than in the UK. Note the reluctance of the courts to restrict medical autonomy of decision-making in *Sidaway v Board of Governors of the Bethlem Royal and Maudsley Hospital* [1984] 2 WLR 778 (CA); [1985] 2 WLR 480 (HL); also M Brazier *Medicine, Patients and the Law*, Penguin Books, Harmondsworth 1992, pp 78–89.
8   See Menkel-Meadow, op cit, also Chapter 9 of this book.
9   We discuss these concepts in Chapter 9. See also C Menkel-Meadow 'Toward Another View of Legal Negotiation: The Structure of Problem-Solving', (1984) 31 *UCLA Law Review* 754. Cf Andy Boon's comment that solicitor's negotiating tends to be a 'low intensity, positional activity' – 'Co-operation and competition in negotiation: the handling of civil disputes and transactions' (1994) 1 *International Journal of the Legal Profession* 109 at 118.
10 Cahn, op cit, p 44.

Care and the codes

The relationship between the codes of conduct and an ethic of care is hard to envisage. It might be argued that the ethics of care is so much an ethic of virtue that it only operates to fill in the many gaps and areas of discretion left by the rules. In this way an ethic of care could go towards resolving some of the contradictions surrounding the present codes. A less adversarial advocacy ethic would thus reinforce the lawyer's status as an officer of the court, engaged in a search for 'truth', rather than as an individual litigant's hired gun.

Overall, this position seems somewhat disingenuous, however.

A fully-fledged ethic of care would create conflicts with the codes as they stand. Ideas of association and connectedness with clients sit uncomfortably with notions of lawyer autonomy and the professional distance implicit in notions such as the cab-rank. Moreover, if an ethic of care translates simply to a client-centred ethic, then it can also be dangerous because it simply replaces assumptions about the nature of the good lawyer with an idealised model of the good client. As Schneyer has pointed out, codes of conduct are in part designed to help lawyers withstand rather than legitimise the illegitimate aims of clients.[1] Having said that, we take the view that the 'caring' lawyer is not simply client-centred. Her perspective is holistic, recognising that her actions on behalf of her client will affect a range of relationships. Indeed, from a client's perspective, the problem with an ethic of care may be that it is not client-centred enough!

Such difficulties do not necessarily mean that an ethic of care is untenable without a change in the regulatory basis of legal ethics. The American studies indicate that there are practitioners who attempt to practise from a similar position to the one we have outlined.[2] Having said that, the potential conflicts in lawyering styles created by contrasting rights and care ethics probably make it impossible – and pragmatically undesirable – for a lawyer to adopt whole-heartedly an ethic of care in the present environment.[3]

Whether or not you should re-evaluate your notions of professional ethics along such lines is a question only you can answer. In reflecting on what you have read, you might like to consider the following concluding comments made by one American law student at the end of a paper much influenced by the ethics of care:

> . . . I can be accused of further perpetuation of 'female' stereotypes, or triviality and failure to recognise power relationships, or utopian idealism in believing that thinking about the world differently will change it, or insignificance for lack of universality . . .
>
> I consider and struggle with many of these critiques frequently. In the end, however, I reject them because they always seem to be used to justify passivity . . .
>
> Actively striving for personal and social freedom makes life exciting . . . I cannot be sure that thinking about the world differently will change it, but I can be sure that apathy will doom me to an existence of perpetual submission . . . Who knows what we may discover in ourselves and others if we learn to break free of the myriad, repressive, ideological constructs we have internalised and justified for so many years. Of course there are risks. Who knows whether we will inadvertently box ourselves into new and equally stifling ideologies in our attempts to break free from old ones? I don't. But I do find using fear of the unknown to justify inaction against known and present forms of oppression pathetic and offensive.[4]

1   T Schneyer 'Moral Philosophy's Standard Misconception of Legal Ethics' (1984) *Wisconsin Law Review* 1529.
2   C Menkel-Meadow 'The Comparative Sociology of Women Lawyers: The "Feminisation" of the Legal Profession' (1986) 24 *Osgoode Hall Law Journal* 897; N Tarr 'Two Women Attorneys and Country Practice' (1992) 2 *Columbia Journal of Gender & Law* 25.
3   Cahn 'Styles of Lawyering' (1992) 43 *Hastings Law Journal* 1039; Bergman 'Is that a fact? Argument in problem-solving negotiations' (1994) 1 *International Journal of the Legal Profession* 81.
4   Worden 'Overshooting the Target: A Feminist Deconstruction of Legal Education' (1985) 34 *American University Law Review* 1141, at p 1155.

Exercise 4.17   Concepts

The procedure for learning these concepts is as follows:

1. *Divide into pairs.*
2. *Each pair is to:*
    (a) *define each concept, noting the page(s) on which it is discussed, and under-taking any additional research that is necessary, then*
    (b) *make sure that you both understand the meaning of each concept.*
3. *Combine into groups of four. Compare the answers of the two pairs. If there is disagreement, look up the concept and clarify it. Make sure you are all agreed on the definition and understand it.*

bureaucratisation	*collegiality*
cab rank principle	*common morality*
ethics of care	*ethics of rights*
Fordism	*hired gun*
legalism	*nonviolence*
role morality	*routinisation*
separatist thesis	*system ethics*

Exercise 4.18   Review questions

1. *Legal education, according to Roger Cramton, suffers from:*

    > *. . . a pragmatism tending toward an amoral instrumentalism . . . an individualism tending toward atomism, and a faith in reason and demo-cratic processes tending toward mere credulity . . .* [1]

    Do you agree?
2. *Go back to the questions raised in Exercise 4.2. Without looking at your previous answers, write out answers to questions (1) to (4) afresh. Now compare these with your original answers. What have you learnt?*
3. *Consider the rule of conduct laid down in CCB para 203(a). Redraft that to reflect an ethic of care. What does this exercise tell you about:*
    (a) *the differences between an ethic of rights and an ethic of care; and*
    (b) *the possibility of legislating for an ethic of care?*

---

1 'The Ordinary Religion of the Law School Classroom' (1978) 29 *Journal of Legal Education* 247, 262. On ethics in American legal education generally see the symposium on Teaching Legal Ethics in (1991) 41 *Journal of Legal Education* 1–119.

Further reading

The American literature is vast, the English virtually non-existent. The following is a small selection of papers which highlight a number of the many cross-currents and issues in the debate. Not all of these references have been cited in this chapter.

R L Abel *The Legal Profession in England & Wales*, Blackwell, Oxford 1988

R L Abel 'Why Does the ABA Promulgate Ethical Rules?' (1981) 59 *Texas Law Review* 639.

J Allaker & J Shapland *Organising UK Professions: Continuity and Change*, Research Study No 16, The Law Society, London 1994.

N R Cahn 'Styles of Lawyering' (1992) 43 *Hastings Law Journal* 1039.

C Gilligan *In a Different Voice: Psychological Theory and Women's Development*, Harvard University Press, Cambridge, Ma & London 1982.

G C Hazard 'The Future of Legal Ethics' (1991) 100 *Yale Law Journal* 1239.

D Luban *Lawyers and Justice: An Ethical Study*, Princeton University Press, Princeton, NJ 1988.

D L Rhode 'Ethical Perspectives on Legal Practice' (1985) 37 *Stanford Law Review* 589.

W H Simon 'Ethical Discretion in Lawyering' (1988) 101 *Harvard Law Review* 1083.

5   Law talk and lay talk: lawyers as communicators

The primary purposes of this chapter are to examine why communication skills have become such an important issue for professional
practice; to explore the nature of communication processes; to consider ways in which various communication problems arise, and
hence to identify opportunities for increasing communicative effectiveness.

Objectives

To:
- Increase your awareness of the part played by communication skills in
  legal education and practice.
- Enable you to obtain greater technical understanding of the communica-
  tion process.
- Encourage you to experiment with a number of communication processes,
  and reflect on those processes.
- Enable you to articulate your own principles for effective communication.
- Enable you to reflect critically on the nature and role of communication
  skills in legal practice.

Lawyers need to talk!

Our ability to communicate in language rather than just signs is perhaps the
most distinctive feature of human evolution, and central to our ability to order
and make sense of our world. To say that communication skills are important
to all of us is therefore an incredibly trite understatement.

The importance of communication skills for the lawyer should be equally
obvious, but, until recently, this aspect has tended to be neglected by legal
education and training. The academic image of the lawyer is of someone por-
ing over textbooks and law reports, or perhaps arguing some fine point of
principle before the Court of Appeal or House of Lords. The need to communicate actions and ideas to people, other than through the very rarefied
medium of appellate argument, does not figure highly in the traditional

model. Indeed, though legal education offers plenty of practice in certain, structured, kinds of writing – notably essay writing – oral skills and the other dimensions of writing skill are frequently taken for granted (at least at the academic stage). The reality of lawyering is usually very different.[1]

Lawyers talk to clients; they negotiate and do deals with other lawyers; they mediate and arbitrate; they act as advocates before courts and tribunals. Of course, written communication is also important in most lawyering processes: letters have to be written; pleadings and other documents drafted. But initial impressions are made, and outcomes often determined, by spoken language. As we shall see, however, communication – both written and spoken – is more problematic than we think. Even in the most general of circumstances, communication can be disrupted by distractions, distortions and misperceptions.

To provide a foundation for your communication skills, we address four key issues in this chapter:

(1) why communication skills matter;
(2) how the communication process operates;
(3) what the bridges and barriers to effective communication are; and
(4) the importance of intra-group communication.

1   For recent research emphasising the primacy of orality, see J Morrison & P Leith *The Barristers' World*, Open UP, Milton Keynes 1993. In legal theory, the concern with (oral) communication is particularly apparent in the hermeneutic and rhetorical concerns of Critical Legal Theory – see eg B de S Santos 'The Postmodern Transition' in A Sarat & T R Kearns *The Fate of Law*, Michigan UP, Ann Arbor 1991.

Why communication skills matter

Let's begin with something you are all familiar with.

Exercise 5.1   What makes a good teacher?

In this exercise we want you to think about your experiences in education – either in university or at school or college, if you prefer. It is unlikely that you will have uniformly good impressions of all the teaching you have received, so:

(a) *What, from your experience, are the characteristics of a good teacher? Make a note of the main skills and attributes you would expect of a good teacher.*
(b) *Consider how many of those features are aspects of communication skills.*
(c) *Now, by analogy, identify the communication skills you would expect a lawyer to display.*

We would guess that most of the skills and attributes you have discussed will have at least a communicative dimension. For teachers and lawyers, being knowledgable about the area is not enough – most of us have come across the problem of the teacher who 'knows his stuff, but can't put it across' to understand why that is the case. The ability to explain a problem, to recognise where and how comprehension problems will arise, to give meaningful feedback (orally and in writing) all depend on communication. Even intangibles like 'enthusiasm' are conveyed, at least in part, by the way teachers communicate. And we shall see that most, if not all, of these attributes are relevant to lawyers as well.

However, the weight of evidence points to the conclusion that lawyers are not effective communicators. As long ago as 1979 the Benson Commission commented that:

> We consider that more should be done to emphasise the importance of gaining the client's confidence and establishing a sound professional relationship with him . . . To establish good communications with another person is a professional skill which must be, and is learnt by many others besides lawyers.[1]

In a representative sample survey conducted for the Law Society in 1988, about a third of the people surveyed thought of solicitors as easy to talk to, and even fewer – only a quarter – described them as easy to understand. As the researchers note, this placed solicitors about on a par with bank managers in terms of perceived approachability. That just about says it all! Even among those respondents who had used solicitors, only a third described them as easy to understand, though 45% said that they were easy to talk to.[2]

Given the centrality of communication skills to most legal tasks, a statistic which suggests that one out of every two clients is likely to have had communication problems with their lawyer is rather alarming. It certainly suggests that communication difficulties form part of the crisis of confidence in the professions.

So, why are lawyers poor communicators? The causes are bound to be quite complex, but it might be helpful to try and identify at least some of the factors if we are to improve the situation for ourselves.

1 *Royal Commission on Legal Services, Final Report,* vol I, Cmnd 7648, HMSO, London 1979, para 22.31.
2 J Jenkins, E Skordaki & C Willis *Public Use and Perception of Solicitors' Services,* Research Study No 1, The Law Society, London 1989, pp 9–10.

Exercise 5.2   The problems with 'law talk'

Stop reading at this point and write down no more than three general reasons why lawyers might be poor communicators. Then compare your list with the comments that follow.

We suggest that the following are key considerations.

1   DIFFERENCES BETWEEN LEGAL AND EVERYDAY LANGUAGE

These differences are, of course, an underlying cause of our problems. They are most obvious at the semantic level. As lawyers we have a distinctive vocabulary which uses words from outside of the general language, and words which are part of the general language, but which have radically different meanings in legal and general usage – like the term 'consideration', for example.[1] There are also a number of more subtle, but equally fundamental, differences in the grammatical and discourse[2] features of legal language which also serve to restrict its comprehensibility, especially in written as opposed to spoken communications.[3] In legal writing the differences include unusual phrase order in sentences, *nominalisations* (ie the use of nouns created from verbs), repetition of whole phrases and sentences, etc. Take, for example, the following extract from a consumer contract:

> . . . and to consent to immediate execution upon any such judgment and that any execution that may be issued on any such judgment be immediately levied upon and satisfied out of any personal property of the undersigned . . . and to waive all right of the undersigned . . . to have personal property last taken and levied upon to satisfy any such execution.[4]

It is too easy to say that the problem is just one of language, however. The *real* problem is the apparent incapacity of lawyers to overcome the communication barriers that these linguistic differences create. We cannot assume we are effective translators between legal and everyday English, but of course that does not make it any the less our *responsibility* to ensure we are understood.

2   THE PROFESSIONALISING PROCESS

This in itself is a substantial part of the problem. We spend three (or more) years in law school where the emphasis is on thinking – and sounding – like a lawyer. Julius Getman,[5] for example, has stressed the way law school introduces us to, and expects us to use, a variety of rhetorical styles, which he terms 'professional', 'critical' and 'scholarly' voices, while 'human voice' – 'language that uses ordinary concepts and familiar situations without professional ornamentation'[6] – becomes lost and undervalued. How is this so?

During this period most of our 'law talk' is directed at other lawyers: students and teachers who are themselves immersed in the legal language. This is an obvious feature of classroom interaction where, crucially, the law is normally presented and discussed on the assumption that the participants have command of a shared legal language. But, as research has shown, the closed nature of law talk can also spill over into, and be reinforced by, less formal interaction among lawyers. The law school and its members are often socially and spatially self-contained.[7] Many law faculties have their own buildings and separate library facilities; law teachers and students frequently emphasise the importance of their identity and distinctiveness as 'lawyers'. Law students themselves may structure a significant part of their social lives separately from other students – the success of many student law societies is a testament to this.

There is a tendency, therefore, for lawyers to emerge as a race apart from the rest of the institution. However, once qualified, the shift to a practice environment involves a radical change in communicative context. Much of our law talk must now be directed to lay clients who do not share our common legal language.

3 DIFFICULTIES IN IDENTIFYING AND RESOLVING COMMUNICATION PROBLEMS IN PRACTICE

We need to recognise that the ability to communicate is the classic tacit skill. This has two implications.

First, we tend to assume that we all communicate more or less effectively with each other on a day-to-day basis. Furthermore, having qualified, we tend to assume that we are pretty clever, articulate, human beings, and therefore efficient communicators. Unfortunately, as a vast body of research into individual psychology and organisational behaviour has shown, this is not necessarily so.

Second, we rarely reflect on what or how we are communicating except when things go wrong (if then). If a communication failure is not identified at the time, there is no obvious reason to try and modify our behaviour. In the professional context, clients do not always articulate their dissatisfaction and, even if it is clear that the client is displeased, the cause – if it is poor communication – may not always be identified as such, even by the client. Sometimes communication failures may not emerge simply because the client does not come back.

The availability of advice and training once we are in the working environment tends to be variable in both quantity and quality. This will affect a firm's capacity both to identify poor communication, and to do anything about it.

4 THE LACK OF TRAINING IN COMMUNICATION SKILLS

There has been a serious lack of training in this area until relatively recently. Communication skills training is now incorporated into vocational training and available through continuing education courses, as well as in a growing number of undergraduate programmes. It remains to be seen how great a difference this makes.

What does this exercise tell us about our potential to be effective communicators? Well, we would suggest that it shows how necessary it is to start thinking more deeply about the communication process, and to question the linguistic assumptions which we tend to make as students (and teachers) of law. In this sense it may require us to unlearn some of the established practices of traditional legal education. Let us begin this process by going back to basics.

1 This point is developed more fully by J A Holland and J S Webb *Learning Legal Rules*, 2nd Edition, Blackstone Press, London 1993, pp 88–101.
2 For present purposes we use 'discourse' simply to mean the use of language in a 'succession of related sentences, as in a conversation or text' – S Pinker *The Language Instinct*, Penguin, Harmondsworth 1994, p 475.
3 We discuss written communication in greater depth in Chapters 7–8.
4 Cited in V Charrow, J Crandall & R Charrow 'Characteristics and Functions of Legal Language' in R Kittredge & J Lehrberger (eds) *Sublanguage: Studies of Language in Restricted Semantic Domains*, de Gruyter, Berlin 1982, p 175 at p 178.
5 'Voices' (1988) 66 *Texas Law Review* 577.
6 Ibid, p 582.
7 Susan Urmston Philips 'The Language Socialization of Lawyers: Acquiring the "Cant"' in G Spindler (ed) *Doing the Ethnography of Schooling: Educational Anthropology in Action*, Waveland Press, Prospect Heights, Il 1988, pp 176–209.

How we communicate

When we communicate with someone we are actually putting into operation quite a complex process of social interaction, involving perception, articulation, response, etc. Psychologists have attempted to describe this communication process through the construction of communication models. Can you devise your own model?

Exercise 5.3   Communication models

Illustrate, diagrammatically or pictorially, your view of what is happening in (i) a conversation between two people; and (ii) writing a letter to a friend (you are advised to try and describe each process separately).

If possible, do this exercise in a group environment so that you can compare your different models.

Now compare your own models with those devised by psychologists: see, for example, the models presented by Michael Argyle,[1] and by Hargie and Marshall,[2] which emphasise the dynamic nature of social interaction in rather different ways.

When you have done this, consider:
(a)   *What differences, if any, exist between the two models of communication you have considered?*
(b)   *Are there particular aspects of the process which the formal models emphasise, but yours does not?*
(c)   *Do the formal models you have considered give a 'full' picture of the communication process or, in your view, do they miss anything important?*

We will leave you to work out the differences for yourselves, but do remember that the existence of such differences does not make either form of communication better or worse than the other. It simply tells us that each will serve some purposes better than others. This does mean that we have to be sensitive to what has to be conveyed through and achieved by each particular communication.

1   *The Psychology of Interpersonal Behaviour*, 5th Edition, Penguin, Harmondsworth 1994.
2   O Hargie & P Marshall 'Interpersonal Communication: A Theoretical Framework' in O Hargie (ed) *A Handbook of Communication Skills*, Croom Helm, London 1986, pp 24–6.

Barriers and bridges to effective communication

Good communication is not just about the right choice of medium or message. There are many other aspects of the communication process which, if taken for granted, can destroy effective communication, but which equally, if used constructively, can increase our potential as communicators.

In this section we consider factors that are important in constructing bridges or barriers to effective communication. We cannot realistically hope to regulate all of them all of the time, but an awareness of their impact can help us to sustain the quality of interaction.

Underlying all of these factors is one basic problem. That is, of course, that creating a climate for good communication is rather more difficult than we generally realise. We can begin to see why, via a further exercise.

Exercise 5.4 A Martian description[1]

For this exercise you need two participants: (A) – your tutor – plays the Martian visitor, (B) the helpful Earthling. We find it works best if the participants sit back-to-back, so that there is no possibility of eye contact.

> A friendly Martian is visiting the planet Earth and is eager to find out more about the daily lives of its people. You (participant B) are in radio contact only with the Martian. Your Martian friend speaks basic English reasonably fluently, but has only a rudimentary understanding of the language, and may not fully comprehend the meaning behind many words. S/he (ie participant A) will ask you to describe a typical day in your life, and, during the course of your description, may ask you to explain or clarify words/activities s/he does not understand.

After running this exercise, you should:

(a) *get the participants to describe the communication problems they confronted, and to explain how those problems made them feel; then*
(b) *reflect on the implications this exercise has for lawyer–client communication.*

The kind of problems you are likely to identify in this exercise reflect a number of generic difficulties which we shall now explore in more detail under the following four headings. In these sections we have deliberately focused on things that you can do to increase your general effectiveness as (legal) communicators.

1 Loosely adapted from P Bergman, A Sherr and R Burridge 'Games Law Teachers Play' (1986) 20 *Law Teacher* 21 at 25–6.

The effect of non-verbal cues

The Martian exercise was made more difficult by the lack of face-to-face conversation. This cut out any reliance on things like facial expression or hand gestures, which can greatly facilitate communication. These are both examples of *non-verbal communication (NVC)*. NVC is simply a global term that is used to describe ways of conveying meaning other than by words.

NVC is extremely important to the communication process. Birdwhistell, for example, has estimated that the verbal component of face-to-face conversation accounts for only 35% of the total 'message' while 65% of the average communication is non-verbal.[1] In part this reflects the fact that *NVC* is 'multichannelled'[2] – ie it can be transmitted and received by visual, auditory, tactile or olfactory means. It is not restricted to the auditory channel of verbal communication, nor to the visual channel of written communication. By recognising the interplay between verbal and non-verbal communication we can begin to appreciate just how much we communicate with *all* our senses, not just the obvious ones.

Research also suggests that the verbal and non-verbal components of a message are used to convey different things: the verbal element mainly conveying information, while *NVC* more often conveys mood, feelings and attitudes.

In this section we shall focus on two key aspects of *NVC*. The least commonly known of these is properly called *prosody*, or sometimes *paralanguage*. This term describes the non-verbal vocalisations we all use to express things. Sighs are thus a form of prosody, as are all the other grunts and snorts we use to express our feelings – eg the sort of things that appear in comics as 'Erm' or 'AAARGH!!' Other more subtle modifications, such as changes in stress and intonation, or rhythm, and pauses in speech are also an aspect of prosody. As an example, try saying the following statements out loud, first as a command:

You're not going out there!

then as a question:

You're not going out there?

In this example you can hear how prosody serves the same function as punctuation in written communication.

The more widely known form of *NVC* is, of course, *body language*. An awful lot of academic material has been produced about the importance and meaning of body language; some of this, often in a very partial and misleading form, has found its way into general folklore. It is particularly dangerous. Much was written on the meaning of body language in the 1970s and early 80s that lacked rigour. Do remember that the meaning of body language is largely dependent on the specific context, culture and status of the actors; it must be viewed as part of the whole communication process – both verbal and non-verbal – and meanings cannot safely be reduced to the checklist approach favoured by some textbooks.

What is important is to try and ensure that your own body language does not serve as a possible barrier to communication. It means, as a minimum, that you need to raise your own awareness of the kinds of signals we send out. The next two exercises are intended to help in this process.

1   R L Birdwhistell *Kinesis and Context*, Allen Lane, London 1971.
2   T Singelis 'Nonverbal Communication in Intercultural Interactions' in R W Brislin & T Yoshida (eds) *Improving Intercultural Interactions*, Sage Publ, Thousand Oaks, Ca 1994, p 268 at 275.

Exercise 5.5   The lights are on . . .

This exercise is in two stages. For the first phase, you need to divide into pairs. Then follow your tutor's instructions.

Now, for the second phase, divide into groups of three. Then, again, follow your tutor's instructions.

Feedback from this exercise before moving on to Exercise 5.6.

Exercise 5.6   Body talk[1]

This exercise works with pairs or groups of three. If you are working in a threesome, one person should act as observer for each 'experimental' part of the exercise. In our own workshops, we like to get two pairs/threes working on each set of exercises independently, and then reporting their findings to the group as a whole. We have laid out the exercise in a way that encourages you to work through the first three phases of the learning cycle. Some of the exercises may only serve to remind you of some fairly basic precepts of social behaviour, so we have not automatically included a final testing phase to close the circle. If you feel it is helpful to do that for yourselves, then you should go ahead and do so. To help you we have given some indication with the first exercise of the kind of things that ought to go under each heading. With each category you might also like to think of its relevance or significance for legal practice.

1   PROXIMITY

(a) Experience: *Carry on a brief conversation with a partner –*
                      (i) standing too close for comfort;
                      (ii) standing too far apart for comfort;
(b) Reflection: *(Describe your feelings. Why did you feel like that?)*
(c) Rule-making: *(What appear to be the rules about physical distance between*
                      people in our society).

2   POSTURE

(a) Experience: *Practise –*
                      (i) tense and relaxed postures;
                      (ii) welcoming and rejecting postures.
                      Without identifying your choice of posture verbally, get your
                      partner to describe what they see/feel.
(b) Reflection:
(c) Rule-making:

3   ORIENTATION

(a) Experience: *(i) Compare the orientation of students and teacher(s) in the*
                      room. What do you see?
                      (ii) Choose an appropriate moment for one member of the
                      pair/team to turn their back on the rest of the group. Wait
                      for comments.
(b) Reflection:
(c) Rule-making:

4   PHYSICAL APPEARANCE

(a) Experience: *(i) Think back to your first impressions of someone else in the*
                      group. Do you think your first impressions were right?
                      (ii) Describe somebody you know well. What elements of the
                      description are most important to you?
                      (iii) Contrast the sets of characteristics you have used.

(b) Reflection:
(c) Rule-making:

5   HAND/HEAD MOVEMENT

(a) Experience: Look around the room; what can you infer from –
                            (i) hand movements (especially hand to head or face);
                            (ii) position and movement of heads.
(b) Reflection:
(c) Rule-making:

One of the things this exercise (indirectly) emphasises is the potential for the communicative context to be manipulated, and for non-verbal communication to be used to convey very powerful messages about the speakers. While you might wish to question the ethics of some such practices, note that lawyers are becoming increasingly conscious of the importance *NVC* can have in presenting a person in a particular light. This is illustrated in the following extract, which shows how video-taped evidence enabled counsel in one major American lawsuit to use witnesses' *NVC* to reinforce their theory of the case. The issue in *Pennzoil v Texaco* was whether Texaco had fraudulently induced a third company, Getty Oil Company, to break a binding merger contract with Pennzoil. This required the Pennzoil lawyers, Terrell and Jeffers, to establish that Texaco management had *actual knowledge* of Pennzoil's deal with Getty. As is commonly the case with American fraud trials, the issues of fact were to be determined by a jury, from a bewildering array of evidence – lengthy depositions and extremely dense and unexciting corporate communications . . .

> Of the sixty-three depositions spanning fifteen thousand pages of transcript during the 'discovery' phase of the case, fifteen had been video-taped by Jeffers and Terrell to assure the jury got a first-hand look at 'the flavour of these people'. Besides permitting Pennzoil to introduce exhibits, the video depositions also enabled it to retell the story of the Getty Oil war – a story intended to depict Petersen [Getty Oil's chairman] and his people as double dealers.
>
> Gordon Boisi, the investment banker who solicited Texaco's bid to defeat [Getty's] deal with Pennzoil, fluttered his eyelids, sniffed and chuckled at the lawyers' questions and held forth in the gobbledygook of the takeover game. When asked in the video-tape whether he would be testifying as a live witness at the trial, Boisi replied, 'If my schedule allowed' – not the kind of answer that impresses jurors who by that time had given up nearly a month of their lives to the case. And when he was asked in the video whether he had come and gone during Gordon [Getty]'s absence from the 'back door' board meeting, he swallowed before answering, 'I guess that occurred'.
>
> Bart Winokur, the outside counsel for Getty Oil who had entered the Getty Oil board meeting in Houston in Gordon's absence, gave intelligent and straightforward responses but appeared a little shifty. He fidgeted in his seat. His eyes darted around the room. His voice at times

adopted a somewhat sassy tone . . . There was something just a little unconvincing about Winokur; while he testified that it was not his practice to take notes during meetings, he was holding a pen in one hand.

Sid Petersen, an executive whose career had been scuttled just as it was reaching its peak, came off as smug and defensive, tossing his head, folding his arms across his chest, heaving sighs. When he was asked a question about [Pennzoil chairman, Hugh] Liedtke's agreement to honour his golden parachute, Petersen snapped, 'I don't give a damn what Mr Liedtke approved. He had nothing to say about it. *I* had a contract.'[2]

1   Adapted from S Habeshaw and D Steeds *53 Interesting Communication Exercises for Science Students*, Technical and Educational Services, Bristol 1987, pp 25–9.
2   From Thomas Petzinger Jr *Oil & Honor: The Texaco–Pennzoil Wars*, 1987, cited in K Roberts & D Hunt *Organizational Behaviour*, PWS–Kent Publ, Boston, Ma 1991, p 242. The jury found in Pennzoil's favour and ordered Texaco to pay the extraordinary sum of $10.53 million to Pennzoil for the loss of access to Getty's oil reserves.

Environmental factors

Communication can be influenced by a huge range of environmental or situational factors. These are commonly lumped together under the term 'noise' which rather graphically describes the distracting effect that such extraneous factors can have on communication. 'Noise' in this sense will include obvious factors such as interruptions, the comfort of our physical environment, the layout of a room or office, or the impact of *real* noise (a pneumatic drill outside the office window!), etc.

Subtler elements, like the absence of face-to-face communication (as in the Martian exercise), or whether or not we are on 'home territory' will also influence the quality of communication.

Note that these are all factors which tend to be more or less controllable, which means we almost always have some capacity to improve the environment within which we communicate.

Cultural factors

It can be argued that the very fact you are a trained lawyer presents a culture gap between you and your clients. This gap is created by the very training and professionalisation processes we talked about at the beginning of this chapter. These can have a number of effects on your communication. We have identified three main issues here.

First there is the matter of what Gutman terms *voice*: the use of conventional professional or scholarly voice has a number of effects on lawyers' discourse.

It encourages the use of more complex sentences than we tend to use in informal speech situations. Examples of what we mean include the obvious, like legalistic (or pseudo-legalistic) phraseology (eg 'Now, Mr Smith, can you tell me what you were doing on the night in question?'). It also covers the adoption of unusual grammar, such as the use of the passive in question construction (eg 'Who was chased by the policeman?' rather than 'Who did the policeman chase?'). We know that people are far more likely to make mistakes in answering passive than active questions.¹ Even if the grammar you are using does not make you harder to understand (neither of the examples here are difficult), it can emphasise difference or social distance.

It also encourages you to fall into the trap of using 'jargon' or technical terms of art where that is unnecessary. Clients do not usually need to know that they might have an action under s 2 of the Unfair Contract Terms Act; nor are comments like 'We need to ask for further and better particulars' likely to leave them much the wiser about the progress of their case. The same problem does not, of course, arise in communications with other lawyers, where technical language can actually facilitate communication by acting as a kind of shorthand. Other lawyers will generally understand references to 'TWOC-ing', 'discovery', etc.

Next there is *linguistic ability*. Distinct from the problems of officialese, you will have to face the fact that your use of language may be different from some, perhaps even most, of your clients. This may be apparent in the respective breadth of your vocabularies; the fluency of your speech; the range of sentence structures you use. This may not only serve to heighten apparent social difference, but may serve to emphasise the powerlessness of a particular client – even if the client comprehends the language you are using, she may be unable to use it effectively to converse with you or to exercise her rights against another.

Lastly, legal practice also involves a number of *'translation' problems*. This does not simply mean that lawyers confuse by jargon, though that may be part of it. Rather, it means that, in talking about problems, lawyer and client are essentially on different wavelengths, focusing on different objects in their discourse. This is because law serves as a *meta-language* – a mechanism, as Mulholland puts it, for 'declaring in words what is happening in words'² – a different language for describing what has already been described.

In part, translation is a necessary feature of legal work. As Maureen Cain has pointed out, the discrepancy between legal and everyday discourse goes beyond mystification. The lawyer has first to translate the client's ordinary-language problem into an object that has some legal identity. So, a problem relating to the joint ownership of a house can only be resolved once it is clear to the lawyer whether the property is held on a joint tenancy or tenancy in common. As Cain explains:

> . . . [t]he house which in everyday discourse the wife and husband regard as 'theirs' turn[s] out in legal discourse to be capable of being theirs in many different ways . . . if the legal discourse had exactly paralleled the everyday discourse it would not have been possible to achieve a solution in one but not the other . . .³

Further translation is then required for the lawyer to convert the objective in legal discourse (eg transfer of ownership from joint tenancy to tenancy in common) into the outcome desired by the client (eg the ability to dispose of the share in the property by will). As Cain concludes: '[a]bility to translate is the specific skill of lawyers, and . . . their definitive practice'.⁴ For lawyers it is this ability to move between discourses that has to become tacit, yet, perhaps for the reasons we have already discussed this frequently does not happen.

Moreover, there are at least two particular problems that can arise during the translation process. To understand how each of these problems arise, we need to understand a bit about how communication works. This takes us first into what is technically termed the 'pragmatics' of communication, and then into the structure of what are called 'communication episodes'.

At one level, communication tends to build on certain shared expectations. As Pinker puts it:

> . . . listeners tacitly expect speakers to be informative, truthful, relevant, clear, unambiguous, brief and orderly. These expectations help to winnow out the inappropriate readings of an ambiguous sentence, to piece together fractured utterances, to excuse slips of the tongue . . . and to fill in the missing steps of an argument.[5]

If communicative action is based on these assumptions of good faith, then failure to meet the expectations created by the communication will clearly be damaging to the relationship between the communicators. To give an extreme example, if Caroline tells a student 'no one has ever failed Julian's Welfare Law course' the student might be less than pleased to discover, on starting the course, that no one had failed because the course had not run before. While one cannot say strictly that Caroline's statement is untrue, the reasonable expectation created by that speech act is that the course *has* run and no one has failed.

However, we also have the capacity to break these good faith rules *without* destroying understanding. In certain situations we deliberately use what is *not* said to convey covert layers of information. Stephen Pinker provides a good example with the following letter of recommendation:

Dear Professor Pinker,
    I am very pleased to be able to recommend Irving Smith to you. Mr Smith is a model student. He dresses well and is extremely polite. I have known Mr Smith for three years now, and in every way I have found him to be most co-operative . . .[6]

This is the sort of reference that is guaranteed not to secure you a job. The letter contains no information relevant to the employer's needs. The covert message sent out by this breach of expectation is: 'this is not the person for you'. The necessity for the disguise is understood on both sides. One does not lightly engage in the breach of trust implicit in writing a reference that actually says, in Pinker's memorable phrase 'Stay away from Smith, he's dumb as a tree'.[7] So long as these conventions are understood, there is no failure of communication. So much for the theory, now back to the problems.

Our first problem is that the complexity of the translation process can lead to a mismatch in lawyer and client expectations. In essence, we get problems of incomplete translation, where the implications of a lawyer's statement do not 'connect' in lay terms, because the 'what-goes-without-saying' for a lawyer needs to be said for a lay person to appreciate it. We cannot break the good faith rules here, because there is not the shared understanding necessary to convey the covert message. Mismatched expectations about legal costs and how they are to be met are a perennial favourite in this context.[8]

Now, to return to the theory again, we said that we also need to consider how communications are constructed as stories or 'episodes'.

We tend to communicate events and feelings by organising them into particular narrative, story, structures. These psychologists call *communication episodes*.[9] Communication episodes display the following 'ERAC' (Events – Response – Actions – Consequences) features:

- Stories are initiated by something happening or something being said: *Events*.
- A character in the story will have a psychological *Response* to those events.
- The character will use that response to construct goals which are reflected in later *Action*.
- These actions will then have certain *Consequences*.

For example: Laurel and Hardy go to a nightclub. Laurel's girlfriend Fay meets them there. Fay really fancies Hardy and spends most of the evening dancing with him. Laurel is jealous; he sits glowering at the bar and gets more drunk as the night goes on. He finally snaps and 'glasses' Hardy in the face. Hardy is taken off to hospital.

This short story conforms to all the characteristics of an episode. The initiating event is Hardy and Fay dancing. Laurel responds by getting more and more jealous. Laurel's jealousy apparently leads to more and more drink and then to the moment of violence (action) and Hardy's injury and hospitalisation (consequences). The causal links between the ERAC stages ensure that it rings true. Theory suggests that even complex narratives correspond to this structure, because they contain sets of embedded episodes – stories within the story.

So, let's apply this particular bit of theory to law as well. First, as we will argue further in Chapter 10, lawyers need to understand how stories are constructed so as to reconstruct and use them in a way that makes sense to the audience – for example, the jury in your client's trial. Research suggests that we are not always effective as professional storytellers. Second, at an ideological level, the translation process this involves can significantly change the nature and even the 'ownership' of the client's story. This is a difficult idea, so let us try and explain.

In traditional practice,[10] a point will come in a case where the lawyers take possession of the client's story and translate it from a lay into a legal narrative. In translating it for a legal audience, the lawyers will frequently change aspects of the communication episode on which it is based. This may be because the client's version of the story does not seem to fit the legal argument in the way the lawyers want, or it may be that the parts of the story that are of the greatest social relevance to the client are not of great legal significance. This, it is argued, has a number of disempowering consequences for the client. If this sounds overly dramatic, then think back to Sara Thornton's case, discussed in Chapter 4.

One of the problems which emerged in the Thornton trial appears to have been a problem of incomplete translation. Thornton's defence had decided to develop a theme of diminished responsibility. Given that the law of provocation did not provide a defence where the killing was premeditated (as was arguably the case here), the defence, perhaps understandably, chose not to follow that line. Yet Thornton's testimony in court was far more consistent with a 'lay' theme of provocation (ie provocation in response to a long period of abuse, rather than a single incident), than with either of the 'legal' defences of provocation or diminished responsibility. The result was that the story did not fit the legal frame. While the lay version provided the necessary causal links between the ERAC features (husband's long term violence (E) – created a 'pressure cooker' response (R) – pressure finally 'blew' with the stabbing (A) – husband died (C)), the legal version did not. For whatever reason, it looks suspiciously as if her lawyers had failed to carry their client with them in their translation of the case from one of 'lay' provocation to 'legal' diminished responsibility.

We shall return to the issues of client narrative and empowerment in Chapter 6.

1   See eg P Wright 'Is Legal Jargon a Restrictive Practice?' in S Lloyd-Bostock (ed) *Psychology in Legal Contexts: Applications and Limitations*, Macmillan/SSRC, London & Basingstoke 1981, p 121 at p 123.
2   *The Language of Negotiation: A Handbook of Practical Strategies for Improving Communication*, Routledge, London & New York 1991, p 78; see also M Cain 'The General Practice Lawyer and the Client: Towards a Radical Conception' in R Dingwall and P Lewis (eds) *The Sociology of the Professions: Lawyers, Doctors and Others*, Macmillan, London & Basingstoke 1983, p 106 at 111.
3   Cain, op cit, p 117.
4   Ibid, p 118.
5   *The Language Instinct*, Penguin, Harmondsworth 1994, p 228.
6   Ibid, p 229.
7   Ibid.
8   See eg G Davis *Partisans and Mediators: The Resolution of Divorce Disputes*, Clarendon Press, Oxford 1988.
9   D E Rumelhart 'Understanding and summarizing brief stories' in D La Berge & S Samuels (eds) *Basic Processes in Reading: Perception and Comprehension*, Lawrence Erlbaum Associates, Hillsdale, NJ; T Winograd & F Flores *Understanding Computers and Cognition*, Ablex, Norwood, NJ 1986.
10 From an ethic of care perspective, ownership of the narrative is recognised as a participation issue. The lawyer needs to be open to the needs of the client, even if this means that your strategy becomes focused on how you lose the case, rather than whether you win.

Personal factors

Personal factors may also create considerable disruption to effective communication by, for example, creating misunderstandings or by generating a sense of social distance between lawyer and client. Examples of personal factors which can influence communication include:

- APPEARANCE
  Whatever the rights and wrongs of this, clients tend to expect their lawyers to look like their image of the typical lawyer. Going against that expectation is risky. Too casual an appearance will raise questions about your professionalism; equally, in some contexts, dress that is too 'slick' or expensive will emphasise the social distance between you and your client.

- CREDIBILITY
  Your effectiveness as a communicator depends in part on your credibility. This will be enhanced by evidence of reliability, consistency and trustworthiness on your part. It will be damaged by your failure to respond

promptly, or appropriately, to other communications; by poor quality work and by inconsistent advice and decision-making.

● EXPERTISE

Generally individuals who are perceived to have expertise on the topic in question are thought to be more credible and effective as communicators. As recent research by Avrom Sherr[1] into lawyers' interviewing skill casts some doubt on clients' capacity to rate the communicative competence of their lawyers, the emphasis here appears to be very much on *perceptions* of expertise rather than the reality. Perhaps it doesn't matter so much what you know, so long as you sound convincing!

● SINCERITY

Insincerity can often become apparent through a lack of congruence between verbal and non-verbal communication. The lawyer who makes all the appropriately sympathetic noises when interviewing, but manages to look totally uninterested in the whole business is not going to convince.

● STEREOTYPING

This is a device we all use to some degree to form impressions about people. Our stereotypes will commonly provide some basis for our opinions of others as good, bad, friendly, reserved, honest or dishonest, etc.[2] Such stereotypes can then influence the messages we send out to or about those individuals. Since stereotypes are often based on characteristics like gender, race, disability, body size, or language,[3] they can be potentially prejudicial, if not downright discriminatory. The dangers are obvious: beware of acting on stereotypical information.

For the client in particular, such personal failures can be alienating, contributing to a sense that the lawyer is not interested in her problem.

One other particular personal factor than can influence communication is *emotion*. How we react to certain people or situations has a tremendous impact on our social interaction. At one level this is obvious: our mood, level of stress, etc, all affect the way we react, and are things that we seek, consciously or intuitively, to display or suppress according to the nature of particular situations. But our concern with emotion goes deeper than that. Once you start to think about it, it is also fairly obvious that connections exist between a person's emotional state, their behaviour and their 'cognition' or thought processes. For example, think how extremes of emotion, like fear or anger, can interfere with our capacity to 'think straight'.[4]

As professionals, often dealing with people in stressful situations, we need therefore to develop ways of coping with both our own emotions and those of others, particularly our clients. The emotional dimension of the lawyer's work cannot simply be ignored.[5]

1   'The Value of Experience in Legal Competence' (forthcoming, 1995). Our thanks to Professor Sherr for allowing us access to his paper in advance of publication.
2   Cf, in the legal context, R Bull 'The Influence of Stereotypes on Person Identification' in D P Farrington, K Hawkins & S Lloyd-Bostock (eds) *Psychology, Law and Legal Processes*, Macmillan/SSRC, London & Basingstoke 1979, p 184.
3   For example, the concept of *standard language ideology*, ie that there is only one 'proper' way to speak English, serves as a classic form of social stereotyping – see generally E B Ryan &

H Giles (eds) *Attitudes towards language variation: Social and applied contexts* Edward Arnold, London 1982. Cf Chapter 7 below.
4 This commonsense notion is supported by psychological research – see D Meichenbaum & L Butler 'Cognitive Ethology: Assessing the Streams of Cognition and Emotion' in K Blankstein et al (eds) *Advances in the Study of Communication and Affect*, Vol 6, Plenum Press, New York 1980.
5 We return to this theme in the next chapter.

Group communications

So far, we have tended to consider communication as a 'one-on-one' exercise. However, in modern organisations, including the law firm, much of the communication process operates within a group dynamic. Even though all communication within groups is interpersonal, the group context introduces some subtle, but significant, changes to the way we communicate.[1]

1 For an overview of the issues from a psychological perspective, see H H Blumberg, M F Davis & V Kent 'Interacting in Groups' in O Hargie (ed) *A Handbook of Communication Skills*, Croom Helm, London 1986, p 269.

The professional context of group interaction

The nature of legal practice has changed substantially in recent years as firms have had to adapt to changes in their scale of operation, their clientele (and client expectations), and the various professional demands for improved quality and efficiency. Particularly in the larger corporate and commercial practices, such external pressures have led to the creation of new internal management structures and working practices:

> As the nature and focus of work has changed, commercial firms' traditional departments have been complemented by new speciality groups, sometimes within a department, but frequently drawing members from across the firm. Also, lawyers increasingly work as members of teams instead of as Lone Rangers, or at least that is an expressed aspiration.[1]

Even outside of this specialised context there is often a group dynamic to certain aspects of the lawyers' work, particularly litigation, which is increasingly characterised as involving team work between solicitor (or solicitors), support staff and paralegals, barrister and client.[2] The problem is that, as one of the practitioners interviewed by Andy Boon put it:

> . . . Team management skills are important and something which many solicitors are not good at; it is not something they are ever coached in or shown how they should go about it. It is also an area of human behaviour where the average lawyer thinks they are doing all right; they do not need to be shown how to do it. They think it is second nature to them and it is not . . .[3]

1 E H Greenebaum *Coping With a Turbulent Environment: Development of Law Firm Training Programs*, Legal Skills Working Papers, Institute of Advanced Legal Studies, London 1991, p 8.

2   See eg E H Greenebaum 'Law Firms and Clients as Groups: Loyalty, Rationality and Representation', (1988) 13 *Journal of the Legal Profession* 205; also Boon 'Assessing Competence to Conduct Civil Litigation: Key Tasks and Skills' in A Boon, A Halpern & K Mackie *Skills for Legal Functions II: Representation and Advice*, Legal Skills Working Papers, Institute of Advanced Legal Studies, London 1992, seriatim.
3   Boon, op cit, p 43.

Communication in a problem-solving group

As we have suggested already, lawyers do not work in teams just for the sake of it. Group work in practice exists because it adds an extra dimension, in terms of available skills and expertise, to the individuals' ability to solve the problem at hand. These advantages may be bought at some cost, in communication terms. Information within a problem-solving group is not all shared equally. Some members of the group will know more about the case than others. Only one or two members, in coordinating roles, are likely to have the whole picture. The efficacy of any team will thus depend on the quality of communication within the group. This will turn not only on the quality of coordination, and the establishment of appropriate procedures for communication within the group, but also on the abilities of each group member to send and receive messages.

Exercise 5.7   The story[1]

This exercise takes about 20 minutes and needs a minimum of six participants – a team of five and at least one observer. A tutor or member of the class is also needed to co-ordinate the exercise.

1.   *The co-ordinator should start by asking the team of five to leave the room.*
2.   *Copies of the story and the accompanying observation sheet should be handed out to the observer(s).[2] Each observer should listen to the proceedings and complete the observation sheet for the team.*
3.   *The co-ordinator will ask the first team member to enter the room, and will read the story once only to the first team member. The co-ordinator will then ask the second team member in, and have the first person repeat the story to the second; the second will then repeat it to the third, and so on until the fifth repeats it to the observers.*
4.   *Once all the team members are in the room, the co-ordinator should re-read the original story, and get each observer to relay their results to the group.*
5.   *Ask the group how they would explain what has happened.*

ONE-WAY COMMUNICATION IN GROUP CONTEXTS

This exercise illustrates the effects on a message of a one-way communication process. One-way communication is common in group situations, and particularly those which are organised around an authoritarian hierarchy,[3] so that messages tend to be conveyed down the hierarchy, rather than communicated direct. One-way communication tends to suffer from three interrelated psychological disadvantages termed 'levelling', 'sharpening' and 'assimilation'.[4]

Levelling describes the way in which messages become simplified by the receiver, thereby reducing the amount of information she has to retain.

Sharpening is the reciprocal of levelling. It describes the process whereby the key points of the message are retained and the other information is either grouped around those points, or else forgotten.

Assimilation explains how these processes are determined by the receiver's own frame of reference – ie her personality, experience, the tasks she is undertaking. The choice of what is remembered and what is not will be influenced by that frame of reference. Sometimes new information will even be substituted in the original message, because that gives the message meaning to the receiver.

TWO-WAY COMMUNICATION

Two-way communication can overcome some of the limitations of the one-way model. To start with it is, by definition, reciprocal. There are routes and procedures for all group members to exchange information, and productive discussion is encouraged. Leadership also tends to be distributed rather than centralised, with an emphasis on consensual decision-making.

Nevertheless, effective two-way communication requires a number of pre-conditions for its success:

Co-operation

A co-operative group climate encourages equal participation by all group members. This can be difficult to achieve in the law school (and practice) context, where there is still a strong emphasis on individual effort. Indeed, it is not unusual for us to think of our peers as competitors as much as colleagues. Competitiveness is very much a two-edged sword in this kind of environment. As Chris Argyris notes in one of his case studies, competitiveness can become linked with cohesiveness within a group.[5] Members of the group get a competitive 'spark' by trying to outdo the others. Ironically, in such an organisation, the more successful group members are in relying on their own resources rather than on the help of others, the more valued they feel. Nevertheless, competitiveness may create defensive forms of practice (eg a reluctance to share knowledge, or to admit to problems) and levels of non-communication that become counter-productive. Competition can be highly destructive both by limiting the group's capacity to define or reach its goals, and on a more personal level, where it can have a corrosive effect on working relationships.

Working constructively in a group can require considerable adjustment and is one area of interpersonal skill which you may need consciously to work on. As one of our own students noted in his learning diary after his first workshop session:

> A certain amount of personal exposure is inevitable with the format of this workshop . . . I must approach the module with an open mind and subdue my competitive instincts to an extent. I do not know if I can become 'pro-social' (sic) and contribute to the group in a positive way, but I have an opportunity to try.

Our experience of running a course which is heavily dependent on team-working is that it is probably the thing the groups think about least when starting out and end up worrying about most. This a mistake. It is vital to plan and to share out team tasks. It is equally important that you make arrangements for meetings, etc, early on in any practical work you do, because once case work gets under way, you may have less time than you would like to reflect on group dynamics and effectiveness.

Ground rules

Try to establish procedures and group norms that facilitate communication. Meeting times, procedures for agreeing deadlines, procedures for contacting other members of the group should all be formulated early on. Think about communication structures within the group. Openness is essential in this kind of context. A classic form of distancing which arises, especially within competitive environments, is what Argyris terms 'discounting'.[6] This is where members of the group attempt to maintain cohesiveness by disregarding the negative aspects of a member's actions or statements: 'She's just letting off steam' or 'If you ignore the whingeing, he actually has some good ideas'. Such discounting does not help the organisation unless both the discounting and the behaviour which creates it are discussable. Double loop learning means being able to reflect on distancing and blocking behaviours and then trying to change those behaviours: that is a prerequisite to progress.

Feedback

It follows that group work depends crucially upon good quality (positive) feedback between members. The hardest environment to work in is one where there is no feedback on progress or performance. A lack of feedback will reduce self esteem, motivation and participation. However, do remember the rules on giving feedback,[7] and try to avoid giving purely negative feedback.

1   Taken from D W Johnson & F P Johnson *Joining Together: Group Theory and Group Skills*, 4th Edition, Prentice-Hall, Englewood Cliffs, NJ 1991, pp 124–6.
2   Contained in the Appendix.
3   Cf the discussion of hierarchy in the law firm in Chapter 4. In terms of law firm organisation both centralised and distributed management systems appear to exist – see eg the discussions in Greenebaum *Coping With a Turbulent Environment: Development of Law Firm Training Programs*, Legal Skills Working Papers, Institute of Advanced Legal Studies, London 1991, p 9.
4   Johnson & Johnson, op cit, pp 134–5.
5   *Reasoning, Learning, and Action*, Jossey-Bass, San Francisco 1989, p 308.
6   Argyris, op cit, pp 308–9, 446.
7   Introduction.

Exercise 5.8   Concepts

After working through this chapter, see if you can come up with your own definitions of the following technical terms. The procedure for learning these concepts is as follows:

1. Divide into pairs.

2. Each pair is to:
   (a) *define each concept, noting the page(s) on which it is discussed, and*
   (b) *make sure that you both understand the meaning of each concept.*
3. *Combine into groups of four. Compare the answers of the two pairs. If there is disagreement, look up the concept and clarify it. Make sure you are all agreed on the definition and understand it.*

   (a) *body language*   (f) *meta-language*
   (b) *cognition*   (g) *NVC*
   (c) *communication*   (h) *prosody*
   (d) *discounting*   (i) *translation*
   (e) *ERAC*

Exercise 5.9   Learning points

If you are doing group work as part of your course, meet with your colleagues and draft a 'contract' outlining the general obligations you will owe and expectations you will have of each other in the course of that/those task(s). Make sure that everyone agrees the terms and signs the contract. Now use it!

Further reading

M Argyle *The Psychology of Interpersonal Behaviour*, 5th Edition, Penguin, Harmondsworth 1994.

J G Getman 'Voices' (1988) 66 *Texas Law Review* 577.

J Gibbons (ed) *Language and the Law*, Longman, London & New York 1994.

D W Johnson and F P Johnson *Joining Together: Group Theory and Group Skills*, 4th Edition, Prentice-Hall, Englewood Cliffs, NJ 1991.

J Mulholland *The Language of Negotiation*, Routledge, London & New York 1991.

6 Interviewing: building the relationship and gaining participation

Client interviewing is probably the single most important context in which lawyers apply their oral communication skills yet, historically, lawyers have shown relatively little aptitude for it. In this chapter we enable you to identify and practise the skills of interviewing and counselling a client and provide a practical framework (WASP) through which you can develop your competence. The chapter also addresses research into and theories of lawyer–client interaction and uses these as a reflective tool for assessing practice. We conclude by offering a prospective model of client-centred lawyering building on notions of 'empathy' and 'community participation'.

Objectives

To:
- Provide an understanding of the aims and objectives of the initial client interview.
- Explore critically the relevant assumptions underlying the lawyer–client relationship.
- Encourage you to develop an empathic understanding of that relationship.
- Examine and practise techniques of questioning, listening, advising and counselling in the context of lawyer–client interviewing.
- Identify the basic steps necessary to take a case beyond the initial interview.
- Explore the potential for greater client participation in the lawyer–client relationship.

The functions of the lawyer–client interview

Imagine your client is about to walk through the door in the next five minutes.

Exercise 6.1   The objectives of interviewing

Make a note of what your main objectives will be when interviewing that client. Don't worry for now what the subject matter is – just think about what you need to achieve in general terms.

Assuming it is a first interview, the key objectives are fairly easy to identify: you obviously want various categories of information. You need to know why your client is here – either what has happened to her or what she wants to achieve that needs the services of a lawyer. You need enough basic information about her situation to open a file and to advise her about possible costs. You will also probably have noted the need to give some advice or indication of future action on your part. That, after all, is what clients generally go to lawyers for. Even though you may not be able to give the client an answer to all their problems at this stage, it would be an unusual meeting which ended without some advice or information being imparted by the lawyer.

Those are, if you like, the 'macro' functions of client interviewing, but there are other important functions implicit in the processes of lawyer–client interaction. We would like you to read the following extract, and then we will use it to reflect on the process it describes:

Mrs Celeste came to the legal aid office early Monday morning. By 8:00 am a line, two and three across, had formed in front of a small wooden table in the centre of the waiting room. A woman standing behind the table gave instructions in English and Spanish. The line grew throughout the morning . . .

When the woman called out her number, Mrs Celeste stood up and walked to the door of the main office . . . she entered a small room with doorways on three sides, plexiglass windows, and a large desk against the wall. In the adjacent space, a telephone switchboard rang. Mrs Celeste sat down in a chair next to the desk. When she started to tell the woman about the food stamps, the woman interrupted: 'Please just answer the questions. If you don't understand, you can see the lawyer for help.'

'What is your full name?' the woman asked, looking down at a case card. 'And your address? Telephone number? Age? Are you married? Hispanic? Do you need an interpreter? Are you here alone or with a group? Employed? Have you ever been here before? Whom were you referred by? Are you a citizen of the United States? What is your monthly rent? How many live in the apartment? Do you have any wages or income? What about welfare? SSI? Disability? Unemployment? Food stamps? Do you have any bank accounts, automobiles, assets or real property?'

Mrs Celeste answered questions for five or ten minutes. When she tried to expand her answers, the woman interrupted. After several interruptions, Mrs Celeste learned to keep her answers short. Once her case card was fully marked, the boxes checked, lines filled, and statistics compiled, Mrs Celeste was told to return to the waiting room. Two hours later she was called again.

'Good morning. My name is Tony Alfieri. I am a welfare lawyer here. Before we begin, let me explain how our office works. Every Monday morning we see about thirty or forty people with welfare problems. Although we would like to help everyone, we just don't have enough lawyers to go around. So in the afternoon, all the lawyers sit down and make hard choices about who we can and cannot help. That is an office decision. It is not my decision alone. *Do you understand?*

'At this moment, I cannot tell you whether our office will be able to help you. That decision will be made later. In the event we cannot help you, we will make every effort to refer you to another legal aid office or give you enough advice so that you can help yourself. With legal advice from us many people are able to help themselves. *Do you understand?*

'The first thing I'd like to do is check the information on your case card to make sure it is correct. That will save us time later. Let's begin with your name and address. Do you live in an apartment or a house? How long have you lived there . . . ?'[1]

1   A V Alfieri 'Reconstructive Poverty Law Practice: Learning Lessons of Client Narrative' (1991) 100 *Yale Law Journal* 2107 at pp 2112-3.

Exercise 6.2   The other side . . .

Pretend that you are Mrs Celeste. Describe in a letter to a friend, what you felt about your experiences at the legal aid office.

(You may assume, if it helps, that the office has now agreed to help you in your case, which concerns the federal government's decision to reduce your food stamps (a kind of welfare payment) because you are in receipt of foster care payments).

Read some of your group's letters out loud, or exchange letters with other members of the group.

What, in summary, are the feelings and reactions that you ascribe to Mrs Celeste?

You might like to contrast what you have written with the comments of an English solicitor's client:

The first one I went to – I was very distressed at the time – I think he just took my name, address and age and noted how long I'd been married. He was totally disinterested. He didn't want to know. It felt as though I was talking to a brick wall. There was no offer of help, no 'come back and see me next week'. I just walked out of that office and burst into tears. I thought 'well, who the hell can I go to?' and that's when I phoned up the clerk to the justices . . . I just didn't know where to turn.[1]

What more do these clients' experiences tell you about the functions of the lawyer–client interview?

The point is an obvious, but nonetheless vital, one. The interview is not solely for information gathering. Being a lawyer is not just about dealing with the legal problem, it is about responding appropriately to the person as well. A lawyer–client interview is centrally concerned with developing and sustaining the relationship between lawyer and client, which, although it is a professional relationship, is also ultimately a *personal* one.

So, taking these elements together, we can suggest that the functions of the interview are essentially:
- to establish the interpersonal dimensions of the lawyer–client relationship;
- to identify the issues and obtain sufficient detailed information to advance the matter;

- to determine the client's objectives, and, so far as possible, advise accordingly;
- to prepare the way for further action on behalf of the client.

We can translate these aims into a broad structure for the interviewing process. A number of such models have been developed by writers in this field.[2] You may well find it helpful to use these models as your competence – and confidence – as an interviewer increases. However, we take the view that they over-complicate the process for novice interviewers. Our own students have said that such models leave them feeling a bit overwhelmed by the number of things they feel they have to remember to do.

We take the view that it is better to start off relatively unstructured; to identify your weaknesses through the process of reflection, and try to improve your skills gradually, concentrating on one major aspect at a time. If you try to do it all at once, you are far more likely to come unstuck.

We suggest you start by using a relatively simple model of the stages of an interview to guide you, like **WASP**:
- **W**elcome.
- **A**sk questions and **A**dvise.
- **S**ummarise facts and advice.
- **P**lan next steps and **P**art.

We will use this as the basic framework for the rest of the chapter, once we have dealt with one final preliminary issue.

1 Taken from National Consumer Council *Making good solicitors: The place of communication skills in their training*, NCC, London 1989, p 3.
2 Notably Avrom Sherr's '13 tasks' in *Client Interviewing for Lawyers*, Sweet & Maxwell, London 1986, p 21; also D Binder P Bergman & S Price *Legal Interviewing and Counseling*, West Publ, St Paul, Minn 1991.

Assumptions about the relationship

First we need to consider the assumptions we bring to the lawyer–client relationship. The key suppositions, we suggest, are about control and participation. In recent research Avrom Sherr[1] asked a sample of practising solicitors and their clients who they felt was in charge during an interview that had just taken place. The responses he obtained were as follows:

'WHO'S IN CHARGE?'	LAWYER RESPONSE	CLIENT RESPONSE
Client	2%	2%
Lawyer/Client equally	33%	51.4%
Lawyer	59.5%	38.5%

Are you surprised by those figures, or do they suggest the sort of response you would expect? Is there anything that bothers you about the responses?

The finding that the vast majority of lawyers and clients agreed that the client was not in control might be pretty much as we would expect. But the fact that more clients than lawyers thought they had joint charge of the interview is interesting. Of course, these data reflect a particular experience. We should not automatically assume they tell us who the various parties thought *ought* to be in charge. However, they may still indicate that there is at least some confusion between lawyers and clients as to where control over the relationship actually lies. The potential for misunderstanding and dissatisfaction is obvious.

But what exactly do we mean by 'in charge', and what should the relationship be? Consider the following exercise.

1   'The Value of Experience in Legal Competence', 1995, forthcoming.

Exercise 6.3   Who's in charge here?

One view of the professional role is to describe it as follows:

> Professionals, in contrast to members of other occupations, claim and are often accorded complete autonomy in their work. Since they are presumed to be the only judges of how good their work is, no layman or other outsider can make any judgment of what they can do. If their activities are unsuccessful, only another professional can say whether this was due to incompetence or to the inevitable workings of nature or society by which even the most competent practitioner would have been stymied. This image of the professional justifies his demand for complete autonomy and his demand that the client give up his own judgment and responsibility, leaving everything in the hands of the professional.[1]

(a)   Do you agree/disagree with this view?
(b)   Why?

Now consider the following example of lawyer autonomy, as expressed by an American attorney interviewed by Rosenthal:

> Theoretically, it's unethical not to report accurately negotiations with an insurer to the client. But you can't, and no lawyer does. You tell him about it in such a way that he is prepared to be satisfied. Say the other side offers $5,000. You tell the client that they offered $3,000. He'll say, 'That's no good'. You agree and say, casually, that you will try and get $4,500 out of them which would be fine. He's still not so happy, but reluctantly agrees. Two days later you call him back with the 'good news' that you got him more than he expected, $5,000. Now the client is prepared to be happy. You know what is a good settlement and what he should take. If it is necessary to lie and cheat him to get him to accept what's good for him you do it.[2]

Some issues for reflection:

(c)   Would you consider it appropriate for any other professional – eg a doctor – to be selective in the information she gives the client/patient?
(d)   Solicitors (but not barristers, or Health Service doctors) have a contractual relationship with their clients. Should that make any difference?
(e)   Can you think of any other relationship where one individual presumes, without the other's explicit consent, to decide what is best for that other?

(f)　How did you feel when a parent or guardian last told you that you had to accept what was best for you?

Before finally leaving this exercise you might find it helpful to reflect on Rosenthal's riposte to the traditional view of professionalism:

> Pressures, especially economic ones, often work against the lawyer's providing disinterested service to his client in making a personal injury claim. In many cases the lawyer's financial interest lies in an early discounted settlement while the client's interest lies in waiting out the insurer. The traditional ideal of professional service assists the lawyer in managing the claim so as to make it appear that no conflict of interest with the client exists. Lawyers do not disclose potential sources of conflict and the traditional model inhibits those active client requests for information that could expose issues of conflict, by making such requests appear to be mistrustful client behaviour. Although the norms of professional responsibility invite client participation, most lawyers believe that a lawyer–client relationship in which client collaboration is to be encouraged by extensive disclosure of critical issues would be inappropriate.[3]

Since the early 70s, when Rosenthal completed his study, there have been growing calls for more 'participatory' or client-centred approaches to lawyering, to the extent that this has, particularly in terms of skills-training, become very much the new orthodoxy.[4] Participatory approaches, it is claimed:[5]

● reduce the potential for conflicts of interest between lawyer and client;
● increase client satisfaction with the lawyer's work (this may be particularly important as a way of encouraging clients to become 'repeat players'[6] – ie to use you regularly for their legal work);
● enable clients to do better, in terms of case outcome, than non-participating clients.

In addition, it might also be argued that a participatory approach underpins any attempts to engage in 'empowering' professional practice. By this we mean:

> . . . a process by which individuals, groups and/or communities become able to take control of their circumstances and achieve their goals, thereby being able to work towards maximising the quality of their lives.[7]

The main practical implications of the participatory model are that it requires:

● an increase in information exchange between lawyer and client, to facilitate a process of 'informed consent' by the client;[8]
● an emphasis on being accessible to the client and responsive to her needs;[9]
● a sensitivity to the human, rather than just the legal, dimensions of the client's problems.

We will work through the implications of this participatory approach for each of the WASP stages.

1　H S Becker *Education for the Professions*, National Society for the Study of Education, Chicago 1962, pp 38–9.
2　D E Rosenthal *Lawyer and Client: Who's in Charge?*, revised ed, Transaction Books, New Brunswick, NJ 1977, p 111. We are not aware of any systematic research on this issue in

England, but our own conversations with practitioners have suggested that similar 'cooling out' practices are sometimes adopted by solicitors in this country.

3   Ibid, p 115. Rosenthal's research suggests that contingency fee arrangements account for much of this pressure. Given debates over conditional and contingent fee systems in England, it is perhaps worth noting that later research in America suggests that, while there is a correlation between the choice of hourly or contingent fee and the amount of effort the lawyer puts into the case, the relationship is probably more complex than Rosenthal suggests – see the discussion in H Kritzer, W Felsteiner, A Sarat & D Trubek 'The Impact of Fee Arrangement on Lawyer Effort' (1985) 19 *Law & Society Review* 251.There are differences between the US contingent fee and the conditional fee system in England which make it impossible to apply the US findings by simple analogy to the UK.

4   See eg Binder, Bergman & Price, op cit; A H Sherr 'Lawyers and Clients: The First Meeting' (1986) 49 *Modern Law Review* 323; M Spiegel 'Lawyering and Client Decisionmaking: Informed Consent and the Legal Profession' (1979) 128 *University of Pennsylvania Law Review* 41.

5   See eg Rosenthal, op cit, seriatim.

6   This term is taken from Marc Galanter's seminal article on how the legal process favours those who use it most frequently – 'Why the "Haves" Come Out Ahead: Speculation on the Limits of Legal Change' (1974) 9 *Law & Society Review* 95.

7   R Adams *Self-Help, Social Work and Empowerment*, Macmillan, London & Basingstoke 1990, p 43. The notion of 'empowerment' has, since the late 1980s, become an important concept in many areas of professional practice. In the UK, it has developed extensively in a number of areas of health and welfare practice, and in management contexts. Similar trends are apparent in the United States, and parallel notions are emerging in the literature on radical legal practice – though not necessarily under the label of empowerment; it would seem, for example, implicit in the ethic of care. We develop the issue further in the final section of this chapter.

8   Spiegel, op cit (cf also Chapter 4, above).

9   Rosenthal, op cit, p 27.

Welcoming: establishing a relationship in the interview

Assume now you are about to meet a new client for the first time. What do you think is the right environment, and what will you do to create it?

As always there are a number of aspects you might have stressed here. As we saw in the previous chapter, getting the physical environment right is obviously important. You should think about the following as a matter of course:

● Arrange to prevent interruptions from a secretary, colleagues, or incoming phone calls.[1]

● Present an organised and uncluttered appearance – which will boost your client's confidence.

● What about seating arrangements? Staring at your client directly across a desk can be intimidating, though it may help your own confidence in the early days. Experiment with various seating arrangements[2] to find one that is efficient and that you feel comfortable with.[3]

Other aspects of what Boon has called 'personal presentation' are also important in creating a client-centred environment. One of the litigators he interviewed in his research summed it up like this:

. . . the critical point, when you are first meeting a client, is to be open in your demeanour and approach; you are there to receive information that they want to impart about their problem . . . you have to elicit the right level of information. It is a combination of trying to put the client at ease so that they feel they are going to get the help they are looking for, plus displaying that you understand the area in which they are working or in which the problem lies so that they have confidence in what you are doing . . . It is important to try and achieve a rapport with the client so that they feel at ease and feel as if they can work with you . . .[4]

There are many practical ways of building rapport. Opening the interview in a manner that is appropriate is an important part of this process. Have a go at the next exercise.

1   If this seems too obvious to be worth stating, it should be noted that in Sherr's latest study of 143 initial interviews, interruptions were recorded in over a quarter of them.
2   See, for example, the suggestions in Helena Twist's *Effective Interviewing*, Blackstone Press, London 1992, p 42.
3   Though ultimately, in practice, your working environment may limit your flexibility to some degree – eg whether you actually have the physical space to ever interview away from your desk.
4   A Boon 'Assessing Competence to Conduct Civil Litigation: Key Tasks and Skills' in Boon, Halpern & Mackie *Skills for Legal Functions II: Representation and Advice*, Legal Skills Working Papers, Institute of Advanced Legal Studies, London 1992, p 9 at pp 36–7.

Exercise 6.4   Meet, greet and seat

Pair up with a colleague; one of you agrees to be the lawyer, the other the client. The client may either use a fictitious persona that s/he has invented for the purpose, or one of the roles in the Appendix (p 375). Your tutor will give the lawyer nothing more than the client's name, and a very general idea of the problem (eg road traffic accident, etc). Now:

(a)   *Practice the Welcoming phase of the interview, up to and including the point where the lawyer begins to elicit information about the problem.*
(b)   *Reflect together on the appropriateness of the lawyer's welcome: what worked well? What worked less well?*
(c)   *Try to consolidate the ideas in (b) into a set of written guidelines for opening an interview.*
(d)   *Compare your guidelines with those of other pairs. What do you find?*
(e)   *Lawyer and client should choose another case from the Appendix and switch roles. The aim of this is to test your consolidation in stages (c) and (d).*

Some of the points you have identified may seem very basic, even obvious, but our own experience has shown that it is often the most basic and taken for granted steps that people forget! Did the lawyers remember the social graces? For example, did they stand up to greet the clients, or did they greet them at the office door, or reception area? Did the lawyers introduce themselves by name? What did they do to 'break the ice'? Offer you refreshments? Engage in 'small talk'? Both? Neither? How did the lawyers open the questioning? Did they ask about the client's personal details, or did they ask about what had happened, or for some more particular piece of information? The questions you ask at this point can make a great deal of difference to the way the rest of the interview proceeds, as we shall see in the next section.

There are a number of other factors which may have occurred to you.

Three which commonly arise are the issues of note-taking, of discussing costs, and of 'territory'.

NOTE-TAKING

This is often one of the hardest tasks to get right.[1] It is extremely important that you obtain a good record of the events leading up to the interview, and of your client's relevant personal details, but it needs to be sensitively done. Excessive note-taking, especially in the first phase of the interview, breaks eye-contact and can become generally quite distracting for the client. Can you think how you might structure the interview to overcome this problem?

We suggest you listen first, then make notes as you start to probe for information. At the other extreme, do not attempt to rely purely on a note written up from memory after the interview. You will not retain detail that may well prove critical later on.[2] It does not do a lot for your credibility if you have to keep going back to clients to find out things they have already told you.

DISCUSSING COSTS

The appropriate moment for discussing costs might also need to be considered.[3] Costs are inevitably a matter of concern for clients, and an area, relative to other aspects of client care, where practitioners' performance is quite poor. A study by Neville Harris for the National Consumer Council in 1993 showed that over 25% of the fee-paying clients surveyed received no information on costs until they received their bill.[4] The same study asked whether the adviser had checked that clients who had received information on fees or legal aid understood it. Forty-nine per cent of respondents in that category said that the lawyer had not asked if they understood.[5] Moreover, less than half the clients who told the lawyer they did not understand the costs felt that their adviser tried hard to explain it more clearly.[6]

The best approach, we suggest, is to be very matter of fact about costs. Ultimately, a lawyer is a person providing a service for a fee, and it is usually as well to recognise this and address the issue of cost sooner rather than later. Clients are well aware that services have to be paid for, even before they get the bill! Equally, if a client is entitled to legal aid, it is in the client's interests to ascertain that this is so. Having said that, there is no absolutely 'right' time to discuss fees. You must use your own judgment to pick the moment. But never assume that, because the client does not mention the fees, she is not interested in – or worried by – how much it will all cost. You should also be aware that the Law Society Written Professional Standards specify the information solicitors should give clients about their charges.

TERRITORY

So far, we have tended to assume that client interviewing takes place on your own home territory all the time, but this is not the case. Both in commercial and criminal work, you may find yourself working on someone else's territory, be it a witness's or the client's or, in the case of criminal work, at the police station. This shift of territory can make subtle but important differences to how you perceive others, and how they perceive you. Relationships can be shaped, at least partly, by territorial considerations, which will affect the power balance between the various people involved.

In police station work, for example, the solicitor's role undergoes some important changes. Not only is the solicitor in the station to get instructions from a client detained in custody, she is often there to protect that client's interests in a very real way – by sitting in on police interrogations of that client. As Sanders and Young have pointed out,[7] the solicitor is in a difficult position. On the one hand, the adversarial nature of the process means that solicitors might be expected to act positively as advocates of their client's cause.[8] On the other hand, for regular defence solicitors, the police station is very much part of the work-place, and while this may mean that they are more likely to feel comfortable in (or at least familiar with) the surroundings, it also means that they have a vested interest in not upsetting the police by their tactics. As one solicitor interviewed by David Dixon has put it:

> You've got to do the best for your client, but you've still got to live with the system many years on. So . . . most solicitors do their best for their clients, but they also . . . won't generally upset the police.[9]

It seems to us that, fundamentally, there is a contradiction between those objectives. You cannot have it all ways all the time. How do you handle those situations where, arguably, the *only* way of doing your best for a client involves upsetting the police? This is an interesting question that goes beyond technique and centres, again, on the ethics and duties of the lawyer:

> The proper role of the defence lawyer is not, as some would have it, merely that of an observer. If that were the case, the lawyer could be replaced by a video camera. Neither is it to maintain some kind of balance between police and suspect – it is unlikely that the defence will ever have the powers and resources to match those of the police. Rather it is, as the Law Society states, 'the vigorous protection' of the rights of the suspect, whether those rights are based on the provisions of PACE and the Codes of Practice or on a wider notion of civil or human rights. If we have an adversarial system, with the police actively pursuing the interests of the prosecution, then the defence lawyer must actively pursue the interests of the defendant. To the extent that s/he does not do so, the lawyer will, as the Lord Chief Justice indicated in the case of *Miller*, be doing a disservice to the client, becoming in effect an arm of the prosecution.[10]

1 Cf Sherr 'Lawyers and Clients: The First Meeting' (1986) 49 *Modern Law Review* 323, pp 329–30. On the sources of information you need see Chapter 4.
2 On note-taking techniques specifically, see Twist *Effective Interviewing*, Blackstone Press, London 1992, pp 42–5.
3 On some academic courses, you may find you are instructed to ignore the question of costs because it can distract you from the interpersonal or skills elements of the exercise.
4 'Do Solicitors Care for their Clients?' (1994) 10 *Civil Justice Quarterly* 359 at 365.
5 Ibid, pp 366–7.
6 Ibid, p 367.
7 See *Criminal Justice*, Butterworths, London 1994, pp 142–4.
8 This is now reinforced by the new Code of Practice C under the Police and Criminal Evidence Act 1984 (in force from April 1995) which states: 'The Solicitor's only role in the Police Station is to protect and advance the legal rights of his client . . .' (Note 6D).
9 'Common Sense, Legal Advice and the Right to Silence' [1991] *Public Law* 233 at p 239.
10 E Cape *Defending Suspects at Police Stations: The Practitioner's Guide to Advice and Representation*, Legal Action Group, London 1993, p 2.

Listening and questioning

The ability to listen and question effectively is obviously central to the interviewing process. Neither skill is as easy to acquire as we tend to think.

Listening

The importance of listening is something we tend to overlook in much of our daily lives. Partly this is just habit: listening is simply part of our daily interaction and, unless something goes wrong, we function quite instinctively. Equally, for many of our normal activities we do not have to attend that closely to what is being said around us. We live and work surrounded by the talk of friends and colleagues, or by the radio or TV, etc, and switch in and out of 'listening mode' much as we choose. Even the lectures we listen to as students can often be taped for later consumption, or copied up from someone else or even, in some cases, read up in a textbook, if we find ourselves drifting off into a more interesting world . . .

In a professional context you do not really get that second chance. Failure to listen to the client's story will not only limit the accuracy of your information gathering and advice, but may damage your ability to build up a rapport and gain the client's confidence. Try the next exercise to see what we mean.

Exercise 6.5 Is anybody there?

(a) Divide into pairs: one speaker and one listener.
(b) The speaker may choose any subject to talk about for two minutes (it's probably best to choose some interesting event or experience, rather than a technical topic).

Phase 1: The speaker should tell their story to the listener. The listener must remain completely passive: do not give any verbal or non-verbal encouragement to the speaker but, unlike Exercise 5.6, do not respond negatively to the story either.

Phase 2: Repeat Phase 1, but this time with the listener responding normally to the story – ie using the verbal and non-verbal 'listening behaviour' you would normally adopt in such a situation. Listeners must remember two things, however:
  (i)   You must not ask any direct questions of the speaker.
  (ii) You should try not to exaggerate your listening behaviour.

Now, in the same pairs:

(c) Discuss the different feelings/responses evoked in the speaker by the listener's behaviour in each of the above processes.
(d) Make a list of the different types of verbal and non-verbal behaviour used by the listener in Phase 2.

What this exercise identifies in a rather extreme way is some of the differences, and the links, between *active* and *passive* listening.[1]

Phase 1 illustrates neatly the extent to which we rely on some kind of positive feedback when talking to someone. Non-response can be as distracting as negative feedback. The dividing line between non-response and *passive listening* can be a relatively fine one, though it is a distinction that most of us manage to negotiate quite happily on a daily basis. Passive listening techniques include:

● *Constructive use of silence* We all know how uncomfortable silences can be when we are with people we do not know well. In interviewing, however, if carefully managed, silence can be helpful. Can you think of some ways in which you might use silence in an interview?

● *Using NVC to encourage further disclosure* In Phase 2 you will have almost certainly noted the ways in which the listener used NVC to show that they were listening – eg by smiling, nodding or using prosodic responses to encourage the speaker to continue.

Obviously, it would be a strange interview if you were just to sit there listening to the client's story, nodding and grunting occasionally! So what does active listening require?

Certainly it implies a particular kind of listening for content. Active listening involves attention not just to the words being used by the client, but the feelings and intentions underlying what the client is saying.

1 These are not precise terms of art, and the boundaries between active and passive listening tend to be drawn differently by different writers on the field – cf Sherr *Client Interviewing for Lawyers*, pp 31–2 and Twist *Effective Interviewing*, pp 15–16. It does not much matter where you draw the line, so long as your use of the different techniques remains appropriate.

Exercise 6.6 Hyperactive?

For this exercise follow your tutor's instructions.

Active listening also needs to be reflected back to the client. This can be achieved by a variety of verbal techniques. You can use *paraphrasing* to confirm your understanding of an event, and to help the client clarify their thoughts and feelings. Helena Twist gives the following example:

Client:	I was absolutely furious when she walked out. How was I supposed to manage? Looking after the kids, working long hours, how could I take care of them properly?
Lawyer:	So, you were worried you wouldn't be able to manage your job and look after the children?[1]

Paraphrasing can also be developed as a reflective technique where you summarise not just what the client is saying but what they are feeling. Sometimes this is relatively easy, where the client makes feelings an explicit part of the story, thus:

Client:	I mean, I don't want to fight and I do want to fight, right? That's exactly what it comes down to.
Lawyer:	Yea, you're ambiguous.
Client:	Oh, boy, am I ever. And I have to live with it.[2]

But often you need to depend on other things to help identify feelings – the client's body language, the pace and modulation of their speech, for example; and it is these as much as the words that need to be reflected back. This can have empathic value and can serve as a basic form of what counsellors would call 'catalytic intervention'. We will develop ideas of empathy and intervention later in this chapter.

1   *Effective Interviewing*, Blackstone Press, London 1992, p 16.
2   Interview cited by A Sarat & W Felsteiner 'Law and Strategy in the Divorce Lawyer's Office' (1986) 20 *Law & Society Review* 93 at p 123.

Questioning

There are a number of basic question styles which can be used interchangeably during an interview to achieve different ends. In this section, we consider the kinds of questions you can use, and their effects.

Open questions are basic introductory questions which are intended to encourage the client to talk, while leaving the client to determine the parameters, eg:

> 'You said you wanted to see me about a road accident you were involved in. Perhaps you could just tell me what happened?'

> 'Is there anything else you think I ought to know?'

These can sometimes yield a lot of information, particularly if the client is reasonably talkative, but they do not work well with all clients, or in all contexts. Sometimes a question (especially of the rather vague 'anything else' variety) can be so general that your client may feel unable to answer it because she has no idea of what you are after. Even with talkative clients, you will also need to use more precise, structured questioning to be sure of getting the information you should have. Structured questions fall into two broad categories: closed and probing questions.

As the term suggests, *closed questions* tend to be narrow, and designed to elicit a particular piece of information. The style of questioning is direct and encourages the client to give a fairly precise answer, and sometimes no more than a yes/no response:

> 'Did you see what he looked like?'

The trick in interviewing is to try and get the right kind of balance and approach between open and closed questioning. Consider the following exercise.

Exercise 6.7   Me and Mrs Jones

Here is an extract from a real client interview. Read the extract, then consider these questions.

(a)   How effective was the lawyer's questioning?
(b)   What, if anything, might he have been done better?

1. Lawyer:	Come on in and sit down.
2. Client:	Thank you very much.
3. Lawyer:	Right now, Mrs Jones what can I do to try and help you?
4. Client:	Er, its a long story.
5. Lawyer:	All right, it's a matrimonial problem is it?
6. Client:	Yes it is.
7. Lawyer:	How long have you been married?
8. Client:	Nearly eight years.
9. Lawyer:	Have you any children?
10. Client:	Yes one, this is the problem, now um, as I say, I've been married for, I think it's eight years, I'm not divorced yet, by the way, because my husband committed adultery and you know all what's involved with that.
11. Lawyer:	Yes, yes.
12. Client:	Well the divorce just hasn't sort of been started, to my knowledge anyway. Now after we separated . . .[1]

Here the lawyer began with an open question (at no 1), but that did not have the desired effect. The client did not get into her story, but rather gave the response noted at no 4. The lawyer responded by going into a set of fairly for-mulaic closed questions, which were finally interrupted by the client beginning to tell her story (at no 10). This was an example of the client taking over the initiative from the lawyer, and it cannot be guaranteed, in such a case, that the client will have the confidence to do this. We have both observed interviews where the interviewer has continued with closed ques-tioning for 10–15 minutes before it becomes apparent what the client's real concern or objective is. With students especially, this behaviour is often asso-ciated with an almost slavish reliance on long, detailed checklists.[2] The effect on performance is dire. The interview becomes a form-filling exercise. There is virtually no eye contact between interviewer and interviewee, and no real opportunity for dialogue and the building of rapport.

Whether this behaviour reflects a lack of confidence on the part of the lawyer, or a fear that the client will just talk on endlessly about irrelevances is hard to say. If it is a fear of the latter, then that tends to be misplaced. Research indicates that clients rarely give information that is irrelevant (though, initially, it may appear irrelevant to the lawyer).[3] It has also been cal-culated that the average time clients take to tell their story is about seven minutes[4] – hardly an age, even by a lawyer's standards!

How might the lawyer in Exercise 6.7 have dealt with this situation, other than by closed questioning? See if you can think of a more effective way to get to the real issue (ie what emerged at no 10).

In our view, the critical intervention is clearly no 5. The client could well have been embarrassed or uncomfortable about the subject-matter, and was probably using her statement (at no 4) as a gap filler as she composed herself, and thought about what she was going to say. The lawyer could have assisted her more effectively here by using some encouraging or enabling statement, rather than the closed question he chose. For example, something like 'Okay, that doesn't matter' or even 'All right, why don't you start from the begin-ning' would probably have had the desired effect. The moral is clear: do not use closed questions too soon; they may only serve to impose your own agenda on the interview.

A special form of closed question is the *leading question*. It is a question which is designed to elicit a specific response. For example, the question 'You saw the accident happen, didn't you?' clearly implies that you expect the answer 'Yes'. For that reason you should be very careful in using leading questions, particularly in respect of any matter which is contentious. If you have prompted your client's answer in respect of a contentious issue, you will need to look for verification of her version of events. We shall consider the role of leading questions again in the context of advocacy.

The other generic category of structured questions, we said, are *probing questions*. These serve to 'flesh out' the client's story by taking the client through the particular points which you consider necessary to develop.

You may find it helpful, as you develop an awareness of your own questioning style, to focus more specifically on the different kinds of probing question you can use, and to try and extend your repertoire of techniques. The following typology may prove helpful.

Interrogatory questions are the simplest form of probing question, hence:

'Why did you say that?'

'How long ago did this happen?'

These can be useful in moving the story along to a rather more specific level of analysis, while retaining some of the characteristics of open questions. Do bear in mind that the style of questioning is important here: too many interrogatory questions, or the wrong intonation, can make your client feel as if she is being cross-examined!

Keyword questions perform a rather more specific function, based upon your use of active listening skills. With this technique, you listen for words or ideas that seem sufficiently important for you to want the client to focus on them. You then repeat the keyword(s) to the client as part of a question. For example, imagine the following dialogue is part of an interview with the victim of a mugging, thus:

Client:	I wasn't really sure what was going on at first, but then he grabbed my arm and tore the bag out of my grip.
Lawyer:	You say he grabbed your arm?
Client:	Yes, really hard, hard enough to leave bruises . . .

This is not just a good device for narrowing in on specific issues, but also provides the client with some reinforcement of their story. By mirroring the client's language, you can signal not only that you are listening closely to what is being said, but that you accept the importance of the client's own language and choice of narrative.

Reflective questions can be used to probe beyond the basic facts and to clarify a client's feelings or perception of a problem. As we have seen, questions form an important part of the active listening process. Reflective questions tend to be prefaced by terms such as 'How did you feel when . . .' or 'Did it seem to you that . . .' (though note that in the latter version there is a risk of leading your client). Reflective questions can not only clarify your client's position, they can also be an important way of testing your evaluation of the case, or of indicating some level of empathy with your client.

Hypothetical questions are really too well known to require much explanation. They take the form 'What if . . .', 'How would you feel if . . .', etc. Hypotheticals can be a useful vehicle for testing your theory of a case on a client, or for proposing a variety of solutions as part of your advice. However, they need to be used with a little caution, particularly if they might encourage a client to concoct a version of events which matches your hypothetical scenario.[5]

1   Sherr *Client Interviewing for Lawyers*, Sweet & Maxwell, London 1986, p 27.
2   We are not against the intelligent use of checklists, it is just that what we describe here is not very intelligent.
3   Sherr, op cit, p 44.
4   We have been unable to track the source of this statement beyond the notes accompanying the LNTV (Legal Network Television) programme, *Solicitors as Communicators*. See programme notes for 16 September 1993, Programme 60, p 3.
5   Aiding the client to concoct a defence etc, will constitute a breach of the professional Codes of Conduct.

Exercise 6.8   Tell me why

(a)   *Form groups of three: two participants and one observer. There are two participant briefs in the Appendix. Your tutor will issue a different brief to each participant. The third person in the group will be given the observer briefing sheet.*

(b)   *Each participant should interview the other, using questions starting only with the words in their brief.*

The aim is for the participants each to find out what the other did last weekend.

(c)   *At the end of the exercise, the whole group should consider:*
   (i)   *Who got the most information?*
   (ii)   *Why did they get more information than the other?*
   (iii) *Who had to work the hardest for information?*
   (iv)   *What do we learn from this exercise about questioning styles?*

Pulling it all together

Listening and questioning are, clearly, closely interlinked skills and the quality of an interview will depend greatly on the way you deploy those skills. It is important to think about the following.

First, you must encourage the client to speak freely about the problem. Use open questions to start with and be prepared to listen and not cut in too early in the interview. Too much emphasis on closed questioning may result in you getting a very skewed version of the problem. Many of the skills books thus suggest you should think of the listening and questioning phase of the interview in terms of a funnel or 'T' in which you start with open questions and then probe. You should then summarise and check the information you have obtained. Sherr's research also suggests that lawyers who give their clients a chance to speak from the outset are less likely to have to go back over the factual issues in depth later in the interview, because the client has not 'had her say'.[1] However, you should always check over the key facts and events with the client before you attempt to give advice, for the obvious reason that this helps you avoid giving advice based on a misunderstanding of the situation.

One other key issue is when you take your client's personal details. Clearly you need this kind of information for the file, and it may have further significance for the matter itself. While you need this information, it is not a good idea to get into a routine of automatically taking personal details at the outset of the interview. Certainly, a person who is highly agitated or upset about a situation is likely to be focused on talking about their problem from the moment they walk through the door. It is often a good idea to let them tell their story first, and then go back to get the details you need later. Be guided by your common sense and your awareness of the person's situation: what is the nature of the problem; does the client appear at all agitated or distressed?

In these welcoming and information gathering phases, the client should generally be allowed to lead the way. Your role is facilitative more than directive. As we shall see, the balance changes rather once you go into the next, advisory, phase of the interview, so let's sum up and try another interview before we move on –

PREPARE YOUR TERRITORY IN ADVANCE.	T
REMEMBER TO MEET, GREET AND SEAT YOUR CLIENT.	A K
LET THE CLIENT DO THE TALKING.	E
SUPPORT THE CLIENT – USE ACTIVE LISTENING AND EMPATHIC QUESTIONING.	N O
PROBE FOR DETAIL.	T E
CHECK THE FACTS BEFORE ADVISING.	S

1   Op cit (1986a), p 43.

Exercise 6.9   The client interview

The aim of this exercise is to practise the information gathering phase only.

(a)   *Divide into the same pairs and same roles as for Exercise 6.4.*
(b)   *Conduct a lawyer–client interview only to the point where the lawyer is satisfied that s/he has acquired all the necessary information on the matter, and has checked the facts with the client. Do not give advice.*
(c)   *In your pairs, reflect and feedback in the normal way.*
(d)   *Don't forget to write up your experiences in your learning diary.*

Advising and counselling

In this section we shall stress the interplay between two related lawyer roles. The first of these is fairly obvious. Our clients expect us to give them legal advice, and there are more or less effective ways of doing so. The second, counselling, role is perhaps less apparent, but no less central to a participatory approach.

Lawyers as advisers

The advisory role is one where, conventionally, the balance of participation shifts. This phase is rather more lawyer-dominated – at least in so far as the lawyer, as adviser, needs to take a more active part than before.

What are the essentials of this phase?

Exercise 6.10   Toast

Divide into pairs: one lawyer and one client.

Your client is seeking advice on a relatively simple consumer problem. Neither lawyer nor client should assume that the client has any substantive knowledge of consumer law. The client has already told you (the lawyer) the basic problem, which can be summarised as follows:

The client's story

Fed up with burnt toast in the mornings, I bought a top of the range toaster from a local department store. I have had it two weeks, and the mechanism has jammed, preventing the toast from popping up. I took the toaster back to the shop, and they say the mechanism could only have jammed in this fashion if the toaster had been dropped, or if some other excessive force was applied to the mechanism. There is no way either of these things have happened while I have had it, but the shop has refused to repair or replace the toaster, or to refund my money. They insist it is my fault and that the guarantee is therefore void.

The client's objectives

I want a new toaster or my money back.

(a) *The lawyer's task:*
   (i)   *You have ten minutes in which to prepare your advice.*
   (ii) *You then have a further ten minutes in which to advise your client and close the interview.*
(b) *The client's task:*
   (i)   *In the ten minutes' preparation, make a note of what you consider to be the lawyer's objectives in advice-giving.*
   (ii) *During the interview, be prepared to ask questions if the lawyer's advice seems uncertain or unclear to you in any way.*
(c) *Reflection in pairs:*
   (i)   *Lawyers should consider their own performance – what worked, what did not work. Why/Why not?*
   (ii) *Lawyers – what problems arose which you did not anticipate at the outset? Why weren't they anticipated?*
   (iii) *Clients – how accurately did the lawyer's reflection match your own experience? Did the lawyer meet the criteria on your list? Discuss with your lawyer the appropriateness of your criteria.*

> (iv)   *Discuss the outcomes of this exercise in the whole group, then compare your criteria with ours (below), and don't forget to reflect on and account for any differences you see!*
>
> (v)   *Make sure you draft an entry in your learning diary.*

Most obviously, you would expect the lawyer to give you some indication of your legal rights. It would not, of course, be sufficient to advise in the abstract, academic, sense. The lawyer would need to include some plan of action – ie an indication of the steps you, or the lawyer, would take to enforce your rights. Ideally the lawyer might seek confirmation that you understand the advice and are happy with it, and should indicate whether, and if so when, you should have another meeting. So, in summary, good advice-giving involves four things:

● stating advice (so far as possible);
● devising and agreeing a plan of action;
● confirming client's understanding of advice and next steps;
● setting-up further contact (if necessary).

What does research tell us about the way lawyers approach this phase of the relationship? Sherr's research suggests that trainee solicitors are generally very poor at this phase, with, for example, 45% of his sample failing adequately to give advice or to state a plan of action; 59% failing to check for client understanding and agreement with that course of action; and 67% failing to set up further contact.[1] In fact Sherr found that this phase of the interview was the least well done of all. That might help you place your own performance in context! But what is it that makes advising so difficult? Let us use the four elements listed above to analyse this phase in more depth.

GIVING ADVICE

This is obviously central to the interview. It should also be something with which you are reasonably familiar from traditional academic study. But somehow that academic experience does not seem to help you a great deal. Why not? See if you can jot down three or four reasons.

Here are our own ideas.

First, you may never have had to use that book knowledge in action before. This has a number of consequences: (i) it means that by the time you come to do a live interview you may have forgotten most of the actual law; (ii) you will have to try and do a translation exercise to convert your academic knowledge into practical advice – this is quite complex because you have both to think through the legal consequences of the particular facts, and translate your advice into lay (rather than legal) language 'on the spot'.

Second, the 'law in action' that you need in order to give advice may be very different from the 'law in books' that you have encountered to date. The impact of procedural law, evidence, costs, and all sorts of other practical consequences, may make the academic law of more limited utility.

Third, as an extension of this second point, the client may not actually be helped by 'black-letter' legal advice. A variety of practical or 'non-legal' solutions may be far more appropriate than conventional legal action (we discuss this in more detail below). These may include referrals to other agencies, or advice on forms of self-help that might be available. Practitioners develop a network of such contacts through their own experience and through that of their colleagues. This takes time to develop, and can be difficult to replicate in a clinical context.

You must be realistic about your own limitations. There are three key mistakes you must try and avoid in giving advice.

The most fundamental error you can make is to give advice that is clearly wrong in law. If you do not know the answer, you must find a way of explaining this to the client (without totally undermining your own position!) and build the need to clarify or confirm your advice into your action plan.

The next most critical mistake you can make is to give a client advice they do not understand, particularly if you expect them to act on it in some way. It is essential therefore to think about how you deliver your advice:

● Try to use language the client understands.
● Give the client some kind of structure, for example use the '3Ts'.[2]
● Confirm your advice with the client.

This last stage is crucial, but, in our experience, commonly forgotten. We shall return to it again.

The third, or perhaps equal second, major error is to give clients advice they do not want. By this we do not mean advice they do not want to hear – there will be times when you have to give bad news: that is part of the job. What we do mean is that you must take account of your client's objectives. This is the essence of participatory, client-centred, practice.[3] Yet there is a strong tendency among lawyers to 'talk past' their clients and focus on their own agendas for action, ignoring the central concerns of those clients.[4] As Sarat and Felsteiner put it, cases proceed 'without the generation and ratification of a shared understanding of reality'.[5] This seems to us to indicate, at the least, a failure in the willingness of lawyers to negotiate outcomes with their clients. We should ensure that the client is adequately informed of the options, and given the opportunity to assess those options on her own terms.

DEVISING AND AGREEING THE ACTION PLAN

There is no point in leaving the client with a blanket piece of advice which does not translate into a set of concrete tasks and expectations. A major cause of client concern is likely to be their ignorance of what the lawyer intends to do next. An action plan can include a whole variety of elements: your commitment to carry out some research, which will lead to fuller advice; an agreement to write a letter for the client, and/or a set of tasks for the client – eg to supply certain documents, or to contact some other person. It may even be no more than getting the client to reconsider her position in the light of your advice. Whatever it is, the critical point is that both lawyer and client have some shared knowledge of and commitment to future action.

CONFIRMING UNDERSTANDING AND NEXT STEPS

Within the structure of a participatory interview it is important that you get the client's informed consent to any next steps. The client should be aware (so far as you can advise) of the cost and other implications of alternative courses of action. To ensure this, it is important that you restate your advice in the context of the action plan – to show how the advice translates into alternatives for action, and to give the client a clear opportunity to ask questions and decide what they want to do. There is no reason why both lawyer and client should not make a note there and then about what has been agreed and what needs to be done, and by whom. In addition, your advice should always be confirmed in writing as part of your client care policy.[6]

SETTING UP FURTHER CONTACT IS ESSENTIAL

It would be a relatively unusual transaction that could be disposed of wholly within one meeting. Uncertainty about what is happening with their case, and when contact ought to be made, will only add to a client's other anxieties about the problem, and may reinforce any worries the client has about your competence. As Sherr notes:

> Research with clients in other fields shows that the immediate 'blush' of satisfaction at the end of a consultation begins to change during the few days afterwards. Clients tend to review in their minds what occurred during the consultation and may become more anxious than they were on leaving the professional's office. It therefore seems good policy to give the client something to look forward to in terms of the next contact.[7]

It may be that the immediate next steps can be conducted by post or phone, but the time scale should, so far as possible, still be made explicit during the first meeting.

1   'Lawyer and Client: The First Meeting', pp 339–40. These findings, of course, pre-date the introduction of direct skills training on the Legal Practice Course.
2   '3Ts': 1. tell them what you are going tell them;
        2. tell them; then
        3. tell them what you have told them (ie check for understanding).
    Cf Sherr's idea of 'advance organisers', *Client Interviewing for Lawyers*, p 83.
3   See Rosenthal, op cit, p 27.
4   See eg S Macaulay 'Lawyers and Consumer Protection Laws' (1979) 14 *Law & Society Review* 115; A Sarat & W Felsteiner 'Law and Social Relations: Vocabularies of Motive in Lawyer/Client Interaction' (1988) 22 *Law & Society Review* 737. This view is not inconsistent with Sherr's finding (forthcoming) that lawyers are generally competent at discovering the client's goals – the issue is, how the lawyer negotiates those goals subsequently.
5   Ibid p 742.
6   See further the final section in this chapter, and Chapter 7 on writing.
7   *Client Interviewing for Lawyers*, p 107.

Lawyers as counsellors

> The traditional ideal of a lawyer is one of a person who is sharp, objective, takes charge, and wins arguments. The ideal of a counselor, as Carl Rogers puts it, is of someone who is accepting, understanding, and congruent. The two ideals are not entirely compatible. Lawyers suffer some difficulty in reconciling them. Maybe, as a result, we lawyers often function poorly with people.[1]

The essence of legal counselling is that you do not allow yourself to get into a mind-set which sees a problem across the desk, not a person. The lawyer–client relationship is a working relationship. It is important in sustaining that relationship that the client feels that she is a special person – in the sense that the lawyer is able, visibly, to respond to her personality and perspective on the case. This does not necessarily require particular 'counselling' skills in a therapeutic sense. Sherr makes the point that 'counselling' in the legal context may indicate little more than presenting clients with the options and enabling them to choose.[2]

This may sound obvious good practice, or it may not. Either way it is not something that we should take for granted. Consider the following description of one highly committed and technically able lawyer:

> After watching Boz, you can easily come away with the impression that she sticks closely to technical legal issues to maintain control over both the boundaries of her relationship with a client and her overall workload. By sticking to technical issues, she can more readily draw the line between where she will help clients and where she wants nothing to do with them. 'Legal' and 'non-legal' become firm categories that play a particularly important function for Boz. Legal designates what the office does and what a lawyer should spend time doing. Non-legal designates everything else, all those things that Boz shouldn't be held responsible for not dealing with or handling badly . . .
>
> Boz's attitude can be as off-putting as her methods. During the Betty Bejarano interview, for example, she never seemed willing to acknowledge the legitimacy of Mrs Bejarano's problem or to credit her for taking steps to correct it herself. She missed virtually every opportunity to give Mrs Bejarano the sense that she had legitimately recognised a wrong that deserved to be righted and that trying to do something about it mattered a lot. She didn't expect anything more than a beaten down, resourceless, uncooperative client, and probably that's often all she ever ends up with. Its chilling to see that sort of behavior in someone who has dedicated herself to helping people.[3]

Would you agree with the author's conclusion after reading that description, or is 'Boz' just recognising what she does best and doing it? How far should lawyers get engaged in the 'non-legal' when advising a client? How would you begin to distinguish the 'legal' and 'non-legal'? You might like to compare your ideas with ours.

THE LEGAL ALTERNATIVES AND THEIR CONSEQUENCES

Consider – whether to proceed to trial/negotiate, arbitrate, abandon action, etc; what time factors exist and what their potential impact on resolution of the dispute will be; the impact each alternative is likely to have on costs; the possibility of further litigation (eg any claims brought by the other side/third party; appeals). How well can your client handle the stresses and strains of each of these?

THE 'NON-LEGAL' ALTERNATIVES AND THEIR CONSEQUENCES

Consider – scope for professional mediation or conciliation of disputes; forms of self-help that may be available without the (further) intervention of lawyers or other professionals; advice and assistance that may be obtained from a non-legal agency; note also the need to consider non-legal alternatives in conjunction with legal action.

Now consider what solutions you would offer in the following situation?

1   T L Shaffer 'Lawyers, Counselors, and Counselors at Law' (1975) 61 *American Bar Association Journal* 854 at 855.
2   'Lawyer and Client: The First Meeting', p 353.
3   G López *Rebellious Lawyering*, Westview Press, Boulder, Col 1992, p 110. The interview referred to is reproduced at pp 103–9.

Exercise 6.11   Home sweet home

Imagine you are interviewing a client who is a single parent with a child at primary school. Your client is living in private rented accommodation – a first-floor flat she shared with her former partner until their relationship broke down, with considerable acrimony on both sides. She has a rent book, in her name, pays rent monthly and has to give a month's notice to leave. The rent is significantly below current market rates.

Her landlord is a friend of her 'ex'. He (the landlord) lives in the flat below, and has clearly taken sides against your client. He has sought without success to evict your client (the tenancy is protected) and is now engaged in harassing her. So far this has taken the following forms: playing loud music late into the night, leaving rubbish on the landing to impede her access to the flat, refusing to undertake such maintenance of the property as is required, and being generally aggressive and unpleasant. She wants your advice.

Make a note of:
(a)   the possible legal courses of action your client has;
(b)   non-legal steps you might advise (if any);
(c)   relevant facts which may effect the utility of those courses of action.

In brief, your answer would probably incorporate most of the following: (a) private and local authority action in respect of noise pollution; the possibility of county court action for quiet enjoyment; (b) a lawyer might well offer advice and assistance in applying for alternative accommodation (eg either council or housing association); (c) if she takes legal action, she should be counselled as to the risk of on-going problems thereafter, but the practicalities of moving out would also need to be considered, eg in terms of the time it might take to get rehoused; whether re-housing would disrupt her child's schooling (would it involve changing schools, for example?) and its impact on her own work/social activities. The cost implications of both options would also need to be considered.

We take the view that, when thinking about consequences, you need always to consider the impact of any advice on the client's financial, social and psychological welfare. If you do not assess these, you are giving legal advice in a vacuum, and possibly doing more harm than good. As part of your advice you should give an assessment of risks inherent in any potential course of action. It is not sufficient simply to present a client with a range of alternatives, spell out the consequences of each and, in effect, say 'take your pick' without giving the client some assessment of the likely outcome of the case. As Binder et al suggest, there may be as many as five possible outcomes which you should seek to identify to your client; they term these:

  (i)   the best possible;
  (ii) the best likely;
 (iii) the most probable;
 (iv) the worst likely;
  (v) the worst possible.

At a minimum, you should make sure your client is aware of and understands the middle three options; these will at least give her an idea of the range of likely results in her case.

Arguably, however, the approach we have outlined so far understates the extent to which even a limited understanding of counselling technique more generally can have a positive influence on lawyer–client interaction. Consider the following scenario.

Exercise 6.12 Car trouble

The group should divide into pairs – a lawyer and a client. Each client should prepare the relevant role in the Appendix. The aim of the interview is to counsel and advise only. The lawyers can assume that the following facts are known and agreed.

Your client is Janet/John Jones, and s/he lives in Bristol.

About three months ago your client lent a car to a friend to use, as a favour. The car is a 1972 Volkswagen Beetle 'soft-top'; it is in extremely good condition for its age and is, now, becoming highly collectable. You are not sure of its current value, but the client has it insured for £2,500. Apart from its market value, your client has made it clear that the vehicle is of strong sentimental value.

The friend has now moved to Taunton, taking the car with him/her. Despite numerous verbal promises, the friend has not returned the car, and has not replied to a letter from your client (posted two weeks ago) asking for the immediate return of the vehicle.

Your client now wishes to resolve the problem and has made an appointment to discuss the options that are open to him/her.

(a) Role play the interview.
(b) Feedback in the usual way.

There are many different general theories and approaches to counselling. We propose to use one approach as a basis for what follows, which is John Heron's 'Six Category Intervention Analysis'.[1] This has the advantages of being a model that has been used in a variety of professional contexts, and also one that is consistent with our own approach to experiential learning.

Heron points out that a counsellor may adopt one of two roles, which he describes as *authoritative* and *facilitative*. In an authoritative mode, the counsellor takes a more dominant or assertive role, whereas in a facilitative mode, the counsellor plays a less obtrusive, enabling or empowering, role. The two approaches are not mutually exclusive. A counsellor may shift from authoritative to facilitative modes as dictated by the client's needs. In the lawyer/client context these styles of intervention may be used within the interview context

to improve the quality of the interaction. Heron calls his six categories:
1. Prescriptive.
2. Informative.
3. Confrontational.
4. Cathartic.
5. Catalytic.
6. Supportive.

The first three are authoritative and the second three facilitative interventions. We shall now consider each of them in turn.

PRESCRIPTIVE

The counsellor will actively give advice or attempt to direct the behaviour of the client. In professional counselling, the counsellor may take a judgmental or evaluative stance in this process. In the lawyer/client relationship, an evaluative stance is often an integral aspect of advice-giving; however, it is best to avoid being judgmental of the client's behaviour. Inevitably, perhaps, prescriptive interventions are widely used in the lawyer–client relationship.

INFORMATIVE

The counsellor takes on a didactic role, imparting new knowledge or information to the client, usually in the hope that the client may then use that information constructively – so ultimately having a more facilitative effect.

CONFRONTATIONAL

A confronting intervention is intended to challenge directly the assumptions or behaviour of the client, eg by pointing out inconsistencies in the client's story, or by picking up on things which have not been said. Remember that confrontational does not equate with aggressive – the confronting must be carefully managed if you are not to lose the trust of your client.

CATHARTIC

Here, the counsellor encourages the client to revive forgotten or repressed ideas about an earlier event which had a strong emotional impact. The aim of a cathartic intervention is to resolve some unconscious conflict in the client. Cathartic intervention needs to be very carefully managed and, as a technique, probably has little place in legal, as opposed to psychotherapeutic, counselling.

However, do remember that you will often be in a position where you are requiring a client to re-live an event that they have strong feelings about. Like genuinely cathartic intervention, this needs careful management. Be prepared to listen. Ask neutral questions which encourage the client to explain things literally – this can make a painful event easier to recount. Be sympathetic, but do not negate the client's feelings by saying things like 'cheer up' or 'never mind'; reflective statements showing an acceptance of the client's feelings (eg 'that must have been difficult for you?') are more empathic and can also encourage the client to continue her narrative – the same is true of a nod and a sympathetic smile! You should also try to avoid following such disclosures with uninvited prescription ('What you need to do is . . .').

In your professional careers you can confidently expect to be confronted with clients who are emotionally highly charged. Anger may be aimed at you directly, or you may be the target for displaced aggression. When confronted by such behaviour, you may feel wronged, defensive, intimidated even. You should try to avoid your own feelings being reflected in an inappropriate or defensive response to the client. This will only hinder the development (or recovery) of a good working relationship with the client. Distress is also very difficult to respond to. You may feel uncomfortable or embarrassed by a client breaking down in your office; or you may find it difficult to maintain professional detachment – in an extreme situation you may experience what Helena Twist calls 'emotional contagion'.[2] This is the situation where you have reached a high level of empathy with the client, to the extent that you are sharing some of the emotional charge with her.

1 For an overview, see J Heron 'A Six Category Intervention Analysis' (1976) 4 *British Journal of Guidance and Counselling* 143. The model is more fully explored in Heron's *Helping the Client*, Sage, London 1990.
2 *Effective Interviewing*, p 85.

Exercise 6.13   Handling emotion

Divide into discussion groups of three or four people.
(a)   Each of you should then take a few minutes to describe a moment in your personal or professional lives when you had to manage the great anger or sadness of another. Talk about how you felt in that situation. What did you do to help that person? Did you attempt any interventions that were clearly counterproductive?
(b)   As a group, try to generalise from these experiences and produce some guidelines for dealing with emotion in a professional context.

CATALYTIC

A catalytic intervention aims to encourage reflection and self-directed problem-solving in the client – eg by helping the client to identify the problem and potential resolutions. Listening is again a crucial element of catalytic interventions – a useful technique, as we have seen, is to listen for verbal cues which seem to carry particular significance for the speaker and feed those back to her.

SUPPORTIVE

In Heron's schema there are many forms of supportive intervention which are intended to show care and concern for the person or welfare of another.[1] Supportive interventions can have some applicability in the legal context, where they serve to confirm or validate the client's actions and worth. Never underestimate the importance of such support: many clients will be in your office precisely because they feel (at least) partly responsible for something going wrong. Supportive interventions affirm the worth of the client at a time when she may be at a 'low ebb'. Be careful that anything you do approve is not subsequently going to rebound and cause problems – qualified approval can be safer, but is obviously less affirmative of that person's worth!

A (fairly obvious) word of warning: to become a proficient counsellor requires specialised training. Practising law does not demand that level of proficiency and you should not seek to confuse your role with that of a professional counsellor. If a client needs specialist counselling, that is one course of action which you may recommend – do not try to usurp that role yourself.

Used carefully, however, we suggest that these techniques can serve a positive role in building and protecting the human dimensions of the lawyer–client relationship.

By way of conclusion, use the following exercise to build on what you have learnt, and to practise any counselling techniques you consider appropriate to the case.

1 See *Helping the Client*, Sage, London 1990, pp 118–20.

'You may find that the problem lies with you, not the client'

Exercise 6.14   Pressing problems

Again, the group should divide into pairs – a lawyer and a client. Prepare the relevant roles in the Appendix.
Role play the advising and counselling phase, and feedback as normal.

As a final point, do not forget the importance of experience in developing your skills. Advising and counselling can be one of the most individualised professional activities you undertake. It is often not amenable to 'off pat' solutions. It is important to reflect on your experience over time. Compare strategies that did and did not work in similar situations. Look for patterns among problem cases and 'difficult' clients. You may find that the problem lies with you, not the client.

Parting, and beginning the continuing relationship

In the professional context, parting is not just a question of saying 'goodbye' nicely. It involves a number of discrete steps.

Ending

First you need to consider how you start to move towards closure. Looking at your watch pointedly is one of the less subtle mechanisms that we have seen employed, but this is not usually recommended!

In all interviewing and counselling contexts, it is important to remember that a client may need some recovery time at the close of the interview. This may be particularly the case where the client has been taken through past events which are distressing, and she must now reorientate herself to the present. It is not appropriate to bring the interview too abruptly to an end in such situations. Establishing or recapping on a plan of action can help in this process; so too can some 'small talk' about everyday matters, so long as you can avoid making the transition seem false.

Second, it is also important to give the client a final opportunity to say anything else that might be of concern or importance to them. Although clients will usually be anxious to talk about the issues, cases will arise where clients are reluctant to disclose the real problem. In the medical literature there is a recognised tendency for the 'presenting symptoms' – ie the initially expressed reason for going to see the doctor – to turn out to be secondary to reasons that only emerge during or at the end of the consultation.[1] There is certainly anecdotal evidence of similar experiences in the law.[2] A final open question may help draw out anything that might otherwise remain unsaid.

Lastly, it should be unnecessary to say that we ought to close the interview in an appropriate fashion, but, again, research shows that we all have the capacity to forget the social graces when we get into the office, despite the fact that final impressions are important. So, do remember to see the client out before you start writing up a file note of the interview!

---

1   See eg P Byrne and B Long *Doctors Talking to Patients*, HMSO, London 1976.
2   In, for example, Sherr 'Lawyer and Client: The First Meeting', p 342n.

Beginning

The end of the initial interview is, in most cases, only the beginning of the continuing relationship. This needs to be recognised in a number of ways.

First, intuitively or drawing on your own direct experience, what specific steps do you think you ought to take in the immediate aftermath of an interview?

Exercise 6.15   Planning your next steps

Make a short list of what action you consider necessary following a client interview.

To some extent your tasks will be determined by the context. The steps which follow taking instructions for a conveyancing transaction will differ somewhat from litigation, for example. Even so, the following steps are normally required across most, if not all, transactions.

MAKE UP A FILE NOTE FOLLOWING THE INTERVIEW

This should contain:
● full details of the client's personal information;
● the events leading up to the consultation etc;[1]
● work to be done by lawyer and by client;
● advice given and advice to be confirmed.

Most firms have a standard format. Sherr also advises including some note on the lawyer's impressions of the client, and the problem.[2]

REVIEW ACTION PLAN AND MAKE DIARY ENTRIES

These should be in respect of:
● next contact; and
● deadlines agreed (if any) for later tasks/stages in the transaction.

SEND OUT CLIENT CARE LETTER TO THE CLIENT

For solicitors this is an obligation under Rule 15 of the Practice Rules.[3]

These steps are merely preparatory to carrying out the tasks required, but should help ensure that you have a good professional basis on which to build. From here on, however, the emphasis in your relationship with the client is likely to shift (certainly in contentious work) away from focusing on the client as an information resource, and on to the discussion of strategy and objectives. This places an emphasis on the lawyer's counselling role.

---

1   See the listing in Chapter 3, above.
2   This is rather more contentious – see Sherr's justifications in *Client Interviewing for Lawyers*, pp 130–3.
3   See further Chapter 7, below. Additional follow-up letters should be sent after each subsequent meeting, confirming what has been agreed.

Participating

We have already seen that a commitment to counselling is a commitment to giving clients choices in the conduct of their cases. We would like to close this section by reflecting more deeply on what this means.

How far this commitment to counselling goes is an interesting and, some would say, highly politicised question. As we have seen, the classic image of the lawyer as 'professional thing-maker' (to paraphrase Maureen Cain) is one in which the lawyer is an autonomous agent whose task is to take control of the client's social problem, translate it into a legal one and resolve it. But by this act of agency, it is argued, the lawyer behaves rather like the marines who charge into occupied territory, shoot the 'baddies', liberate the 'natives' and sail away again at the first opportunity – until the next time.

Like the marines, we may have changed the material situation for the present, but we have not necessarily enabled those we have 'helped' to take command of the situation and to maintain control over their future. Moreover, it is sometimes said that counselling itself, as presently envisaged, operates as part of a 'politics of control' between lawyers and clients.[1] Counselling, it is suggested, can become another, more subtle, form of control than that exercised in non-participatory forms of practice. It is very easy for the lawyer to give a semblance of choice and control to the client, while in reality she stays firmly in charge.[2]

Perhaps a more genuinely counselling-orientated role is a logical outcome of the participatory approach, and our failure to recognise this need in our clients and ourselves is explanatory of both some of the client dissatisfaction lawyers face, and of the deeper inequalities in power disclosed by current practices of lawyering. Sarat and Felsteiner have started to address this issue in the context of divorce practice:

> The vocabularies of motive used by clients in divorce cases excuse and justify their conduct and place blame for the failure of their marriage, as well as for problems in the legal process, squarely on their spouses . . . Their vocabulary serves to add sympathy to fees as a basis on which their lawyers' energies can be commanded . . .
>
> This emphasis poses an awkward choice for lawyers. If they were to join with clients in the project of reconstructing the marriage failure . . . they would be dragged into a domain that is, in principle, irrelevant to no fault divorce . . . and is in fact beyond their expertise. On the other hand, if they directly challenge client characterisations . . . they risk alienating their clients or deepening client mistrust. Thus most of the time lawyers remain silent in the face of client attacks on their spouses. They refuse to explore the past and to participate in the construction of a shared version of the social history of the marriage . . .
>
> . . . lawyers' refusal to engage with client efforts to give meaning to the past is not without consequences. It often means that clients end up dissatisfied with lawyers who do not understand or empathise with them. Furthermore, the legal construction of social relations may go far in explaining how contentious and difficult the settlement process becomes . . .
>
> The vocabularies of motive used in lawyer/client interaction in divorce respond to the distinctive characteristics of that social relationship. Lawyers deploy the resources of professional position; they emphasise their experience and the expertise that experience provides as they try to limit involvement in the client's social world. While this limitation gives

power to lawyers' interpretations of the social world, it cannot guarantee acquiescent clients. By repeatedly expanding the conversational agenda, clients resist their lawyers' efforts to limit the scope of social life relevant to their interaction. They manipulate attributions of blame and victimisation to counter professional authority and claims to expertise on which lawyers rely. Thus in divorce as elsewhere, law, and the images of social life with which it is associated, is deeply embedded in a conflicted and unequal social relationship.[3]

Certainly, in our view, the counselling dimension of the lawyer's role remains underdeveloped in current practice, perhaps because there is so little training that is genuinely counselling-oriented, and because there are perceived (and perhaps real) tensions between the role of lawyer-as-counsellor and lawyer-as-independent adviser.

1   Sherr *Client Interviewing for Lawyers*, pp 150–3; for a wider analysis of the politics of control in action, see P Harris 'The Politics of Law Practice' in I Grigg-Spall & P Ireland *The Critical Lawyers' Handbook*, Pluto Press, London 1992.
2   These concerns, and others, are echoed in current debates about empowering practice in the caring professions: see eg K Baistow, 'Liberation and regulation? Some paradoxes of empowerment' (1994/95) *Critical Social Policy*, Issue 42, Winter, p 34.
3   A Sarat & W Felsteiner 'Law and Social Relations: Vocabularies of Motive in Lawyer/Client Interaction' (1988) 22 *Law & Society Review* 737 at 764–7.

Interviewing and empathic lawyering: a (re)vision of practice?

In bringing this chapter to a close we want to move even further beyond the narrow question of interviewing skills, in order to think about the wider implications of the participatory approach to legal practice. In so doing, we will use the notion of empathy as a unifying discourse to review our approach to interviewing and to consider some radical alternatives for legal practice.

Empathy and participation

I only wish I could have found somebody else, a better solicitor, because I honestly thought they just didn't give a damn, couldn't care less, as though it's an everyday occurrence. Probably it is in their case but I didn't want to feel that. I mean, I didn't think that I was special, but I just wanted a little bit of – not sympathy – just concern, I think, to know what was best. I was going to them for help. I didn't know the legal position.[1]

Reading this statement, what do you think was the client's primary complaint about her solicitor?

What we think is interesting about that quote is the way in which the client's feelings about the lack of 'personal service' and 'concern' came to be translated into broader fears about the whole service she was getting. You need to think how you would prevent such a situation arising. Your ability to relate to your client at a personal level is important, as we saw in the previous chapter, in maintaining the channels of communication, and in maintaining the professional relationship once it is established.

A very important characteristic in this context is the notion of *empathy*. We have touched on this at various points in the discussion, without really explaining it. In this final section we shall suggest that empathy is the one thing that really holds the participatory approach together. Empathy operates reflexively, ie it informs both our perception of clients, and their perception and reception of us.

Lynne Henderson[2] has identified three distinctive features of an empathic capacity:

- the ability to perceive others as having their own interests or goals;
- the capacity imaginatively to experience the situation of another;
- the distress response which accompanies the imaginative experiencing of another's pain.

The conventional expectation of the professional role we adopt as lawyers is often one in which we maintain a safe 'professional' distance from our clients and their problems. This is often justified as a personal defence mechanism – we simply cannot afford to get 'involved'. We are lawyers, not social workers, it is said. Very true, but empathy does not mean actively *sharing* your client's problem/pain at a deep, personal, level: it means *understanding* and *responding* to it. At the same time it is not the same as *sympathy*. You do not have to 'take sides' to be empathic – to recognise the 'otherness' of that person's experience. Indeed, empathy can help you develop a capacity for seeing when the client might mislead you (innocently or otherwise) and help you to understand why that happens.[3] Distancing the client and objectifying her problems does not achieve that, and does not make you a 'good' lawyer. The capacity to relate to the client can be as vital as your legal knowledge, not just in terms of your own relations with those clients, but also in establishing your professional reputation:

> One of the solicitors we spoke to told us of how she had dropped one barrister from her firm's stable in favour of another who was less technically able but prepared to talk to clients in a way they were able to relate to.[4]

Empathy is something you can display throughout the relationship, not just as part of some more or less discrete 'counselling phase'. An empathic approach to interviewing also creates practical benefits in terms of the quality of information that is obtained.[5] Again, this is a good point to stop and think.

1 Divorce client quoted in G Davis *Partisans and Mediators*, Clarendon Press, Oxford 1988, p 104.
2 'Legality and Empathy' (1987) 85 *Michigan Law Review* 1574 at pp 1579–82.
3 Psychologists see a close link between empathy and the accuracy of person perception: the greater the empathy the greater the accuracy. See eg P Hinton *The Psychology of Interpersonal Perception*, Routledge, London & New York 1993, p 127.
4 J Morison & P Leith *The Barrister's World*, Open University Press, Milton Keynes 1992, p 71.
5 See L Graves 'Sources of individual differences in interviewer effectiveness: a model and implications for future research' (1993) 14 *Journal of Organizational Behaviour* 349.

Exercise 6.16   Empathic interviewing

Reflect on (a) the listening, and (b) the questioning techniques we have considered so far.
  Which, if any, are particularly useful in giving an empathic response to a client?

As you have probably gathered by now, empathic responses to the client may be many and varied. They are reflected in all the active listening techniques we have discussed in this chapter. Similarly, questioning techniques like mirroring and reflective questioning serve empathic as well as informational ends. Statements which show that you understand what the client is telling you and 'motivational statements'[1] (eg explanations of why particular steps are necessary, or why you need to know certain things) also emphasise that the relationship is an empathic one.

Of course, empathy plays a central part in the lawyer's advising and counselling functions too. An empathic approach is one which recognises that legal advice has to take account of the needs of the 'whole client'. Legal problems inevitably have an emotional impact on the client, and that does not just apply to the more obvious situations in family, personal injury or criminal practice. Commercial cases too involve interaction with people who may have a strong personal commitment or involvement in a matter, and this needs to be acknowledged.[2]

1   Binder, Bergman & Price *Legal Interviewing and Counseling*, pp 107–10.
2   See by way of illustration the comments in Boon 'Assessing Competence to Conduct Civil Litigation' in Boon, Halpern and Mackie *Skills for Legal Functions II: Representation and Advice*, Legal Skills Working Papers, Institute of Advanced Legal Studies, London 1992, p 39.

Towards a (re)vision of the relationship

At a deeper level, we would argue that empathy is central to any process of redefinition. Empathy, at least as it is starting to emerge in the academic literature, involves a call for greater contextualisation of legal disputes and legal discourse – a greater willingness to hear and engage with client stories on the client's terms, rather than just the lawyer's. In critical legal discourse this is being seen as a necessary first step in the empowerment of the client.

This may sound fine within the rarefied atmosphere of academic law, but what about the realities? Sharing power between lawyers and clients is not simply a question of saying, 'Here you are, I value your involvement, you make the decision'. Clients can, and will, turn round and say, 'Hang on, that's what I'm paying you to do'. Lawyers need to consider how they might develop practices which recognise and value the experience both sides bring to a problem, and then enable clients to participate in ways that do not smack of tokenism. Ironically, perhaps, this is already commonplace (in a sense) within large-scale commercial and corporate practice, as one practitioner has commented:

> In company/commercial work the client is aware through their own experience and so the solicitor is helped by the client. Also the possible permutations of problems have been explored before.[1]

In this context there is commonly some empathy deriving from shared values and experience – lawyers and clients are quite likely to share the same sort of background, and speak the same sort of language. It is easiest to build an empathic understanding with those who are most like ourselves. Rather more cynically one can point out that, here, the power relationship also tends to be reversed, with the client possessing the greater bargaining power and often at least equivalent social status to the lawyer.

In 'high street' and legal aid practices the situation may be very different (though it is not inevitable). The lawyer–client relationship may be more hierarchical in social and educational terms. Opportunities for empowering and co-operative forms of practice may be more difficult to discover, perhaps not least because our empathic capacity is limited by our experience. As Massaro suggests:

> . . . we can share in only some lives, and relate to only some voices. We are part of some communities, but not others. I may be bigger than my single physical self, but I am not the world . . . This vanishing point – the limit of self and the exhaustion of connection – is often the beginning point for law.[2]

If we are to move towards a more participatory style of lawyering, it will require commitment to change. We need to develop our capacity for reflection about our role as lawyers and the way we intervene in client lives.

If we are to change or develop our practices, it is important that reflection is focused and critical. It is not sufficient to stop at the level of 'Why did I do that?' Irving & Williams talk of using a 'ladder of inference'[3] as a reflective tool which is capable of drawing out the differences between your espoused theory and your theory-in-use.[4] Ask yourself these questions:[5]

- What was I trying to achieve here?
- What was it about the expected outcome that I valued?
- What assumptions am I making here?
- What beliefs do these assumptions depend on?
- Did I put those beliefs into action?

The key issue is the way in which we prioritise and implement agendas – our own and our clients. Various academics and practitioners (chiefly in the United States) have proposed a variety of more or less radical practices to empower clients in these situations. At the heart of many of these developments[6] is a commitment to honouring client narrative and experience and using it as part of a collective endeavour between lawyer and client. Such practices aim to 'help the client help himself'.[7] These ideas have been operationalised in forms of community action, in local law centres and other activist work. This is not that novel, though it is now dressed up in the discourses of postmodernity. There has long been a tradition of pro-active and communal legal work outside of traditional private practice. As Stephens, for example, has pointed out in the English context, pro-active law centres place emphasis

> . . . on communal control and on the use of people-working strategies in order to encourage clients to play an active role in the processing of their claims and in the running of their organised groups . . .[8]

There are interesting and important ways in which we can link these notions to the debate over access to justice, and the lawyer's role in facilitating access. Marc Galanter has used the participatory approach as a starting point in developing access to justice strategies. Galanter argues that access to justice may be improved by making changes at one of four levels in the legal system: he calls these levels *rules, courts, lawyers* and *parties*.[9] He suggests that the greatest scope for increasing access lies at the level of parties.

The lack of party capability is a key barrier to greater access. Most individual litigants are 'one-shotters',[10] isolated players engaged in one-off actions who lack the institutional and structural power/access of repeat players (such as the large corporations). Lawyers could increase access by 'upgrading'[11] the party capability of litigants who would otherwise be reduced to 'one-shot' status. These techniques particularly require the organisation of parties into common interest groups, which would then enhance their capacity to seek both legal and political redress of grievances. In this sense, the lawyer's role becomes far more catalytic, and involved with 'people-working'[12] rather than just rule-using. Bringing litigants together, helping set up community-based groups and initiatives, educating as well as giving legal advice – a significant re-defining of the lawyer–client relationship.

Putting it bluntly, however, these are developments that are currently quite marginal, and divorced from the traditional centres of legal practice and experience. The challenge over the next few years will be to see whether these new discursive practices can have something to say at the centre as well as at the margin of both academic work and practice.

1   Cited in Boon 'Assessing Competence to Conduct Civil Litigation', p 28.
2   'Empathy, Legal Storytelling, and the Rule of Law: New Words, Old Wounds?' (1989) 87 *Michigan Law Review* 2099 at 2122.
3   'Critical thinking and reflective practice in counselling' (1995) 23 *British Journal of Guidance and Counselling* 107 at 113.
4   If you cannot remember the difference, See Chapter 2, pp 23–4, above.
5   Irving & Williams, op cit, p 113.
6   See eg Alfieri 'The Antinomies of Poverty Law and a Theory of Dialogic Empowerment' (1987–88) 16 *New York University Review of Law & Social Change* 659; C D Cunningham 'A Tale of Two Clients: Thinking About Law as Language' (1989) 87 *Michigan Law Review* 2459; P Gabel & P Harris 'Building Power and Breaking Images' (1982–83) 11 *New York University Review of Law & Social Change* 369. There is an extraordinary dissonance in some of this work between high theory and low practice, so that when it comes to thinking about using client narrative, the analyses lapse into pessimism or banality – see eg the papers by Alfieri and Cunningham.
7   López *Rebellious Lawyering*, Westview Press, Boulder, Col 1992, p 52.
8   M Stephens *Community Law Centres: A critical appraisal*, Avebury Press, Aldershot 1990, p 26.
9   'Why the Haves Come Out Ahead' (1974) 9 *Law and Society Review* 95.
10 Ibid, p 97.
11 Galanter 'Delivering Legality, Some Proposals for the Direction of Research' (1976) 11 *Law & Society Review* 225 at pp 230–1.
12 Cf the discussion in Chapter 3, above.

Exercise 6.17   Concepts

1. *Divide into pairs.*
2. *Each pair is to:*
   (a) *define each concept, noting the page(s) on which it is discussed, and undertaking any additional research that is necessary; then*
   (b) *make sure that you both understand the meaning of each concept.*

3. *Combine into groups of four. Compare the answers of the two pairs. If there is disagreement, look up the concept and clarify it. Make sure you are all agreed on the definition and understand it.*

active/passive listening	*counselling*
empathy	*empowerment*
hypothetical questions	*keyword questions*
mirroring	*motivational statements*
open/closed questions	*participatory approach*
probing questions	*reflective questions*
six category intervention analysis	

Exercise 6.18   Review questions

1. *In interviewing, experience means making the same mistakes with greater confidence. Do you agree?*
2. *During an interview a client makes a racially derogatory comment about a third party involved in his case. How do you respond?*
3. *How far can we, or should we, go in empowering our clients to make their own decisions?*

Learning points

Following the model used at the end of the second section of this chapter, produce a brief summary of the principles you have derived from
  (i) *the section headed* Advising and counselling; *and*
  (ii) *the section headed* Interviewing and empathic lawyering.

Further reading

D Binder, P Bergman & S Price *Legal Interviewing & Counselling: A Client-Centred Approach*, West Publ, St Paul, Minn 1991.

J Heron 'A Six Category Intervention Analysis' (1976) 4 *British Journal of Guidance and Counselling* 143.

G López *Rebellious Lawyering*, Westview Press, Boulder, Col 1992 (ch 2).

A Sarat & W Felsteiner 'Law and Social Relations: Vocabularies of Motive in Lawyer/Client Interaction' (1988) 22 *Law & Society Review* 737 .

A Sherr *Client Interviewing for Lawyers*, Sweet & Maxwell, London 1986.

H Twist *Effective Interviewing*, Blackstone Press, London 1992.

7 Clarifying language: making sense of writing

All of you who read this book are experienced writers. But how well do you write? This can only be judged by looking at a text through the eyes of the reader. You will analyse a number of texts to identify their audiences and purposes. We encourage you to pick out organisational and linguistic features which clarify or obscure meaning. We explore the concepts of correctness, appropriateness and standard English. We provide exercises and examples which allow you to reflect on, articulate and develop your tacit knowledge of how to write clearly, concisely and correctly.

Objectives

To:

- Identify and describe differences between the spoken and written language.
- Recognise different styles of writing and judge when each is appropriate.
- Identify strengths and weaknesses in your writing and develop strategies for improvement where necessary.
- Plan your writing to take account of the needs of your reader.
- Emphasise the need for clarity and the value of plain English at all times.
- Use style, grammar and vocabulary which is appropriate to your task.

Why it is important to write well

Practising lawyers and law students spend a lot of their time writing. By now, you are well-versed in the skills of legal discourse (the language and method of reasoning used by lawyers), practising it constantly in essays, problem analyses, exam answers and lecture notes. It has become part of your tacit knowledge.

These forms of writing are read and evaluated by your tutors, who are themselves lawyers. As practising lawyers, however, you will also be writing for others who are not familiar with the language and reasoning of the law.

Exercise 7.1   What, when and why?

List the forms of written communication you think you will need in your work as a lawyer. Then compare your list with ours which follows.

You will need to be able to:
- take a clear, comprehensible set of *notes* (in what circumstances, and why?);

- write *letters* which the recipients (who are they?) will understand;
- *draft* (compose) *legal documents* (such as, and who for?);
- Write *opinions* (barristers) (who for?).

As we saw in Chapter 3, communication is about getting the message you want across to your recipient. Developing a fluent written style will save you and your reader a lot of time, irritation and misunderstanding . . .

. . . with writing, you don't get a second chance to get your message across . . .

Exercise 7.2   Which is dense? The reader or the text?

Below are three written texts. For each one:
(a)   Read quickly to discover the meaning, then more carefully to get the detail.
(b)   Did you sort out the meaning after
   (i)   the first reading?
   (ii)   the second reading?
(c)   Who do you think are the intended readers?
(d)   Note down which features you think make the text difficult to understand, giv-
   ing reasons.

1.   Where particulars of a partnership are disclosed to the Executive
     Council the remuneration of the individual partner for superannua-
     tion purposes will be deemed to be such proportion of the total
     remuneration of such practitioners as the proportion of his share in
     partnership profits bears to the total proportion of the shares of such
     practitioner in those profits.[1]

2.   SECTION 21, CONSUMER PROTECTION ACT 1987

     Meaning of 'misleading'
     21(1) For the purposes of section 20 above an indication given to
     any consumers is misleading as to a price if what is conveyed by the
     indication, or what those consumers might reasonably be expected
     to infer from the indication or any omission from it, includes any of
     the following, that is to say –
     (a) that the price is less than in fact it is;
     (b) that the applicability of the price does not depend on facts or
         circumstances on which its applicability does in fact depend;
     (c) that the prices covers matters in respect of which an additional
         charge is in fact made;
     (d) that a person who in fact has no such expectation –
         (i)   expects the price to be increased or reduced (whether or
                not at a particular time or by a particular amount); or
         (ii)   expects the price, or the price as increased or reduced, to
                be maintained (whether or not for a particular period); or
     (e) that the facts or circumstances by reference to which the con-
         sumers might reasonably be expected to judge the validity of any
         relevant comparison made or implied by the indication are not
         what in fact they are.

3.   . . . ideas which stress the growing importance of international co-
     operation and new theories of economic sovereignty across a wide
     range of areas – macro-economics, trade, the environment, the
     growth of post neo-classical endogenous growth theory and the
     symbiotic relationships between growth and investment in people
     and infra-structure, a new understanding of how labour markets
     really work and the rich and controversial debate over the meaning

and importance of competitiveness at the level of individuals, the firm or the nation and the role of government in fashioning modern industrial policies which focus on maintaining competitiveness.[2]

1 Taken from Sir Ernest Gowers *The Complete Plain Words*, Penguin, London 1986, p 2.
2 Taken from a speech made by Shadow Chancellor Gordon Brown and quoted in the *Daily Mail*, 28 September 1994, and the *Guardian*, 7 December 1994. The *Guardian* further reported that Gordon Brown won the Plain English Campaign No Nonsense Award 1994 for this 'long-winded drivel'. It appears the speech might have been composed by a researcher, Ed Balls. This prompted President of the Board of Trade Michael Heseltine to announce to the 1994 Tory Conference: 'It wasn't Brown's – it was Ball's.' (See *Daily Mail*, 7 December 1994).

ANALYSIS OF TEXT 1

This text was written for ordinary people, not experts. Writing like this is inefficient, because the writer, or someone else, will have to take time to explain the meaning. Why is it so difficult to grasp the meaning on a first reading?

First of all, it is all one sentence (57 words), so that by the time you get to the end, you have forgotten the beginning.

Secondly, any sentence should contain one or more verbs. These tell you what is happening, to whom, where, when, etc. Verbs give life and movement to the ideas being expressed. In this text there are only three verb phrases:

. . . are disclosed . . .

. . . will be deemed to be . . .

. . . bears . . .

Furthermore, the first two are passive verbs. Active verbs are made passive by inverting subject and object and changing the form of the verb, as in the following example:

ACTIVE: *The dog* (subject) *bit* (verb) *the man* (object);
PASSIVE: *The man* (now the subject) *was bitten* (verb) *by the dog* (now called the agent!).

Although these two sentences appear to have the same meaning, the passive draws your attention to what happened at the expense of the person or thing carrying out the action. It therefore has the effect of making the message impersonal. Moreover, the passive form increases the length and complexity of the sentence. This may make it more difficult to understand.

In 'officialese' often no subject is expressed, so that the active form can't be used. Try putting this phrase from Text 1 into the active form:

Where particulars of a partnership are disclosed to the Executive Council . . .

Congratulations if you managed it and it still sounds acceptable. We couldn't. This device of omitting the subject is common in such writing. It gives the impression that a sequence of actions takes place without any human intervention causing them, or seeing them to a conclusion. This is why such writing seems to represent the cold, remote, inhuman face of bureaucracy. Moreover, there is no obvious person to blame when things go wrong!

Thirdly, Text 1 makes up for the lack of verbs with cumbersome and complicated noun phrases:

> . . . particulars of a partnership . . .
> . . . the remuneration of the individual partner for superannuation purposes . . .
>
> . . . such proportion of the total remuneration of such practitioners . . .
> . . . the proportion of his share in partnership profits . . .
> . . . the total proportion of the shares of such practitioner . . .

The effect is to make the meaning obscure, and the content dry and uninteresting. It reads like a list rather than a series of dynamically connected ideas.

We suggest the following plainer English translation, but only tentatively: we aren't sure the meaning is right. We use 'your' because this text is taken from a reply to a letter of inquiry.

> Your superannuable income will be proportionate to your share in the partnership profits.

Sir Ernest Gowers suggests the following as a possible meaning:

> Your income will be taken to be the same proportion of the firm's remuneration as you used to get of its profits

You will see that we don't agree on the meaning of the text. Is it because we are stupid, or because the text is incomprehensible?

ANALYSIS OF TEXT 2

The paragraphing and numbering in this text aids clarity to the extent that a large block of print is broken into smaller blocks which are easier on the eye. However, smaller chunks do not make the text any more digestible. Why not?

The main point of the text is made in the first few lines. The rest is a list of situations which qualify the main point. We assume that the intention of the writer in sub-dividing the points was to make the message clearer, but the use of subordinate clauses (sentences within sentences) and repetitions spoils the intention. The effect is to pack in far too much information to grasp at a first reading.

Unlike Text 1, this text is written for experts who will take time to scrutinise it in great detail to discover its meaning and check for ambiguity. The drafter therefore has to ensure that the text is precise, unambiguous and comprehensive. She will use words and phrases that have acquired special meanings through legal convention and precedent. For example:

> For the purposes of section 20 above . . .

In the view of Sir Ernest Gowers:

> If it is readily intelligible, so much the better; but it is far more important that it should yield its meaning accurately than that it should yield it on first reading, and legal draftsmen cannot afford to give much attention, if any, to euphony or literary elegance. What matters most to them is that no one will succeed in persuading a court of law that their words bear a

meaning they did not intend, and, if possible, that no one will think it worth while to try.

All this means that their drafting is not to be judged by normal standards of good writing . . .[1]

Do you agree with this view? We will be looking in detail at the language of legal documents in Chapter 8.

ANALYSIS OF TEXT 3

We would like to put Text 3 into plain English for you, but we don't know what it means. This is the kind of obfusc babblegab you will probably have come across in articles and textbooks, and which we hope you do not imitate!

Much of the discussion we had about Text 1 is relevant here. In a sentence (or part of a sentence) of 93 words, there are only three verbs: stress, work, focus. Ponderous and inelegant noun phrases proliferate, for example:

. . . the growth of post-neoclassical endogenous growth theory . . .

There is a danger that once you allow these streams of noun phrases to pour forth, they form themselves into lists and give you little flexibility to vary the structure and rhythm of your writing. This is, inevitably, a turn-off for the readers. Any stimulating ideas the writer intended to communicate have been lost in their expression.

The writer could liven the text up and make it more intelligible by breaking it into smaller units and using fewer abstract words and more verb phrases. How many people understand the terms 'post-neoclassical' and 'endogenous growth theory'? It's one thing to use these terms amongst the small group of people who understand them, it's quite another to use them in a speech intended for wider circulation. This speech was delivered to economists, but the writer must surely have anticipated that information on Labour Party economic policy would be widely reported.

Let's now look at a text that gets its message across in quite a different way.

1   Sir Ernest Gowers, op cit, p 6.

Exercise 7.3   Lord Lucid

Read Lord Denning's judgment in *Mitchell (George) (Chesterhall) Ltd v Finney Lock Seeds Ltd* (1982) 3 WLR 1036 (CA). In particular, read 1043A to 1045F, and in pairs, discuss the following:

(a)   *Who are the likely readers?*
(b)   *When this case reached the House of Lords, Lord Bridge referred to Lord Denning's 'uniquely colourful and graphic style'.[1] Using examples from the text, identify the features of this style and compare the text with those you studied in 7.2.*

This text is a brief summary of the law on exemption clauses, intended for other lawyers to read, so you might expect it to be as inelegant and unexciting as the texts in 7.2. On the contrary, one can't help wishing Lord Denning had written a textbook on contract law. What makes it such an enjoyable read?

Because it is not a struggle. Sentences are a reasonable length, and simple in structure. There are no surplus words or phrases. Lawyers deal in abstractions, and Lord Denning is no exception. However, he uses an old device to catch our imagination and keep our attention. He tells us a story of heroes and villains. The story is full of illustrations and imagery. He turns abstract concepts into images which become tangible and real to the reader. The notion of freedom of contract, which law students spend some hours conceptualising and attempting to understand, becomes an 'idol', worshipped by the legal establishment. The 'true construction of contracts' is a 'secret weapon' with which to stab the idol in the back:

> Faced with this abuse of power – by the strong against the weak – the judges did what they could to put a curb upon it. They still had before them the idol, 'freedom of contract'. They still knelt down and worshipped it, but they concealed under their cloaks a secret weapon. They used it to stab the idol in the back. This weapon was called 'the true construction of the contract'.[2]

Masses of verbs move the text along, and there is hardly an abstract noun phrase in sight.

What distinguishes this writer from those in 7.2 is the impression that this writer has a clear point of view about the subject. Is Lord Denning less objective than his colleagues in the House of Lords, with their 'indigestible' speeches? Or is he just more open about the values he brings to bear on his decisions?[3]

To reinforce the points made so far, we end this section with part of a bible story and Richard Wydick's translation of it into gobbledegook:

> (A)s the Lord commanded . . . he lifted up the rod and smote the waters of the river . . . and all the waters that were in the river were turned to blood. And the fish that were in the river died; and the river stank, and the Egyptians could not drink the waters of the river; and there was blood throughout all the land of Egypt.
>
> *Exodus 8:7*

Here is the information described in the language of a modern environmental impact report:

> In accordance with the directive theretofore received from higher authority, he caused the implement to come into contact with the water, whereupon a polluting effect was perceived. The consequent toxification reduced the conditions necessary for the sustenance of the indigenous population of aquatic vertebrates below the level of continued viability. Olfactory discomfort standards were substantially exceeded, and potability declined. Social, economic and political disorientation were experienced to an unprecedented degree.[4]

1   (1983) 2 All ER 737 at 741.
2   At 1043.
3   For further discussion on this point, see J Holland and J Webb *Learning Legal Rules*, Blackstone, London 1993, pp 99–101.
4   R Wydick 'Plain English for Lawyers', (1978) 66 *California Law Review* 727 at p 737.

Learning from your writing experience

The purpose of Exercise 7.2 was to encourage you to pick out characteristics of effective and ineffective writing. Those we identified which help to obscure meaning were:

Long sentences

Complex sentences   – passives

                                  – verbs turned into nouns/noun phrases
                                          (nominalisations)

                                  – subordinate clauses

Repetition

Difficult vocabulary   – abstract concepts

                                  – technical terms

It should now be clear that to get your message across you must have your readers and their feelings in mind. If the readers are bored, irritated, frustrated or switched off, they are less likely to be persuaded by the message – if indeed they can grasp it.

If you are faced with a text that you find almost impossible to grasp, don't lose confidence in your intellectual abilities. It may be that ideas expressed in some texts are intellectually very demanding, but in many cases the fault will lie with the writer. It is not that you are too stupid to grasp the thoughts of a great expert. Rather, obscure writing is at worst a sign of the writer's muddled thinking or pretentiousness, or at best the result of bad planning.

Think now about your own writing skills. You are all writers of 15 or so years of experience. Or have you had one year's experience 15 times over? Are you complacent about your writing ability? How consciously do you reflect on and refine your writing? Do you make the kinds of mistakes poor writers make? Writing is so much a part of our tacit knowledge that it is easy to take the skills involved for granted. Think about your essay-writing. Are your arguments fluent and clearly linked? If not, why not? Is it because you don't express yourself well, or because you haven't clearly thought them out, or a bit of both?

Exercise 7.4   Do you suffer from verbal diarrhoea?

(a) *Choose a partner, and an extract from an essay you have written recently.*
   (i) *Read your text carefully.*
   (ii) *Note down which features aid or impede clarity, giving reasons.*
   (iii) *Give your text to your partner and ask her to do the same.*
   (iv) *Compare notes with your partner and discuss ways of improving your text.*
(b) *If you are still on speaking terms with your partner, carry out stages (a)(i)–(iv) with your partner's text.*
(c) *Make an entry in your learning diary. Make sure you include an action plan on what changes to make to the next piece of writing you draft.*
(d) *Remember to carry out your action plan.*

As we have seen, poor writing is a reflection of the writer's failure to take her readers into account. The proficient writer's aim is always to make sure the reader understands the message easily and precisely. This involves:

- KNOWING EXACTLY WHAT YOU WANT TO SAY;
- SELECTING THE FORM OF ENGLISH THAT IS APPROPRIATE FOR THE READER AND THE PURPOSE;
- SAYING EXACTLY WHAT YOU MEAN TO SAY.

Know exactly what you want to say

Exercise 7.5   The brick exercise

(a)   *Briefly note down what you think are the main differences between the spoken and written language.*

(b)   *For this part of the exercise, follow your tutor's instructions.*

Differences between the spoken and the written language

Many writers (does this include you?) think that in writing you use less common words and phrases. Why? They add formality, courtesy, dignity, and demonstrate the writer's high level of education, adherents to this mistaken belief might reply. Unfortunately, adherence to this view is the main source of gobbledygook and babblegab. We analysed some examples in Exercise 7.2. Here are some further examples of officialese:

> Prior to collecting your vehicle, please ensure you pay for your parking at the machines located in each bus stop in the car park. Credit card payments in excess of £130 and payment by cheque can only be dealt with at the administration building situated at the exit.

> We are embarking on measures to resolve the issue at the earliest opportunity.

> Please ensure noise is restricted to an absolute minimum in the vicinity of the quiet study locations.

The Brick Exercise should have demonstrated the necessity for clarity and precision in writing. Certain features which aid understanding in a conversation are absent from written communication. What are these missing features? You should remember them from Chapter 5.

- *Body language*   This tells the participants the state of mind and level of understanding and interest of the other participants.
- *Prosodic features*   These include stress, intonation, pauses and wordless sounds – ugh, ooh, ouch, um, which convey meanings such as disgust, surprise, excitement, embarrassment, the need for time to think, and so on.
- *Immediate response*   In conversation, the participants can respond immediately

to what is said, and a speaker can modify what she says in the light of that response.

It is this combination of body language, prosodic features and immediate response which makes speech so much easier to understand than writing. Whereas in speech you can think as you go along, in response to the reactions of your listener, when writing you need to get it right first time. To do that, you must think and plan in advance.

Since your aim will always be clarity and precision, as a general rule you should avoid less common words and phrases. Otherwise your reader may think you pompous, ponderous, prolix and over-formal. This is not a good way to start or maintain a relationship.

Planning

Research into successful writing strategies tells us that writing is not a linear process. Instead, writers use a circular, reflective approach:

> Perhaps the most powerful writing strategy is to take a problem-solving approach to writing which focuses on the three goals common to every writer: understanding of the issues to be discussed, effective communication of that understanding to the reader and persuading the reader to respond. Implicit in this approach is thinking the problem through, generating ideas and revising them, organising ideas in a logical framework, analysing the reader, monitoring whether the paper achieves the writer's goals and making the necessary changes.[1]

So why not begin by having a good think about the purpose of the communication?

WHY ARE YOU WRITING?

What do you want to happen as a result of it? For example, are you writing to persuade a client to take a particular course of action? If so, your message must be sufficiently comprehensive and clear that the client can make a decision quickly, preferably with no need for further discussion.

WHO ARE YOU WRITING TO?

You will be more likely to get the response you want if you aim to establish and maintain a fruitful relationship with your reader. Be aware of her needs as well as her status, and vary your language and style accordingly. Put yourself in her shoes and ask yourself what's in it for her.

The following factors will determine the way you write:

(a) *How well do you know your reader?* Are you on first name terms? Would he like to be addressed as J Webb Esq, or would he find such formality unfriendly?

(b) *What is his attitude towards you?* Is he on your side or the other side? Is he a fellow-professional?

(c) *What will his attitude be to the message?* Is the news good or bad? Is he likely to be hostile?

(d)   *How easily will he understand the information?* Is it very technical or detailed?

(e)   *How well can he read?*

(f)   *How well does he understand English?* Is it his mother tongue?

1   A Hasche 'Teaching Writing in Law: A Model to Improve Student Learning', 1992 3 *Legal Education Review*, 267 at p 270.

Exercise 7.6   Plain thinking

1.   (a)   *A client has instructed you to petition for divorce. In a letter to her describing the legal procedure, explain the term DECREE NISI.*

(b)   *A friend of yours runs a business designing computer software. He wants to know what emergency measures could be taken to stop a rival organisation selling his designs. He would like you to fax him your reply. You want to suggest the use of an ANTON PILLER ORDER. How would you express this?*

(c)   *Your legally aided client is about to embark on a long and complex personal injury claim. Write and explain to her what is meant by the STATUTORY CHARGE.*

(d)   *You occasionally write for a local newspaper as their legal correspondent. They have asked you to write a piece for their readers about a recent case where a man was pushed down the stairs by his sleepwalking wife. How would you explain the defence of AUTOMATISM?*

(e)   *A fellow-student has been seriously injured during a rugby match and wants compensation. Write and tell him about VOLENTI NON FIT INIURIA.*

2.   *In small groups:*

(a)   *Compare your written versions.*

(b)   *Discuss the methods and techniques you used to explain the legal terms.*

(c)   *Discuss and note down what you have learnt from this exercise.*

(d)   *If you were asked to repeat Exercise 1, what changes would you make to your approach?*

One fundamental point you may have discovered from this exercise is that you have to be absolutely clear about the meaning of technical terms yourself, before you can convey their meaning to others! Legal language is part of your social knowledge, yet it is only when you have to explain its meaning to lay people that you realise much of it is not yet tacit knowledge. You may have mugged up *statutory charge* for an English Legal System exam in the first year, and promptly forgotten it when you moved on to 'learn' Contract. It is only when you have had to deal with it in the swamp that it gradually becomes part of your tacit knowledge.

Exercise 7.7   Who is my reader?

Below are three letters written by solicitors, and a notice. Read these texts and in small groups discuss the questions that follow.

1.   Dear Sirs,

Burke v Melford Limited

WITHOUT PREJUDICE

Thank you for your letters of 20 March and 2 April.

We note that Ms Burke has rejected the payment into court and that the matter may well have to proceed to trial.

Incidentally, we think the cases you have pointed out in Current Law have quite the opposite effect from the one you intended. We think those reports show that rather more serious injuries than those suffered by your client might achieve awards in the region of £10,000 to £15,000. Ms Burke's injury was not in the same category as the other plaintiffs you referred us to.

For example, your client suffered a fracture which was only slightly displaced and this is why it was left to unite naturally. Your client was in hospital for only two days.

Mr Maple sustained a triple fracture of the ankle which needed fixing internally with plate and screws. His walking was limited to about half a mile, and there was a 5% risk of osteo-arthritis developing.

Mrs North underwent no less than five operations under general anaesthetic over a period of four years. The serious and permanent disabilities and disfigurement she suffered put her in a wholly different category to Ms Burke.

The same comment applies to the award to Ms Hazelwood by the CICB last July.

We will put your proposal to our clients and will let you know their response shortly.

Yours faithfully,

. . . .

2.   Dear Mrs Thornhill,

Road Traffic Accident – 25 June 1994

We understand from the Police Report that you were present at the scene of this accident and made a statement to the police.

We are acting for Molars Ltd, the company whose van was involved in the accident. The driver of the other vehicle has begun legal action against Molars Ltd, alleging that their employee, the van driver, was negligent.

As you were a witness to the accident, it is possible that we will want to call you to give evidence at the trial. We would like to fix the date of the trial at a time which is convenient to the people involved.

Could you therefore please let us know if you move house, and any dates that you will be unavailable for the rest of this year.

We will do our best to inconvenience you as little as possible. A pre-paid envelope is enclosed for your reply.

If you would like to discuss this further, please feel free to contact Ms Zoë Smith at this office.

Yours sincerely,

. . . .

3.   Dear Sir,

Copyright Claim

WITHOUT PREJUDICE

Thank you for your letter dated 22 February 1995.

In response to your claim for £200, we are prepared to offer £50 in full and final settlement of all your claims in relation to the multiple reproduction of the print of the cassette sleeve. This represents the notional royalty which you would have received for all prints made and represents your likely loss in law if a copyright claim was successfully made out by you. We do not accept that the items listed by you next to your claim for £150 represent any part of your likely loss in law if a copyright claim was successfully made out by you.

This offer remains open for acceptance for 14 days from the date of this letter. Acceptance is only valid when received in writing by us.

We hereby put you on notice that we are aware that you have been making recordings of some of our concerts without our permission. We consider this activity to be in breach of our rights in our live performances as contained in the Copyright Designs and Patents Act and give you formal notice to refrain from this activity forthwith. In addition, we hereby reserve all of our rights in relation to your unlawful recordings of the concerts concerned.

Yours faithfully,

. . . .

4.   This notice was sent to a resident who was late with her council tax:

PLEASE NOTE

YOU HAVE LOST YOUR RIGHT TO PAY BY INSTALMENTS.

IF PAYMENT OF THE FULL AMOUNT SHOWN IS NOT MADE WITHIN SEVEN DAYS A SUMMONS WILL BE ISSUED. THIS WILL INCUR ADDITIONAL COSTS OF £24.50.

QUESTIONS

(a)   *What is the purpose of the communication?*
(b)   *Who is the reader?*
(c)   *What do the language and style tell you about the relationship between writer and reader?*
(d)   *What do you think will be the attitude of the reader to the writer and the message?*
(e)   *To what extent does the writer take the reader's needs into account?*
(f)   *If you were the recipient, how would you respond to the communication?*
(g)   *Has the writer achieved her purpose?*

Now that you know your reader, move on to consider:

DO YOU HAVE ALL THE *INFORMATION* YOU NEED?

Is it accurate, or is there anything that needs checking? Is it complete?

WHAT IS THE BEST WAY TO *ORGANISE* THE INFORMATION FOR THIS READER?

You won't achieve your purpose if the recipient throws your letter in the bin or puts it on one side, probably to be forgotten. To get a quick response, you need to capture her interest and keep it. You can do this by making it clear why the message is important to her and how a reply will benefit her. Look again at the letters in Exercise 7.5. The writers are concise and get straight to the point. The recipients should be able to read, understand and act on the information at one reading.

If your purpose is to provide information, consider the effect the information will have on your reader. Is the news good or bad? If good, don't waste the reader's time with preliminaries. Get straight to the central point. If the news is bad, prepare the recipient for disappointment by giving some neutral or positive information first. Try to end on a positive note, for example, by offering a possible alternative solution.

If your purpose is to persuade the reader to a course of action, you need to make the benefits to the reader clear straight away. Point out the drawbacks of failing to follow the course of action.

Whatever your purpose, you must structure the content of the message so that it can be understood easily and unambiguously. Each paragraph should deal with one main topic, and should be clearly linked to the preceding and following paragraphs. We look at paragraphing in detail later in this chapter.

HOW SHOULD THE INFORMATION BE *PRESENTED* ON THE PAGE?

Closely spaced, unbroken blocks of print are hard on the eye and will turn the reader off. Use headings, subheadings and a numbering system if you are presenting a large amount of information.

Summary

Knowing what you mean to say involves:
● KNOWING YOUR PURPOSE;
● KNOWING YOUR READER;
● KNOWING YOUR INFORMATION;
● KNOWING YOUR ORGANISATION;
● KNOWING YOUR LAYOUT.

Selecting appropriate language

Exercise 7.8   Who speaks good English? It is I!

In groups of three or four, discuss the following:
–   What is good English?
–   Who speaks it?

- *What is bad English?*
- *Who speaks it?*
- *What are your pet hates in language use?*
- *Why do you hate them?*

Select an appropriate variety of English

Language experts agree there is no satisfactory definition of a 'language'. This applies as much to English as it does to any other language. Some form of English is the first language of about 700,000,000 people worldwide, and the second language of most of the rest of the world. As you know, there are significant differences in this language, depending on where it is spoken. The English of an American is not quite the same as the English of a person from the Indian sub-continent, and that of an Australian differs from the language of an English person. American English, Indian English and Australian English are different *varieties* of English.

Differences in spoken English can be heard at a much more local level. Many people in the UK learn a language as children which is very different from the kind of English heard on the BBC. These local varieties, or dialects, of English are highly complex, rule-governed ways of communicating. In other words, they have grammars.

When asked who speaks good English, many will say 'the Royal Family', or 'BBC newsreaders and commentators', because they speak standard English, which is 'accent-free', and therefore superior to other varieties.

How do language experts respond to this?

It is well-known to nearly everybody in the English-speaking world that most of us pronounce the language very badly. But, here again, the strongest complaints are usually reserved for the way in which other people pronounce, since it is obviously people from other cities, countries, age groups and social classes who really make a mess of things and have the most appalling accents, voices, drawls, twangs, whines and burrs. As linguists, we think that this widespread belief, like so many others that have to do with language, is mistaken. In fact, almost all of us pronounce our native language, whatever it is, very well indeed . . .

Some words in English have more than one pronunciation. Some of us, for instance, say 'ecconomics' while others say 'eeconomics'. This doesn't seem to bother anybody. With other words, however, passions are roused, and one pronunciation is condemned as wrong, illogical, ignorant, ugly and careless, while the other is praised as correct. Should we say 'con*trov*ersy' or '*con*troversy'? Should it be 'Covventry' or 'Cuvventry'? Is it 'offen' or 'offten'? Does it matter? Will it make any difference to anything important if everyone starts saying 'irre*vocc*able' rather than 'ir*revv*ocable'?

(Accent) refers . . . to the way particular vowels and consonants of a language are pronounced, and to the intonation or sentence melodies employed. Because accent refers in this way to pronunciation, everybody, without exception, has an accent. Complainers, of course, often talk as if only other people have accents – and usually rather funny ones at that – but if they pronounce vowels and consonants when they speak, and we have to assume that they do, they must have accents also. An accent, then, is not something to be ashamed of, because *everyone speaks with an accent.*

. . . we use people's accents to find out things about them. If you can tell whether somebody is a Geordie, Australian, Cockney, upper-class, etc, when they speak, then you are able to do this mostly – and most quickly – from the accent . . .

But we do more than use accents as clues. We also pass judgments on them. We say that some people are 'nicely spoken', that others are 'affected' in their speech, and that yet others have 'ugly' accents. As linguists, we believe that judgments of this type are almost entirely social judgments, based on what we know, or think we know, about the accent in question and where it comes from. We do not believe that these judgments are in any way truly aesthetic.[1]

One example of a pet hate, particularly amongst older people, is the use of the glottal stop: *-?* instead of *-t.* They regard this as 'lazy' or 'sloppy' pronunciation. In fact, speakers using glottal stops follow quite clear linguistic rules. Their use depends on the position of *-t* in the word. So, for example,

bu?er (butter), bo?om (bottom), bi?e (bite), biscui? (biscuit),

but not

?ank (tank), ?eacher (teacher).

In the UK the standard English accent, or 'Received Pronunciation' (RP) is perceived as the the most prestigious, because it is used by the influential, the wealthy and the educated. An experiment was carried out with a lecturer who could speak both RP and a strong regional accent. He gave the same lecture several times to a series of different audiences who did not know the real purpose of the experiment. The lectures given in RP were judged by most listeners to be superior in content to those delivered in the regional accent![2] Do we therefore judge the authenticity of news reporting by the accent of the newsreader? Are witnesses in court who speak RP more believable than those who don't?[3]

Of course, standard English doesn't only differ in pronunciation from other accents. You will hear lots of people speak the standard language, not in RP but in regional accents. Standard English is also a dialect, which differs grammatically from other dialects of English. Although it is only one dialect among many, like RP standard English is perceived as superior to non-standard forms, because it is the dialect used in all our national institutions, taught in school, learned by non-English speakers and used in international communication.

No matter which spoken variety you learned as a child, you are expected to be able to use the standard written variety. However, in your work as a lawyer you will probably communicate with people who do not speak or write standard English. Will you perceive them as inferior for that reason? Or their language as incorrect?[4]

1   L Andersson & P Trudgill *Bad Language*, Blackwell, Oxford 1990, pp 19–20, 21–2. See also D Freeborn, P French & D Langford *Varieties of Language; An Introduction to the Study of Language*, Macmillan, Basingstoke 1986, pp 81–4.
2   This experiment is described in Freeborn, French & Langford, op cit, p 17.
3   We discuss this particular question in more detail in Chapter 10.

4   For opposing views on the status of standard and non-standard forms, see extracts from
    P Trudgill *Accent, Dialect and the School*, Edward Arnold, London 1975, and J Honey *The
    Language Trap: Race, Class and the 'Standard English' Issue in British Schools*, 1983, both cited
    in Freeborn, French and Langford, op cit, pp 20–1. See also S Pinker *The Language Instinct*,
    Penguin, Harmondsworth 1994, Chapter 12.

Select an appropriate register

Register is a technical term used in linguistics to refer to the language we use
in situations. Suppose, for example, that your dialect is standard English. In
one day you will use and move between a number of registers of standard
English, depending on where you are and who you are talking or writing to.
You will use different language to your child, your partner, your law lecturer,
your employer, your best friend, your clients, the judge, and your colleagues.
As a barrister you will use different language with your colleagues in court
from that you would use with them in chambers or over lunch. You adapt
your standard language to suit each occasion and to reflect the kind of relationship you have with your audience.

Occupations and activities have their own specialised language registers.
Thus, rugby players perform *flying wedges* and enjoy(!) *loose mauls*. Linguists
discuss *syntax, whiz deletion* and *register*. And lawyers? *For the purposes of the
aforesaid it is submitted that the said professionals may be in flagrante delicto here-
under. Res ipsa loquitur.* As this example demonstrates, we are not talking only
about vocabulary. Grammatical structure also changes between registers. This
is clearly illustrated in the following extract from a radio sports commentary:

> . . . and again cries of 'England' ringing round the stadium – Wilkins
> takes the free kick short to Brooking five yards outside the Belgian
> penalty area – good running by Brooking – down to the bye-line – cuts
> the ball back – Meeuws is there to head the ball away – not very far –
> Wilkins trying to get the shot in – Wilkins going forward – a chance for
> Wilkins here – and – oh! what a superb goal by Ray Wilkins.[1]

A register may also contain slang. Police officers may talk of sending out the
yobbo van, and teachers in higher education may refer to 'resource-based learning' as *fo-fo* (unabbreviated form unprintable – please consult your tutor).

Command of a register can signify your membership of a closely-knit group
and increases group cohesion by keeping out those who don't belong. For
example, users of technical language justify the need for it in the interests of
precise and accurate definition, and shorthand. However, we need to think
long and hard about how much of it is actually necessary, and to what extent
we use it to mystify outsiders.

Outsiders, and some insiders, refer to specialised vocabularies as *jargon*.
This word was:

> . . . first used, in the late fourteenth century, in the sense of the twittering
> of birds. From this it passed on naturally to mean talk one does not
> understand, or gibberish, and so to any form of speech or writing filled
> with unfamiliar terms or peculiar to a particular group of persons.[2]

1   Adapted from Freeborn, et al, op cit, p 136.
2   K Hudson *The Jargon of the Professions*, Macmillan, London 1978, p 10.

Exercise 7.9   Le mot juste

Here are some words and phrases which lawyers are fond of using. Which are essential to the legal register, and why?

ultra vires	*Mareva*	*inter alia*
Calderbank letter	*aforementioned*	*certiorari*
affidavit	*pursuant to*	*fee simple*
conveyance	*disbursements*	*lessor*
the said agreement	*hearsay*	*voire dire*

Select an appropriate style

Style is one aspect of register in that it is determined by context. When we advise you to select an appropriate style for your communication, we are talking about degrees of formality and informality, and tone.

For example:

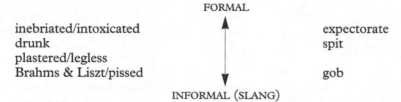

FORMAL	
inebriated/intoxicated	expectorate
drunk	spit
plastered/legless	
Brahms & Liszt/pissed	gob

INFORMAL (SLANG)

As we have said, the level of formality and the kind of tone you adopt will depend on the relationship you want to establish or maintain with your reader.

You may choose to use a formal style with plenty of legal language to resolve a dispute quickly. For example, the tone of Letter 3 in Exercise 7.7 is hostile. A lawyer drafted it, but it was signed by the clients. They wanted to make it clear to the recipient that they had taken legal advice. The tone puts the recipient in a very poor bargaining position. Since it may cost him more than £50 to consult a solicitor, he has little choice but to accept the offer.

Used in this way, legal language and style can be extremely powerful. If the writer had conveyed the message in a friendly, courteous style the recipient might still be prevaricating. We discuss the power of legal language in more detail in Chapter 8.

Select gender-neutral language

The well-known rule that the masculine includes the feminine is based on the belief that language is neutral. It is not. Look at the following three examples:

Every solicitor in private practice should ensure his complaints procedures are clearly set out in writing.

There are so many conflicting cases in this area of contract law that the businessman cannot be certain what the law is.

Anyone who has reasonable grounds for complaint should send his objections to Head Office.

The constant use of *he, his, him* perpetuates an ancient linguistic convention[1] which many people now find offensive. When we want to refer to a person whose gender is unspecified, what good reason is there to choose the masculine pronoun instead of the feminine? For those of us who hold stereotypical views about gender roles in society, perpetual use of the masculine pronouns serves only to reinforce them. In the sentences above, try changing the masculine forms into feminine. Does it sound strange? If so, why? Interestingly, of those qualifying as solicitors in 1993, 51.1% were female.[2]

There are a number of ways to avoid masculine forms. Many writers prefer to use *they* and *their*, etc:

> Anyone who has reasonable grounds for complaint should send their objections to Head Office.

Others may choose to rewrite the sentence using *you, your*, etc:

> If you think you have reasonable grounds for complaint you can send your objections to Head Office.

The plural may be possible:

> All solicitors in private practice should ensure their complaints procedures are clearly set out in writing.

Some writers use roughly equal numbers of *he, she, his, her*, etc. Others deliberately use the feminine forms to challenge the stereotypical view. In this book we use the feminine forms most of the time.

The following is gender neutral, but inelegant, so we don't recommend it:

> Anyone who has reasonable grounds for complaint should send his or her objections to Head Office.

Other gender neutral usages are criticised for their ugliness and inelegance: for example, *humankind, significant other*. In this book we reluctantly use *drafter* for *draftsman*. There seems to be no elegant alternative.

Businessman, salesman, fireman, policeman, when used generically, can be replaced by *businesspeople, salespeople, fire fighters, police officers*.

1   Some Romance and Germanic languages have gender neutral pronouns: for example, French *on*, English *one* and German *man*. Both the French and English versions are derived from the Latin *homo*, meaning *man*. Throughout the ages people have extended the meaning to include both genders, so *homo* comes to have the general meaning of *human*, irrespective of gender (cf *homo sapiens, homo erectus*, etc). The fact remains, however, that these words are derived from a word which means *man* and is grammatically masculine.
2   Law Society Annual Statistical Report, 1993, p 56.

Summary

Selecting appropriate language for your communication means thinking about:
- VARIETY;
- REGISTER;
- STYLE;
- GENDER NEUTRALITY.

Say exactly what you mean to say

Exercise 7.10 Grasping grammar

Note down in a few sentences what you understand by the word 'grammar'. Discuss your answers with your group. Can you reach a consensus about the meaning? If so, what is it?

Getting the fundamentals right

Do you remember our earlier discussion about the status of standard English and other dialects? Grammar is at the heart of this debate. For linguists, the main meaning of 'grammar' is a *description* of the rules which underlie a speaker's ability to understand, speak and (possibly) write a given language. Linguists therefore treat all grammars as equally valid, and prefer to talk of 'appropriate' and 'inappropriate' grammar.

In its popular sense, 'grammar' is a set of rules which *prescribe* how users should speak and write. Those who believe in the superiority of standard English tend to talk of its grammar as 'correct' whilst the grammars of other dialects are 'incorrect'.

Exercise 7.11 Bad grammar

In small groups, discuss the examples of written English below. Identify the features which make each text 'inappropriate', or 'incorrect'.

1. Graffiti from the London Underground:

   > I woz ere
   > Ere I woz
   > Woz I ere?
   > Yes, I were

2. want pizza don't any on I anchovies my
3. He failed to entirely avoid the oncoming car.

In 1 the meaning is clear, and the text is perfectly punctuated. However, we can all recognise this as non-standard English, because the spelling is incorrect. There is also a grammatical mistake of subject/verb agreement in the last line.

Example 2 is nothing more than a meaningless list of words. If someone said it to you, you would need time to sort it out into some logical meaning. And this is a very simple sentence. Imagine the difficulties of sorting out much more complex and abstract sentences. This example illustrates the most fundamental rule of English grammar: that relationships within sentences are governed by rules of word order. Break this rule substantially and you get nonsense. Native English speakers whose language has developed normally do not make mistakes like this. The rules of word order are part of our tacit knowledge, and we apply them correctly, even though we might not be able to say what they are.

199

There appears to be a problem with word order, too, in 3. It may look perfectly all right to you. It seems to get its message across clearly (and more concisely than the first example!). However, it breaks a well-known 'rule':

Never split an infinitive.

Those who cleave to this rule would say the 'correct' form is

He failed entirely *to avoid* the oncoming car.

However, a change in the word order here changes the meaning. The first version suggests a slight impact, whilst the second suggests a full impact. Thus, splitting or not splitting in such a case may communicate the wrong information.

The rule about not splitting the infinitive is not a grammatical rule at all. It is a stylistic preference, and is therefore a matter of taste rather than correctness or incorrectness.

Nobody is born with the written variety of English as their mother tongue, so for all of us there is an element of 'foreignness' about it. Admittedly, if we are used to using standard English in our everyday lives, the similarities between that and written English help us enormously.

The point, however, is that when we learn a new language we need rules and conventions which we can follow and trust. Some of these are plainly necessary, others are not. Those that are plainly necessary are to do with 'grammar'.

The following are the most important rules you must abide by: otherwise you will be using this variety of English incorrectly.

USE COMPLETE SENTENCES

Unlike the spoken language, written English demands that we use full sentences to convey our meaning. If you are not using these you are not respecting the way that the language encompasses elements of sense and meaning. Here is the final paragraph of a letter sent to Caroline by a former bank manager:

I trust that this letter will put things in perspective and *where in finality you find it needful for our offered support to come from elsewhere.*

When you have read to the end, you expect more words, not a full stop. The italicised part is not a full sentence. By full sentences we mean ones that contain a *subject* and a *verb* and any necessary *objects*.

The SUBJECT usually appears before the main verb in statements and after the main verb in questions:

Jim was stopped by the police on the way home last night.
Where was *Jim* stopped by the police?

All the following can be subjects:

A noun:	*Hang-gliding* is dangerous.
A noun phrase:	*Endogenous growth theory* is dangerous.
	The cost of mortgages is going up.

A pronoun:	*It* isn't possible.
	Who wrote that rubbish?
A subordinate clause:	*What you wrote* was perfectly acceptable.

The VERB must agree with its subject. In standard English there is little variation in the form of verbs. An exception is the third person singular of the present tense. For example: *I sing, she sings.*

Other exceptions are the verb *to be*, for example:

I am, she is, you are, etc.
I was, you were, etc.

Modal verbs don't change at all:

must, can, may, might, shall, will, ought, should, would, could.

Some verbs have to be followed by an OBJECT, others don't. For example,

He sang is correct, but
I don't want is not.

The following are all acceptable sentences:

He sang.

He sang the national anthem (object: *WHAT* did he sing?).

He sang in the bath (adverbial phrase: *WHERE* did he sing?).

He sang out of tune for several hours (adverbial phrases: *HOW* did he sing, and for *HOW LONG*?).

He sang everything that we wanted him to sing (object: *WHAT* did he sing?).

Note that some sentences may be complete though they omit the subject. The subject is implied, for example, in the politeness formula sentence *Thank you*, and in commands:

(I) *Thank you for your letter.*
(You) *Go to your room.*
Don't (you) *park on double yellow lines.*
Never (don't you ever) *split an infinitive.*

The following sentences are unacceptable. What is missing?

With reference to your letter of 21 March.

Thanking you for your kind attention.

Unfortunately being unavailable at the time I wanted to see her.

The first has no verb at all. In the second, *thanking* does not imply the subject *I* and so is not a verb. It would be acceptable to say:

Thank you for your kind attention.

The first part of the third sentence is wrong. *Being* does not imply the subject *she*, and so the subject must be expressed, and then the verb must agree with it:

Unfortunately *she was* unavailable at the time I wanted to see her.

In some contexts, such as story-telling and conversational style, incomplete sentences may be acceptable in written English. For example:

Out of winter into spring.

I sat in the public gallery, studying the defendant's face, as the jury gave their verdict. *Guilty.*

What do you think of this chapter so far? *Rubbish.*

OBSERVE THE RULES OF SYNTAX (WORD ORDER)

In highly inflected languages, like Latin, the meaning is derived from the different word endings, which indicate the relationship between one word and another. English has very few inflections. We noted above that English verbs vary their form very little. They add *-s* or *-es* for the third person and and most add *-ed* for the past. Most nouns add *-s* or *-es* to make the plural. That's about all. We therefore derive the meaning of an English sentence not from word endings but from the order of the words in the sentence.

Using word order intelligently therefore enables you to write your meaning more correctly. To tie yourself down with unnecessary rules like not splitting the infinitive restricts your capacity to be precise, as the example on page 199 demonstrated.

Some words may look benign but can cause trouble. For example:

The prosecutor *only* stood up when the magistrates entered the court room.

This sentence can have several meanings:

- The prosecutor had been sitting down up until that point.
- Nobody stood up except the prosecutor.
- The prosecutor did nothing except stand up: she did not speak, smile, etc.

Careful planning of the word order will enable you to express the meaning you want. Where would you put *only* to get each of the three meanings above? Or do you have to make more radical changes to the sentence?

In the next chapter we shall see the liberties legal drafters take with word order to try to ensure precision.

USE APPROPRIATE PUNCTUATION

Punctuation helps us make sense of written language by breaking it up into smaller units. Furthermore, as we noted during the Brick Exercise (7.5), the prosodic features which aid our understanding of the spoken language are absent from the written. If spoken, the meaning of

The prosecutor only stood up when the magistrates entered the court room,

would be understood quite clearly from intonation and emphasis on particular words and syllables. Precise word order is one way of compensating for loss of prosody; punctuation is another. See how punctuation alters the meaning in this sentence:

The judge said the accused was the most heinous villain he had ever met.

The judge, said the accused, was the most heinous villain he had ever met.

Intonation and emphasis would make the meaning clear if either of these sentences were spoken.

Exercise 7.12   Some people just don't know when to stop

Briefly write down when you would use the following punctuation marks:
(a) *a full stop,*
(b) *a comma,*
(c) *a semi-colon,*
(d) *a colon,*
(e) *an apostrophe.*

FULL STOPS don't usually cause trouble. The rule is straightforward as long as you understand the rules for sentences. We use full stops to separate sentences. Each new sentence starts with a capital letter and ends with a full stop.

I met Mrs James in the supermarket. We decided to go for a cup of coffee together. Over coffee she began to tell me about her divorce.

COMMAS separate words, phrases and clauses. They signify short pauses and changes in intonation in the spoken language.
The example above of the judge and the accused shows how using and not using commas can affect meaning. Moreover, your meaning may be obscured if your sentence is top-heavy with commas. For example:

There may be some difficulty, as I have already indicated, if, as you wish, you insist on inserting Clause 5b, in its present form, into the contract, without some modification, which takes account of the present law.

We wouldn't want this writer to draft our contracts. She is extending the sentence length to accommodate new thoughts as they come to mind. The comma is not a substitute for thinking and planning. What would you do to make this message readable?
Cutting out a few commas won't do. The sentence needs re-thinking. Here is one possible alternative:

If you wish to include clause 5b in the contract, we will have to alter it to make it comply with the law.

Commas don't function as full stops and so shouldn't be used to link sentences. You can link two sentences with a co-ordinating conjunction (eg *and, but, for*), or make a sentence break with a full stop. For example,

(a) I shall discuss two recent cases, the first was decided a month ago, the second only yesterday

can be rewritten as:

I shall discuss two recent cases. The first was decided a month ago and the second only yesterday.

Similarly,

> (b) You must put your application in within 28 days, otherwise you will lose the right to make a claim

should be rewritten thus:

> You must put your application in within 28 days. Otherwise you will lose the right to make a claim.

Alternatively, it is possible to use a co-ordinating conjunction which means the same as *otherwise*:

> You must put your application in within 28 days, or you will lose the right to make a claim.

If you don't want to make a complete break between the sentences in (a), can you use a stop that is less full – a colon or semicolon? You can use a SEMI-COLON where you think a sentence is too closely related to what has gone before to be cut off by a full stop. However, these situations are rare.

> I could hear footsteps behind me; then they stopped.

Use of the semicolon here heightens the tension. Generally, however, they aren't necessary because we have the full stop.

The COLON is used to precede an explanation, and so can be used in sentence (a). A colon can also introduce a list. For example:

> There are three main ingredients for batter: flour, milk and egg.

APOSTROPHES cause a lot of trouble. You find them in all sorts of places where the rules say they should not appear at all. This is probably because apostrophes represent nothing that is heard in the spoken language. Other punctuation marks intonation, emphasis or pauses. Apostrophes are purely a written convention.

In fact, the rules are quite straightforward. In spoken English we generally indicate possession by adding *-s* to the 'possessor'. In writing the *-s* is retained, but we add an extra feature – an apostrophe. For example:

> The dog's biscuits
> The dogs' biscuits
> Mary's paintings.

In speech the first two examples sound exactly the same and we would have to judge the precise meaning from the context. The written form tells at a glance whether we are talking about one or more dogs.

Because apostrophes are usually unnecessary to understanding, many people think them old-fashioned. It may be because attitudes are changing that there is so much uncertainty about how to use them. Some people mistakenly add apostrophes to verb endings and noun plurals:

> This shop offer's fresh vegetables' at very low prices.

Apostrophes should never be used in this way. If you want to be thought of as an educated writer, you need to learn to use them correctly. The rules are as follows:

1. Singular nouns and plural nouns which don't end in 's': put the apostrophe before the 's':

    > The *dog's* biscuits
    > A *woman's* right to choose
    > *John's* neighbours
    > The *men's* changing room.

2. Plural nouns ending in 's': put the apostrophe after the 's':

    > The *judges'* wigs
    > The *dogs'* biscuits.

3. Singular nouns ending in 's': put the apostrophe after the 's'. You can add another 's':

    > *James'* knuckles, or
    > *James's* knuckles.

We also use the apostrophe to measure a period of time:

> five *weeks'* work,
> seven *days'* holiday;

to refer to places and premises:

> Make an appointment at the *dentist's*
> Shall we go and eat at *Brown's*?

It is also, rather unexpectedly, used in the following way:

> He is a friend of *George's*.

This seems mainly to be used for relationships and in sentences where an alternative would be to use *one of*, as in

> He is one of George's friends.

Where we combine subject and verb to make one word, we use an apostrophe. This is called elision. For example:

> *She's* never going to marry him!
> *John's* going to Australia.
> *Who's* going with him?
> *Who'd* want to go there?

A second kind of elision is when some verbs are made negative:

> *haven't, couldn't, don't, mustn't, wasn't,* etc.

Note that the apostrophe goes where the *-o* should be, not between the words. It marks the dropping of the letter *-o*, not the boundaries between the words.

A frequent mistake is to confuse the following:

> *whose* (the possessive pronoun) and
> *who's* (short form of *who is* or *who has*)

as in

> *Whose bike is this?* (answer: Kate's)
> *Who's coming to lunch?* (Who is coming to lunch?)
> *Who's got the Watson file?* (Who has got, etc)

If the version you are using cannot be expanded to *who is* or *who has*, then you must use *whose*. The same rules apply to *its* and *it's*.

Exercise 7.13   Whose who?

Put the appropriate form into the following:

> Have you heard who__ been made redundant?
> Do you know who__ writing that is?
> You know Jenny's car? Well, it__ for sale.
> It__ mileage is very low.
> Can you tell me who__ taken my wig?
> Put that down. You don't know where it__ been.

Many of you probably apply the rules of punctuation correctly, even if you are not in the habit of articulating them. If we insult your intelligence, we apologise. However, it is important to remember that selecting appropriate punctuation marks is not a matter of taste or cosmetics. These marks carry meaning and so have an important grammatical function. Punctuation is part of your 'grammar'.

We shall see in Chapter 8 how the traditional reluctance of lawyers to use punctuation in legal documents has contributed to the unintelligibility of these texts.

Use correct spelling

Sorry, folks! Spelling is one of those conventions we just have to observe. It is not acceptable to experiment: it is either right or wrong.

What makes English spelling so difficult is that words are not spelt as they are pronounced. There are two main reasons for this: firstly, that the spelling system introduced by the Normans was mixed with the system we used before the Conquest. This accounts for two different spellings for the same sound, for example *-se* and *-ce*:

> *mouse, mice.*

Furthermore, we also have two sounds for the same spelling, for example *-g*:

> *get, gender*
> *gift, gin.*

The second reason is that pronunciation has changed, but spelling hasn't. In the Middle Ages those few people who could write spelt words in different ways. However, a fixed and uniform system of spelling began to be established with the introduction of printing in the fifteenth century. In the eighteenth century English dictionaries adopted this standard system. This is largely the system we use today: a fossil, unaffected by major changes in pronunciation which have taken place since the fifteenth century.

We see examples of this fossilisation in

liGHt, Knee, douBt, saLmon.

We spell *meat* and *meet* differently because in the past *ea* and *ee* were two different sounds. Can we therefore say that all words where *ea* and *ee* occur sound the same? Think of other examples:

read, reed
dear, deer.

But compare:

great, greet
head, heed.

We therefore can't rely on a clear rule. English spelling has few 'rules', and those there are may be outnumbered by the exceptions to them. No wonder writers have problems. Since there are so few rules, learning to spell in English is largely a matter of memorising. We do not use the intellectual processes which are necessary to acquire the complex linguistic skills of grammar and punctuation.

It is therefore quite untrue to say, as many do, that poor spelling is a sign of intellectual incompetence. Nevertheless, incorrect spelling is unacceptable in written standard English. If you send a letter to a client asking:

Where woz your daughter the night your house woz burgled?

your client is likely to withdraw her instructions, thinking you uneducated, incompetent or unprofessional. If you have difficulties with spelling, always use a dictionary or a spell-checker.

Summary

Saying what you mean to say means getting the fundamentals right:
- USE APPROPRIATE GRAMMAR (STANDARD WRITTEN ENGLISH):
  WRITE COMPLETE SENTENCES
  WITH CORRECT WORD ORDER
  AND APPROPRIATE PUNCTUATION;
- USE CORRECT SPELLING (STANDARD WRITTEN ENGLISH).

Moving towards artistry

Following the fundamentals will not of itself lead you to write acceptable and comprehensible English. Good writing is the result of good judgment about:

CLARITY;
PRECISION;
ELEGANCE.

There are no hard and fast fundamentals for this. You have to develop your own views and test them in practice. However, there are certain things you should concentrate on which will help you develop your judgment.

Vocabulary

You may find it useful at this point to go back and re-read the texts and discussion on Exercise 7.2. Remember, what you should be aiming for is to make your meaning clear as rapidly and straightforwardly as possible. What you should avoid is the appearance of pomposity and formality which certain words and phrases tend to give to writing. This can create a barrier between you and your reader. For the same reason you should avoid long-windedness, unnecessary technical terms and antiquated language, particularly Latin! This 'legalese' has given lawyers a bad name.

When we discussed the Brick Exercise (7.5) we suggested that writers should avoid infrequently used words and phrases. The words and phrases below, once rarely used, have become common both in speech and writing, particularly officialese. For example:

Commence (begin);
Utilise (use);
Facilitate (help, assist);
At a later date (later);
Prior to (before);
On a regular basis (regularly);
In the final analysis (finally);
Subsequent to (after);
Until such time as (until);
At this moment in time (now);
As a matter of urgency (urgently);
And while we are on the subject (furthermore);
In the vicinity of (near);
For the purpose of (to).

Richard Wydick has some sensible advice:

Every time you see one of these pests, swat it.[1]

Can you think of others? Pests which you are in the habit of using?

In speech some of these phrases are used as gap fillers while the speaker prepares to introduce a new topic or thinks out what she is going to say next.

In writing this padding device is often used to introduce a new topic, or to link paragraphs. For example:

As far as your purchase is concerned, we will deal with it as a matter of urgency.

With regard to your request for further and better particulars, we enclose herewith a statement . . .

As I have already said, . . . (so why repeat it?)

As I mentioned earlier, . . .

Try to avoid these clumsy devices. Concise language will bring elegance to your writing. Imprecise language will dilute the force of your message.

The same goes for redundant words and phrases. What we are talking about here is the insertion of unnecessary words and phrases as padding. For example:

close proximity
duly incorporated
I enclose herewith
forward planning
unfilled vacancy
null and void
last will and testament.

If it is possible to cut out a word without altering the meaning of the sentence, cut it out.

Which words are redundant in this sentence?

Relatively few people can afford the cost of taking a case through the civil courts.

1   R Wydick 'Plain English for Lawyers', (1978) 66 *California Law Review* 727 at p 731.

New use or misuse?

Another problem with using big words to impress the reader is that you have to be absolutely sure you know what they mean. Can you spot the fault in the following sentence?

I have been invited to partake in a group session on experiential learning.

The writer uses *partake* when she means *participate*. This is what is known as a *malapropism*, named after the character Mrs Malaprop in Sheridan's play *The Rivals*. Sheridan took her name from the French *mal à propos* which means 'inappropriate'. She kept using and misusing long, learned words.

The *partake/participate* confusion is now quite common in speech. So is it still a malapropism, or does it denote a change in the meaning of *partake*? Linguists Lars Andersson and Peter Trudgill address this problem:

If a single person such as Mrs Malaprop misuses a word, this is a problem for her. As we have seen, languages are socially based systems and individuals cannot unilaterally decide to change the meaning of words. In the case of Mrs Malaprop herself, the usual effect is comic, but of course confusion could also result. The moral is that trying to use fancy language can easily lead someone into looking very foolish. Mrs Malaprop would have been much better advised to stick to her own everyday language.

Notice, however, that if everybody used the same malapropism, then it would by definition no longer be a malapropism . . . The fact is that words mean what speakers use them to mean. Formerly, for example, all speakers of English . . . used the word *nice* to mean 'ignorant', 'foolish'. Gradually the usage went through a series of changes so that the meaning became by turns 'shy', 'delicate', 'fine', and finally 'pleasant'. Anyone wanting these days to use *nice* with its original meaning would be making just as bad a mistake as Mrs Malaprop.[1]

Andersson and Trudgill comment that although confusion may arise whilst words are changing their meanings, complete misunderstanding is unlikely.[2]

Grammatical forms also undergo change. For example, the prescriptive rules on *less* and *fewer* tell us to use *less* with uncountable nouns (which because they are uncountable, have no plural forms), as in

If you drive at a steady 55mph, you use *less petrol*.
Everyone should pay *less income tax*.

Countable nouns, which have plurals, should be preceded by *fewer*:

There are *fewer people* here than there were yesterday.
Higher pay settlements mean *fewer jobs*, says the government.

However, it is now very common in speech to say *less* instead of *fewer*:

less people,
less jobs.

This usage is finding its way into writing, too. It looks like a sensible language rationalisation – why have two forms when we could use one, without any misunderstanding? The problem is, when a language change like this is happening, it is difficult to know at what point the new usage becomes acceptable. Some people see the 'misuse' as a sign of poor education.

Another grammatical change which makes Caroline particularly ill is now found very frequently in writing, as well as speech. Here is an example of this loathsome usage:

If you require any assistance, please contact *myself* or my assistant.

Your tacit knowledge, once surfaced by yourselves, will tell you that these reflexive pronouns *-self*, *-selves*, as in:

She washed herself in ass's milk.
Go and clean yourselves up.
We can't go there by ourselves.
He has a very fine opinion of himself

are grammatical because in each case the pronoun refers to the subject of the sentence. We'll call this Rule 1. Note that the rule is not always consistently followed. For example,

Have you got any money on yourself?

sounds distinctly odd!

Rule 2: The reflexives can also be used in another way to give emphasis, as in:

Are you sure he got my message? Yes, I took it round there *myself*.

However, the traditional rules do not allow their use as object pronouns *you*, *me*, *him*, *her*, *us*, *them*. Yet this is what is happening. If words mean what people use them to mean, then the frequency of this usage signifies a language change. But is this usage acceptable in standard written English? It certainly makes many people grind their teeth. Why?

We looked for this usage in an up-to-date grammar book[3] and found a reference to it after certain words and phrases, such as *as for, like, but for, except for*:

As for me/myself, I'm going home now.
Heavy drinking is not a good idea for someone like me/myself.

and in co-ordinated noun phrases, such as:

He showed us a picture of *him and Kate.*
He showed us a picture of *himself and Kate.*

Is *please contact myself or my assistant* covered by this second situation? *Myself or my assistant* is a co-ordinated noun phrase, like *himself and Kate.* But can you spot the difference? In the latter *himself* points back to the subject *he.* This sentence can therefore fall into our Rule 1, as would

He showed us a picture of himself.

However, in

If you require any further assistance, please contact myself or my assistant,

the subject of the sentence is *you.* Similarly, in the repellent

Your tacit knowledge, surfaced by yourselves, will tell you, etc . . .

the subject is *your tacit knowledge.* The 'misuse' therefore does not seem to be a gradual extension of pre-existing rules, but a complete defiance of them. This is what boggles the mind and grinds the teeth, particularly of prescriptive grammarians.

So the next question is: should you use it? We think that a change as profound as this will take a long time to become accepted in standard written English. Avoid it. There is nothing wrong with:

Please contact me or my assistant.

1   L Andersson & P Trudgill *Bad Language*, Blackwell, Oxford 1990, p 150.
2   For an illuminating example of this, see their discussion of the development in meaning of the word *interested* and its negative forms *disinterested* and *uninterested*: ibid, pp 151–4.
3   G Leech & J Svartik *A Communicative Grammar of English*, Longman, London 1994, pp 335–6.

Sentence length and complexity

As you have learnt from your own reading experience, long sentences tire and confuse the reader. Yet too many short sentences one after another make the content disjointed and your writing look simplistic. The secret of good writing is to vary the length of your sentences. However, it is difficult to say what makes a 'long sentence' because readers have different levels of reading ability. One reader might find a sentence of 12 words difficult to understand, while another might find it childish and patronising. The average reader seems happy with sentences of 15 to 20 words, but this is only a rough guide.

Moreover, the number of words alone doesn't determine the level of understanding. This will depend also on how complex the sentence is. In Exercise 7.2 we noted that lengthy abstract noun phrases (nominalisations) are difficult to process because they compress a number of ideas into few words. If we replace them with verbs, the sentence will probably be longer, but more comprehensible.

The passive is another grammatical feature we looked at in Exercise 7.2 which can obscure meaning. Should you use it, and if so, when? You can use the passive to emphasise an action, irrespective of who carried it out if the action is clearly more important than who did it. For example, a newspaper reporter at the scene of an accident might well write:

The injured woman was taken away in an ambulance,

because she is more interested in reporting the events at the scene. A close friend or relative of the injured woman, however, would probably look at it differently. They might say:

They took her to hospital in the ambulance.

In scientific and academic writing we use the passive because we are not usually interested in who carried out the activity:

Water was mixed with mud and heated.

This style of writing is supposed to denote academic rigour, because it appears to be impersonal and objective. For example:

It is submitted that . . .
It is argued that . . .

is preferred to:

I think that . . .
I feel that . . .

Bear in mind that the passive puts distance between you and the recipient of your message. Use it sparingly.

Another very confusing feature is the overuse of negative forms. For example:

Members of the jury, is it not improbable that in the circumstances he would not have been unable to avoid the attack?

As members of the jury are we supposed to think that he could or could not have avoided the attack? It will take us some time to decide, by which time the advocate will have gone on to the next point, or beyond.

The sentence is not particularly long, but there are five items in it which convey negative meaning: *not, im-, not, un-, avoid*. The reader has to decipher which negatives cancel each other out. Furthermore, when you compose something as complicated as this, how can you know you are expressing the meaning you want to express? Make sure your sentences make sense.

Other difficult sentences to grasp on a first reading are those with a number of subordinate clauses. Subordinate clauses are 'sentences within sentences' and consequently make heavy demands on the reader's memory. For example:

Mr Hughes, who is a well-known local solicitor, having been stopped by the police on his way back from lunch at a nearby pub where he had had some drinks with a few colleagues, will have to go to court because of the positive breath test and could lose his licence.

Far too much information is packed into this one sentence, and it is hard to keep track of the sequence of events. It doesn't help that the subject, *Mr Hughes*, is separated from its main verb *will have to* by several other ideas.

There are seven separate ideas in this sentence. You could write each of them as a separate sentence, but your writing would look childish. You don't need to avoid subordinate clauses altogether, but the more you put into your sentence, the harder it will become to understand it. Why not start from scratch with this one and sort out the order of events?

If you do this, you will probably find you don't need to put each idea into a separate sentence. Most readers are capable of taking in more than one idea for each sentence. You have to use your judgment about whether you are overloading them or not.

Just as we have to take care about expressing different ideas within sentences, so we have to make sure our sentences are linked in some way. Each sentence, either in its sense, or by the use of linking words, should follow logically from the sentence which preceded it. What is the problem with these two sentences?

Vicky failed her degree. She did very well in Trusts.

They seem to be contradictory because they are not linked in a way which shows the desired relationship between the two ideas. We can rewrite them to show that there is a logical relationship between the two ideas:

Vicky failed her degree, although she did very well in Trusts.

Exercise 7.14 Sense and nonsense

1. *Rewrite the text below, making sure the sentences follow logically from each other. You don't have to use the same number of sentences.*

   Usually a litigant will only go to court if advised that she has an arguable case. Do their lawyers read the same law? Why are people prepared to go to court when statistically they only have a 50% chance of success? What is it about legal disputes which means that both parties can be certain enough of the truth of their claim and the legal merits of their case to go to court? In any legal argument that gets to court someone wins and someone loses.[1]

2. *Choose a partner and compare versions:*
   (a) *Does your new version make sense? If so, why? If not, why not?*
   (b) *What have you learnt from this exercise which you will use in your own writing?*
   (c) *Record an action plan in your learning diary.*
   (d) *Remember to put your plan into action the next time you write anything that will be read by others.*

1   Adapted from J Holland and J Webb *Learning Legal Rules*, Blackstone, London 1993, p 78.

Paragraphing

Paragraphing is the skill of constructing documents whose contents flow in a logical order. Each paragraph should deal with one main topic, which is then developed in the rest of the paragraph. You probably all know this, but do you do it?

The rules for linking paragraphs are the same as for sentences. To give your text a coherent structure, each paragraph should be linked to the previous and the following paragraphs.

Some people write a series of paragraphs of just one sentence.

This is a sign of poor writing.

This is because the writing seems disjointed.

The reader has to struggle to make connections.

It looks simplistic.

Get the picture?

However, long, unbroken blocks of print which contain a large amount of information also put a strain on our information processing abilities. We must struggle to extract and make connections between pieces of information.

Above we advised you to vary the length of your sentences. Do the same with your paragraphs. A paragraph consisting of one sentence is therefore perfectly acceptable once in a while, but not as a general habit.

Every paragraph has a topic sentence, usually at or near the beginning. This sentence encapsulates the main point of the paragraph. As long as you have planned your content carefully you should not find it difficult to decide what goes into the topic sentence of each paragraph. What is more difficult is to relate the other sentences in the paragraph to the topic sentence and to each other.[1]

1   If you find paragraphing difficult, try the exercise on paragraph analysis in C Maughan & M Maughan 'Legal Writing' in P A Jones *Lawyers' Skills*, Blackstone, London 1994, pp 59–63.

Exercise 7.15   Link-hunting

Read this text carefully and answer the questions that follow. Then compare your answers with others from your group.

THE THRILL OF THE MANHUNT

The abolition of hunting is, quite literally, a Utopian ideal. The inhabitants of Sir Thomas More's island rejected the thrill of the chase 'as a thing unworthy to be used of free men'.

Nearly 500 years on, John McFall MP hopes that Parliament will follow their example by giving a second reading to his Wild Mammals (Protection) Bill. His opponents, predictably enough, have accused him of hypocrisy. Why ban fox-hunting but allow shooting and fishing? Why legislate to 'protect wild mammals from certain cruel acts including being taken, killed or injured by the use of dogs' while doing nothing about the cruelty of other predators? It is 'disgraceful', one pro-hunting man thundered this week, that the RSPCA hasn't lifted a finger to campaign on behalf of wild birds, which are 'lured to bird tables with peanuts, then caught by domestic cats and taken half-alive to be tortured'.

Fair enough. Our attitudes to animals are indeed inconsistent. People who seethe with indignation at the sight of a fur coat made from farmed mink will happily swagger about town in leather jackets. Many self-styled 'vegetarians' are quite willing to gorge themselves on smoked salmon. Even vegans may be on shaky ground: after watching David Attenborough's Secret Life of Plants, can anyone be sure that cabbages and carrots have no feelings? In a real Utopia, we should all eat nothing but salt – except that, as G K Chesterton once predicted, some smart aleck would then ask 'why should salt suffer?'

Hunters should, however, think twice before making too much of these inconsistencies, lest they be expected to follow through the logic of their own position. If, as they say, it is wrong for Parliament to outlaw blood sports, why don't they demand the repeal of laws against bear-baiting and otter-hunting? And why hasn't the British Field Sports Society reintroduced the noble art of pig-sticking – which is a far more equal battle of wits, setting a lone hunter against a large and dangerous hog?

Why, come to that, should the nanny state prevent us indulging in the ancient and once popular pastime of cock-fighting? When I proposed this the other day to a hunting zealot of my acquaintance, she squealed with outrage: 'Oh no, it's cruel!'

Quite so. The solution, I suggest, is to find humane – or rather human – alternatives. Near where I live in East Anglia there is a pack of bloodhounds which pursues runners across the fields every weekend, to the great enjoyment of all concerned. Sub-aqua enthusiasts could be recruited to swim around Scottish lochs, occasionally rising to the bait of a dry-fly. Viscount Whitelaw showed what could be done on the grouse-moors when, a few years ago, he fired a volley of shotgun pellets into the backside of Sir Joseph Nickerson; Sir Joseph seemed none the worse for the ordeal.

And here's an even better idea: why doesn't some animal-lover invent a 'sport' in which two men climb into a ring and punch each other to a pulp? It might lack the gory excitement of the old cock-fights and dog-fights, but at least no one would try to ban it.[1]

1. (a) *Identify the topic sentence in each paragraph.*
    (b) *Taking each paragraph in turn, identify the words and phrases which:*
         (i)   *link sentences within paragraphs, and*
         (ii) *link paragraphs.*
         For example: and, or, but, however, moreover, on the other hand, therefore, although.
    (c) *Are there any sentences which are not linked by such words or phrases? If so, how are they linked?*
2. *Now try this exercise, with a partner, on some of your own writing.*
    (a) *Separately, look at two or three paragraphs you have written.*
    (b) *Then compare your results.*
    (c) *Do you agree on the topic sentence? What linking devices are used? Do they help clarify or obscure the meaning?*
    (d) *Now do the same with two or three paragraphs written by your partner.*

It is of course possible that you will disagree with your partner about which sentence is the topic sentence. Your interpretation of a paragraph may differ from the one the writer intended. The lesson to be learned here is that there is more likely to be agreement on the meaning when the text is written clearly and coherently. It is much more difficult to agree where the writer's meaning is obscure.

So far in this chapter we have considered a number of characteristics of writing. It may be useful now to formulate a 'rule' for *SAYING WHAT YOU MEAN TO SAY*. We call ours the *THREE Cs*:

       BE   –   CLEAR
              –   CONCISE
              –   CORRECT

This involves:
● WRITING COMPLETE SENTENCES, BUT
● AVOIDING OVER-LONG AND COMPLEX SENTENCES;
● USING FREQUENTLY USED WORDS AND PHRASES INSTEAD OF INFREQUENTLY USED ONES;
● CUTTING OUT REDUNDANT WORDS AND PHRASES;
● AVOIDING CLUMSY AND INELEGANT WORDS AND PHRASES;
● NOT USING THE LEGAL REGISTER UNLESS
   (a)   there is no alternative, and
   (b)   the reader will understand it;
● MAKING SURE YOU KNOW WHAT YOUR WORDS MEAN;
● USING ACCEPTED GRAMMATICAL FORMS;
● USING CORRECT SYNTAX;
● USING APPROPRIATE PUNCTUATION;
● SPELLING CORRECTLY;
● STRUCTURING PARAGRAPHS WITH TOPIC SENTENCES;
● STRUCTURING PARAGRAPHS WITH LINKING DEVICES.

Now, in the next exercise, try applying these guidelines to some poor writing.

1   Taken from the *Guardian*, 1 March 1995. The author is Francis Wheen.

Exercise 7.16   Take out the rubbish

In small groups:
1. *Note down what is wrong with the following texts. Give reasons for your answers.*
2. *Then rewrite each text so that it is clear, concise and correct.*

   (a)   The defendant denied that she was in breach of contract as alleged by the plaintiff.
   (b)   It is of supreme and paramount importance to our education pro-gramme that classes be kept at minimum levels.
   (c)   Prior to collecting your vehicle please ensure you pay for your park-ing at the automatic machines located at the administration building which is situated at the exit.

(d) We look forward to meeting with you next week. In the meantime do not hesitate to contact Ms Bloggs or myself at any time should you have any specific queries.

(e) Whenever there is a body laying in front of his jurisdiction, the coroner must be informed.

(f) I have given implicit instructions to my staff to keep noise to an absolute minimum due to the close proximity of residential properties.

(g) A recent report complained that the Crown Prosecution Service was the victim of a great deal of unwarranted criticism. Whenever there is a cock-up they always get the blame.

(h) The jury also provide a freshness to our system of justice because they are unbiased and therefore their mind is open and enables them to be objectionable.

(i) The conclusion which has been reached by my client is that if there is a continuation of your insistence on this position, the termination of the contract will be taken into serious consideration by her.[1]

(j) It would appear that such critical allegations are not without substance as no satisfactory answers regarding queries as to the purpose of consideration. Any proposed suggestions can be dispelled, either by the existence of legal rules relative to the other essential contract elements or by the accepted definition and nature of consideration itself. (Best of luck with this one!)

(k) We are embarking on measures to resolve the issue at the earliest opportunity.

(l) He is a distinguished academic and an imminent politician.

(m) There was a discussion yesterday on the worrying of sheep by dogs in the minister's room.

(n) Mr Maplethorpe, a magistrate, who was well-known for the severity of his views on drunk driving and who made it a point of principle to give the maximum sentence for such offences, particularly when faced with re-offenders, being absent from the meeting that day, a very unusual occurrence for him, was elected chairman of the bench.

(o) The defendant was arrested for fornicating under a little-used state statute.[2]

(p) The remedies for innocent misrepresentation are rescission and damages, awarded at the courts discretion.

---

1 Our thanks to Richard Wydick for this one, which 'clanks along like a rusty tank': op cit, p 745.
2 Ibid, p 747.

Self-edit your writing

Self-editing helps you to develop the skill of looking at what you have written through the eyes of your reader. Getting into the habit of self-editing is a matter of attitude. It can be frustrating and time-consuming to have to rewrite sections of your draft, but the more strict you are with yourself about this, the faster you will achieve artistry.

You may have learned from doing these exercises that it helps to read a draft aloud to yourself, or preferably, to someone else. Better still, ask them to read it aloud to you. This is probably the most revealing strategy to use, because you will hear all your mistakes read out and you will know immediately whether the content is clear and logical. This can be very embarrassing, but at the same time illuminating and instructive.

By now you should be able to draft your own self-editing checklist. This should contain questions you must ask yourself about your text after you have composed one. Try to answer the questions honestly.

Exercise 7.17   Self-editing

1. *In pairs, draft a self-editing checklist. Be clear, concise, correct.*
2. *Compare your list with ours at the end of this chapter. If you think it necessary, revise your list.*
3. *Try your list out on your next piece of writing. Is it adequate? If not, make any necessary changes.*

Writing letters

There is certain technical information you need to know before you begin to practise drafting legal letters.

Writing to clients: client care[1]

Practice Rule 15 aims to improve communications between solicitors and their clients. It imposes obligations on solicitors to give their clients certain basic information early on in the relationship and throughout the case:

(1)   Every principal in private practice shall operate a complaints handling procedure which shall, inter alia, ensure that clients are informed whom to approach in the event of any problem with the service provided.

(2)   Every solicitor in private practice, shall, unless it is inappropriate in the circumstances:
    (a)   ensure that clients know the name and status of the person responsible for the day-to-day conduct of the matter and the principal responsible for its overall supervision;
    (b)   ensure that clients know whom to approach in the event of any problem with the service provided; and,
    (c)   ensure that clients are at all relevant times given any appropriate information as to the issues raised and the progress of the matter.

Under the Law Society's revised Written Professional Standards (1991) a client must know at the time of instructing a solicitor what the solicitor is going to charge for her services. As the case progresses, the client must be kept informed about costs.

---

1   See The Law Society *Client Care: A Guide For Solicitors,* 1991.

Writing to other people

(A)   THE LETTER BEFORE ACTION

This is a letter which threatens to begin legal proceedings against the other side. It should state the facts of your client's case, the cause of action she wants to pursue, and the remedy she is seeking. Look at the following example:

Mr J Webb
Jules's Cafe
37 Doyle St
London W33 4PL   6 March 1995

Dear Mr Webb,

Work Carried out by CM Plumbing

We have been instructed by CM Plumbing to recover £2,565.25 from you for work they carried out at your premises in September 1994. You were sent an invoice on 25 October 1994 which asked for payment in full within 14 days.

Our clients have sent you four reminders asking for this sum to be paid, but to date you have not paid anything.

Our clients will not accept any further delay and have instructed us to begin proceedings in the County Court if payment in full does not reach this office by 13 March.

We advise you to consult your solicitor if you are unsure of your legal position.

Yours sincerely,

. . . .

(B)   THE REPLY TO A LETTER BEFORE ACTION

Imagine Mr Webb consults you and engages you as his solicitor. How are you going to reply to this letter? You will need to consider your response very carefully. You may want to deny the allegations or seek further details. You might want to make a counterclaim. If so, you should state the facts, cause of action and remedy, as in a letter before action.

If a matter goes to court, any letters before action or replies will form part of the bundle of documents put before the court. Careful and accurate drafting is therefore essential.

Exercise 7.18   Something wrong with the plumbing?

In small groups:
(a)   *Draft a reply to the letter before action. Assume Mr Webb wants to counterclaim because the work was not properly completed. Invent any necessary details.*
(b)   *While composing, don't forget to use any diary entries, action plans and your self-editing checklist.*
(c)   *Exchange drafts with another group and compare. Is there anything you would do differently next time?*

You will of course write lots of different kinds of letters. Some will seek information, others will provide information, negotiate or set out the terms of a settlement. Negotiations towards the sale or purchase of land, for example, should be headed *SUBJECT TO CONTRACT*.

WITHOUT PREJUDICE at the top of the letter allows parties to negotiate freely without the risk of damaging their case. If negotiations subsequently fail and the case goes to court, no 'without prejudice' correspondence will be included in the bundle of documents for court.

Exercise 7.19   Joyless in the Maldini

You have been instructed by Margaret Foster, who came to ask your advice about a possible claim against a tour operator. Ms Foster told you she booked a package holiday for her family with Joyful Tours Ltd in April 1994. The holiday was for two weeks in the Maldini islands, from 14 July to 28 July 1994. The hotel was described as follows:

> All 60 rooms are air-conditioned and comfortably furnished. Each has a mini fridge-bar, shower and wc. All rooms have a verandah opening on to the beach. There is an air-conditioned restaurant, a bar and a club house. There is a wide range of water sports, including scuba diving. Regular evening entertainment includes live bands. For a change of scene a ferry service operates to the neighbouring island of Voss.

The air-conditioning in the Fosters' hotel rooms did not work. The children's verandah opened on to a noisy building site, with no sea in sight. The bar was closed for nine nights of their stay. Bob, Margaret's son, particularly wanted to learn to scuba dive, but was told this facility was not available. No other water sports were offered either. There was only one disco held in the club house, and not one live band appeared during their stay. Desperately searching for a change of scene on Voss, they found there were no ferries operating.

Margaret complained several times to the Joyful Tours representative in the hotel, but nothing was done. The family came home miserable and depressed. One of Joyful Tour's booking conditions states:

> . . . In the unlikely event that matters cannot be resolved to your satisfaction in the resort, details of your complaint should be notified in writing to our Customer Relations Department at our Manchester Head Office within 28 days of returning from the resort. We will not accept liability in respect of claims which we receive after that date.

Margaret wrote to Joyful Tours to complain, but not until 19 September 1994.

In pairs:
(a)   *Carry out the necessary research. Mind map or flow chart the information you think you need to give Ms Foster.*
(b)   *Draft a letter to Ms Foster, confirming her instructions and explaining the legal position.*
(c)   *Draft a letter to Joyful Tours' insurers.*
(d)   *Give your letters to your tutor.*

Good writing makes sense

We hope we have made it clear in this chapter that you should never under-estimate the importance of good writing. Because you have been writing for so long as part of your education, it is easy to assume you are good at it, or at least that your skills are adequate. We have seen many examples in this chapter of poor writing composed by ostensibly well-educated people who must have been writing for years.

We hope your study of this chapter has provided you with some insight into how language works. In our experience, students frequently recognise that they are poor writers, but cannot pinpoint their weaknesses. We think that it helps to identify weaknesses and put them right when you have some idea of the functions of grammar and punctuation.

We have tried to dispel some of the popular misconceptions about language. That punctuation is part of your grammar, for example, may have come as a surprise to some of you. It is easy to think that punctuation errors are unimportant, whereas they are necessary and useful markers of meaning.

Similarly, it may have surprised some of you that you learn the fundamentals of grammar without being formally taught. Or that writing which makes the reader struggle to get the meaning denotes ineptitude or muddled thinking rather than elegance and sophistication. Remember too that if you have a problem with writing, it may not be because of linguistic expression alone. It may be that you have not thought through clearly in advance what it is you want to say.

Exercise 7.20   Concepts

In this chapter we have discussed a number of concepts. We list the main ones below. The procedure for learning these concepts is as follows.

1. *Divide into pairs.*
2. *Each pair is to*
   (a) *define each concept, noting the page on which it is defined and discussed, and*
   (b) *make sure that both members of the pair understand the meaning of each concept.*
3. *Combine into groups of four. Compare the answers of the two pairs. If there is disagreement, look up the concept and clarify it until all agree on the definition and understand it.*

register	*dialect*
syntax	*grammar*
accent	*malapropism*
sentence	*topic sentence*
officialese	*jargon*
standard English	*correctness*

Exercise 7.21   More rubbish

In small groups:
1. *Note down what is wrong with the letter below. Give reasons for your answers.*

221

2. *Rewrite the letter. (You should be able to infer the context).*
3. *Exchange redrafts with another group.*
4. *Mark their redraft. Underline or highlight good and bad points, and give a mark out of 10.*
5. *Return the redraft to the group and give constructive oral feedback.*
6. *Note down anything you will do differently next time.*

Fleeceham & Bankitt
Solicitors
Blur Buildings
Narrow Street
Bristol BS45 5OJ

6 March 1994

Dear Sirs,

Re: Gary Francis Dobbs

We are in receipt of your communication dated 28 February 1994, for which we are grateful. As is doubtless known to yourselves, the discussions between myself and the aforementioned client attract Legal Professional Privilege which it is incumbent on the client to waive, rather than ourselves.

In order to facilitate your enquiries, we have taken it upon ourselves to take matters further by re-establishing contact with Mr Dobbs, at present resident in Grabham remand centre. Mr Dobbs expressed to us his lack of opposition to such waiver of Privilege, the effect of which being that we are enabled to bring the content of such Privileged information to your attention.

My initial personal contact with this client took effect at 7.57 pm precisely, in a cell at Grasston Police Station. During this brief interlude between interviews Mr Dobbs gave me the impression, in somewhat garbled dialect, that he was not a well man. I apprised him of the forthcoming situation of the interview and reassured him that my presence there was assured. Mr Dobbs did not make any admissions at this premature stage. Nor did he appear, to my surprise, unduly becalmed by my assurance of accompaniment at the interview.

Mr Dobbs continued to seem somewhat disfunctional throughout DC Binks's postulations, and rather lacked self-composure in my view, in consideration of the fact that the posture on the part of the Police Officers did not convey an impression of undue pressure or threatening aspect.

During the interval, we had time for a little chat. Mr Dobbs told me that he had indeed taken the Car and driven it for some distance, as alleged by the Police Officers. I must say at this point, however, that comprehension of Mr Dobbs's strange speech patterns was not automatic. Probing for understanding did not appear to be received with equanimity on his part, for some reason I know not what of.

I advised him in plain and simple English to come clean with me on the Aggravated Vehicle Taking business. The great proportion of my time was taken up in attempting at considerable length and clarity to put across the merits as regards sentencing of admitting the aggravated facts in issue if indeed facts they be. If not, however, I explained at great length, he should be forearmed to treat the stipulations and ramifications of the Officers with considerable disdain in pursuit of denial.

What I said to him I fear made little sense. He was in a condition of extreme agitation and dejected. His replies to my exhortations were convoluted and to some extent non-existent. Thus I cannot report them to you with any precision or intelligibility.

I wish to inform you that should you require any further assistance from myself, from the 15th until the 22nd of March I shall be attendent and presenting a Paper at a symposium in Seattle, USA, the subject of which is delineated as 'Solicitor–Client Discourse: Semantic and Lexical Variables in Police Station Narratives'. I shall therefore unfortunately be unable to attend upon any needful requirements of yourselves.

Yours faithfully,

. . . .

Review question

Discuss the following quotation:

(T)here are no important propositions that cannot be stated in plain language . . . The writer who seeks to be intelligible needs to be right; he must be challenged if his argument leads to an erroneous conclusion and especially if it leads to a wrong action. But he can safely dismiss the charge that he has made the subject too easy. The truth is not difficult. Complexity and obscurity have professional value – they are the academic equivalents of apprenticeship rules in the building trades. They exclude the outsiders, keep down the competition, preserve the image of a privileged or priestly class. The man who makes things clear is a scab. He is criticised less for his clarity than for his treachery.[1]

1   J K Galbraith *Writing, Typing & Economics*, Atlantic, 1978, p 105.

Learning points

(a)   Select an assignment that you are planning to write in the next few weeks.
(b)   What changes will you make to your approach, and why?

Further reading

Sir Ernest Gowers *The Complete Plain Words*, Penguin, London 1986.

Lars Andersson & Peter Trudgill *Bad Language*, Penguin, London 1990.

C Maughan & M Maughan 'Legal Writing' in P Jones *Lawyers' Skills*, Blackstone, London 1994, pp 51–78.

Margot Costanzo *Legal Writing*, Cavendish, London 1993.

H Brayne & R Grimes *Professional Skills for Lawyers: A Student's Guide*, Butterworths, London 1994, pp 19–84.

D Freeborn, P French & D Langford *Varieties of English: An Introduction to the Study of Language*, Macmillan, Basingstoke 1989.

Self-editing checklist for writing

Purpose:

What is the purpose of this communication? . . . .
Have I adapted style and content to suit the reader's needs? . . . .
Have I dealt with all the issues? . . . .
Have I answered all the questions raised? . . . .
Have I gone into enough/too much depth? . . . .
Have I repeated myself unnecessarily? . . . .

Content:

Is all the information accurate? . . . .
Is all of it relevant? . . . .

Style:

Is the style too formal/informal? . . . .
Will my tone produce the desired response? . . . .
Is it friendly, courteous, helpful, frank? . . . .
Is it peremptory, hostile, rude? . . . .

Layout:

Is the layout appropriate for the purpose and content? . . . .
Is it set out in manageable blocks? . . . .

Structure:

Are the sentences short enough? . . . .
Does the order of sentences and paragraphs make sense? . . . .
Does each paragraph contain just one main idea? . . . .
Is there a link between each paragraph and the next? . . . .
Are there links between sentences in each paragraph? . . . .

Language:

Have I used plain language – clear, concise, and
   correct language that the reader can easily understand? . . . .
Have I omitted words and phrases which are
(a)   infrequently used,
(b)   inelegant, ...
(c)   redundant, ...
(d)   unnecessarily technical, ...
(e)   unnecessarily abstract, ...
(f)   verbose? . . . .
Is the grammar appropriate for the purpose? . . . .
Are punctuation and spelling correct? . . . .

8 Manipulating language: drafting legal documents

The language of legal documents has unique features which are closely linked with its purposes. A legal draft is a correct and complete statement of a legal relationship, so legal drafters are much more concerned with making that statement comprehensive than comprehensible. A drafter wants to guard against the possibility of litigation arising from her draft more than she wants it to be elegantly written and easily understood. The extent to which the often complex requirements of the draft can be rendered in elegant, easily understood English is the measure of the drafter's artistry.

Objectives

To:
- Examine the purposes of legal document drafting.
- Analyse the linguistic, organisational and contextual features of legal language.
- Determine what is essential for precision and clarity, and discard what is not.
- Establish a general set of principles for drafting in plain English.
- Apply these principles when redrafting and drafting documents.

Legal documents are precision instruments

In Chapter 7 we argued that clarity and precision are at the heart of artistry in writing. In legal document drafting, however, these two elements are apparently in conflict. Why is this so? To answer this question we must look at the functions of drafting.

Legal language does not only have a communicative function. In both its written and oral forms, it is the primary *tool* of the legal professional. Unlike physicians who have instruments and procedures, engineers who have blueprints, computers and processes, and scientists who have laboratories, lawyers have only legal language. In fact, lawyers call their legal documents 'instruments'. True, all professions have a body of thought and theory that is embodied in language, but for lawyers there is only *one* way of accessing this knowledge – through legal language.[1]

Let's have a look at one of these 'instruments'.

1   V Charrow, J A Crandall, R Charrow 'Characteristics and Functions of Legal Language' in
    R Kittredge & J Lehrberger (eds) *Sublanguage: Studies of Language in Restricted Semantic
    Domains*, De Gruyter, Berlin 1982, p 181.

Exercise 8.1   Runaway trolleys

Read the following text and answer the questions:

The Litter (Northern Ireland) Order 1994 Schedule 1: Abandoned Shopping and Luggage Trolleys

1. (1)   Subject to sub-paragraph (2), this Schedule applies where any shopping or luggage trolley is found by an authorised officer on any land in the open air and appears to him to be abandoned.

   (2)   This Schedule does not apply in relation to a shopping or luggage trolley found on the following descriptions of land, that is to say –

   (a)   land in which the owner of the trolley has an estate;

   (b)   where an off-street parking place affords facilities to the customers of shops for leaving there shopping trolleys used by them, land on which those facilities are afforded;

   (c)   where any other place designated by the district council for the purposes of this Schedule affords like facilities, land on which those facilities are afforded; and

   (d)   as respects luggage trolleys, land which is used for the purposes of its undertaking by a statutory undertaker.

Power to seize and remove trolleys

2. (1)   Where this Schedule applies in relation to a shopping or luggage trolley, the district council may, subject to sub-paragraph (2), –

   (a)   seize the trolley; and

   (b)   remove it to such place under its control as the council thinks fit.

   (2)   When a shopping or luggage trolley is found on any land appearing to the authorised officer to be occupied by any person, the trolley shall not be removed without the consent of that person, unless –

   (a)   the council has served on that person a notice stating that the council proposes to remove the trolley; and

   (b)   no notice objecting to its removal is served by that person on the council within the period of 14 days from the day on which the council served the notice of the proposed removal on him.

1. *Can you grasp the meaning on a first reading?*
2. *Why/why not?*
3. *Who is the text written for?*

4.   Who are the likely readers?
5.   What is the purpose of the document?

Nobody reads documents like this out of choice. We only read them if we have to. Their purpose is to provide a comprehensive and correct statement of the law. Legal drafters know that their creations will be scrutinised at length and in silence by legal experts who will often be intent on finding some loophole or ambiguity which will advance their argument or their client's case. It is therefore vitally important to get the law right.

There are those who take the view that any thought or idea can be expressed in an immediately comprehensible way. We don't agree. Haven't you ever had a thought which you couldn't put easily into words? Sometimes our thoughts are too sophisticated to be rendered by the language we have at our disposal. Legal drafters often find themselves in this position and consequently have to stretch, twist and curl the language to embrace all possible meanings and interpretations which can be ascribed to their documents. Headline writers do this to create ambiguity:

STIFF OPPOSITION EXPECTED TO CASKETLESS FUNERAL PLAN
DRUNK GETS NINE MONTHS IN VIOLIN CASE
QUEEN MARY HAVING BOTTOM SCRAPED
COLUMNIST GETS UROLOGIST IN TROUBLE WITH HIS PEERS
IRAQI HEAD SEEKS ARMS[1]

Presumably the headline writers knew which meaning of *stiff, violin case, bottom, peers* and *head* they had in mind. This is precisely the kind of ambiguity that legal drafters need to avoid. How are they to do this?

To be so precise as to avoid ambiguity, whilst at the same time covering every foreseeable eventuality is extremely difficult. This is why many drafters stick to boilerplate.[2] It is certain and therefore safe. They don't want to take the risk of litigation which could arise if in the name of clarity, brevity and elegance they experiment with untested language.

This is the key issue in this chapter. Up to this point we have argued that getting your message across to your recipient quickly and easily is the primary purpose of speech and writing. We have recommended respect for the needs and abilities of your audience and the use of plain English in writing. In drafting, we have to make sure that what we say is comprehensive and correct in law and fact, before considering the likely needs of the reader. In fact, we have to assume that our readers are capable of understanding what we write, because we are not going to alter it to make it more accessible.

Naturally, we believe you should aim for clarity as well. Mastering the techniques of precision will make you technically competent, but add clarity and you will be developing your artistry. You can be innovative with language without having to experiment with untried forms.

So you should still have your reader in mind. An 'authorised officer' or 'statutory undertaker' may need to read the trolley regulations. She may not have time to consult a lawyer or indeed may not have access to one.

1   Taken from S Pinker *The Language Instinct: The New Science of Language and Mind*, Allen Lane, London 1994, p 79.
2   The language of formbooks. See Charrow, Crandall & Charrow, op cit, p 178.

Exercise 8.2   Is the drafter off her trolley?

1. *Read the text of 8.1 again and paraphrase it. Note down how long this process took.*
2. *In small groups, discuss:*
    (a)   Which features aid understanding and which do not? Give reasons. In particular, consider:
        (i)   content;
        (ii)   layout;
        (iii) syntax;
        (iv)   sentence length and complexity;
        (v)   punctuation;
        (vi)   archaic words and phrases;
        (vii) superfluous words and phrases.
    (b)   Identify the words and phrases which have special legal meanings. Define them.
    (c)   Which of these have different meanings in standard English? Define them.
    (d)   How would a lay person find out a specific legal meaning if for some reason they couldn't consult a lawyer?
    (e)   Agree definitions of 'luggage trolley' and 'shopping trolley'. Draft your definitions in the style of the Schedule.
    (f)   Compare your draft with the original; s 5 of the Schedule.
    (g)   In conclusion, do you think a lay reader will grasp the meaning of these provisions without having to consult a lawyer?

Legal documents and the three Cs

Imagine a council employee wants to deal with a complaint from a resident who keeps finding empty shopping trolleys in his garden. How easily will she find her way round this document? In comparison with many older statutory instruments, this one is a model of clarity. There is plenty of punctuation which breaks up sentences into manageable blocks and helps with meaning. No block of print is longer than three lines, and generally, each section and sub-section deals with only one idea. The word order follows the patterns of standard English with one or two exceptions: s 1(2)(d), for example. It would be more usual to say

> . . . land which is used by a statutory undertaker for the purposes of its undertaking.

Nevertheless, some parts of the document are long-winded. For example:

1(2)(d):	. . . which is used *for the purposes of* its undertaking . . .	Won't *for* do?
1(2):	. . . in relation to . . .	Won't *to* do?
and	. . . that is to say –	Is this necessary?

A bit of tinkering in these examples will reduce redundant words and phrases.

However, we have to think a little harder before we abandon the cumbersome phrase at the end of the following section:

> 1(2)(c) where any other place designated by the district council for the purposes of this Schedule affords like facilities, *land on which those facilities are afforded*;

A more elegant rendering produces:

> any other land designated by the district council which affords like facilities;

The ambiguity here makes it clear that the cumbersome phrase is not superfluous. Using *which* or *who* will bring elegance to writing, but these words can be dangerous for legal drafters. It must be quite clear which preceding item these words refer back to. This is why legal drafters have avoided the usual ways of linking an item either to what follows or what has gone before. Legal documents therefore seem to be unnecessarily repetitious, and hard to read as a result.

An unfortunate by-product of this concern for precise reference is a host of ugly words and phrases which have come to characterise boilerplate: *aforesaid, hereinbefore, the said facilities*, for example. These allow the drafter to avoid ambiguities which could arise from using ordinary English linking words like *he, she, it, them, their, this, that, which, who*, etc. However, these archaic usages have become so entrenched in the legal register that lawyers use them in situations where no ambiguity would arise. For example:

> By a written contract dated . . . . . . between you and the Defendants, you agreed to undertake repairs and redecoration work at the Defendant's premises known as . . . . . . , for a total cost of £ . . . . . .
>
> It was an express term of the said contract that you would choose appropriate decorations for the said hotel, and that you would guarantee the quality thereof, . . .[1]

Couldn't we use '*this* contract', '*this* hotel', '*their* quality'?

Or would the gravitas of the law be irredeemably shaken by the use of these ordinary words? We shall return to this point shortly.

Now have a look at s 1(2)(b):

> where an off-street parking place affords facilities to the customers of shops for *leaving there shopping trolleys used by them*, . . .

On first reading you are tempted to think the drafter has mistaken *there* for *their* – until you read on. *Used by them* is ghastly. Can't we rewrite the part in italics 'leaving their shopping trolleys there'?

We can't, can we? We should be grateful that modern drafting is beginning to abandon forms like *by the said customers* and use *by them* instead where it is quite clear who is referred to. The plain English campaign is clearly making its mark!

There are other examples in this text. In s 2(2)(b) we have *that person* and *by him* rather than *the said person* and *by the said person*, or *by that person*. In s 1(2)(c) the drafter uses *like facilities* instead of repeating the whole phrase

> to the customers of shops for leaving there shopping trolleys used by them.

230

Is *like* sufficiently safe? Why didn't she use *such*, a very common word in such writing? Do they mean the same?

As respects in s 1(2)(d) is a usage we haven't come across before. It seems to replace the officialese *in respect of* but does not improve on it.

Let's turn now to a sub-section that is hard to grasp. In s 2(2)(b) the drafter crams a number of ideas into one sentence. No wonder the sentence lacks clarity. How many ideas can you list in this sentence? We counted at least four: the trolley 'shall not be removed unless' –

1   that person has not served a notice on the council;
2   this notice objects to removal;
3   this notice must be served within 14 days;
4   from the date the council served its removal notice on that person.

Not surprisingly, the normal rules of English syntax cannot cope. The rules have to be bent and twisted, and the reader has to study the text carefully to sort out the grammatical relationships which give the clues to meaning.

Interestingly, Latin would have coped much better with s 2(2)(b). Meaning in Latin is determined not by the word order, as in English, but by word endings. Deciphering long sentences was therefore not difficult. The noun and case forms of Latin showed quickly and concisely the internal relationships of ideas in a sentence. An idea which might need eleven words in English could be expressed in five. For example:

de minimis non curat lex: the law does not concern itself with things
                               of little importance

Many legal documents used to be written in Latin, where it is possible to incorporate a large number of ideas into one sentence. To do the same in English needs far more words. Perhaps it is the old lawyers' love of Latin which has left us the legacy of interminable legal sentences which only an expert can understand, and then with difficulty.

Turning now to the vocabulary of these regulations, you won't have found any archaisms. Nevertheless, there are words and phrases with technical meanings which a lay person may not have come across. For example:

estate;
land;
authorised officer;
statutory undertaker;
under its control;
thinks fit.

Seize is an interesting, metaphorical usage. It doesn't sound like legalese. Rather, it conjures up an image of an authorised officer grabbing hold of a trolley, shouting 'come here, you . . .' Do you think the drafter should have used the more neutral *take possession of*?

Reading s 1(2)(d), a lay reader may be forgiven for missing the connection between luggage trolleys and funeral parlours. As far as we know, corpses are not transported in luggage trolleys!

Help is at hand in the interpretation section, which defines *statutory under-taker*. Moreover, our council employee will find herself described in the definition of *authorised officer*. The other terms in the list are not defined. Can she get the meaning from the everyday English definitions? If not, will a dictionary help?

Let's try this out with the word *estate*. The Oxford English Dictionary gives us thirteen meanings. Number 11 is the legal meaning:

> The interest which anyone has in lands, tenements, or any other effects; often with qualifying words or phrases as *an estate upon conditions, in fee, for life, of inheritance, tail from year to year, at will,* etc. *Real estate,* an interest in landed property; *Personal estate,* an interest in moveables . . .

Will a law dictionary explain this definition in terms comprehensible to the lay person?

> 'Estate' has two meanings. In its narrower meaning it denotes the fee simple of land and any of the various interests into which it could formerly be divided at law, whether for life, or for a term of years or otherwise: and, where there was an estate at law, there could be a corresponding estate in equity. In its wider meaning it denotes any property whatever and is divided into real and personal estate.[2]

To interpret these entries correctly you surely have to be familiar with the legal register.

Under its control: will the officer tie the trolley up to prevent it escaping? This phrase has a specific legal meaning which will probably elude anyone not well-versed in the discourse of law. The same is true of *think fit*.

We can't comment on how the information is organised in this document, because we have only quoted two sections of it. However, we can see that the information itself is not particularly complex. You probably paraphrased the content very quickly. It is therefore relatively easy to draft it in a manner that the reader finds comprehensible. Although you may have concluded that a lawyer will need to explain certain terms to a lay person, this shouldn't be too difficult a task.

Nevertheless, when the drafter tries to cover a number of ideas in one sentence, as in s 2(2)(b), it obscures the meaning. Do you remember Text 1 in Exercise 7.2? How could you forget it?

> Where particulars of a partnership are disclosed to the Executive Council the remuneration of the individual partner for superannuation purposes will be deemed to be such proportion of the total remuneration of such practitioners as the proportion of his share in partnership profits bears to the total proportion of the shares of such practitioner in those profits.

This text is so impenetrable that we weren't able to agree on the meaning. Normal English structure can't do justice to such complex subject matter. Let's look now at part of a Regulation which is not as immediately accessible as the trolley regulations.

1   This is an extract from a Third Party Notice, an example draft in S Blake *A Practical Approach to Legal Advice and Drafting*, Blackstone, London 1993, p 367. These archaic

forms are still quite common in pleadings.
2   J Saunders (ed) *Words and Phrases Legally Defined*, Vol 2, Butterworths, London 1989,
     pp 175–6.

Exercise 8.3   Unravelling the regs

Gerry is a family friend who comes to ask your advice. His father, George, is 87 years old and lives in a residential home for the elderly. Gerry is legally entitled to act for George in matters of social security.

Income support was paid to George from the date he entered the home (December 1992). At that time George's house was put on the market, but was not sold until July 1994. All but £4,000 of the proceeds of sale were paid to Gerry and his sister, Jane. This was to repay them:
(a)   for money they spent on looking after George and his house for several years until he entered the residential home,
(b)   for money they had spent renovating and decorating the house to get it ready for sale,
(c)   for legal fees and selling costs.
Therefore, only £4,000 was paid directly to George.

Gerry has received the following notification from the Social Security Adjudication Officer:

> The claimant is not entitled to Income Support from 14 July 1994. This is because he is treated as possessing capital which exceeds the prescribed amount of £8,000.

When Gerry phoned the social security office for an explanation, he was told that the Adjudication Officer considered that items under (a) and (b) were not proper deductions, but had been made solely to secure George's entitlement to income support. Gerry was referred to the following provisions:
–   Section 134 of the Social Security Contributions and Benefits Act 1992;
–   Regulations 45 and 51 of the Income Support (General) Regulations 1987.
Gerry started to read Regulation 51, but gave up after sub-section 2 and consulted you:

NOTIONAL CAPITAL
   51(1)   A claimant shall be treated as possessing capital of which he has deprived himself for the purpose of securing entitlement to income support or increasing the amount of that benefit except –
        (a)   where the capital is derived from a payment made in consequence of any personal injury and is placed on trust for the benefit of the claimant; or
        (b)   to the extent that the capital which he is treated as possessing is reduced in accordance with regulation 51A (diminishing notional capital rule).
   (2)   Except in the case of –
        (a)   a discretionary trust;
        (b)   a trust derived from a payment made in consequence of a personal injury; or

> (c)   any loan which would be obtainable if secured against cap-
>   ital disregarded under Schedule 10,
> any capital which would become available to the claimant upon
> application being made but which has not been acquired by him
> shall be treated as possessed by him but only from the date on
> which it could be expected to be acquired were an application
> made.[1]

Gerry wants you to tell him how the Adjudication Officer could have reached this decision.

In small groups:
(a)   *Paraphrase s 51(1) and (2), noting how long this process took you.*
(b)   *What features make this text more difficult to understand than the trolley regulations? Give reasons.*
(c)   *When you have done the research, draft a letter to Gerry, explaining the legal position.*
(d)   *Compare your draft with another group's draft and feed back.*
(e)   *Discuss the purposes of Exercises 8.1 to 8.3, and what you have learnt from the exercises about drafting.*

What has to be put down in words in Regulation 51 is extremely complex. To start with, you have to grasp the central notion: that the law treats you as having capital even though in reality you haven't! It is not easy to get your head round this apparently illogical proposition.

Your work on Chapter 7 and your analysis of the trolley regulations here will have enabled you to identify the linguistic features which impede understanding, so we don't propose to discuss them again here. The tortured sentence structure speaks for itself.

To add to the complexity, the reader may have to refer to other sources (regulation 51A, Schedule 10). After the further six sub-sections in s 51 which we haven't quoted, there is a list of words and phrases in which the reader is referred to various other pieces of legislation to find their definitions. To interpret the meaning, it is therefore necessary to refer to sources other than the provision itself.

Why have we asked you to analyse legislation in three exercises, when you are much more likely to be drafting contracts, wills and pleadings? Since we can't expect lay people to find their way round this legislation without expert help, it is vital that the experts understand it. Then they have to be able to explain its meaning to non-experts. How sure are you that your explanation to Gerry was completely accurate and comprehensive? If as a result of your investigations you concluded that Gerry could successfully appeal the Adjudication Officer's finding, would you suggest to him that he argues the appeal before the tribunal himself? Or will he need representation?

Working through these exercises should have made it clear that with subject matter as complicated as this and where it is necessary to cross-reference from a number of sources, drafting a version which makes sense (even to lawyers) will be impossible. Yet your client is going to expect that you can do this even if in many cases we would have to consolidate all the sources before we could attempt something intelligible.

Consolidation, of course, is a task for a higher authority. This brings us to our next point of discussion on the purpose of drafting.

1 Income Support (General) Regulations 1987.

Legal language is powerful stuff

It is axiomatic that ignorance of the law is no excuse. Yet the provisions we have quoted demonstrate that ignorance of the law ought to be a very good excuse. We are governed by regulations that may be inaccessible to those appointed to enforce them, as well as to all of us who are expected to obey them. For reasons we have discussed, the designers of these instruments are not concerned about the reader's level of understanding. Their creations put the law into action. If what you do is contrary to regulation A which must be read in conjunction with regulation B as amended by regulation C, you are guilty. Likewise, if you put your signature to a contractual document you may experience the full force of the Law (note capital L) if you don't keep to its terms.

> . . . because bureaucrats communicate with the rest of the world on unequal terms – because they possess the power – they do not have to listen to non-bureaucrats. Outsiders must deal with the bureaucracy on its own terms. Consequently, bureaucrats may forget how to organise their ideas, write, and speak like ordinary people. Sometimes, they may consciously use bureaucratese to exclude outsiders, or to enhance their own power by mystifying outsiders.
>
> Because of the power of the government over ordinary people, bureaucratic language (including the written variety) is effectively a prestige dialect. Even though many people dislike it, even ridicule it, many others consider it valuable, and worth emulating. The news media are quick to take up bureaucratic jargon and use it as their own, contributing to its spread and further enhancing its prestige.[1]

As Veda Charrow says, many bureaucrats are lawyers, who both interpret and perpetuate the legalese that gives life to the bureaucracy. But can we expect them to stop using this high status dialect? Learning to think like a lawyer takes years of training, and some years of experience to refine. However, if the examples on pages 232 and 234 represent how lawyers think, law schools should be very worried indeed. As American attorney Ronald Goldfarb puts it:

> Something very strange happens when human beings enter law school. At some point during their three years, students pick up the notion that in order to be a lawyer, one must learn to speak and write like a lawyer. No one actually tells law students this is a requirement to pass the Bar, but inevitably the message reaches them.
>
> Nothing is done in law school to cure the problem, in fact it is compounded. What students read in law school are law review articles, legal treatises and judicial opinions. In the most part this is a collection of turgid, overblown, pompous, technically incompetent prose.
>
> By the end of three years, students can barely get through a letter or a conversation without dropping a few 'notwithstandings', 'heretofores'

and 'arguendos'. Everything they have seen and heard for three years leads them to assume this lingo is expected of them.[2]

James D Gordon III quotes a lawyer's 'supernatural incantation' for the simple statement *I give you this orange*:

> Know all men by these presents that I hereby give, grant, bargain, sell, release, convey, transfer, and quitclaim all my right, title, interest, benefit, and use whatever in, of, and concerning this chattel, otherwise known as an orange, or citrus orantium, together with all the appurtenances thereto of skin, pulp, pip, rind, seeds, and juice, to have and to hold the said orange together with its skin, pulp, pip, rind, seeds, and juice for his own use and behoof, to himself and his heirs in fee simple forever, free from all liens, encumbrances, easements, limitations, restraints, or conditions whatsoever, any and all prior deeds, transfers or other documents whatsoever, now or anywhere made to the contrary notwithstanding, with full power to bite, cut, suck, or otherwise eat the said orange or to give away the same, with or without its skin, pulp, pip, rind, seeds, or juice.[3]

This may be humorous exaggeration, but the point is made. Using this dialect shows you are an expert. Expertise denotes power and prestige. By relinquishing their boilerplate lawyers reduce the gap between them and ordinary mortals.

We referred earlier to the gravitas of certain legal English. There are features of legal discourse and culture which are reminiscent of religious ritual. In a statement of claim, for example, the remedies the plaintiff seeks are listed in what is known as the 'prayer'.[4] When judges or magistrates enter the court room, we are ordered to 'all rise'. We half expect them to ask us to remove our hats. The majesty of the court is reinforced through the unusual form of headdress worn by judges and barristers. Anyone who wore this somewhere other than a court room would probably be the object of ridicule. Recently, however, newly-appointed solicitor-advocates wanted to adopt this ritual. The Bar objected.

> And as in some religions, where it is not necessary (or perhaps even desirable) to understand the meaning of the rituals in order to be impressed by the power of the deity, it is not necessary for the lay person to understand the law in order to be impressed by the power of the law. As with religion, the law has trained intermediaries – lawyers – who will interpret, even intercede for us.[5]

It is not only the bureaucracy that deals with us on unequal terms. Since the use of standard form contracts became widespread, there has been concern that the recipients of these have no choice but to accept the terms, however unreasonable.[6] Judicial attention has focused particularly on exemption clauses. Judicial decisions, statutes and, more recently, EC Directives have sought to redress the balance.

Boilerplate has played its part in inventing these complex and incomprehensible documents. The example below sets out BT's conditions for telephone service. In 1990 you would have been required to sign this document if you wanted to use a telephone in your home.

Conditions for Telephone service

(applicable only to telephone exchange line customers)

1 For definitions see paragraph 27

2 Provision of service

 2.1 We agree to provide you with service on the terms and conditions of this contract.

 2.2 For operational reasons we may vary the technical specification of service.

 2.3 It is technically impracticable to provide service free of faults and we do not undertake to do so. We do undertake however certain obligations with regard to a failure of your line: see paragraph 8 below.

 2.4 Requests made to us relating to the provision of service are to be made or confirmed in writing if we ask.

 2.5 We accept liability for failure to provide your line by any date agreed for its completed provision or to restore service after a failure of your line subject to sub-paragraph 21.2 and the other terms and conditions of this contract but any other date proposed by us or you is to be treated as an estimate only and we accept no liability for our failure to meet it.

 2.6 If we agree any change in service, this contract is to be treated as varied accordingly.

3 Classification of lines

We will classify or reclassify your line as a business or residential line according to the main purpose for which the line or your premises are used.

4 Shared lines

On occasion we may, for operational reasons, change a shared line to an exclusive line.

5 Minimum period of service

The minimum period of service (beginning on the day when service is first made available) is 12 months or the applicable period set out in our Price List but it does not prevent us from exercising our rights to suspend service, or you or us from terminating this contract or the provision of a service or facility under it.

6 Our general powers

We may:

 6.1 whenever necessary for operational reasons, change the name or number of the exchange serving your line, or its number, or any other name, code or number allocated in connection with service;

 6.2 in an emergency, suspend service temporarily in order to provide or safeguard service to a hospital or to the emergency, or other essential, services;

 6.3 temporarily, suspend service for the alteration of our apparatus to permit the passage of vehicles with abnormal loads;

 6.4 temporarily suspend service for repair maintenance or improvement of any of our telecommunication systems and any poles, brackets, cabinets or ducts supporting or enclosing them; and

 6.5 give instructions about the use of service which we think reasonably to be necessary in the interests of safety, or of the quality of service to our other customers;

but before doing any of these things we will give as much written or oral notice as is reasonably practicable in the circumstances, and we will restore service as soon as is reasonably practicable after temporary suspension.

7 Your responsibility for your line

You are responsible for your line (including any associated poles, brackets, cabinets or ducts) within the boundary of your premises and for its proper use: if it is lost, destroyed or damaged (except for fair wear and tear) you must pay our charge for its replacement and/or repair. You must not interfere with it nor permit anybody else (except someone authorised by us) to do so.

8 Failure of your line

 8.1 If you report a failure of your line, we undertake, subject to paragraph 21 and other terms and conditions of this contract, to correct it not later than two whole working days after it is reported.

 8.2 if we do work to correct a reported failure of your line and find there is none, we may charge you for the work.

 8.3 if we agree to attend to a fault outside the normal working hours of the fault repair service we are otherwise contracted to provide for you, you must pay a charge based on our applicable Time Related Charge set out in our Price List.

9 Connection and use of your equipment with our telephone system

You may connect your equipment to your line only by means of a socket installed and maintained by us unless we agree otherwise and we may withdraw our agreement by reasonable notice. Your equipment must not be used with your line (whether connected or not) except in accordance with our appropriate terms and conditions for the attachment of customers' equipment to our telecommunication systems in force from time to time, which form part of this contract. You can see or obtain copies at any of our District Offices. In addition, you must not allow any other person to do any of the things forbidden by this paragraph.

10 Electricity

If we ask you, you must provide at your expense a suitable mains electricity supply, with connections where we need them, to enable us to provide you with service.

11 Phone Books

We will allocate a number to your line and, unless you ask otherwise, we will make a free standard form entry for each line or line group identified by the same telephone number as soon as is reasonably practicable in your appropriate area Phone Book. Any special entry is agreed subject to the additional terms and conditions and relevant charges in our Price List.

12 Mis-use

12.1 You must not use or permit anyone else to use service:

12.1.1 to send a message or communication which is offensive, abusive, indecent, obscene or menacing, or

12.1.2 to cause annoyance, inconvenience or needless anxiety; or

12.1.3 in breach of instructions we have given under sub-paragraph 6.5.

12.2 If we suspend service for contravention of sub-paragraph 12.1, we can refuse to restore it until we receive an acceptable assurance from you that there will be no further contravention.

13 Charges for service, your responsibility for them and value added tax - general

13.1 You must pay on demand the charges for service which appear, or are calculated according to the rates which appear, or are otherwise mentioned, from time to time in our Price List. When we make a change to those charges or rates we will publish details (including the operative date) in our Price List as soon as possible and in any event not less than 2 weeks before the change is to take effect unless the charge is payable only by you in which case we will give you not less than 2 weeks' notice of the change.

13.2 Unless this contract provides otherwise you are responsible for all charges set out in our Price List for service provided for you; in particular, for charges for calls and other telephone services and facilities made or requested from your line, or obtained by the use of any name, code or number allocated to you under this contract or of one of our British Telecom Charge Cards associated with your line, whether they are made, requested or obtained by you or any other person.

13.3 Unless our Price List provides otherwise, all charges for service are exclusive of value added tax for which, if it is applicable, an amount will be added to your bill.

13.4 The charges for any call are those calculated by us using details recorded at our exchange only.

13.5 We may allow you to pay charges by instalments, but you must pay all unpaid instalments when this contract is terminated.

13.6 If at your request we apply a special low user tariff to your line, we will cease to apply it immediately without notice if we become aware that your line does not qualify and may charge you retrospectively at the normal rate.

14 Rental

14.1 You become liable to pay rental on the day on which we first make service available for you.

14.2 Except for temporary service you must pay rental in accordance with our billing cycle. If we begin, or cease, service on a day which is not the first or last day of the period by reference to which we charge rental we apportion rental on a daily basis for the incomplete period. Rental is normally payable in advance but we may on occasion bill you in arrears.

15 Deposits and payments in advance

15.1 We may ask you for a payment in advance not exceeding the connection charge and rental for the minimum period of service for the service requested, before service is provided.

15.2 We may ask you for a deposit at any time, as security for payment of future bills, in accordance with guidelines which we publish from time to time. We can hold it until payment of all you owe us, though we may use all or part of it for payment of any charges due. When we repay a deposit or part of a deposit we will add interest at the rate, whether expressed as a percentage or a formula published in our District Offices for the period in question.

16 Cancellation

You may give us notice to cancel this contract, or a service or facility asked for under it, before service or the particular service or facility is provided as the case may be but we may make a charge for abortive work done and/or money spent to meet your requirements.

17 Default

17.1 If you:

    17.1.1 do not pay any charge within 28 days of it falling due or break this contract in any other way; or

    17.1.2 do not pay any charge for any Telephone, Telex or Private Service within 28 days of it falling due to us under another contract with us; or

    17.1.3 are subject to bankruptcy or insolvency proceedings;

we can (without losing or reducing any other right or remedy) suspend service (including partially) temporarily without notice, though you remain liable to pay rental during the suspension, or terminate this contract by immediate notice. If we suspend service because you do not pay any charge, then any further suspension within a period of 12 months following restoration of service may take place 14 days after your failure to pay instead of after 28 days.

17.2 "Bankruptcy or insolvency proceedings" means bankruptcy proceedings or in Scotland sequestration proceedings, becoming insolvent, making any composition or arrangement with creditors or an assignment for their benefit, any execution, distress, diligence or seizure; or if you are a company, being the subject of proceedings for the appointment of an administrator, going into liquidation whether voluntary or compulsory (except for the purpose of amalgamation or reconstruction) or having a receiver or administrative receiver of any assets appointed.

17.3 On termination under this paragraph, as well as other sums payable up to the end of the contract, you must pay us the rental which would have been payable for the remainder of the minimum period of service at the rate in force at termination but we will make due allowance for any rental you have paid in advance for a period ending after the termination date or the end of the minimum period of service whichever is later, and make a repayment where appropriate.

17.4 You continue to be liable to pay all charges which are due for service during any period in which you do not comply with this contract.

17.5 If we waive a breach of contract by you, that waiver is limited to the particular breach. Our delay in acting upon a breach is not to be regarded in itself as a waiver.

18 Termination of service by notice

At any time after service has been provided this contract or the provision of any service or facility under it can be ended:

18.1 by one month's notice by us;

18.2 by 7 days' notice by you, unless this contract provides otherwise.

If we give notice, you must pay rental up to the expiry date of the notice. If you give notice, you must pay rental until 7 days after the date we receive the notice or until expiry of the notice, whichever is later, except that you must pay rental for the remainder of any minimum period of service at the rate in force at termination unless you have given notice because of an increase in the rate of rental. Your notice does not avoid any other liability for service already provided. Whoever gives the notice, we will repay or credit to you the appropriate proportion of any rental paid in advance (unless it is for part of the minimum period of service) for a period ending after your liability for rental ceases.

19 Permission to enter property

You must allow anyone accredited by us, on production of official evidence of identity and authority, reasonable access to your premises at all reasonable times for the purposes of this contract, and you must obtain the permission of any other person which is needed. We will try to comply with your reasonable requirements as to safety of people on your premises.

20 Arbitration

If a dispute between you and us about this contract does not involve a complicated issue of law, an issue of quantification or of mitigation of loss, or a sum exceeding £5,000, you may refer it to arbitration by the Chartered Institute of Arbitrators under procedures agreed between us and the Institute, details of which appear in our Code of Practice for Consumers.

21 Our liability

21.1 We do not exclude or restrict liability for death or personal injury resulting from our negligence.

21.2 Our liability for default in the provision of service whether in contract, tort, delict or otherwise (including liability for negligence) is limited to loss or damage caused by our failure:

21.2.1 to provide your line by any agreed date for its completed provision; or

21.2.2 to restore service after a failure of your line;

and arises on the third working day after the agreed date or after the day on which you report the failure of your line to us. It is limited to:

21.2.3 £5 without proof of loss for each complete working day (or part of a day) once liability has arisen until your line is provided or service is restored excluding any working day (or part of a day) in a period of failure by us caused and/or continued because you do not provide us with any access to your premises or other reasonable assistance necessary for the purpose and under your control or because you

agree to the delay; or (at your choice)

21.2.4 damages for breach of contract consisting of the actual financial loss sustained by you on or after that third working day, and caused by our failure continuing on or after that day, up to £5,000 if your line is a business line or up to £1,000 if your line is a residential line;

for each line concerned (whether provided under this or another contract), subject to a maximum of £20,000 for all such lines for each incident or related series of incidents at any one set of your premises;

but we are only liable if you make your claim in writing, unless we agree otherwise, within 2 months of the completed provision of your line or the restoration of service.

21.3 We will not be liable under or in connection with this contract whether in contract, tort, delict or otherwise (including liability in negligence):

21.3.1 for any default in the provision of service; or

21.3.2 for any indirect or consequential loss, corruption or destruction of data, any loss of business, revenue or profits, anticipated savings or wasted expenditure or for any financial loss whatever;

except as provided by sub-paragraphs 21.1 and 21.2;

and any liability or ours whatever its nature except liability under subparagraph 21.1 whether in contract, tort, delict or otherwise (including liability for negligence) is limited to £1,000,000 for any event or related series of events and £2,000,000 for all events in any period of 12 months.

21.4 In performing any obligation under this contract our duty is only to exercise all the reasonable care and skill of a competent telecommunication service provider and in a case falling within sub-paragraph **21.2** (but not in any other case) the burden of proof that we have done so is upon us.

21.5 Each provision of this paragraph limiting or excluding liability operates separately in itself and survives independently of the others.

21.6 Sub-paragraph **21.2** does not apply to a line providing automatically for the recording of calls to you for which you are to pay all or part of the charges or used primarily in connection with a service which you provide to callers and where we pay you for each call made to that service.

21.7 We may pay a sum payable under sub-paragraph 21.2 not exceeding £25 by a credit to your account.

21.8 In our Districts where 24 hour fault reporting is available for all customers, a fault reported outside the working hours of a working day for our fault repair service applicable to you will be regarded as reported during the working hours of the next working day.

22 Indemnity

You must indemnify us against any claims or legal proceedings arising from your use of service which are brought or threatened against us by another person.

23 Variation of terms and conditions

We can from time to time change the terms and conditions of this contract other than the charges payable under it by a document referring expressly to this paragraph and signed by a duly authorised employee of ours. We will publish details of any change (including the operative date) in each of our District Offices as soon as possible and in any event not less than 2 weeks before any change is to take effect, except that if the change is made to a provision of this contract limiting or excluding our liability for breaches of our duty to you (in contract, tort or delict) we will give you not less than 2 weeks' notice of the change.

24 Limitation on assignment

You must not assign the benefit of this contract in whole or in part.

25 Giving notice

A notice given under this contract, except under paragraph 6, (including a bill sent by us to you) must be in writing and may be delivered by hand or sent by telex or prepaid post to the addressee at the following addresses.

25.1 To us: the address of our District Office shown on our order form which leads to the making of this contract or on your last bill or any alternative address which we notify to you at any time.

25.2 To you: the address to which from time to time you ask us to send bills, the address of your premises, or if you are a limited company, your registered office.

26 Matters beyond our reasonable control

We are not liable for any breach of this contract where the breach was caused by Act of God, insurrection or civil disorder, war or military operations, national or local emergency, acts or omissions of government, highway authority or other competent authority, our compliance with any statutory obligation or an obligation under a statute, industrial disputes of any kind (whether or not involving our employees), fire, lightning, explosion, flood, subsidence, weather of exceptional severity, acts or omissions of persons for whom we are not responsible (including in particular other telecommunication service providers) or any other cause whether similar or dissimilar outside our reasonable control.

27 Definitions and application

27.1 In this contract unless the context otherwise requires:

"we" and "us" means British Telecommunications plc;

"you" means the customer with whom we make this contract including a person reasonably appearing to us to act with that customer's authority;

"failure of your line" means any failure of your line causing you continuous total loss of the ability:

– to make a call; or

– to receive a call;

"line" means a telephone exchange line and ancillary apparatus and in particular, does not include your equipment;

"provision of your line" includes reconnection of your line after temporary disconnection at your request;

"service" means telecommunication service provided by means of the line connecting your premises to our telephone exchange and the rest of our public switched telephone network and telephone service provided to you when you use a British Telecom Chargecard associated with your line and any ancillary or related services but not AccessLines together with, where applicable, services or facilities listed in the Telephone Service sections of our

Price List provided by or in connection with your line;

"working day" means a complete calendar day on which we would normally do work to provide an exchange line for you or to repair faults in accordance:

– with our standard fault repair service (work carried out 0800-1700 hours Monday to Friday excluding Bank and Public holidays which we observe); or

– with any alternative fault repair service we have contracted to provide for you;

except that if the working hours of the fault repair service applicable to your line are 24 hours per day seven days per week, for the purpose of sub-paragraph 21.2 a working day is each period of 24 hours calculated from the time a fault is reported;

"your equipment" means equipment, including in particular additional sockets and related wiring, which is not part of our public switched telephone network and which you use or intend to use for service;

"your premises" means the premises at which service is or is to be provided under this contract; and

words in the singular include the plural and vice versa.

27.2 Our Price List contains definitions, notes, terms and conditions which form part of this contract where relevant. You can see copies or obtain extracts at any of our District Offices.

27.3 We will provide you with telephone service only on these "Conditions for Telephone Service" which set out our entire contract with you.

NOTE
(This note is for information only and does not form part of our contract with you).

We run our public switched telephone network under a licence, issued under the Telecommunications Act 1984, which contains conditions which we must observe in providing service and which are enforceable by the Director General of Telecommunications. Copies are obtainable from HMSO.

AccessLines
AccessLines are provided on British Telecommunications plc's Conditions for Private Service. They contain limitations and exclusions of liability, in particular (but not only) for loss of profits, business or anticipated savings, or for any indirect or consequential loss whatsoever and those limitations and exclusions differ from those for Telephone Service. The Conditions may be seen or obtained from any District Office. Charges for AccessLines will appear on the bill for you Telephone Service.

Does it really need to be so long and dense? Don't worry, we won't ask you to analyse it – yet.

Pressure from politicians, judges, and consumer groups over issues of bargaining power have been effective in encouraging the move towards plain English in legal documents. The trolley regulations we analysed earlier are evidence of this. Recently BT launched its new plain English Conditions for Telephone Service (see the Appendix). But what is plain English? What is legal English? And how can we reconcile the apparently conflicting demands of clarity and precision? Answers to these questions will provide us with a strategy for drafting.

1   V Charrow 'Language in the Bureaucracy' in R Di Pietro (ed) *Linguistics and the Professions: Advances in Discourse Processes* Vol 8, Ablex, Norwood, NJ 1982.
2   R Goldfarb 'My Secretary, Hereinafter Referred to as Cuddles . . .', (1978) 5 *Barrister*, 40.
3   Quoted in James D Gordon III 'How Not To Succeed in Law School', (1991) 100 *Yale Law Journal*,1678, at p 1689.
4   See S Blake, op cit, p 147.
5   V Charrow, J A Crandall, R Charrow, op cit, p 181.
6   See for example F Kessler 'Contracts of Adhesion – Some Thoughts About Freedom of Contract', (1943) *Columbia Law Review* 629; Lord Reid in the *Suisse Atlantique* case (1966)

2 All ER 61 at 76; Lord Diplock in *Schroeder Music Publishing Co Ltd v Macaulay* (1974) 3 All ER 616 at 624; Law Commission *Second Report on Exemption Clauses in Contracts* (1975) No 69; G Gluck 'Standard Form Contracts: The Contract Theory Reconsidered', (1979) 28 *International & Comparative Law Quarterly* 72.

Legal language is not plain language

Exercise 8.4   Plain reflection

(a) Write a definition of plain English, then compare your definition with another student's. If it helps, refer to Chapter 7 again.

(b) Think about what you have so far read of this chapter. Make a list of the factors you think contribute to the impenetrability of legal writing.

Lawyers themselves are not as expert in language as they would have us believe. They seem to misunderstand the nature of linguistic complexity. Studies have shown that when lawyers are asked what makes legal documents incomprehensible, they tend to put it down to technical vocabulary and the complexity of legal concepts.[1] Moreover, until recently, lawyers who have researched legal language largely concentrated on vocabulary – terms of art, latinisms, and archaic, formal and infrequent words and phrases.[2]

Cutting out archaisms and superfluous expressions will help, but is only tinkering with the problem. You should remember from your analyses of officialese and academic writing in Exercise 7.2 that there are also grammatical and organisational features of the language which inhibit understanding. These are common in legal language too. Veda and Robert Charrow isolated a number of these features in their study of the comprehensibility of Californian standard civil jury instructions.[3] These instructions are given orally by the judge before the trial starts. The Charrows then redrafted the instructions, eliminating the features that apparently gave trouble. Comprehensibility increased on average by 35–40%. These results don't seem particularly encouraging. Is it because the concepts are so complex? Here is one of the original instructions:

> You must never speculate to be true any insinuation suggested by a question asked a witness.

We have come across this before: poor organisation. There are too many ideas pushed into one sentence and normal syntax can't take it. Nobody would normally speak or write like this. In the jargon of linguistics, this writer uses multiple embeddings with whiz deletion! This means there are sentences within sentences which leave out the *Wh-* words *which* or *who*. It is these words which help us process the information more easily by showing the relationship between the ideas:

> any insinuation *which* is suggested by a question *which* is asked a witness.

There are three ideas in the sentence:

1   when a lawyer questions a witness;
2   if the question contains insinuations;
3   you must never think that those insinuations are true.

It is what is left out which increases the unintelligibility, along with the passive verbs *suggested* and *asked*. These are truncated passives, ie passives where we aren't told who the agent is. Charrow and Charrow rewrite as follows:

> If a lawyer's question to a witness contained any insinuations, you must ignore those insinuations.

This example destroys another common preconception about language: that the longer the sentence, the more difficult it is to process. Rewriting sentences like this in comprehensible English will mean making them longer.

Here is another jury instruction:

> Discrepancies in a witness's testimony or between his testimony and that of others, if there were any, do not necessarily mean that the witness should be discredited. Failure of recollection is a common experience, and innocent misrecollection is not uncommon. It is a fact, also, that two persons witnessing an incident or a transaction often will see or hear it differently. Whether a discrepancy pertains to a fact of importance or only to a trivial detail should be considered in weighing its significance.

Again, you should be familiar with the grammatical features which obscure the meaning:

- abstract nouns and noun phrases in place of verbs (nominalisations)   'failure of recollection, fact of importance',
- multiple negatives   'innocent misrecollection is not uncommon',
- unusual word order   'Whether a discrepancy . . . its significance'.

A feature that we haven't discussed before is the misplaced adverbial. This is a word or phrase which is inserted into a part of the sentence where you would not expect to find it. It may break up the normal subject–verb–object word order and the break is often marked with commas. In legalese you often find these between subject and verb. For example:

Discrepancies . . .	(Subject)
if there were any,	(Adverbial)
do not necessarily mean . . .	(Verb)

There is also an organisational problem in this paragraph. It is not clear how the subject matter relates to the jurors. 'What's this got to do with me?' a juror might ask. 'What am I supposed to do?' The Charrows' modified version makes this relationship clear by directly addressing them:

> As jurors, you have to decide which testimony to believe and which testimony not to believe.
>
> You may be tempted to totally disbelieve a witness because he contradicted himself while testifying. Keep in mind, however, that people sometimes forget things, and end up contradicting themselves.
>
> You might also be tempted to totally disbelieve a witness because another witness testified differently. But keep in mind also that when two people witness an incident they often remember it differently.
>
> When you are deciding whether or not to believe a witness, you should

consider whether contradictions or differences in testimony have to do with an important fact or only a small detail.

These examples show that understanding does not depend on the ease or difficulty of comprehending individual words and sentences, but on how they relate to each other in a text.

Let's apply this knowledge to a small piece of boilerplate.

1 For example, R Charrow & V Charrow 'Investigating Comprehension in Real-World Tasks', paper presented at Linguistic Society of America Annual Meeting, Philadelphia, December 1976.
2 For example, D Mellinkoff *The Language of the Law*, Little, Brown & Co, Boston 1963.
3 'Making Legal Language Understandable: A Psycholinguistic Study of Jury Instructions', (1979) 79 *Columbia Law Review* 1306–74.

Exercise 8.5 Clause analysis

The text below is taken from a precedent which the author suggests can be used for drafting a contract of employment in the publishing and multimedia business.[1] We have numbered the lines of the text to give you points of reference in your analysis.

(a) *Read the text and paraphrase the content. Note down how long this process took you.*

(b) *What is its purpose?*

(c) *Who is it written for?*

(d) *Who are the likely readers?*

(e) *Comment on:*

   (i) *layout;*

   (ii) *punctuation;*

   (iii) *sentence length;*

   (iv) *word order;*

   (v) *sentence complexity;*

   (vi) *vocabulary.*

(f) *Imagine you have to explain the meaning of the clause to a newly-engaged employee of the company. What would you say?*

(g) *Redraft the clause.*

15. INTELLECTUAL PROPERTY	
The entire copyright and all other rights	1
including without limitation design rights registered	2
design rights patent rights trade mark rights rights	3
of action and all other rights of whatsoever nature	4
in and to any and all material invention or process	5
of whatever description created or produced by you	6
whether alone or in collaboration with others in the	7
performance of your duties whether or not during the	8
working hours specified in paragraph 1 and whether or	9
not at the location referred to in paragraph 9.1 or	10
at any other location shall vest in the Company	11
absolutely from the moment of creation and the	12

Company its successors assignees and licensees shall	13
be the sole absolute unencumbered legal and	14
beneficial owner throughout the world of all rights	15
in all such material for the full period during	16
which such rights may now or at any time in the	17
future subsist under the laws in force in any part	18
of the world.	19

The main grammatical features we have been discussing:
- nominalisations;
- multiple embeddings;
- truncated passives;
- noun lists;
- unusual word order;

are all found in other professional varieties, such as academic and bureaucratic writing. There are features, however, which we find only in legal English. For example, a rule of English word order tells us that an adjective precedes its noun:

legal language
ugly expressions.

In the term of art *fee simple*, however, we use French word order, but we pronounce it as English, not French. Is there something about the development of legal English that accounts for such unique usage?

1   Taken from M Henry *Publishing and Multimedia Law*, Butterworths, London 1994, p 792.

Legal language is unduly peculiar

Richard Wydick tells us that criticism of lawyers' writing is not new:

> In 1596 an English chancellor decided to make an example of a particularly prolix document filed in his court. The chancellor first ordered a hole cut through the centre of the document, all 120 pages of it. Then he ordered that the person who wrote it should have his head stuffed through the hole, and the unfortunate fellow was led around to be exhibited to all those attending court at Westminster Hall.[1]

Although we don't deal with poor writers in this way now, probably the characteristics of prolixity then were much the same as they are now. Legal language has not changed in the way that the standard variety has.

1   R Wydick 'Plain English for Lawyers', (1978) 66 *California Law Review* 727 at p 727.

Lawyers, not the people, decide what words mean

Ordinary language changes through usage. New forms take the place of old ones, and other forms change their meaning. In Chapter 7 we looked at the meaning of *nice* and how it has changed over time. The word *gay* is another example. No one would now use this word in its former meaning of *cheerful, lively* because it would confuse the recipient of the message. Old forms we no longer use include, for example, the third person singular present tense of verbs -*th*, as in *he hath*, (he has). The new forms then become acceptable in the standard written variety.

Because we do not normally speak or write legal English, it has developed much more slowly. Meanings are imposed on the users by courts, legislatures and other agencies. To ensure precision, lawyers are reluctant to depart from them and create new forms. Reliance on these past, static forms gives legal language its archaic flavour. Lawyers won't let them die! They prefer to retain archaisms like *hereinafter*, *aforesaid* and *witnesseth*.

Lawyers have also shown a liking for tautology. For example:

null and void
goods and chattels
terms and conditions
perform and discharge
will and testament.

These usages show the dominance of Latin and French over legal language for centuries. Where there were English and Latin or French words for the same item, there was often doubt as to whether the words meant exactly the same. To be safe, lawyers used both.

The legal register still contains both Latin and French legal terms which survive in their original forms, though not in their original pronunciation. What examples can you think of? Are you sure you use them all correctly?

If a Minister has ultra virus the Divisional Court will squash it

Imposing specialised meanings on particular words and phrases has led to differences between ordinary and legal English concepts. The concepts of *negligence*, *assault*, and *consideration*, for example, all have specific legal meanings which are different from those understood by non-lawyers. What other examples can you think of?

Nevertheless, drafters do not set out specific meanings all the time. They may have good reasons for being imprecise. Consider the following example, taken from our old friend, the Litter (Northern Ireland) Order 1994:

4. (1)   Subject to paragraph (4), if any person, being a person in charge of a dog, permits the dog to deposit its excrement in any place prescribed by regulations, he shall, subject to paragraph (2), be guilty of an offence.

   (2)   It shall be a defence for a person charged with an offence under paragraph (1) to prove that –
     (a)   he took all reasonable precautions and exercised due diligence to avoid the commission of the offence; or
     (b)   he made a reasonable attempt to remove the excrement.

Exercise 8.6   Shovelling excrement

You are a local councillor. The Responsible Dog Owners Association asks you to explain this regulation to them in plain English. What will you say?

You won't have found it easy to be precise, because the deliberate use of the elastic concepts *reasonableness* and *due diligence* allow matters to be decided on a case by case basis. The Association, which wants a straight answer about what constitutes a valid defence, will not be happy.

Do you think this regulation should provide a defence at all? We are sure many of you will have strong views on this. Inhabitants of Britain either love or hate dogs but are rarely indifferent, even if we can all agree to hate their deposits. Legislatures and government agencies have to balance up conflicting interests, about which there may have been widespread public discussion and intensive lobbying by pressure groups. In situations like this it will be left to the courts to set the boundaries, so decisions will not be seen as 'political'.

Contract terms may be drafted in such a way as to leave their meaning unclear. This is usually done to give an advantage to the party drawing up the contract. For example:

The Company reserves the right to make alterations to your normal working hours in order to meet its business commitments.

Put yourself in her position: deriving meaning from context

In ordinary English writing readers infer meanings from context. We imagine ourselves or others in the situation described either by the words themselves, or by what went before. If we replaced leaving there shopping trolleys used by them

in s 1(2)(b) of the trolley regulations with

leaving their shopping trolleys there

as we briefly threatened to do on page 230, we would infer that *their* means *customers'* shopping trolleys, but that the customers don't own them, because shopping trolleys are always owned by stores, never by customers. The relationship between customer and shopping trolley is quite clear.

Because lawyers have to make the words themselves clear in case other lawyers challenge the meaning, their discourse demands that they try to derive meaning entirely from the words they use. They must therefore avoid the possibility of alternative interpretations from context. Only when the meaning is ambiguous or uncertain do they turn to context for an interpretation.

Exercise 8.7   Natural meanings

In small groups, discuss:
(a)   Which devices of statutory interpretation exclude inferences from context?
(b)   Which don't?

It isn't easy to exclude context when it plays such an important part in helping us to process meanings. Because lawyers have to go to some lengths to obliterate it, they have developed the skills of understanding and classifying information without using it. Unfortunately, this can lead them to make assumptions about lay people's abilities to do the same.

The jury instructions we looked at earlier are an example. Drafters of documents assume readers (or listeners) know the purpose of the document, and so don't state it. However, people who are unfamiliar with the criminal justice system and who are not clear about their role in it will not be able to work out how the instructions relate to them unless they are clearly told what their role is.

You are all familiar with the police caution given to suspects before questioning. This has recently been revised. The first draft for the revised PACE Code of Practice C was as follows (Para 10.4):

> You do not have to say anything. But if you do not mention now something which you later use in your defence, the Court may decide that your failure to mention it now strengthens the case against you. A record will be made of anything you say and it may be given in evidence if you are brought to trial.

Apparently it was discovered in a survey that 60% of A level students could not understand it, so an attempt was made to simplify the draft. Here is the final version:

> You do not have to say anything. But it may harm your defence if you do not mention when questioned something which you later rely on in

court. Anything you do say may be given in evidence.

The main criticism of the first draft was that there were too many words in it. Is this the problem?

Exercise 8.8   Caution! Unforeseen hazard ahead!

In small groups, answer the following questions:
(a)   What was the wording of the caution before it was revised?
(b)   What was the legal position of a suspect who declined to answer police questions?
(c)   Why has it become necessary to draft a new caution?
(d)   Which features impede understanding in the first version above? Give reasons.
(e)   To what extent is the final version an improvement on the first? Give reasons.
(f)   If you think the final version has deficiencies, how would you remedy them?

The way this problem has been dealt with demonstrates once again that lawyers misconceive what is complex in legal language. The problem here is not sentence length, but that both these drafts are pieces of legal discourse. As such they cannot be easily understood by outsiders. You have to be familiar with the world of the lawyer and the legal register to grasp these concepts.[1] *It may harm your defence* – what will this mean to someone who has never been inside a criminal court and knows nothing of criminal procedure? Similarly, *something which you later rely on in court* – what is meant by *rely on*?

How can it happen that with something as important as this, when in many situations a lawyer will not be there to advise, the drafter is talking to a lawyer when she should be addressing the suspect?

In setting the scene in the courtroom it appears the writer has ignored the listener's perspective. If she had put herself in the suspect's shoes, she would have been able to anticipate the barriers to understanding. Is this simply a failure to grasp the importance of context, or is it a reflection of the view held by many lawyers that legal concepts are too complex to be understood by ordinary people?

As part of the Document Design Project at the American Institutes for Research, a group of researchers redesigned the District of Columbia Medicaid form. People on welfare had to fill in this form to get money to pay for health care. One factor the researchers found which impeded the recipients' understanding of the original form was that they understood a term differently from the meaning the drafter intended:

> One kind of change which we made was simply at the word level, to take account of special audience characteristics. The MRF audience is comprised of people who are poor, not well-educated, often old, and frequently speakers of a non-standard dialect, or not native speakers of English. Problem analysis showed that these people tend to misinterpret the term 'family member', which recurs in important questions throughout the form. Or rather, they misinterpret the term relative to the dialect of the document designer. The designer intends the phrase to refer to people in

the immediate, nuclear family of the Medicaid recipient, all covered by a common Medicaid card. This meaning is not spelled out, but is implied by listing the names of the people covered and placing them in a box labelled 'family members' near the top of the form. The designer assumes the meaning is clear not only because of this graphical definition, but also because the phrase itself is simple, familiar, and has a unique meaning to the designer. People in the Medicaid population, however, have extended families – a network of kin, often reared together, and all considered immediate family. As might be expected, many respondents answered questions about family employment and resources as if those questions referred to nephews, cousins, sisters-in-law, and others not covered by the recipient's Medicaid.[2]

This presumably happened because the drafter either knew nothing of the experience and way of life of the readership, or for some reason decided to ignore these.

People who have to explain complex ideas and procedures to others often help them understand by making abstract concepts concrete. Jesus and other religious leaders have done it for thousands of years. Lord Denning did it with freedom of contract, as we saw in Chapter 7. Even law teachers do it. Revision of the Medicaid form at the sentence level was based on a particular method called the 'scenario principle'.[3] Readers were asked to explain the meaning as they went along, in an effort to understand. They tended to convert the information into a small dramatised scenario – a scene in which somebody does something:

> Take, for example, a paragraph headed 'Applying for Bank Loans,' and starting 'The procedure to apply for bank loans consists of . . .' A reader might turn the preceding into, 'Now say I wanted to apply for a bank loan, then I would . . .', or 'Now this fellow wanted to apply for a bank loan, then he . . .' In trying to understand what the regulation said, readers expressed abstract definitions (with a nominalisation like 'procedure' as subject) in the form of a story-like event (with a human agent as subject doing an action in a time and place context). The event frame makes information concrete, imageable, and familiar through relationships like agent–object and action–goal. This frame seems to be a basic structure of experience and a way we naturally think.[4]

Nobody (apart from law students?) reads legal documents to learn definitions. We read them to engage in human activities: to find answers to questions, to make decisions and carry them out. In the earlier exercises where we asked you to paraphrase and explain legal provisions, did you use the scenario principle? Or did you fiddle about with abstract legal concepts and then attempt to translate them into real life contexts? Which will be your starting point for your drafting?

---

1   For more discussion on this, see R Eagleson 'Plain English: Some Sociolinguistic Revelations', in S Romaine (ed) *Language in Australia*, Cambridge University Press, New York 1991, pp 362–72 at p 369.
2   V Charrow, V Holland, D Peck & L Shelton *Revising a Medicaid Recertification Form: A Case*

Study in the Document Design Process, American Institutes For Research, Washington DC 1980, cited in L Campbell & V Holland 'Understanding the Language of Public Documents Because Readability Formulas Don't', in Di Pietro op cit, pp 157–72.

3   See L Flower, J Hayes & H Swarts 'Revising Functional Documents: The Scenario Principle', *Document Design Project Technical Report No 1*, Carnegie–Mellon University, Pittsburgh, Penn 1980.

4   Campbell & Holland, op cit, p 165–6.

Does it matter what it looks like? Layout and punctuation

According to Crystal and Davy,[1] the content of early legal documents was usually set out on parchment in one solid block of writing, the lines extending from margin to margin. This unbroken format may have been used to economise on parchment, or to defeat fraudulent insertions or deletions by leaving no spaces. The advent of printing did nothing to make the format more accessible.

Most early documents were written in Latin, which as we noted earlier, has a periodic structure. This means that the relationship between main and subordinate clauses is clear from the word forms and endings. It was therefore quite acceptable to draft long sections of a document, or even a whole document, in one sentence.

As these documents were read, not spoken, there was no need for punctuation to show the reader where to pause. It is interesting that proclamations, written to be spoken out loud, were always properly punctuated.[2] Furthermore, punctuation could be added to change meaning, and so having none at all prevented forgeries.

The regulations we have looked at in this chapter reveal the modern tendency of legislation to use punctuation, headings and numberings to separate provisions. It recognises that the reader will rarely want to read the whole instrument and thoroughly digest all of it. Breaking the provisions up into separate items makes it easier to scan the document and find the provisions you are looking for.

Isolated sentences

Besides being long and complex, legal sentences are self-contained. This means they stand on their own, neither linked to what precedes or follows them. This is necessary because each action or requirement is dependent on a series of conditions which must be fulfilled before it can happen. That's it. Nothing else is relevant. You then go on to the next action or requirement, and then the one after that.

Earlier in the chapter we suggested that this lack of linking is responsible for cumbersome repetition in legal writing. In standard written English ideas are linked by logical progression and the use of linking words and phrases. This gives coherence to a text. We discussed this in some detail too in Chapter 7.

By treating each sentence as a separate item, legal ideas are isolated from each other. The writing is disjointed and may read like a list. Documents therefore seem to lack coherence. The reader has to struggle to make connections between items and their place in the text as a whole, as well as put up with unnecessary repetition.

In fact, legal documents are coherent, in a way which is closely linked to their purpose. They are written records which lawyers use for reference. This means that, for example, readers will not normally scan a new piece of legislation to get a rough overview – they can get this from journals and commentaries. They will scan to find out which sections of the document are likely to give them the answers they want to specific questions, then take time to study those parts in detail. This process is easier if each section is set out separately from every other.

Coherence and word order

In everyday writing (and speech) the subject appears at or near the beginning of the sentence, followed closely by its verb. Legal drafters, however, put words, phrases and clauses in unusual positions. The usual underlying logical structure of a legal sentence is

If (or when) X, then Y shall be Z, or Y shall do Z.

–   X is a set of conditions or circumstances (if? when? where?);
–   Y is the agent (who?);
–   Z is the state or action (what?).

This structure is sometimes known as a *legislative sentence*, or *legislative thought*.[3] Here is a simple example:

If the work is cancelled by the customer,   (X)
the contractor   (Y)
is entitled to make the following charges . . .   (Z)

Look back to regulation 51(2) on notional capital in Exercise 8.3. It begins with a list of exceptions. Besides feeling confused, a lay reader might well wonder why it takes so long to get to the point.

Normal English word order would be Y, Z, X. Why the difference? In legal sentences the X component often appears at the beginning of the sentence to enable the reader to discover early on whether she is interested in this provision or not. If not, she is spared the agony of having to read on! If she is unfortunate enough to have to struggle on, by the end she may well have been floored by a monstrous and nightmarish sentence which spawns vast strings of embedded clauses and phrases. These overwhelm the subject of the sentence and swallow up part of its verb. She may hunt in vain, but won't find the verb until it is disgorged many lines further on.

Can you make out the underlying structure in this complicated legislative thought? Section 2(1) of the Official Secrets Act 1911:

If any person having in his possession or control any sketch, plan, model, article, note, document, or information which relates to or is used in a prohibited place or anything in such a place, or which has been made or obtained in contravention of this Act, or which has been entrusted in

confidence to him by any person holding office under His Majesty, or
which he has obtained owing to his position as a person who holds or has
held office under His Majesty, or as a person who holds or has held such
an office or contract, –

(a) communicates the sketch, plan, model, article, note, document or
information to any person, other than a person to whom he is
authorised to communicate it, or a person to whom it is in the interest of the State his duty to communicate it, or

(b) retains the sketch, plan, model, article, note, or document in his
possession or control when he has no right to retain it or when it is
contrary to his duty to retain it:

that person shall be guilty of a misdemeanour.

The X component in Section 2(1) is introduced by *If*. The subject of this
clause is *any person*. We then have to read another 96 words before we come
upon its verb *communicates*. You therefore have to keep the opening words in
mind all the way to (a). The X component is made up of a number of sub-
clauses, so that by the time we get to Y and Z, the drafter thought it necessary
to remind us who the subject is: *that person* (Y).

Why not use normal English word order? Components Y and Z are so simple and brief that the reader can easily check the provision for relevance. Here
is the underlying structure, using normal word order:

a person(Y) is guilty of a misdemeanour(Z) if . . . (X).

This does not help with the complexity of the X component, however. Now
try and work out the relationship of the sub-clauses in the X component to
each other. You will see then that the relationships between the numerous *or*
and *which* clauses can be clarified by using lists and numbering.[4]

But is it that simple? Where drafters use a co-ordinating conjunction, such
as *or* or *and*, they appear to join two legislative sentences in one provision.
This can be confusing for the reader, who has to work out whether the provision covers one right or obligation with a number of X components, or two
distinct rights or obligations. You can find an example of this in the intellectual property clause you redrafted in Exercise 8.5. If you are sure that the
provision deals with two rights, you should split them into two separate legislative sentences.

1   D Crystal & D Davy *Investigating English Style* Longman, London 1969, pp 193–217.
2   Ibid, p 200.
3   See for example P James & R Goncalves *Modern Writing For Lawyers*, Continuing Legal
Education Society of British Columbia, Vancouver 1993, p 154; also N Gold, K Mackie,
W Twining *Learning Lawyers' Skills*, Butterworths, London 1989, p 132.
4   Section 2(1) has been repealed by the Official Secrets Act 1989, which defines six categories
of official information.

Interceding with the Deity: pleadings

Pleadings define the issues for trial and so when drafting them you have to
follow formal rules and conventions which prescribe the form and content of
your draft.[1]

Pleadings inform the other side of the case against them by setting out the material facts which the parties are going to rely on at trial. In civil proceedings the most important pleadings you will draft are:

1. the *statement of claim*, which states the plaintiff's case and the remedy she is seeking, and
2. the *defence*, which sets out the facts denying the plaintiff's claim.

In criminal proceedings at Crown court the offences the defendant is charged with are set out on the *indictment*.

The pleadings limit the issues to be tried, so that if you forget to raise an issue on the draft, you can't raise it unless the court gives you leave. Essentially your draft should:

● Summarise your case	BE CONCISE
● Clarify your case	BE CLEAR
● Be logically organised	BE CORRECT
● Contain all the issues to be raised	BE COMPLETE.

Although pleadings are the most formal documents you will draft, the drafting skills are the same as those you need for other kinds of legal documents. You have to draft pleadings carefully, because a poor draft suggests you haven't prepared your case properly. A concisely-worded, comprehensive draft is more likely to focus the judge's attention on the strengths of your case. If you omit a material fact or get something wrong, the case could be lost. For example, the defendant may go free if you draft the indictment incorrectly.

Note, too, the comments of William Rose:

You may ask, 'Well, what is the *point* of elegant drafting? After all, so long as I have made myself clear, why should style be of any relevance?' The answer can be summed up in one word – *authority*.

Assuming a basic legal competence, the most important additional attribute that will distinguish good pleading (or advocacy for that matter) from the mundane, is authority. To be able to stamp your mark on the case, pick it up by the scruff of its neck, dictate the action, and essentially show yourself to the Court to be in command and the master of your subject, gives you an incalculable advantage over your opponent. For a start, and have no doubt about this whatsoever, it shows! Your opponent will know, the Judge will know, and if you are at the Bar your solicitor will know. In terms of prestige, and sheer psychological 'clout' you are ahead. Don't be mistaken, these things matter.[2]

There are a number of detailed practical guides on the technique of drafting pleadings. Here are a few of them:

– Susan Blake *A Practical Approach to Legal Advice and Drafting*.
– William Rose *Pleading Without Tears: A Guide to Legal Drafting*.
– The Inns of Court School of Law *Opinion Writing and Drafting*.

We suggest you consult at least one of these before you attempt the next exercise. You may also find it useful to look at RSC Order 18, r 7(1).

1 Pleadings in civil proceedings, for example, are governed by RSC Order 18.
2 W Rose *Pleading Without Tears: A Guide to Legal Drafting*, Blackstone, London 1994, p 10.

Exercise 8.9   Major surgery[1]

Read the following draft statement of claim carefully.
(a)   Which material should not be pleaded? Give reasons.
(b)   Is there anything which has been left out?
(c)   Comment briefly on the style.

IN THE SOUTH BROMWICH COUNTY COURT   1995 No 34500

BETWEEN:

RAYMOND BILLICK

Plaintiff

and

FREDERICK FINK

1st Defendant

and

SNOOGS MANUFACTURING LTD

2nd Defendant

PARTICULARS OF CLAIM

---

1.   On Friday 7 January 1995 the plaintiff Raymond Billick had an
     unfortunate accident. The plaintiff had got up early to drive from
     his home at 25 Nuttall Avenue, Gloucester, to London along the
     A40. He was driving his new Ford Mondeo registration number
     M111 NDD and it was still quite dark.
         As he was driving along Macey Road in Cheltenham there was a
     collision between the said vehicle and a Vauxhall Cavalier registra-
     tion number J454 CND driven erratically by the First Defendant,
     who was at all material times the servant or agent of the Second
     Defendant, acting in the course of his employment.
2.   The plaintiff was driving carefully at about 30 mph because his car
     was new and there were schoolchildren about. The accident
     occurred at 8.16 am exactly. Several people at a bus stop witnessed
     the said accident and made statements to the Gloucestershire police.
     One witness, Molly Bigginshaw, of 19 Harkness Road, Cheltenham,
     will say that the said collision was caused by the First Defendant.
3.   The First Defendant went through a red traffic light while the
     Plaintiff's car was crossing. The Plaintiff could not possibly have
     foreseen that a driver would be so stupid. The First Defendant owed
     the Plaintiff a duty of care and failed to take reasonable care in the
     circumstances. The 1st Defendant was therefore negligent (*Donoghue
     v Stevenson* 1932). The Second Defendant is liable because he had

ordered the 1st Defendant to deliver some cartons of stationery to Flippers Newsagents in High Street, Cheltenham. Therefore the First Defendant was acting in the course of his employment when he caused the said accident.

PARTICULARS OF NEGLIGENCE

The First Defendant was negligent because he did not obey the traffic signals which all road users know they should do on the highway. He breached his duty of care.
He was particularly negligent in that he:
(1) Drove his said vehicle along the said road:
    (a)   too fast and aggressively;
    (b)   with a defective tyre;
    (c)   without looking where he was going, apparently; the Plaintiff had his lights on;
    (d)   without reasonable care for other road users.
(2) Failed in time or at all to stop at a red traffic signal; this is a criminal offence and a breach of the highway code.
(3) There are skid marks which show that he failed in time or at all to take sufficient steps to brake, steer or otherwise control his said vehicle, so as to avoid the said collision with the Plaintiff's vehicle.
(4) Collided with the Plaintiff's said vehicle
4.   As respects all the matters aforesaid, as a result of the First Defendant's said negligence the Plaintiff has suffered inter alia a fractured collar-bone.

PARTICULARS OF INJURY

(a) Concussion and shock. The Plaintiff was aged 35 at the time of the said accident.
    The Plaintiff was conveyed several miles by ambulance to the Accident and Emergency Unit at St Charles's Hospital. The ambulance took half an hour to get to the scene of the said accident. The Plaintiff was found to have a fracture of his clavicle and was in severe pain. It was set in plaster under general anaesthetic. The Plaintiff had to keep the plaster on for 6 weeks, and was not able to work during that time. A copy of the doctor's report is attached herewith.

PARTICULARS OF SPECIAL DAMAGE

Loss of earnings for 6 weeks	£1,500 approx
Cost of repairs to vehicle	£3,000
Damage to clothing	£85
Pain killers – whisky and paracetamol	£65
Total	£4,650

5.   Further the Plaintiff claims interest pursuant to section 69 of the
County Courts Act 1984 the amount found to be due to the Plaintiff
at such rate and for such period as the court shall deem just.

AND the Plaintiff claims
  (1)   Damages
  (2)   The aforesaid interest pursuant to section 69 of the County
         Courts Act 1984 to be assessed.

Served, etc   *Karen Squibb*

1   Adapted from the Inns of Court School of Law *Opinion Writing and Drafting*, Blackstone,
    London 1992, p 144.

The illiteracy of the well-educated

Robert Eagleson quotes the following example of typical legalese:

In default of the appearance of the objector before the Tribunal for the
purpose of review, the Tribunal shall . . .

Translated into clear English, this means

If the objector does not appear before the tribunal . . .[1]

Why is it that lawyers and other professionals turn verbs into complex and
ponderous nominalisations and add lots of superfluous words? We don't speak
or write like this when our purpose is to communicate. Has our training and
experience made this our natural mode of communication? Do we think naturally in nominalisations? Or do we translate from the normal to the abnormal?
If so, we tend to make meanings and concepts much more complex than they
are in reality, because, as we have seen, the language is so ill equipped to cope.

What is worrying is that it is the educated who appear to be afflicted with
the disease of gobbledegook. They have a restricted view of language,
allowing its communicative role and the rights of audience to be dis-
counted. They are frequently trapped in their own linguistic conceits,
enmeshed in words, deceiving themselves and others into believing that
they are saying something. As enterprises to rewrite the Takeovers Code
and insurance policies have shown, they are at times saying not what they
intend, but the sheer convolution has hidden the error. The thrust for
plain English reveals that ironically it is the professionals who are linguis-
tically disadvantaged. While sadly they may be disadvantaging others in
the community by not setting out their rights and responsibilities clearly,
it is they who are in need of instant help . . .
      Plain English is not about helping the less well-educated and less fortu-
nate in the community; it is also about releasing the more able.[2]

Now you are released, you can work towards creating a strategy for drafting.

1   R Eagleson 'Plain English: Some Sociolinguistic Revelations' in S Romaine (ed) *Language in
    Australia*, Cambridge University Press, New York 1991, p 366–7.
2   Ibid, p 372.

Defining your drafting principles

By the time you reach this point you should have a clear idea about the purposes of drafting and how to achieve them. Now you are in a position to design a general set of drafting objectives. Use these objectives:

(a)   every time you begin to plan a draft;
(b)   as you revise your draft; and
(c)   after you have completed your draft.

Exercise 8.10   A general checklist for drafting

In pairs, draw up a checklist of your drafting objectives. You may want to use the following materials to help you:

1.   *Your self-editing checklist for writing.*
2.   *The Law Society Legal Practice Course standards for writing and drafting, reproduced below:*

(Students) should be able to draft documents that:

(a)   meet the client's goals, carry out the client's instructions or address the client's concerns;
(b)   accurately address all relevant legal and factual issues;
(c)   where appropriate, identify relevant options;
(d)   where appropriate, demonstrate a critical use of precedents;
(e)   are logically organised;
(f)   form a consistent and coherent whole;
(g)   follow the rules of grammar;
(h)   demonstrate appropriate use of language;
(i)   are succinct and precise;
(j)   meet any formal requirement;
(k)   maintain a standard of care which protects the interests of the client.

The main headings we came up with are:

● PURPOSE
● READERSHIP
● CONTENT
● PROCEDURE
● LAYOUT
● STRUCTURE/ORGANISATION
● LANGUAGE
● STYLE

You may have decided you need a more detailed checklist than the Law Society's, but that some of the detailed questions in your writing checklist are inappropriate for legal documents.

The *Purpose* Heading needs to be adapted to the specific purposes of drafting we have discussed. Most drafting manuals suggest the Law Society guideline (a). However, we have seen that in some standard form contracts the client's goals may not always correspond to those of the readership or the public as a whole. There may therefore be ethical issues you need to think about.

Given our earlier discussion about the organisational characteristics of legal documents, you may have dispensed with the need to link ideas.

Our checklist is more detailed than the Law Society standards, because we think it is helpful to be able to answer very specific questions about your drafts. Some of the questions overlap, but we wanted to make the list comprehensive:

PURPOSE

What are your client's goals?   . . . .
How is the document going to be used?   . . . .
What does the client expect it to accomplish?   . . . .
What are the client's instructions?   . . . .
Have I carried them out?   . . . .
Does the client understand the document?   . . . .
Who are the readers?   . . . .
Will they understand the document?   . . . .
Does it matter if they don't?   . . . .
Is it clear to all readers what the document is for/how it affects them?   . . . .

CONTENT

Have I covered all the relevant law?   . . . .
What legislation applies?   . . . .
What case law applies?   . . . .
What are the possible legal pitfalls?   . . . .
Have I understood the relevant law correctly?   . . . .
Have I drafted it accurately?   . . . .
Does the document cover all contingencies?   . . . .
Is it precise?   . . . .
Is there any ambiguity? in meaning? in syntax?   . . . .
Is it vague in the right places?   . . . .
Have I repeated myself unnecessarily?   . . . .
Do any provisions contradict each other?   . . . .

PROCEDURE

Are there any formal legal requirements?   . . . .
If so, have I met them?   . . . .
Have I used a precedent?   . . . .
If so, have I modelled my draft on it?   . . . .
Or have I checked my draft against it?   . . . .

STRUCTURE

Is the document organised into a coherent whole?   . . . .
Does the material follow a logical sequence?   . . . .
Is the material divided into appropriate categories?   . . . .
Does each category/heading/section/paragraph/sentence contain
(a)   relevant material?   . . . .
(b)   just one idea?   . . . .
Have I used legislative sentences where appropriate?   . . . .
Are any sentences too long?   . . . .
Have I used normal English word order?   . . . .

If not, does the syntax make sense? . . . .
Do I need to make the purpose of the document clear? . . . .
Have I given the same word the same meaning throughout? . . . .

LAYOUT

Is this appropriate for the purpose and content? . . . .
Is it set out in manageable blocks? . . . .
Have I used appropriate headings, subheadings, numbering? . . . .
Do the headings accurately and concisely describe what follows? . . . .

LANGUAGE

Have I followed the three Cs? . . . .
Is my grammar appropriate for the purpose? . . . .
Have I used unnecessary
– sentences within sentences? . . . .
– nominalisations? . . . .
– passives? . . . .
– multiple negatives? . . . .
– misplaced adverbials? . . . .
– word lists? . . . .
Have I omitted words and phrases which are
– redundant? . . . .
– unnecessarily technical? . . . .
– archaic? . . . .
– verbose? . . . .
Is punctuation correct? . . . .
Have I used too much/too little for the purpose? . . . .
Is spelling correct? . . . .

STYLE

Is the style too formal/informal for the purpose? . . . .
Will the tone produce the desired response? . . . .

EFFECT

Have I done everything possible to protect the client's interests? . . . .
Do I understand what I have drafted? . . . .
Do I find it convincing? . . . .

You may find the length of this list daunting. As you become more confident and experienced in drafting, you will find you can discard much of the detail.

Putting principles into practice

Exercise 8.11   Have a go

You are legal adviser to Long Haul Tours, a newly-formed company setting up in the travel business. They have instructed you to draft a booking form for their new 199– package holiday brochure. The company is a member of the Association of British Travel Agents.

The company is particularly concerned to have maximum protection against possible claims by customers should the company cancel or make last minute alterations to bookings. On the other hand, it is keen to prevent customers cancelling or altering bookings, if possible.

1. *In small groups, brainstorm how to go about the task and discuss possible approaches and methodologies.*
2. *Individually, decide which methodology you prefer and why. Make a note in your learning diary on your preferred methodology.*
3. *In your group:*
   (a) Decide which methodology you are going to use.
   (b) Draw up an action plan and show it to your tutor, remembering to define your objectives.
   (c) Do the necessary research.
4. *In preparation for a meeting with the client, draft notes explaining the content and effect of the cancellation clauses you are preparing to draft.*
5. *Draft these clauses. Check you have achieved your objectives.*
6. *Exchange drafts with another group and analyse their draft.*
7. *Feed back to the group on their draft, and receive feedback on yours.*
8. *Discuss with the whole group what problems you experienced in the exercise and what you did to overcome them. Use this information for your learning diary entry.*
9. *Your tutor will give each group a booking form. Read it carefully. Would you make any changes to*
   (a) your draft, and
   (b) the booking form
   as a result of the practical work and analysis you have carried out for this exercise? If so, what changes?

Defining your approach

There are a number of ways you could go about planning this draft. Pragmatists will probably favour dashing off to the nearest travel agent to get specimen booking forms. Theorists may have suggested researching the relevant law first. Activists will have taken a leading role in the brainstorming session and might even have suggested having a go at drafting from scratch. Reflectors will have thought carefully about all the approaches you discussed before deciding eventually which one to go for.

All these methodologies are equally valid. Select whichever one you think will work best for your group.

Aim to be a critical composer, not a complacent copier

One thing you will need to decide is how to use formbooks and precedents. Formbooks are useful for getting started on a draft, as are examples of booking forms in this particular case. They will save you a lot of time and will help to boost your confidence. Furthermore, they help you check you haven't left anything out. As you become more confident and experienced, however, you will not improve your drafting skills sufficiently to become proficient if you rely too heavily on 'off the shelf' precedents. Try to develop your own style as early as possible.

Slavish copying of formbook precedents can be dangerous. You may fail to recognise or analyse a potential problem if you rely too heavily on them. You must evaluate a precedent as carefully as you do your own writing.

You will find that once you can draft with precision, clarity and elegance, you can draft anything. However, keep in mind that the quality of your drafting will be determined as well by the quality of your research and preparation.

We end this chapter with views on drafting from two practitioners: a barrister in commercial practice and a trainee solicitor. Interestingly, neither view seems to reflect any concern for the readers.

> If you're a novelist or an academic, plagiarism is a dirty word, but if you're a practitioner it isn't ... whether you're copying your own precedent, a textbook precedent or somebody else's precedent or if you get six precedents that are roughly in the area but not quite and you chop and change between them ... so long as you've got a draft that is the right answer and is going to progress that case the step required and you get that back quickly ... that's what you're being paid for – getting the right information down on paper and back to the client as quickly as you can ... yes, the solicitor client ... That's a better service than locking yourself up and attempting to do it all out of your own head.[1]

> ... most drafting exercises on the LPC were unproblematic. The reality is that much drafting in real life is not so straightforward. There are often additional points that must be covered or quirks in the information that you are given so that precedents fail to be of use. Only experience enables you to deal quickly and efficiently with drafting.[2]

We hope that these last two chapters have convinced you of the importance of keeping your reader in mind when planning to draft. We recommend you use formbooks critically and discard bits of boilerplate which are archaic and superfluous. Plagiarism is quick and easy, but the results are almost invariably ugly, ponderous and incomprehensible to the reader.

1 Quoted in J Morison & P Leith *The Barrister's World*, Open University Press, Milton Keynes 1992, p 96.
2 Trainee solicitor Nick Oliver, in *Legal Aide*, Trainee Solicitors' Group, Spring 1995, p 4.

Exercise 8.12 Concepts

In this chapter we have discussed a number of concepts. We list the main ones below. The procedure for learning these concepts is as follows:

1. *Divide into pairs.*
2. *Each pair is to*
    (a) *define each concept, noting the page on which it is discussed, and*
    (b) *make sure that both members of the pair understand the meaning of each concept.*
3. *Combine into groups of four. Compare the answers of the two pairs. If there is*

disagreement, look up the concept and clarify it until all agree on the definition and understand it.

boilerplate	*context*
tautology	*truncated passive*
nominalisation	*scenario principle*
archaism	*legislative sentence*
pleadings	*whiz deletion*
bureaucratese	*misplaced adverbial*
term of art	

Exercise 8.13   Analysis

In your groups: compare Clause 7 of the new BT Conditions for Telephone Service (in the Appendix) with Clauses 13, 14, and 15 of the earlier BT agreement on pages 238–9. In particular, comment on

punctuation
sentence length
word order
sentence complexity
vocabulary

and give examples to show how these features influence readability.

Exercise 8.14   Boilerplate redrafting

(a)   Read the business tenancy clause below.
(b)   Summarise the legislative thought in no more than 60 words.
(c)   Redraft the clause in plain English. When you are satisfied with your draft, write it on an overhead transparency.
(d)   All groups should then show their redrafts to the whole group and feed back.

2.   PAYMENT OF INSURANCE

In the event of the demised premises or any part thereof or any of the adjoining or adjacent premises of the Council or any part thereof respectively being damaged or destroyed by fire at any time during the term hereby created and the insurance money under any insurance effected thereon being wholly or partly irrecoverable by reason solely or in part of any act or default of the lessee its agents servants or workmen or of persons occupying or being upon the demised premises or any part thereof with the authority or permission of the lessee then and in every such case the lessee will forthwith in addition to the rent pay to the Council the whole or (as the case may require) a fair proportion of the cost of completely rebuilding or reinstating the same and any dispute as to the proportion to be so distributed by the lessee or otherwise in respect of or arising out of this provision shall be determined by a single arbitrator in accordance with the provisions of the Arbitration Acts 1950 1975 and 1979 or any statutory modification or reinactment thereof for the time being in force.

Review questions

The following extracts are taken from an article in the *Times* by Francis Bennion, in which he discusses the problem of obscurely drafted legislation.

> A prime cause of the horrendous cost of legal advice and litigation, now under investigation by Lord Woolf, is the obscurity of the law . . .
>
> . . . my advice to Lord Woolf is this. Do not look for savings by trying to make the law easier for lay persons to understand. Instead, make it easier for lawyers to use.[1]

1. *Do you agree with this view? Why/why not?*
2. *How would you make the law easier for lawyers to use?*
3. *Summarise the differences between plain English and legal English. How do these differences reflect the differing priorities of each type of writing?*

1   24 January 1995, p 35.

Further reading

M Adler *Clarity for Lawyers*, Law Society, London 1990.

L Melville *The Draftsman's Handbook*, Longman, London 1991.

S Blake *A Practical Approach to Legal Advice and Drafting*, Blackstone, London 1993.

B Child *Drafting Legal Documents: Principles and Practices*, West Publishing, St Paul, Minn 1992.

H Brayne & R Grimes *Professional Skills for Lawyers: A Student's Guide*, Butterworths, London 1994, pp 265–334.

Inns of Court School of Law *Opinion Writing and Drafting*, Blackstone, London 1994.

W Rose *Pleadings Without Tears: A Guide To Legal Drafting*, Blackstone, London 1994.

9 Managing conflict: negotiation

Negotiation is an interactive social process which we regularly engage in. You have therefore become well versed in the skills of negotiating long before you get to this chapter. Our task here is to enable you to identify your skills and transfer them to the context of legal practice. You will consider the broad range of situations in which lawyers negotiate, and how effective they are as negotiators. You will have a chance to identify what type of negotiator you are before we introduce you to three negotiating strategies: win/lose, win some/lose some, and win/win. You will try out these strategies in specific legal situations and assess their strengths and weaknesses. Finally we ask you to consider your own position in the light of the often conflicting ethical and commercial pressures of a busy law practice.

Objectives

To:
- Recognise the importance of negotiation in legal practice.
- Briefly consider the types of dispute resolution in which negotiation plays a part.
- Identify and analyse your negotiating behaviour and personality.
- Analyse the negotiating process and its ethical implications.
- Examine zero-sum and creative strategies of negotiation.
- Assess which strategies are appropriate in which situations.
- Practise negotiation planning, strategies and skills in legal contexts.

Making decisions and resolving conflict

In its broadest sense negotiation is a form of decision-making. It is the process of bargaining to reach an agreement in any situation where the views of more than one person have to be taken into account. We engage in this interactive process constantly when we are with other people:

- Do you fancy a coffee?
- Yes, please. I'll get them.
- No, it's OK. You paid last time.
- OK.

- Your car looks like a bit of a rust box to me. I'll give you £500, take it or leave it.
- Leave it out. There's not an ounce of rust on it.

- £550, that's my final offer.
- OK. It's a deal.

Exercise 9.1   Conflicts of interest

The Joneses, a close-knit and harmonious family, have just won £20,000 on the national lottery. Not surprisingly, at the time they bought tickets they didn't decide what they would do with the money if they won.

Phil wants to buy a new car. He has to travel a long way to work, and his old banger is always breaking down. His boss is beginning to get angry about his lateness.

Debbie, his mother, wants to spend the money on a good holiday for the whole family. They haven't had a holiday abroad for several years.

Ray, his father, wants to use the money to pay off some of the mortgage on the family home.

Sarah is applying to university and wants the money to tide her over the three years until she gets a job. This would mean she would not have to depend on Debbie and Ray.

Rebecca thinks all the family members who are working should give up their jobs and start their own business, making and delivering pizzas.

The family has arranged to meet and discuss what they are going to do with the money.

(a)   Role play: the family meeting.
   (i)   Form groups of five if possible; four if necessary. Allocate a role to each member of the group, leaving out one of the roles if you are a group of four. Change the gender of the roles as necessary to suit your group.
   (ii)   You have 10 minutes to prepare your role. You can make up facts as appropriate to your role.
   (iii)   Role play as if you were at the family meeting.
(b)   'Families' feed back to large group.
   (i)   Did you reach a decision? If so, what was it?
   (ii)   Did everyone agree with it? Why/why not?
   (iii)   How was the decision reached? Analyse carefully what strategy/ tactics each role player used to try and get what they wanted.
   (iv)   Analyse the thoughts and feelings of each role player during the meeting.
   (v)   Did any role player plan their strategy in advance? If so, did they stick to it in the meeting? Why/why not?
   (vi)   If you didn't reach a decision, why was this?
   (vii)   Have you learnt anything new:
      –   about negotiation within a family group?
      –   about yourself as a negotiator?

The scene you have just acted out involved much more than simply problem-solving. The participants have various needs and goals which are in conflict with those of the other participants. You may have noted that different people use different strategies to try and get what they want. We learn these strategies in childhood. Those of you who are parents will know the subtle means by which your children manipulate you to get what they want and no doubt you have a range of techniques for handling conflicts with them.

How you act in a conflict, or a situation ripe for conflict, will be determined by the relationship you have with the other people involved. If it is a 'one-off' interaction, like advertising your car in the paper and selling it to whoever makes the best offer, you are unlikely to meet the buyer ever again. You may therefore think you can get away with some tough bargaining to obtain the highest price.

If, on the other hand, you have conflict at work, at home or with friends, a harmonious future relationship will usually be more important to you than getting everything you want. You are therefore more likely to compromise to reach agreement.

Before you act you must therefore balance two conflicting desires: to achieve all your goals, and maintain co-operation in the future. Which is more likely to satisfy your longer term needs? Your assessment of the relative importance of achieving short term goals and maintaining relationships will influence your behaviour during negotiation.

Exercise 9.2   The shark and the turtle

The purpose of this exercise is to help you reflect on the ways you have learned to manage conflicts and how they compare with the methods that others use.[1]

(a)   *Form your usual groups of four.*
(b)   *Your tutor will give each of you a questionnaire. Working individually, complete the questionnaire without conferring with the other members of your group.*
(c)   *Read the text on conflict strategies below.*
(d)   *Write the names of the other members of your group on separate slips of paper, one name to a slip. On each slip of paper, write the conflict strategy that best fits the actions of the person named.*
(e)   *Pass each slip to the person whose name is on it. Each of you should receive three slips of paper describing the conflict strategy the other group members ascribe to you.*
(f)   *Add up your score on the questionnaire, using the table given you by the tutor. The highest score will indicate the strategy you use most frequently. The second highest score indicates the strategy you use as a back-up when your first one fails.*
(g)   *Tell the group your questionnaire results, comparing them with their descriptions of your style on the slips of paper. Ask the other group members for examples of how they have seen you act in conflicts. Repeat this feedback procedure for all group members.*
(h)   *Discuss the strengths and weaknesses of each of the conflict strategies.*

STRATEGIES FOR MANAGING CONFLICTS

The Turtle (withdrawing)

The turtle withdraws into its shell to avoid conflict rather than face up to it. Turtles will keep away from anyone involved in a conflict, even if this means

Conflict strategies

damaging a relationship with that person. Their personal goals are unimportant.

The Shark (forcing)

The shark wants to win and the opponent to lose. Sharks will try to force opponents to accept their desired outcome to the dispute and won't mind sacrificing relationships to that goal. Sharks attack, overwhelm and intimidate opponents. They see losing as failure and inadequacy.

The Teddy Bear (smoothing)

Teddy bears smooth over conflict and will abandon their goals in order to preserve relationships. They want others to accept and like them.

The Fox (compromising)

The fox wants to meet in the middle. She wants a mutually acceptable agreement and is prepared to sacrifice part of her goals and relationships to achieve it.

The Owl (confronting)

Their goals and relationships are very important. They view conflict resolution as a means of eliminating tension and negative feelings, and look for a solution which yields the best result for both sides.

Besides your personal strategy, there are external factors which influence how you act. Within the group – organisation, family, friendships, or community – there are rules and conventions which determine how negotiation should operate. These may be explicitly agreed: for example, Standing Orders which determine how local council meetings are to be conducted. Or they may be implicit. For example, it might be acceptable to throw a tantrum at home during a family row, but it would be thought quite unacceptable to do so at a company board meeting.

Moreover, it might be clear to everybody involved that certain things are simply not negotiable. For example, a couple living together may have agreed that infidelity by one or the other is not acceptable, so that if it happens, they will decide to split up.

A further significant factor which can influence the process and outcome of negotiation is the bargaining positions of the participants. Age, gender, education and values may bring about subtle and imperceptible shifts of power from one participant to another and back again. These can affect the course of the negotiation and indeed may be the source of the conflict. By virtue of their position, parents know they can resolve a dispute so that their child gets nothing. Employers can drive hard bargains on pay and conditions when jobs are in short supply. Bosses can sexually or racially harass junior employees or trainees and feel they can get away with it.[2]

Can you think of other factors external to the conflict itself which might influence the course and outcome of negotiation?

1   Taken from D Johnson & F Johnson *Joining Together: Group Theory and Group Skills*, Prentice Hall, Englewood Cliffs, NJ 1991, pp 304–9.

2   An unpublished report by the Bar, which studied over 822 Bar Students completing Bar
    Finals in 1989–90 into pupillage and practice, has found that 40% of the women had suf-
    fered sexual harassment by more senior practitioners: see B Hewson 'A Recent Problem?'
    New Law Journal, 5 May 1995, p 626.

The context of legal negotiation

Exercise 9.3   Negotiate? What for?

In pairs or small groups, discuss
(a)   *In what circumstances do legal practitioners negotiate, and why?*
(b)   *In each circumstance you have identified, who will the lawyer negotiate with,
      and on whose behalf?*
(c)   *In those circumstances you have noted which could lead to trial, what
      advantages do you think negotiation has over court action? Are there any
      disadvantages?*

Negotiation forms an essential part of our social relations. Since the practice
of law is one of the ways we manage those social relations, it is hardly surprising that lawyers in practice spend a great deal of their time planning and
carrying out negotiations. They negotiate with their clients and they negotiate
on their behalf, by phone, letter, fax and face to face. They negotiate with the
other side's lawyer and lay experts such as social workers and doctors. In face
to face negotiation with an opponent they may have the client present and
participating, or do it without the client. They may conduct the negotiation
through a mediator.

Over 90% of civil cases are settled or are withdrawn before trial. In personal
injury claims a number of factors may persuade the client not to go as far as
trial. It may be impossible to predict the trial outcome, facts may be difficult
to prove, a plaintiff may need compensation urgently, the client may not be
able to afford to litigate, or the client may not want to ruin a relationship with
the opponent.

Moreover, empirical research into manufacturing industries in the United
States tells us that business people tend not to use contract law remedies and
court action when resolving disputes. They will find excuses to suppress
potential disputes and will renegotiate contracts in order to preserve long-
term relationships, since only by fostering these will they achieve their
long-term goal: to be, or continue to be, successful in business.

Disputes are frequently settled without reference to the contract or
potential or actual legal sanctions. There is a hesitancy to speak of legal
rights, or to threaten to sue in these negotiations. Even where the parties
have a detailed and carefully planned agreement which indicates what is
to happen if, say, the seller fails to deliver on time, often they will never
refer to the agreement but will negotiate a solution when the problem
arises apparently as if there had never been any original contract. One
purchasing agent expressed a common business attitude when he said,

if something comes up, you get the other man on the telephone and deal with the problem. You don't read legalistic contract clauses at each other if you ever want to do business again. One doesn't run to lawyers if he wants to stay in business because one must behave decently.[1]

Where the parties do not expect to deal with each other in the future, they may well behave differently.

We associate negotiated settlements primarily with civil proceedings, but negotiation may feature in criminal proceedings too. As yet we have no formal procedure of plea bargaining in the UK, yet prosecution and defence lawyers are known to agree deals informally.[2]

1   See S Macauley 'Non-Contractual Relations in Business: A Preliminary Study', (1963) 28 *American Sociological Review* 55 at p 61; also 'An Empirical View of Contract', (1985) *Wisconsin Law Review* 465. Extracts from these articles are cited in S Wheeler & J Shaw *Contract Law: Cases, Materials and Commentary*, Clarendon Press, Oxford 1994 pp 76–81, 607–12, 799–810. See also H Beale & A Dugdale 'Contracts Between Businessmen: Planning and the Use of Contractual Remedies', (1975) *British Journal of Law and Society* 18.
2   The Report of the Royal Commission on Criminal Justice (Cm 2263, 1993, paras 41–58) proposed a more formalised system of plea bargaining along the lines of the American system. This proposal has not been adopted, but s 48(1) of the Criminal Justice and Public Order Act 1994 implements Recommendation 156 of the Royal Commission that earlier guilty pleas should attract higher sentence discounts. When deciding sentence, the court can take into account at what stage in the proceedings the offender indicated his intention to plead guilty, and the circumstances in which he gave the indication.
   For the most important research on plea bargaining to date, see J Baldwin & M McConville *Negotiated Justice*, Martin Robertson, Oxford 1977.

Alternative dispute resolution[1]

There are methods of conflict resolution which do not involve negotiation at all. You can settle a dispute by head-butting the opponent, or you can walk away from it, like the turtle. At the other extreme are the formal methods of adjudication – the courts, whose decisions are not negotiable. In the personal injury and contractual disputes we discussed above, lawyers may negotiate an agreement on their clients' behalf without any other person being involved. However, there are other mechanisms of negotiated dispute resolution in which neutral outsiders play a part.

These mechanisms have expanded rapidly during the last twenty years, principally in the United States. In this country their development is more recent. Some methods, like arbitration, have a long history, whilst others, like the mini-trial, are new. Alternative Dispute Resolution is seen as a means of relieving overloaded courts and improving access to justice.[2] However, its supporters are not only concerned with court reform. Its rapid growth is perhaps a symptom of what Schön calls the crisis of confidence in professional knowledge and status.[3] Resolving disputes in the academic tradition of black-letter law is not always an appropriate response in a society whose citizens and communities expect to regulate their own lives and collaborate in conflict resolution. As Tony Marshall says, painting a conflict in terms of legal rights and wrongs is unrealistic and an over-simplification of conflict. Moreover:

> In practice the law can be said to set a bad example – the use of socially condoned violence. Law is perhaps the most civilised way we have of fighting; but it is still fighting. It is unfortunate that law has become the predominant representation of conflict resolution in modern society.[4]

Of course there are situations where court action is preferred to more informal mechanisms of dispute resolution. Take, for example, abuses of fundamental human rights, serious criminal behaviour, or the need for clear statements of public values and the policies which support them.[5] All these may best be satisfied by a legal judgment. ADR does not declare or develop the law, does not happen in full view of the public, and may not even yield a resolution if the process breaks down. A court hearing always ends in a decision.

Moreover, there are those who take the view that the existence of ADR within a legal system is itself a paradox. There are two possible versions of this argument. One suggests that negotiated settlements are compromises whose effect is to deny justice.[6] The other conversely argues that ADR is a 'justice' that is simply outside the law.[7]

Finally, disputes should not be categorised as either adversarial or non-adversarial. Since most cases are settled before trial, it makes more sense to see all dispute settlement as centred around negotiation. Only if this fails will the case proceed to court. The perception of law as litigation, so all other methods of dispute resolution are 'alternative' is surely mistaken. The range of DR mechanisms is now so broad that it is perhaps more accurate to describe litigation as supplementary to the so-called 'alternative' methods. We stress that this is our view, but there is no evidence which can confirm or deny that practitioners share it.

Of the ADR mechanisms which involve a neutral third party in negotiations, mediation is the most widespread. The mediator's task is to encourage the parties to reach their own mutually acceptable agreement.

Some of you may know of mediation in the context of matrimonial disputes.[8] Its supporters claim that it is a constructive and creative way of reaching an agreement between two parties who have decided to separate but who are often extremely bitter and hostile towards each other. Adversarial processes can foster this hostility and force the couple into more entrenched positions, which can damage not only them, but also their children, relations and close friends.

Mediation starts from a position of neutrality between the parties. This is not true of litigation; in court proceedings, one party will have to bear the burden of proof. The position of neutrality allows the disputants to take more control of the process. This can establish a basis for developing enough trust for them to exchange information which in other circumstances they would have withheld. They have more opportunity to thrash out their grievances, express their needs and weigh them against those of their ex-partner. The mediator can meet with the parties separately or together and can make proposals which may be more likely to be accepted because they come from the neutral party, not from the 'enemy'. She can help them concentrate on what should happen in the future, rather than what has happened in the past.

Mediation is a technique which is adaptable to many kinds of disputes. For a long time it has played a central role in industrial relations conflict and recently it has begun to be used to solve local community/neighbourhood problems and commercial disputes.[9]

However, mediation has its critics. Apart from the general criticisms of informal mechanisms we discussed above, there is debate about the functions of the mediator. How far should the mediator intervene? For example, should she discuss the merits of the case, or predict potential trial outcomes? Should all mediators be legally trained? Will justice be denied to weaker parties if lawyers are excluded from the negotiations? Divorce involves a number of complex and technical areas of law. In cases where there is a serious imbalance of power, how do we make sure the weaker party does not sacrifice her rights? Should mediation ever be mandatory?[10] You will have the opportunity to discuss these questions at the end of the chapter.

1   For a discussion of the development and characteristics of Alternative Dispute Resolution mechanisms, see K Mackie (ed) *A Handbook of Dispute Resolution*, Routledge, London 1991; L Singer *Settling Disputes: Conflict Resolution in Business, Families and the Legal System*, Westview Press, Boulder, Colorado 1994.

2   Recent reviews of the civil justice system have consistently identified delay, cost and complexity as the factors which deny litigants access to justice. See the Report of the Review Body on Civil Justice, Cm 394, HMSO, 1988; Heilbronn-Hodge *Civil Justice on Trial: The Case for Change*, General Council of the Bar and Law Society, 1993. The latest review is being carried out by Lord Woolf, who is due to report in 1996.

3   See Chapter 1.

4   T Marshall 'Neighbour Disputes: Community Mediation Schemes as an Alternative to Litigation', in K Mackie (ed), op cit, p 64.

5   See O Fiss 'Against Settlement', (1984) 93 *Yale Jaw Journal*, 1073.

6   See W Twining 'Theories of Litigation, Procedure and Dispute Settlement', (1993) 56 *Modern Law Review* 384–5, in which he discusses this view held by Jeremy Bentham.

7   Y Dezalay 'The Forum Should Fit the Fuss: The Economics and Politics of Negotiated Justice', in M Cain & C B Harrington (eds) *Lawyers in a Postmodern World*, Open University Press, Buckingham 1994, p 155 at p 158.

8   See eg G Davis *Partisans and Mediators: The Resolution of Divorce Disputes*, Clarendon Press, Oxford 1988.

9   Agencies which offer mediation services are: National Association of Family Mediation and Conciliation Services; Centre for Dispute Resolution and ADR Group (commercial disputes); Advisory, Conciliation and Arbitration Service (ACAS); Mediation UK (neighbourhood disputes).

10   For further discussion of mediation, see L Singer, op cit; K Mackie 'Negotiation and Mediation: From Inelegant Haggling to Sleeping Giant', in K Mackie (ed), op cit, pp 74–94; C McEwen, L Mather & R Maiman 'Lawyers, Mediation, and the Management of Divorce Practice', (1994) 28 *Law and Society Review*, 149–86; C Menkel-Meadow 'Lawyer Negotiations; Theories and Realities – What We Learn From Mediation', (1993) 56 *Modern Law Review*, 361–79; R Ingleby 'Court Sponsored Mediation: The Case Against Mandatory Participation', (1993) 56 *Modern Law Review*, 441–51; H Brown *Alternative Dispute Resolution*, Law Society, London 1991.

What clients want from negotiation

What do you think a client wants most from a negotiation? Clearly she wants the dispute resolved. Research carried out in the United States on client satisfaction with methods of alternative dispute resolution indicates that negotiation procedures weigh more heavily with clients than outcome. In other words, they are less interested in getting everything they want from the negotiation, or even that the settlement is fair. They are more concerned that they are treated fairly.[1] They want to be treated with courtesy and respect, and to participate actively in the process. This means having the opportunity to put their cases and have their views listened to by the lawyers, judges, or mediators who are settling their problems.

> Those with problems value the opportunity to present their problems to authorities. By allowing disputants to bring their problems to them, authorities are reaffirming the disputants' social standing and their right to call on the authorities for help.[2]

If disputants feel they have some control over the outcome of their dispute, then they are more likely to be satisfied that the outcome is fair.

If we look at dispute resolution from the client's point of view, we should not be surprised at these findings. After all, it is the clients, not their lawyers, who have to live with the outcome.

1 For an overview of the research, see T Tyler 'Procedure or Result: What Do Disputants Want from Legal Authorities?, in K Mackie (ed), op cit, pp 19–25.
2 Ibid p 22.

What lawyers want from negotiation

Lawyers are trained to see disputes in 'win–lose' terms. 'Thinking like a lawyer' means thinking adversarially. As we have seen earlier in this book,[1] law school problems are confined to issues of legal principle and ignore the broader problems of the swamp, such as the future relationship of the parties to the dispute or the power relationship between them. Moreover, the professional codes of conduct prescribe the practitioners' duty to act in their clients' best interests.

> . . . within an 'adversarial' system of law, the lawyer's responsibility is to seek to 'win' for the client using every tactic that is professionally allowable (or not explicitly prohibited); and that the object of the process is victory in relation to a carefully defined question of principle as applied to (usually) a definite past incident or incidents. Thus trials issue narrow win–lose outcomes rather than problem-solving solutions which take into account the context of the dispute, the merits of both sides and the wider relationship of the parties, past, present and future; law firms handle cases in 'litigation' departments rather than 'settlement' departments – although most of the time they settle rather than go as far as trial (but often for negative reasons of cost considerations and uncertainties of trial judgment rather than positively negotiated mutually satisfactory outcomes); relations between clients and client attitudes to legal action become soured by legal wrangling and procedural hurdles motivated by lawyer obsession with technical victories.[2]

275

It could therefore come as a surprise to some lawyers that clients may be more interested in fairness than winning or losing.

Furthermore, lawyers' and clients' perceptions of fairness may well differ. You may take the view that the informal procedures of ADR do not offer parties the safeguards provided by the formal procedures of litigation. For example, a common criticism of informal plea bargaining is that the offender's lack of bargaining power in this situation may force him to make a decision against his own best interests. Yet can we assume the offender sees it in the same way? Isn't it possible he may view the chance to have a say in the outcome of his case as far more 'just' than having a decision imposed on him by a court? At the very least the lawyer should check that the client's view of what is fair and just accords with her own.

1   See Chapters 1, 3 and 4.
2   K Mackie 'Dispute Resolution: The New Wave', in Mackie (ed), op cit, p 5.

Mind the gap[1]

Research by Austin Sarat and William Felsteiner, among others, provides evidence that client and lawyer perceptions of the reality and function of negotiation differ in other respects.[2] They recorded conversations between clients and their lawyers involved in divorce cases. From these they formed the conclusion that while clients concentrate on what happened in the past and the failure of their marriage, lawyers focus on the future: the legal issues of getting the divorce and making arrangements about children and property.

> Lawyers avoid responding to these (the clients') interpretations because they do not consider that who did what to whom in the marriage is relevant to the legal task of dissolving it. In this domain clients largely talk past their lawyers, and interpretive activity proceeds without the generation and ratification of a shared understanding of reality.[3]

Here is an extract from one conversation, followed by the authors' comments:

Client: There was harassment and verbal degradation. No interest at all in my furthering my education. None whatsoever. Sexual harassment. If there was ever any time when I did not want or need sex, I was subject to, you know, these long verbal whiplashings. Then the Bible would be put out on the counter with passages underlined as to what a poor wife I was. Just constant harassment from him.

Lawyer: Mmn uh.

Client: There was . . . what I was remembering the other day, and I had forgotten. When he undertook to lecturing me and I'd say, 'I don't want to hear this. I don't have time right now,' I could lock myself in the bathroom and he would break in. And I was just to listen, whether I wanted to or not. And he would lecture me for hours. Literally hours . . . There was no escaping him, short of getting into a car and driving away. But then he would stand outside in the driveway and yell, anyhow. *The man was not well* (emphasis added).

Lawyer: Okay. Now how about any courses you took?

This lawyer does not respond to his client's attribution of blame or characterisation of her husband; no negotiation of reality occurs. The 'okay' seems to reflect the end of his patience with her description, and he abruptly changes the subject.[4]

These conversations took place in the context of no-fault divorce. Engaging with the client in reconstructing the past is therefore irrelevant and time-wasting for the lawyer, because there are no legal issues of marriage breakdown to resolve.

However, in a fault-based system the lawyer will want to discuss the details of the marriage failure with the client. This is necessary to identify the relevant legal issues and to check the accuracy of the client's description of her ex-partner's behaviour and character. Client–lawyer interests therefore seem to coincide. How much does it matter if the client interprets the lawyer's interest in the marriage failure as motivated by sympathy and support, when in fact it is motivated by issues of law and fact?

In the case of no-fault divorce, however, the needs and perceptions of client and lawyer do not even appear to coincide. It is as if they are

in effect largely occupied with two different divorces: lawyers with a legal divorce, clients with a social and emotional divorce. The lawyers orient themselves towards legal norms and institutional practices, the clients towards the social norms of their environment.[5]

When articulating and developing your approach to negotiation, you clearly need to be aware of gaps like these. Can they be bridged, and if so, how? Is it the responsibility of the lawyer to bridge them, for example, by developing an ethics of care?[6] What are the 'business' implications? In a busy practice, will you be given the time to listen to and empathise with your client? Or will there be too much pressure on you to 'process' as many clients as possible to earn more fee income for the practice?

It is essential to keep these questions in mind as we work through the principles and practice of negotiation.

---

1 This phrase is used by C Cunningham 'A Tale of Two Clients: Thinking About Law as Language', (1989) 87 *Michigan Law Review*, 2459 at 2469.
2 A Sarat & W Felsteiner 'Law and Social Relations: Vocabularies of Motive in Lawyer/Client Interaction', (1988) 22 *Law & Society Review*, 737; also 'Law and Strategy in the Divorce Lawyer's Office', (1986) 20 *Law & Society Review*, 93; J Griffiths 'What Do Dutch Lawyers Actually Do In Divorce Cases', (1986) 20 *Law & Society Review*, 135; S Merry & S Silbey 'What Do Plaintiffs Want?' (1984) 9 *Justice System Journal*, 151.
3 Sarat & Felsteiner (1988), op cit, p 742.
4 Ibid, pp 744–5.
5 J Griffiths, op cit, p 155.
6 See Chapter 4, pp 117–20.

Learning the art of legal negotiation

Earlier in the chapter we pointed out that we have all been negotiating from a very early age. Negotiation is such a 'natural' process that we are hardly aware we are doing it a lot of the time. Up until recently lawyers received no training in legal negotiating skills, but were left to pick them up 'on the job'. This they had to do by building on the tacit knowledge they had gained throughout their lives. It was a haphazard and difficult process for many. We want you to begin the process now, so that when you come to negotiate professionally you will have a starting point for the development of your own artistry.

We shall look at the process of negotiation in a series of steps:
1 Identify the critical issues.
2 Select a negotiating strategy.
3 Sort out your ethics.
4 Work out your tactics.
5 Keep your act together during the negotiation.
6 Keep a negotiation journal.

Step 1: Identify the critical issues

By 'critical issues' we mean those issues (legal and non-legal) which must be resolved if the dispute as a whole is to be resolved and the parties are to reach agreement.

Exercise 9.4 What is there to negotiate about?

The purpose of this part of the exercise is to identify the critical issues in the five cases which follow.

(a) *Form groups of four or five. Each group should then split into two sub-groups, A and B. Sub-group A will represent one party to each dispute, Sub-group B will represent the opposing party:*

SUB-GROUPS A	SUB-GROUPS B
Wilf	*Pam*
Employer	*Frances*
Carol	*Bob*
Maxine	*John*

For Case 4, divide your group so that Randall, the Chairman, and Cliff are all represented.

(b) *Each sub-group should list the critical issues in each of the five cases.*

1. Wilf, a third year student, has lived at 9a Woodbridge Way for three years under a tenancy agreement with Pam. Wilf owes Pam £850 in back rent because he has got into debt and hasn't paid any rent at all for the last few months. He is preparing for his final exams in two month's time.

Pam has given Wilf notice to quit, convinced that she will get no more rent out of him. She was reluctant to do this, because up to now Wilf has been a model tenant. Last year when Pam was going to have the flat decorated, Wilf offered to do it for a small charge if she paid for all the materials. He decorated the whole flat and Pam paid him £100.

The neighbours were unhappy at first when they knew a student was moving in, but they have never had any reason to complain about noise, or anything else. All the neighbours are very friendly with Wilf and have told Pam they will be sorry to see him go.

2. Frances is a recently qualified chartered accountant who got a job with a prestigious firm in the City. Two months after she started the job, she found she was pregnant. Her relationship with the baby's father had ended when she moved down to London to take the job.

   Frances decides she wants to have the baby and keep her job, because her career prospects with this firm are excellent. After she has told her employer she is pregnant, the partners meet and decide to terminate her contract. The reason they give her is that the time off she will need for the birth etc, will mean she can't complete her probationary period. They advertise for a new accountant immediately.

3. Bob and Carol have been married for ten years and have three children, aged 8, 6 and 3. Carol is a talented painter who had two successful exhibitions before she got married, but hasn't done any serious painting since she had the children. Over the years she has become increasingly resentful about the lack of opportunity to pursue a career.

   Bob works for an international oil company and is often abroad. He has therefore played little part in looking after the children. However, the family is well off, and Bob repeatedly suggested to Carol that they employ a nanny to live in and look after the children. Carol always refused, saying she didn't want a stranger in their house. She would rather her husband was home more.

   Six months ago, Carol started an affair with Rachel. Bob found out and made her leave the family home. Rachel agreed that Carol could live with her for the time being. The couple are the main source of gossip in the village where they live.

   Bob will not allow Carol to see the children at all, and has begun divorce proceedings.

4. On the eve of a major cup final, Randall Dolph, the captain of Melton FC, was interviewed by the press. Off the record, he called the club Chairman a 'fat old fart, who knows absolutely f*** all about football'. One tabloid newspaper printed the statement, and now the story is headline news. The Chairman is extremely concerned about his public image and credibility, and goes on record as saying he wants Randall sacked from the club. He instructs Cliff, the team manager, to drop Randall from the team. If Cliff refuses, the Chairman says, he will be sacked. The Chairman has also issued a writ against the tabloid newspaper.

In the meantime, the players have refused to play in the cup final unless Randall is reinstated. If the match doesn't go ahead, the club will incur a large financial penalty, and lose important income. They may even be expelled from their league. The supporters club has threatened to boycott all matches unless the Chairman resigns immediately.

5.   When Maxine Krantz was driving down Stapleton Road one evening last May, she knocked a cyclist off his bike. Stapleton Road is quite wide, but there were cars parked on both sides of it. In her statement to the police Maxine said the cyclist pulled out in front of her from behind a parked car as she was beginning to overtake him.

John Rose, the cyclist, said Maxine was driving too fast, otherwise she could have stopped. Also, there was not enough room for her to overtake at that point. John's kneecap was broken, his bike was damaged, and his clothes ruined. Maxine has not been prosecuted.

Maxine doesn't want any publicity, because she is well known in the area and a local magistrate.

John is due to start a new job in Australia in two months' time.

In your sub-groups:
(c)   *Get together with another sub-group which is advising the same parties. Compare findings and try to agree a final list of the critical issues for each case.*
(d)   *Now list what you think are the critical issues for the other side in each case. Then discuss your list with your opposing sub-group.*
(e)   *With your opposing sub-group, try to agree:*
    (i)   *a list of critical issues, and*
    (ii)   *their order of importance.*

Your identification of the critical issues should have provided you with a clearer idea of the possible outcomes of each dispute.

You may not have been able to agree on the order of outcomes. Nevertheless, you should now be in a position to advise your clients what their options are. In real situations you would do the next part of the exercise together with your clients, having discussed their objectives with them.

(f)   *In your sub-groups: rank your options in each case, from the best possible outcome down to the least desirable. Can you justify this ranking? Don't forget that any assumptions you make about your client's needs or interests would, in a real situation, have to be articulated and checked. Try to determine in each case your client's likely bottom line: the lowest acceptable option.*
(g)   *Are there any reasons why negotiations might fail? If so, what are they?*
(h)   *What are your choices, if any, if you don't reach agreement?*

You must be prepared for negotiations to fail. This means you need to work out the best possible and practical course of action – your Best Alternative to a Negotiated Agreement (BATNA).[1] In most situations your BATNA will be court action.

(i)   *Compare your rankings with those of your opponent.*
(j)   *FEED BACK to tutor and whole group.*

You should now be in a position to think out your negotiating strategy – how you intend to get what your client wants.

Incidentally, don't worry that you haven't researched the law yet. We are concerned here to get you thinking generally and creatively about how to use negotiation to resolve legal conflicts.

However, before we move on to strategy, compare your list of critical issues with ours. We aren't going to work through all the cases, but we shall illustrate the purpose of the exercise so far with Case 1, and make some general points.

CRITICAL ISSUES

PAM	*WILF*
Can she evict Wilf?	Can Pam evict him?
Does she want to evict him?	Does he have anywhere to go?
Does she want to lose a good tenant?	Where can he live while doing his exams?
Does it matter if they part on bad terms?	Does it matter if they part on bad terms?
Is there any way she can get the money? – all of it? – some of it? – when? – how?	Is there any way he can pay? – all of it? – some of it? – when? – how?
Can he pay rent in the future?	Can he pay rent in the future?
How long will he stay?	How long will he stay?
Does she mind the bother of getting a new tenant?	

You may have thought of others, or considered some of these not critical.

On the information you have, there are a number of issues the parties have in common which could be a starting-point for negotiation. It may come down to Pam deciding how important this source of income is to her. We can't judge this without knowing more about her financial circumstances. If it is the priority, then negotiations may not be successful.

POSSIBLE OUTCOMES

PAM	*WILF*
Wilf is evicted and she gets a new tenant quickly who can pay. Wilf pays the debt off immediately by getting a loan.	Pam lets him stay rent-free until his exams are over. Either she writes off the debt or he pays it off by instalments.
As above, Wilf pays the debt off by instalments.	As above, he pays a minimal amount until he leaves.

As above, she writes off part of the debt: failing that, all of it.	As above, he owes full rent until he leaves.
Wilf stays until exams are over, pays full rent from now, and arrears by one of the methods above.	He is evicted, debt is written off.
	As above, pays off part of the debt in instalments
Wilf stays as long as he likes; come to some flexible arrangement about rent.	As above, has to get loan to repay debt.
BATNA – Court order for possession.	BATNA – Arranges to stay with friend until exams over.

Wilf's real BATNA could be a moonlight flit, but as his lawyer you shouldn't have advised him to do this!

It is worthwhile identifying the contingent or contextual factors that will have influenced your options in each situation. Four of the cases depend on whether an established relationship should continue. In Bob's and Carol's case, it will have to continue in some form or other. The personal injury claim is a 'one-off' situation, so the relationship of the parties is probably not an issue. On that basis, litigation may look like an attractive option.

However, on the information you have so far on the personal injury claim, the outcome if the matter went to court is very uncertain. The issue of liability is unclear, before you even get to quantum. In Cases 1 and 2 the legal issues are clear. Case 4, however, differs from the others not only because at least three parties are involved; here the legal issue – defamation – is peripheral to the conflict. The parties will have to negotiate, and fast, if they want to avoid a debacle, as sports commentators are fond of describing such an event.

We summarise these contingent factors as follows:

1. DOES THE RELATIONSHIP HAVE TO CONTINUE?
    DO THE PARTIES WANT IT TO?
2. IS THIS MAINLY ABOUT MONEY?
    IS THE AMOUNT CERTAIN OR UNCERTAIN?
3. WHICH IS LESS TROUBLE: SETTLEMENT OR LITIGATION?
    –   NOW? COST, DELAYED DECISION, CONTROL?
    –   THE FUTURE?
4. IF WE GO TO COURT: IS THE OUTCOME CERTAIN?

You will probably have found that your order of preferred outcomes in every case is fairly speculative, because you haven't got enough information to go on. What is more important at this stage, however, is to recognise that your intuition and experience have guided you to prefer some options over others. Your knowing-in-action will similarly inform your choice of negotiating strategy.

1   See R Fisher & W Ury *Getting to Yes: Negotiating An Agreement Without Giving In*, Business Books, London 1991, p 104.

Exercise 9.5 Pam and Wilf

In the large group:
1. *Select two volunteers to do the negotiation, one to role play Pam's lawyer, the other one to represent Wilf. The volunteers have 10 minutes to prepare their roles.*

    To prepare for the negotiation, the role players will need to look at a profile of their client in the Appendix. Naturally they may only look at the profile of their own client! If any more information is needed, they may make it up, provided it is consistent with the information in the profile.

    The rest of the group will be given both profiles.
2. *The lawyers carry out the negotiation.*
3. *Feed back in the following order:*
    (a) Pam's lawyer;
    (b) Wilf's lawyer;
    (c) Members of the group;
    (d) Tutor.
    The lawyers should try to answer these questions:
    (i)   What was the best possible outcome for your client? Did you achieve it?
    (ii)   Are you completely satisfied with the result? Why/why not?
    (iii) Does the outcome benefit both parties? Why/why not?
    (iv)   What kind of relationship did you want to build with your opponent? Give reasons. Did you establish the relationship you wanted? Why/why not?
    (v)   What was your opening stance? Why?
    (vi)   Did you share information with your opponent? Why/why not?
    (vii) Did you obtain any information from your opponent? Why/why not?
    (viii) Did you make any concessions? Which? Why/why not?
    (ix)   During the negotiation, did you feel:
    > *upset?*
    > *angry?*
    > *confident?*
    > *strong?*
    > *weak?*
    > *pressured?*
    > *hostile?*
    > *any other emotion? Which?*

    If so, at what point, and why?
    (x)   Is there anything you would do differently if you carried out this negotiation again? If yes, what and why?

Step 2: Select a negotiating strategy

Should you negotiate on the merits of the case as a whole, or on the basis of getting the best for your client at the expense of the other side? When should you consider compromise? We summarise the negotiating strategies below and then go on briefly to describe their main characteristics. A great deal has been written about these strategies.[1] You will find that writers differ in their descriptions and terminology, and this can be quite confusing. For example, some understand 'co-operative' strategy to mean strategies two and three below, as opposed to the 'competitive' strategy of number one.

1. WIN/LOSE   (competitive, adversarial, positional, zero-sum).
2. WIN SOME/LOSE SOME   (compromising, co-operative, collaborative).
3. WIN/WIN   (problem-solving, integrative, principled, creative).

You may be surprised to learn that there is a fourth strategy which we call LOSE/LOSE; but more of this later.

1.   THE WIN/LOSE APPROACH

This is the courtroom model and so is as admirably suited to lawyers, you may think, as it is to sharks. The participants are adversaries, the goal is victory. The prize is a bigger share of a fixed cake. Therefore, any gain for the winner means a corresponding loss for the loser. Game theorists refer to this model as 'zero-sum'.[2]

The negotiator may not go in hard, but will certainly take control from the beginning. She will try to get the opponent to make the first of a number of concessions. She will be slow to reveal information and will exaggerate the strength of her client's position. She may appear conciliatory so as to get all the information she needs from the opponent. She takes up a strong, uncompromising position and keeps the pressure on the opponent to make concessions. However, she is not overtly aggressive. She may be argumentative, but will remain within the bounds of courteous and ethical conduct.

2.   THE WIN SOME/LOSE SOME APPROACH

This approach recognises that you need to give in order to get. It may start from a win/lose position and then negotiators come to realise that neither party has a chance of winning outright. They therefore have to decide what is important and what can be given away. The objective is to achieve a solution which is satisfactory to both sides. Co-operative negotiators seek to establish and maintain a friendly relationship with the opponent, so that they can look for common ground and shared interests. (The Fox).

3.   THE WIN/WIN APPROACH

This approach favours the co-operative, collaborative style of bargaining, but instead of being satisfied with compromise, its objective is mutual gain. Fisher and Ury describe it as 'principled' negotiation, or negotiation 'on the merits'.[3] They see the process not as a contest in which the parties haggle over their positions, conceding a bit here and a bit there, but as a shared problem in which the best possible solution must be obtained for both sides. The danger of the positional approaches 1. and 2. is that the parties can overlook other options and common interests as they get locked into argument over slight shifts of position. Principled bargaining, on the other hand, is 'designed to produce wise outcomes efficiently and amicably'.[4]

---

1   See for example G Williams *Legal Negotiation and Settlement*, West Publishing, St Paul, Minn 1983; R Fisher & W Ury, op cit; D Lax & J Sebenius *The Manager as Negotiator: Bargaining for Co-operation and Competitive Gain*, Free Press, New York 1986; C Menkel-Meadow 'Legal Negotiation: A Study of Strategies in Search of a Theory', (1983) Am B F Res J 905.

See also the skills manuals recommended in the Further Reading section at the end of this chapter.

2 See for example R Axelrod *The Evolution of Co-operation*, Basic Books, New York 1984.
3 Fisher & Ury, op cit.
4 Ibid, pp 10–11.

Principled negotiation

Fisher and Ury define four key rules of principled negotiation:

1. SEPARATE THE PEOPLE FROM THE PROBLEM.
2. FOCUS ON INTERESTS, NOT POSITIONS.
3. INVENT OPTIONS FOR MUTUAL GAIN.
4. INSIST ON OBJECTIVE CRITERIA.

1. SEPARATE THE PEOPLE FROM THE PROBLEM

This rule appreciates that human beings are creatures of strong emotions who often have radically different perceptions and have difficulty communicating clearly. Emotions typically become entangled with the objective merits of the problem. Taking positions just makes this worse because people's egos become identified with their positions. Hence, before working on the substantive problem, the 'people problem' should be disentangled from it and dealt with separately. Figuratively, if not literally, the participants should come to see themselves as working side by side, attacking the problem, not each other.[1]

Separating the people from the problem is far from easy. Do you have any suggestions as to how to go about this?

2. FOCUS ON INTERESTS, NOT POSITIONS

The parties' interests may not all conflict. You won't discover their compatible interests unless you look behind their apparently opposed positions. To understand their real interests, ask 'why'? not 'what?'. You are then more likely to find out what it is they really want.

> Consider the story of two men quarrelling in a library. One wants the window open and the other wants it closed. They bicker back and forth about how much to leave it open: a crack, halfway, three-quarters of the way. No solution satisfies them both.
>
> Enter the librarian. She asks one why he wants the window open: 'To get some fresh air.' She asks the other why he wants it closed: 'To avoid the draught.' After thinking a minute, she opens wide a window in the next room, bringing in fresh air without a draught.[2]

3. INVENT OPTIONS FOR MUTUAL GAIN

Looking to expand the cake rather than divide it will involve creative processes of brainstorming and lateral thinking. Think up in advance the widest range of possible solutions which advance shared interests and reconcile conflicting ones. We encouraged you to try this in Exercise 9.4.

Why do you think it is important to do this in advance?

4. INSIST ON OBJECTIVE CRITERIA

Negotiations can become a contest of wills or a conflict of opinion in which neither side wants to lose face. You can avoid this if you establish an independent basis for settlement, such as market value, expert opinion, custom or law. A fair settlement based on objective criteria will be more acceptable to both sides.

You may have already decided which of the three strategies we have outlined fits best with your assessment of your negotiating personality. Owls will tend to go for win/win, for example. However, you need to experiment with all three to see how they work. They are not mutually exclusive, and no single strategy will succeed in every case. You must recognise which strategy is appropriate for a particular case and a particular opponent. Aim to become conversant with all of them. Furthermore, you need to be able to recognise which style your opponent is using.

1 R Fisher & W Ury *Getting to Yes: Negotiating An Agreement Without Giving In*, Business Books, London 1991, p 11.
2 Ibid, p 41.

Exercise 9.6 Have your cake and eat it, divide it in two, or eat it and have another one?

In your groups:
(a) Discuss the advantages and disadvantages of each strategy.
(b) List the advantages and disadvantages of each on separate pieces of flipchart. Then compare your list with those of other groups.
(c) Divide into pairs. Choose one of the negotiating scenarios:
> *Frances/Employer;*
> *John/Maxine;*
> *Chairman/Randall/Cliff (you will need to form a threesome for this one);*
> *Bob/Carol;*
> *and prepare the negotiation (20 minutes). For further information, consult the profiles in the Appendix. Remember not to look at your opponent's profile!*
(d) Role play the negotiation.
(e) In your pairs, answer the following questions:
> *(i) Was the negotiation successful? Why/why not?*
> *(ii) What strategy did each of you plan to use, and why?*
> *(iii) Did you alter your strategy during the negotiation? If so, why?*
> *(iv) What, if anything, will you do differently next time?*

We summarise the strengths and weaknesses of the three negotiating styles below. The list is not comprehensive.

THE WIN/LOSE STYLE OF COMPETITIVE BARGAINING

STRENGTHS	*WEAKNESSES*
Makes clear you are out to win.	Can produce tension.

May get result close to
opening position.

May irritate opponent.

Effective against weak
opposition.

May divide parties further.

Most likely to get
concessions.

Can result in deadlock.

Results may impress clients
and colleagues.

Loses sight of mutual
interests.

Can get the best result for
client.

Exchanges may become
emotional.

Negotiator may build up
reputation which antagonises
future opponents.

THE WIN SOME/LOSE SOME STYLE OF CO-OPERATIVE BARGAINING

STRENGTHS

WEAKNESSES

Likely to result in
settlement.

May give away more
than necessary.

Settlement more likely
to be fair.

Strengths of case may
not be pushed.

May improve parties'
relationship.

May appear 'weak' and be
exploited by win/lose opponent.

Friendly, trusting atmosphere
may encourage opponent to
make concessions.

May accept easy option,
not the best one.

Results may benefit both sides.

May not get the best for client.

THE WIN/WIN STYLE OF PRINCIPLED NEGOTIATION

STRENGTHS

WEAKNESSES

Can explore options which
positional bargaining obscures.

Opponent may not use
it and so not respond.

Avoids haggling and
bickering.

No safety net of
'bottom line'.

Can get best possible
result for both sides.

Only works if there are
compatible interests.

Bargains on objective
criteria.

Negotiation stages not
clearly defined.

We hope that by this stage you are beginning to get an idea of these approaches and styles. You may have made up your mind that a particular one does not suit you, and so you won't use it. When you are more experienced at legal negotiation, you will be able to use all three, and if necessary, use them at different points during the same negotiation.

The next exercise should give you some further insight into how the strategies work.

Exercise 9.7   The Red–Blue exercise[1]

In your groups,
(a)   *Discuss what factors make a negotiation successful. Consider in particular the behaviour and characteristics of an effective negotiator.*
(b)   *Summarise your findings on flipchart.*
(c)   *Form yourselves into new teams. There must be an even number of teams, eg A plays B, C plays D, E plays F etc. Each game will need one person to act as a 'go-between'. Each game should be played as far away as possible from the others, as it can get very noisy!*

The rules for each game are as follows:

OBJECTIVE: To end the game with the highest possible score for your team.
1.   There are two teams.
2.   There are ten rounds.
3.   Your team will choose to play either red or blue at each round.
4.   When your team has decided on its colour for that round, tell the go-between. You will be told what your opponents have played only when both teams have decided. It is the combined colours that determine your respective scores.

You will be scored as follows:

PLAY		SCORE	
GROUP A	*GROUP B*	*SCORE A*	*SCORE B*
Red	Red	+3	+3
Red	Blue	–6	+6
Blue	Red	+6	–6
Blue	Blue	–3	–3

5.   You can have a conference with the opposing group after the fourth round. However, this can only take place if both groups wish it.
6.   You can have another conference after the eighth round, if both groups choose to do this.
7.   The ninth and tenth rounds score double, ie:
     –   If both groups play Blue, each scores –6;
     –   If one group plays Blue, the other Red: Red = –12; Blue = +12;
     –   If both play Red, each scores +6.

Use the following score sheet and fill it in after each round, entering both your score and that of the opposing team. Remember that at the conference points you may only negotiate if both sides agree. You are only playing your opponents. The other pairs of groups are not part of your game.

SCORESHEET

Move	Colour played		Score	
	A	B	A	B
1				
2				
3				
4				

Conference point				
5				
6				
7				
8				

Conference point				
9 (double)				
10 (double)				

TOTALS				

Your tutor will put all the scores up on the white board.

(d) *Return to your original groups. Display the flipchart your group did for part (b) of the exercise somewhere where all the other groups can read it.*

(e) *Game teams feed back to the large group:*
  - *What was the objective of the game?*
  - *Does your score reflect that objective?*
  - *How does your score compare with your opponents'?*
  - *Briefly describe the course of your game and why your team acted as it did. Were there any disagreements about strategy within the team? What are your feelings, both towards your opponents and towards other members of your team?*
  - *What do you think was the purpose of the game?*
  - *How does your 'flipchart for effective negotiation' compare with the way you played this game? Do you detect any discrepant reasoning?*

(f) *Further Reflection-on-Action. When you have had more time to reflect, make a detailed entry in your learning diary about this exercise. What have you learned from the experience? Please show your diary to your tutor for comments.*[2]

We dropped a hint earlier about a fourth strategy, which we called Lose/Lose. It has to do with saving face, ie we would rather win than lose, but if we are going to lose, we shall drag the other side down with us. A negotiator will consciously and deliberately decide to outdo her opponent, even if it means ending up with an unsatisfactory outcome herself. These sharks[3] prefer competition so strongly that they will not forgo it in exchange for a mutually much more beneficial outcome, even if this means they and their clients receive substantially less as a result. Win/lose is so ingrained that they think they have won because they haven't lost as much as the other side. Their reward lies in beating their opponents.

This brings us neatly to our third step in learning the art of negotiation.

1   This is one of the many variations on the Prisoner's Dilemma Game (PDG), invented in about 1950 by Merrill Flood and Melvin Dresher. M Deutsch used the PDG to study the issue of trust in situations of conflict: see for example 'Trust and Suspicion', (1958) 2 *Journal of Conflict Resolution* 265–79. The PDG has been studied by mathematical game theorists D Luce & H Raiffa: see *Games and Decisions*, Wiley, New York 1957; see also R Axelrod, op cit.
2   In all the years that we have played Red–Blue with our students, the results are nearly always the same. There are a number of things that you can learn from them about negotiation, but it would give the game away to mention them here. Tutors: please consult the Teachers' Book.
3   Are lawyers and law students included among their number?

Step 3:   Sort out your ethics

> While the official code of conduct prescribes a zealous pursuit of the client's interests, the informal norms and the realities of professional life prompt compromise and co-operation. Unfortunately, clear guidelines for helping attorneys decide which path to take are nonexistent.[1]

This writer is talking about the divorce process in the United States, but the point is a general one. How can you reconcile this conflict? You have probably been discussing these questions already, before you reached this point.

Does it mean you must use the win/lose strategy? You may think that getting a settlement which is fair to both sides is not the same as maximising your client's interests. Is principled negotiation a realistic and ethical strategy in legal disputes? The cake, whatever its size, will have to be shared out in the end. Can you get the best for your client yet avoid positional bargaining?[2] And should you use it where there are serious imbalances of power between the parties?

In 1987 Hazel Genn published a study of negotiated settlements in personal injury claims between plaintiffs' solicitors and defendant insurance companies. She found that plaintiffs are disadvantaged from the start because of the imprecision and uncertainty of the law of negligence and the problems of proof. These factors put pressure on plaintiffs to avoid the risks of trial and compromise their claims. The inequality increases because not only are insurance companies specialist and experienced 'repeat players' in negotiation and litigation; they have greater financial resources to collect the information needed to resist the claim.[3] Therefore, although the parties may have a common interest in saving time and money by not going to court, their fundamental interests are diametrically opposed.

. . . the nature of personal injury claims settlement is inherently adversarial. The plaintiff wants to maximise his damages, while the defendant
wants to avoid or minimise payment . . . In this contest the very idea of
co-operation between the parties appears misconceived and many specialist personal injury solicitors recognise this fact . . . although insurance
companies encourage co-operation rather than confrontation and prefer
matters to be settled without the commencement of court proceedings,
they will take advantage of their opponent if the opportunity is presented.
The desire for co-operation among insurance companies therefore
appears largely opportunistic; and for plaintiffs' solicitors to postpone the
commencement of proceedings in the interests of co-operation, or to be
drawn into longer-term co-operative relationships, may not be in plaintiffs' best interests, unless claims are weak or of low value.[4]

This seems to suggest that the ethical choice is the win/lose approach in
claims against a 'powerful' defendant. If you accept this view, then you will
have to learn to use the strategy effectively if you are acting for the plaintiff.[5]
At least you will probably have fewer ethical dilemmas to worry about!

In theory, win/win lends itself to situations where the relationship between
the parties has to continue after the conflict has been resolved. It is therefore
the appropriate strategy for mediation in matrimonial and commercial disputes, for example, where the conflict is about much more than money.
However, if such disputes are negotiated by lawyers rather than mediated by
a neutral third party, win/win may be thwarted if the lawyers insist on keeping information from the other side as their 'secret weapon', rather than
revealing it.

Talking about divorce process, McEwen, Mather and Maiman give us some
insight into the lawyer's role conflict:

The demands of trial preparation and of negotiation are not entirely consistent . . . Lawyers must decide, for example, between aggressively using
formal legal procedures such as discovery and embarking on co-operative,
informal efforts at information sharing; between taking extreme positions
and making 'reasonable' offers; between being open and honest about
underlying interests and goals or keeping them hidden; and between
engaging in strategic behaviour that imposes costs and pressures on the
other party and minimising posturing and costs for both parties.[6]

Does the sharing of information produce yet another conflict of interest?
Suppose you are representing Bob, and at some stage during the negotiation,
he tells you he has just inherited £50,000 worth of shares from his deceased
grandmother, but Carol mustn't know about it? How will you respond? If you
fail to persuade him to reveal this information, you will have to confront the
fact that it will no longer be possible to reach an agreement that is fair to both
parties. Ironically, the conflict might be resolved for you by Carol's lawyer setting in motion the formal procedures of discovery.

Moreover, what do you do if your client is being totally unreasonable? If you
challenge her expectations, you can leave yourself open to the charge of not
acting in her best interests. Of course, you can use the law as an excuse to give
unwelcome advice in cases where the law is clear. However, in many situations
it isn't. In divorce negotiation you may have to bear in mind the interests of

291

the children and the extent to which they compete with those of their parents. This is an area where strong emotions can influence clients to make unrealistic and unreasonable demands. You have to be clear on where to draw the line between your natural inclination to support your client through a testing and emotional time, and the need to convey possibly unpalatable alternatives.

The final point on the subject of you and your ethics is one we have talked about earlier in the chapter: the extent to which you allow your client to participate in the negotiation process.[7] This will be determined firstly by your duties to advise and inform her, to obtain her instructions and to carry them out. You therefore have to be absolutely clear about what your client wants from negotiation. Remember to 'mind the gap': know, respect and support your client's view of the situation.[8]

Secondly, you will have to make decisions about negotiation strategy and tactics, and whether or not you will let the client have a say in these matters. This is difficult, because you need to be as flexible as possible. For example, you might need to vary your strategy and tactics during the negotiation.

Next, do you want the client to be present during the negotiation? Will she cramp your style? Certainly, until you are experienced, you might prefer to do it without her. If the other side's lawyer is someone you know well and trust, could the client feel left out, or think you too friendly to the opposition?

You at least need to think about these issues, even if you can't easily resolve them.

1   K Kressel *The Process of Divorce: How Professionals and Couples Negotiate Settlement*, Basic Books, New York 1985, p 59.
2   Lax and Sebenius call this 'the negotiator's dilemma': op cit.
3   See H Genn *Hard Bargaining: Out of Court Settlement in Personal Injury Actions*, Clarendon Press, Oxford 1987, pp 161–69.
4   Ibid, p 166.
5   But see A Paton 'How to Create a Win/Win Situation', *Post Magazine*, 28 April 1994, pp 28–9, where the author describes the successful mediation of a personal injury claim.
6   C McEwen, L Mather & R Maiman, op cit, p 157.
7   For a rare example of a paper arguing for a participatory approach to negotiation, see R Cochran Junior 'Legal Representation and the Next Steps Toward Client Control: Attorney Malpractice or the Failure to Allow the Client to Control Negotiation and Pursue Alternatives to Litigation', (1990) 47 *Washington & Lee Law Review* 819.
8   In practice your client cannot participate fully all of the time. She will not be present when you are on the phone to the other side's lawyer and may not entirely understand details of expert evidence and complex legal procedures. Your heavy caseload will mean you may not always be able to explain and inform as often as you would like to.

Exercise 9.8   Hidden messages

The following text contains extracts from a negotiation carried out by two students on Case No 5, John Rose and Maxine Krantz. The defendant insisted that she did not want her insurance company involved. Assume that the lawyers have not met each other before.

In your groups, read the text and discuss the questions which follow.

P: Hello there.
D: Hello.
P: Thank you for instigating this negotiation, I'm sure we can sort

things out. I thought I might kick things off by just running through my client's case – basically put on the table for you the kind of settlement we're looking for, which will make my client happy.

D: That's fine.

P: If we perhaps do a quick résumé of the facts. The accident happened on . . . *(P briefly summarises the facts of the accident and description of the injury. Both agree on these.)* We are alleging your client was negligent under several headings, actually. Basically we're contending that your client was guilty of careless driving under s 3 of the Road Traffic Act, and failed to observe the highway code by not leaving adequate clearance for a cyclist, which should be somewhere in the region of at least three feet.

D: Right . . .

P: So that's the case we're making out. One other thing: as yet we haven't got . . .

D: *(interrupts)* Would you mind me coming in now, and leaving the detail. There are one or two things I want to come back to. First of all, obviously, the facts as you describe them, I'm quite happy with. But the manoeuvring between vehicles – you said what was happening when your client was hit from behind – the evidence I'm looking at . . .

P: *(interrupts)* The accident report, I was going to refer to that . . .

D: . . . the accident report. As you know, Mrs Krantz has disclaimed all responsibility and alleges it was entirely the fault of your client. *(Meanwhile P is murmuring and interrupting.)*

P: Can I just ask in that case: on what grounds is she saying she is not liable?

D: This is what I was coming to – that your client was at fault, that he was negligent himself. Can I . . . *(Lawyers go into the facts of the accident in minute detail, looking at the statements, then do the same with the details of the injury. Then they agree to accept the evidence of the medical reports.)* . . . You quoted to me various provisions of the Road Traffic Act, presumably in support of your claim of negligence.

P: That's right.

D: I too have researched the Road Traffic Act, and though it's a fruitless exercise to read it all, there are offences which Mr Rose might have committed. What I'd like to say is there were no charges brought against my client, so I don't . . .

P: No, and likewise none against my client, but I think we must look at the overall evidence. I don't think that anyone at any stage has been guilty of any offence, and one must realise that as my client was the most likely of the two to be injured, the onus was on your client to drive carefully and considerately. What I would like to do, unless you've got any more points there . . .

D: No, I was responding . . . , right . . .

P: Obviously I refute any allegation that my client was negligent. It's difficult to imagine how he could have been, considering he was actually in front of the vehicle that your client was driving. However, a few points that I can come up with in the road accident report, perhaps you could help me with these . . .*(There follows another detailed examination of the facts of the accident.)*

D: I think I have to concede that given that your client is the more vulnerable road user, that . . . we would like to discuss that there was fault on both sides. I would like you to move towards me and accept that there was fault on both sides. If I continue here . . .

P: Well, um, there are several points that we do have to discuss, can I run through them?

D: Well, yes, can I say then I'm conceding that there was certainly fault on our side. What I want to establish from you is that there was also fault on your side.

P: Um . . . in what way? Can you actually elaborate?

D: Yes, certainly. I won't refer to the Road Traffic Act unless you want me to.

P: No, I just wonder what your general contention of contributory negligence is. *(There follows another detailed discussion of facts and statements.)* I think I tend to agree with you that there may be just perhaps a small amount of blame on the part of my client, because he does actually say that he was manoeuvring in between two parked vehicles.

D: I wonder if we're getting a little bit stuck in that these two statements come down to my client's word against yours and who is the court going to believe. *(Lawyers go on to discuss the independent witness statement and how unhelpful it is.)* Can we see where we are now? We have agreed there is fault on both sides.

P: I'm relatively happy that I've established that my client is not totally to blame if . . .

D: So shall we move on?

P: I believe you've already received a statement . . . *(Lawyers confirm P's figures for the special damages claim.)* We are looking for damages in the region of £3,000 to cover pain and suffering and future loss of amenity.

D: Right.

P: That is obviously on top of the special damages figure, so the total is £4,765 now, and I think we can negotiate on that to a certain extent, but that's my opening gambit.

D: Right. We'll accept the special damages. We are looking for contributory negligence from your client to reduce the overall figure – say 50:50.

P: Right, well there's absolutely no way we can accept 50% liability. If that's your contention, we're quite happy to take it all the way into court and let the court assess the damages, based on the evidence. I think possibly I'd go so far as to say maybe 20% contributory negligence.

D: *(pause)* You've got to move more towards me, Mr Brown.

P: Well, I . . . Good heavens, is that the time? I'm afraid I'll have to leave in a minute. I've got another appointment.

D: If you want me to, I'll make you an offer, then. I'll concede your starting at 20%. I need more from you and we can't agree a settlement like that. I need more from you.

P: I'm not willing to accede to 50%.

D: I'll move to 60:40 if your client is willing to accept that, purely on the grounds that your client is the more vulnerable road user, that should the matter come to court, the sympathy will lie with him.

P: Yes, I feel that really that's still putting too much of the blame for the accident on my client. I don't think we can go quite as far as that. Perhaps you would consider we meet halfway at . . .

D: Well, I've done some figures for you. Would you like to have a look? 50:50; 60:40. I'll make you a final offer, Mr Brown. We will reimburse all special damages to make a flat offer, without any discussion of liability, of £1,500, which will give you a figure of £3,265. Are you prepared to consider that offer? I think it's a fair offer.

P: I'll put it to my client. I'm sorry, I've got to leave now, I'm going to be late for my appointment. I'll be in touch.

D: Goodbye.

P: Goodbye.

QUESTIONS

1. *From what you have read, do you think the parties had prepared properly for their meeting? Why/why not?*
2. *How should you prepare properly for a negotiation? Draw up a checklist of questions you need to answer when planning a negotiation.*
3. *What strategy was each side using? Did it change? If so, why?*
4. *How effective was each side's strategy?*
5. *Was there any risk of deadlock at any point? If so, how was it avoided?*
6. *What tactics did each side use in pursuit of their strategy? Give examples of behaviour and language which specified any of the following:*
   - *opening positions;*
   - *attempts to dictate the agenda;*
   - *willingness to make offers/concede;*
   - *bluff and counter-bluff;*
   - *stalling;*
   - *tactics to put pressure on the opponent;*
   - *signals that you are willing to move;*
   - *signals that you are not willing to move;*
   - *bargain testing ('if you . . . , then I . . .');*
   - *threats.*
7. *Which party set the agenda for the meeting, and at what point?*
8. *How would you describe the relationship between the parties? Is there tension at any point? If so, at what point? What caused it? Do you think the cause was deliberate or accidental?*
9. *Is there anything that you would advise the participants to do differently next time? If so, what, and why?*

Step 4: Work out your tactics

Up to now we have concentrated on identifying the critical issues and selecting a negotiating strategy. It is your strategy which will determine your choice of tactics. By tactics we mean the techniques you use to put your strategy into operation.

However, you won't be able to make decisions about any of these issues until you have researched your case thoroughly. You must know your facts and law inside out before you enter the negotiation. This means knowing its strong points and weak points, along with those of the other side. Identify any aspects of the case or information which need clarification, and try to clarify them with your opponent before the negotiation.

You are already aware of your own strengths and weaknesses as a negotiator. You will be all the better prepared if you can anticipate those of your opponent. If you don't know her or haven't met her, find out as much as you can about her. For example, is she a shark by reputation? This may help you predict the tactics she is likely to use, so that you can determine in advance how to respond to these.

If you plan to use the win/win strategy, an important preliminary tactic is to establish friendly relations with the opposing lawyer. If you are making the arrangements for the meeting, plan the seating so that you are not confronting each other face to face. When you meet, avoid plunging straight into the issues, as your opponent could think you are trying to dictate the agenda. Instead, agree how you both want the negotiation to proceed and, if necessary, set a time limit on it. Setting a framework before you start makes it easier to agree to return to it if you stray off the beaten track or get bogged down in superfluous detail.

The next stage of the negotiation involves you and the other side exchanging information. This will help you assess or re-assess the strengths and weaknesses of the other side's case. You can start by going through the facts and establishing points of agreement and difference. How open you are about your client's objectives will depend on your choice of strategy. Whatever strategy you have chosen, don't make offers or concede anything at this stage.

The third stage is the bargaining stage, where both of you test the ground with offers and counter-offers. If you are using win/win, your objective is to agree an outcome which benefits both sides. Remember to bargain on objective criteria.

At the fourth stage you should be able to finalise an agreement. Tie up all loose ends, so that no peripheral details are omitted. Recap on what you have agreed and make a record of it.

Bear in mind that these stages of the process are flexible. If, after some coffee and friendly chat, you estimate that your opponent will respond positively, why not get down to the 'nitty gritty'? For example:

> Well, as we're here to talk about money, why don't we ignore liability for the moment? What kind of figure are we looking at?

Do you think that taking this line would have altered the course of the *Rose v Krantz* negotiation for better or worse?

Taking such a direct approach does not necessarily mean you are a win/lose negotiator. It means you are a flexible one. Furthermore, some negotiators are much more comfortable with an approach that puts the cards on the table at the beginning. It establishes early on how far apart the two of you are. If you are far apart, you can then concentrate on the discrepancies. Bear in mind, however, that if you use this method of opening, you should have planned for it in advance.

Plan too for the possibility of having misread your opponent's likely response! For instance, by opening in this way, aren't you effectively conceding liability? A competitive negotiator will almost certainly read it in that way. What would be your response? Would you then become a win/lose player yourself? Or can you sustain a principled position?

Where there are issues that you disagree about, you must decide in advance whether to broach the more serious or less serious disagreements first. Again, this will be dictated by your strategy and whether you prefer to get the big issues dealt with first or later on.[1]

John Rose's lawyer seemed to want to dictate the agenda from the beginning. Rather than discuss together how they should proceed, he did not let his opponent get a word in, so that in the end she had to interrupt him. They also failed to determine any time limit for the meeting, so that D was taken by surprise when P suddenly said he had to leave. She could not know whether he had another appointment, or whether he was using it as a tactic to force her into making further concessions. His abrupt closure, together with the inconclusive result of the meeting, left D dissatisfied and frustrated.

Whichever strategy you decide to use, you have to be able to give and interpret hidden messages. These messages convey attitudes and responses in an indirect way. As you know, body language, intonation, stress, wordless sounds and pauses signal such messages. There are also messages hidden in the language of the participants. For example, John Rose's lawyer says

> I think we can negotiate on that to a certain extent, but that's my opening gambit.

Indirectly, he is saying that he is prepared to move towards the other side. D picks up the signal and demands a 50:50 split. Signals which indicate a willingness to move towards the opponent are known as 'Floppies'. They are signals which an effective negotiator will both recognise and know when to use.

P signals another floppy near the end of the negotiation:

> I don't think we can go quite as far as that. Perhaps you would consider we meet halfway at . . .

D, who is in a great hurry to conclude an agreement at this point, misses this signal, which is indicating P's willingness to settle for halfway between 40% and 20% contributory negligence – ie 30%.

Signals which indicate an unwillingness to move and a potential deadlock, are known as 'Flinches'. For example:

> Well, there's absolutely no way we can accept 50% liability.

This is P's response to D's demand for a 50:50 share of liability. So his floppy was followed speedily by his flinch. Did you spot any other floppies and flinches?

When P was reflecting on his performance, he pointed out that he had no intention of starting off in the way he did, not allowing his opponent to get a word in. So why did it happen? Perhaps the answer is that the best-laid plans and thorough preparations can go awry when you are in the thick of it.

1 You need to plan tactics carefully if your opponent is from a different cultural background. If you don't take into account matters like levels of formality, pleasantries, non-verbal signals, and the stages of the process, your behaviour could be misinterpreted. Many Japanese, for example, like a lengthy preliminary phase of informal meetings and social events. According to Ann Halpern,

> it is only when they feel on the same wavelength with you that they will begin to do business with you.

See A Halpern, op cit, pp 82–87 at 85, and J Mulholland *The Language of Negotiation: A Handbook of Practical Strategies for Improving Communication*, Routledge, London 1991, pp 75–97.

Exercise 9.9   Staying cool, calm and collected

In your groups, discuss:
(a)   what you could do in the course of a negotiation if:
  (i)   you don't feel in control of things;
  (ii)   you feel angry with your opponent;
  (iii) you can't concentrate on what your opponent is saying;
  (iv)   the opponent won't let you get a word in;
  (v)   the other side won't respond to your win/win approach;
  (vi)   your opponent threatens to break off negotiations.
(b)   Should you take a checklist into the negotiation with you? Why/why not? If yes, what should it contain, and in how much detail? How should you use it?

Step 5:   Keep your act together during the negotiation

P may have launched in with a monologue because he was nervous and needed to feel in control of the process to increase his confidence. D put up with it for a while, but then felt she had to interrupt, to re-distribute the power relationship and impose her agenda.

When planning, you have to anticipate your opponent's tactics, and deal with them during the negotiation. This is a tall order, when you already have the problem of processing a large amount of information very quickly. You have to use a number of skills simultaneously: active listening, observing non-verbal behaviour, taking notes, thinking out how to respond. To keep on top of things, you want to impose a structure on what is an open-ended interaction, so it is all the more frustrating when you find you are losing concentration, because this signifies to you, rightly or wrongly, that you are losing control.

Your interviewing practice has made you aware of the problems of information overload. In our experience, however, many students find negotiation gives them more anxiety. With a lay client, they say, you are the expert, and that makes you feel secure and more powerful, because you know more than they do – or the client thinks you do. On the other hand, you negotiate with a fellow-expert, so you can't get away so easily with bluff and flannel. In your discussions you will have picked up P's negative response to D:

> D: I would like you to move towards me and accept that there was fault on both sides. If I continue here . . .

P: Well, um, there are several points that we do have to discuss, can I run through them?

P's stalling may have been a tactic to keep the onus on D to carry on making concessions, or he simply may have needed time to absorb the information and make a more appropriate and conciliatory response.

There are no prescribed techniques to cope with information overload, anxiety and other unwelcome emotions. Separating the people from the problem is not easy, as we have said. However, we can suggest some general guidelines:

1. You will feel more confident when you enter the negotiation if you know your case inside out.
2. Aim to be flexible. When planning, anticipate every possible direction the negotiation could take. For example, if you think the issue in a personal injury claim is quantum, don't assume the other party won't want to discuss liability.
3. Don't rush. Remember you don't have to conclude an agreement until you are quite ready. Pause if you need to, to take information in.
4. Hide nerves, anger, frustration and insecurity by speaking quite slowly, keeping your voice low, asking your opponent to justify her unreasonable position, behaviour, etc.
5. Don't get drawn into pointless arguments. Allow your opponent to let off steam.
6. Don't take a checklist with you unless it is short. Some students like to have lengthy checklists with them as security blankets, but they will increase the amount of information you have to try and absorb and so divert your attention from the important skills of listening actively, responding appropriately and questioning. Remember it is a checklist and not a recipe. Use it only to check you have covered everything, not to determine the agenda.
7. Reflect on your negotiation experiences: make an entry in your learning diary.

The reflections of P and D immediately after their negotiation should give you some useful hints about the difficulties you can encounter during negotiation, despite what you thought was careful planning.[1]

During their reflections, both P and D said they intended to use a cooperative strategy, but felt forced to become adversarial when they got into the negotiation. D had planned to talk about quantum, and was not prepared for the very lengthy discussions on liability. Talking about the first few minutes, she said:

> I'd planned my strategy. P departed from that plan. I didn't know what to do. He flattened me. I had to counter-attack, to re-establish my own agenda.

When the tutors asked what each lawyer had planned as their best possible outcome on quantum, it was revealed that they were only £200 apart!

TUTOR: So you've spent twenty-five minutes arguing around liability when you were about £200 apart on your best

	outcome. What does that tell you about your strategy?
P:	I don't quite know how we got so sidetracked on the other issues, because I didn't want to be really discussing those . . .
D:	Nor did I, nor did I. I kept on thinking I didn't want to be talking about this, it's not the issue.

and later . . .

P:	I felt I wanted to be more friendly and not talking so much.
D:	So did I. We wanted the same things. But if I'd said I didn't want to go to court, instead of hiding that, I'd have felt I'd conceded everything.

and later . . .

D:	Last time we practised I was conscious that I had entered the negotiation as myself. For this I wanted to make sure everything was right for the client, but I still wanted to be myself. I could have done that. Instead I felt myself trying to put on a . . . I was consciously trying to be someone I wasn't.
P:	I think that was my problem as well. I wasn't quite sure who the hell I was.
D:	I could still have been myself.
P:	Yes, I wanted to . . . we got stuck on the nit picking . . . not the intention at all . . . Every time I said something, you came back and argued. We started winding each other up.
D:	I'm sorry to think of myself like that, that I did that.
P:	I kept telling myself to be flexible.

Red–Blue all over again?

1   In Chapter 2 you will find an extract from D's learning diary on the subject of this negotiation. See pp 27–9.

Step 6:   Keep a negotiation journal

By now we shouldn't have to remind you to record your learning in your diary. However, we recommend you keep a negotiation journal as well. It is a useful way of recording

● your preparation for negotiation;
● the course of the negotiation (pattern of offers, counter-offers, etc);
● the details of the agreement;
● the implementation of the agreement.

Earlier we asked you to draft a checklist for preparation. You can build your journal around this. You may find it helpful to compare your checklist with ours below.

Planning the negotiation

The critical issues and potential outcomes

What are my client's goals? . . . .
What are my client's instructions? . . . .
What are the factual issues? . . . .
What are the legal issues? . . . .
What are the strengths of our case? Fact? Law? . . . .
What are its weaknesses? Fact? Law? . . . .
What are the opponent's strengths? Fact? Law? . . . .
What are the weaknesses? Fact? Law? . . . .
What do I anticipate are the opponent's goals? . . . .
What do I know about the opposing negotiator? . . . .
What are the options? Priorities:
    What is our best possible outcome? . . . .
    What is the least we will accept? . . . .
    What is unacceptable? . . . .
    What is our BATNA? . . . .
    How would the other side answer these questions? . . . .
CHECK: (a)   Present objective criteria to back up each option. . . . .
          (b)   Client's authority for each option. . . . .
          (c)   Test out what is unacceptable to the other side. . . . .

Our strategy and tactics

What strategy are we intending to use? Why/why not? . . . .
Am I comfortable with our chosen strategy? . . . .
What tactics will we use? . . . .
What is our agenda? . . . .
What will be our opening position? . . . .
How much information will we share/withhold? . . . .
What information do we want from them? . . . .
What offers are we prepared to make? . . . .
What concessions are we prepared to make? . . . .
What concessions do we want the opponent to make? . . . .
Have we anticipated and resolved the ethical issues? . . . .

Their strategy and tactics

Might we need to alter strategy/tactics? Why? How? . . . .
What strategy will they use? Why? . . . .
What tactics should we be prepared for? . . . .
How will we respond to:
    Threats/intimidation? . . . .
    Stalling? . . . .
    Arrogance? . . . .
    Discourtesy? . . . .
    Anger? . . . .
    Floppies? . . . .

Flinches?   . . . .
Obstinacy?   . . . .
Silence?   . . . .
Interruptions?   . . . .

CHECK: Are we thinking of taking this giant checklist into the negotiation
          with us? Don't even think of it.

When the negotiation is over, you can use the list again to check what you did,
at which point, what worked well and what was less effective. Record the details
of the settlement, and which of your client's objectives you achieved. If you
failed to reach agreement, give reasons and note down what is to happen next.

Are lawyers poor negotiators?

We have spent some time identifying a few of the possible pitfalls that professional negotiators can fall into. Remember, though, that negotiation is a skill
you have been developing since you were a baby, so you have a wealth of successful (and unsuccessful) techniques at your disposal already.

So what do legal negotiators actually do in practice, and how effective are
they? The empirical research there is suggests that experienced practitioners
are less effective than you might expect. According to Carrie Menkel-Meadow

> . . . many negotiators persist in wasteful and counter-productive adver-
> sarial or unnecessarily compromising behaviour, . . .[1]

She observed live negotiations conducted through mediation. Her study confirms the pattern established by other researchers whose data is based on
interviews with lawyers: that most negotiation is 'low intensity'. Lawyers
spend little time bargaining, preferring to settle quickly, on the basis of first or
early offers. Any bargaining there is tends to be positional.[2] There is evidence
of co-operative behaviour, but few signs of problem-solving approaches.

She further found that both lawyers and the parties seemed to approach
their disputes from a particular orientation or 'mind-set', and that this prede-
termined how they acted in the negotiation.[3] She concludes:

> . . . that there may be an empirical reality to the polarised models of
> negotiation, but that these behaviours are not limited to lawyers. Parties
> too may have polarised orientations to the world; seeing in each dispute
> or encounter with another human being an opportunity to 'get mine' or
> to 'see what can be done about this problem and work things out'. If, as
> many researchers report, most people are lazy about negotiation, that is
> they seek to 'satisfice' with low intensity contacts and expect to compro-
> mise in the middle, the two polarised orientations will, in reality, meet in
> a compromised middle and may not accurately reflect what the parties
> really need or that they are really entitled to, unless they have made
> explicit choices about the transaction costs of more involved, higher
> intensity negotiation processes.[4]

So what are the factors which inhibit creative solutions? These findings suggest that the personalities of both lawyer and disputant are an important one.

Moreover, the reality of legal practice, with its need to keep costs down and heavy caseloads is likely to encourage routinisation and standard resolutions; tort disputes are about money, divorce settlements about compromise, etc.

Boon's study of 28 specialist solicitors in the UK found that lawyer–client relationships and the firm's culture could limit a lawyer's choice of negotiating style. One specialist in general litigation he interviewed said:

> In litigation over contracts I was required to do some very hard bargaining – not necessarily because I wanted to do it that way but because it was the sort of firm where the solicitor did what the client wanted. Our client profile was 'hard-nosed businessman'. They believed threats would produce results . . . If one co-operated with the other side in any way, or suggested they might have a valid point, this was seen as weakness . . .[5]

The empirical evidence therefore seems to suggest that lawyers' adversarial culture and habits may impede the development of problem-solving strategies. As Boon concludes:

> The questions for negotiation theory which this raises are whether or not legal problems have limited integrative potential, whether lawyers fail to see or to exploit the potential which is there or whether a pervasive adversarial culture limits the scope for problem solving approaches to negotiations.[6]

So in whose interests are they working? And what will your position be?

1   C Menkel-Meadow, (1993) op cit, p 363.
2   For example, H Genn, op cit; H Kritzer *Let's Make A Deal: Understanding the Negotiation Process in Ordinary Litigation*, University of Wisconsin Press, Madison, Wisc 1990; L Ross *Settled Out Of Court: The Social Process of Insurance Claims Adjustment*, Aldine Press, Chicago 1980; C McEwen, L Mather & R Maiman, op cit; A Boon 'Co-operation and Competition in Negotiation: The Handling of Civil Disputes and Transactions', (1994) 1 *International Journal of the Legal Profession* 109 at 118.
3   Cf the discussion of the relational and rule-oriented mind-sets of litigants and judges in the small claims hearings studied by Conley & O'Barr – see *Rules Versus Relationships: The Ethnography of Legal Discourse*, University of Chicago Press, Chicago 1990, and in Chapter 10, below.
4   C Menkel-Meadow, p 377.
5   Ibid, p 115.
6   Ibid, p 119.

Exercise 9.10   Concepts

In this chapter we have discussed a number of concepts. We list the main ones below. The procedure for learning these concepts is as follows:

1. *Divide into pairs.*
2. *Each pair is to:*
   (a) *define each concept, noting the page on which it is defined and discussed; and*
   (b) *make sure that both members of the pair understand the meaning of each concept.*
3. *Combine into groups of four. Compare the answers of the two pairs. If there is disagreement, look up the concept and clarify it until all agree on the definition and understand it.*

repeat players	*mediation*
zero sum bargaining	*flinch*
co-operative strategy	*lose/lose strategy*
floppy	*negotiation journal*
BATNA	*low intensity negotiation*

Exercise 9.11   Yet another negotiation

In pairs:
(a)   From the five cases on pages 278–280, select one you have not yet negotiated and allocate roles.
(b)   Individually, write a detailed plan for the negotiation and show it to your tutor.
(c)   Role play the negotiation and feed back.
(d)   Individually, write up your negotiation journal. Show it to your tutor. Then make an entry in your learning diary, preferably after you have seen the video recording of your negotiation.

Review questions

1.   Discuss the following: [1]
(a)   Should mediators be legally qualified? Why/why not?
(b)   What should be the role of the mediator? Should they comment on the merits of the case/predict trial outcomes? Why/why not?
(c)   In what circumstances, if any, should mediation be mandatory? Give reasons.
2.   Which aspects of your negotiation skills and behaviour do you think you need to improve? Give reasons, and indicate how you will go about making improvements.

1   The following reading may be helpful: R Ingleby 'Court Sponsored Mediation: The Case Against Mandatory Participation', (1993) 56 *Modern Law Review*, 441; S Roberts 'Alternative Dispute Resolution and Civil Justice: An Unresolved Relationship', (1993) 56 *Modern Law Review*, 452; C McEwen, L Mather & R Maiman 'Lawyers, Mediation and the Management of Divorce Practice', (1994) 28 *Law and Society Review*, 149; K Mackie 'Negotiation and Mediation; From Inelegant Haggling to Sleeping Giant', in K Mackie (ed) *A Handbook of Dispute Resolution*, Routledge, London 1991.

Further reading

A Halpern *Negotiating Skills*, Blackstone Press, London 1992.

D Tribe *Negotiation*, Cavendish, London 1993.

Inns of Court School of Law *Advocacy, Negotiation and Conference Skills*, Blackstone, London 1994.

R Fisher and W Ury *Getting to Yes: Negotiating an Agreement Without Giving In*, Business Books, London 1991.

K Mackie (ed) *A Handbook of Dispute Resolution*, Routledge, London 1991.

10 Into court: the deepest swamp?

> Advocacy is often seen as the apogee of the lawyer's skills. This chapter aims to set out the basic skills of the advocate, and to give you the opportunity to practise those skills within the context of a 'narrative' or 'story' model of advocacy. However, that is not all. It emphasises the centrality of planning and preparation in successful advocacy. It shows how evidence and procedure control – or do not control – courtroom strategy and process, and it looks critically at the ways in which a kind of reality is reconstructed through the adversarial process.

Objectives

To:
- Enable you to appreciate the social and institutional context in which advocacy takes place.
- Enable you to appreciate the importance of preparation for advocacy.
- Introduce you to information management techniques that will support your preparation and advocacy.
- Enable you to explore a range of techniques applicable to narrative and interrogatory styles of advocacy.
- Encourage you to reflect on the relationship between advocacy and ethics.

The art of advocacy

In this final chapter we begin to look at the process of advocacy. We say 'begin' deliberately. For reasons that will become apparent, we cannot pretend – and do not attempt – to offer more than an introduction in a book of this kind.[1] We also intend to focus only on trial advocacy. John Mortimer may feel that

> no one has felt the full glory of a barrister's life who has not, in wig and gown, been called to the podium in the committee room of the House of Lords by an official in full evening dress and, on a wet Monday morning, lectured five elderly Law Lords in lounge suits on the virtues of masturbation . . .[2]

but appellate advocacy is too specialised an art form to incorporate here.[3]

Advocacy is probably the most obviously 'artistic' (in Schön's sense) of the

DRAIN skills. It is certainly the most complex to master, because it is a composite skill involving some highly specialised processes and techniques. To see what we mean, think back to your answers to Exercise 1.2. You will see that we identified quite a number of attributes that a good advocate needs. But is advocacy difficult only because of the *range* of skills it involves?

1   In so doing we must admit to a bias towards criminal advocacy. We would explain this on three bases: first, it remains the context where the problems of adversarialism and lay adjudication are most interwoven; second, it is the area where there is the greatest volume of research into the processes involved; third, in the context of our own teaching programme, advocacy is explored largely through a criminal case study.
2   *Clinging to the Wreckage*, Penguin, Harmondsworth 1982, p 12. We should point out that he was talking about an obscenity case in which he was counsel at the time!
3   We have also not specifically addressed a number of common advocacy contexts, such as bail applications, pleas in mitigation, or, on the civil side, the order for directions or application for summary judgment. On all of these see eg A Sherr *Advocacy*, Blackstone Press, London 1993.

Exercise 10.1   Advocacy as communication

On the face of it, advocacy may seem to be just another application of our communication skills, but is that right?

(a)   In pairs, consider what factors, if any, distinguish advocacy from the other oral communication processes in this book.
(b)   Briefly discuss your conclusions with the whole group.

The key point is that, even though all the basic communication skills are there – talking, active listening, appropriate use of NVCs – they have to be put together in a very artificial environment and for highly specialised purposes. Advocacy as communicative action is far removed from our 'everyday' experience of communication, because:
●   the context is relatively formalised, ritualistic even;
●   you are often trying to communicate effectively to very different constituencies (eg judge, jury, opponent, client) at more or less the same time;
●   the scope for interaction is often limited: there is a far greater emphasis on one-way communication than in interviewing or negotiating;
●   the style of your communication may be very different from the more participatory techniques recommended for interviewing or negotiating, eg where you are deliberately trying to control or coerce the person you are communicating with.
Before we consider in detail what constitutes effective advocacy, we want to reflect on the wider issues of context, which have been raised by Exercise 10.1. We think these are essential, given our concern with developing a critical and reflective view of lawyering skills.

Advocacy in context

The adversarial nature of advocacy

The present style of advocacy reflects the adversarial nature of most English legal proceedings. Sir David Napley encapsulated the essence of English

advocacy in the title of his book – one of the first of the advocacy manuals –
The Technique of Persuasion.[1]

Within this model, the essence of the advocate's task is to persuade a sup-
posedly neutral third party (judge or jury) that her view of events (or of the
law) is more correct than her opponent's. The process is adversarial because it
is up to the lawyers themselves to make the running; they choose the territory
to fight on (ie the legal and factual issues in dispute), and each will choose
arguments not so much with a view to establishing an objective 'truth', but
(within the limits that ethics allow) in order to advance their client's version of
events, or to discredit their opponent's. As one experienced criminal practitioner has put it:

> . . . one is really not dealing with a static set of facts at all. It's an area of
> shifting sand. I have been known to say that, when I go into the criminal
> courtroom, I don't expect to hear anybody tell the truth at all. That is
> perhaps again a cynical view, but certainly I don't expect to be able to
> identify readily who is telling the unvarnished truth, who it is who is var-
> nishing it a bit, who it is who is deliberately lying and perhaps what
> difference that is going to make in assessing the totality of the evidence
> being presented.[2]

This is not just a problem in criminal trials. Trials, whether they are civil or
criminal, tend to turn on disputed facts. To give a simple anecdotal example,
Julian once had the (not unusual) experience in one civil case, involving a
road traffic accident, of the parties disagreeing on most issues of fact. For
example, though the case showed incontrovertibly that the accident was
caused by the defendant driving into the back of the plaintiff's car, the plaintiff said the impact pushed the car thirty or forty feet, while the defendant said
about ten or twelve feet.[3] Neither was necessarily lying – that may well be how
they remembered events, but equally either or both may have been reinvent-
ing the details of the accident to their own advantage, as they saw it. The
manner in which these contested versions of 'reality' come to be represented
in court is central to wider concerns about the ability of the trial process to
deliver 'justice'.

1 4th Edition, 1991, Sweet & Maxwell, London.
2 Bill Nash 'The psychologist as expert witness: a solicitor's view' in J Shapland (ed) *Lawyers
and Psychologists – Gathering and Giving Evidence*, Issues in Criminological and Legal
Psychology No 3, British Psychological Society, Leicester 1982, p 32 at p 35.
3 Not surprisingly this was not ultimately at issue; an admission of negligence was obtained by
the defendant's insurers and the case proceeded on quantum only.

Recreating facts in the courtroom

The basic point we need to bear in mind is that courts are places where decisions are made on the basis of available evidence. This fairly innocuous
sounding principle is important for a number of reasons.

First, English courts do not operate on a principle of 'freedom of proof'. As
a lawyer or litigant, you cannot just appear before a court and tell your story.
The parameters of your story may be affected by the complex body of legal

rules which determine what evidence may be heard in court, and for what purposes. That means that a good advocate should have a sound grasp of the law of evidence, though anyone watching a busy magistrates' court in action will recognise that there is often a gap between theory and reality here. How good is your knowledge of evidence? The next exercise gives you a flavour of what the law involves.

Exercise 10.2   Evidential quiz

Answer all the following questions. A word of warning: do not assume that there is only one right answer listed (there may be more); but equally, do not assume that any of the answers are necessarily correct.

	TRUE	FALSE
1. The standard of proof in criminal cases is:		
(a) proof on a balance of probabilities;	[ ]	[ ]
(b) proof so that you are sure;	[ ]	[ ]
(c) proof beyond reasonable doubt;	[ ]	[ ]
(d) proof of a prima facie case.	[ ]	[ ]
2. A confession is:		
(a) any inadmissible statement made by a witness in legal proceedings;	[ ]	[ ]
(b) any admission of fact against his own interests made by a party in civil proceedings;	[ ]	[ ]
(c) any admission of fact made by a witness in criminal proceedings;	[ ]	[ ]
(d) an admission of fact against his own interests made by D in criminal proceedings.	[ ]	[ ]
3. The defence apply for bail. Any statement made by D or his solicitor is:		
(a) admissible evidence;	[ ]	[ ]
(b) a representation;	[ ]	[ ]
(c) incomprehensible;	[ ]	[ ]
(d) hearsay.	[ ]	[ ]
4. A prima facie case is:		
(a) small, red, and carried by the Chancellor of the Exchequer;	[ ]	[ ]
(b) evidence on which a court might convict;	[ ]	[ ]
(c) evidence on which a court must convict;	[ ]	[ ]
(d) evidence on which a court must acquit.	[ ]	[ ]

5. A police officer may refer to his/her notebook
   in giving evidence in order to:

   (a) corroborate his/her testimony;   [ ]   [ ]

   (b) corroborate another witness's testimony;   [ ]   [ ]

   (c) refresh his/her memory;   [ ]   [ ]

   (d) contradict defence witnesses.   [ ]   [ ]

6. A witness is 'hostile' if:

   (a) he attacks the character of another witness;   [ ]   [ ]

   (b) he attacks the judge;   [ ]   [ ]

   (c) he gives evidence which is unhelpful to his side;   [ ]   [ ]

   (d) he gives evidence which is unhelpful to the other side. [ ]   [ ]

7. Which of the following is always hearsay evidence:

   (a) evidence given by a witness stating
   what someone else said;   [ ]   [ ]

   (b) evidence given by a witness of a statement
   made by him/her to someone else;   [ ]   [ ]

   (c) a written statement made by a person
   who is not called as a witness;   [ ]   [ ]

   (d) the video-taped evidence of a child
   who is not called as a witness.   [ ]   [ ]

8. Corroborative evidence is required as a matter of law:

   (a) to confirm the facts in issue in all
   criminal & civil proceedings;   [ ]   [ ]

   (b) to confirm the facts in issue in all
   criminal proceedings;   [ ]   [ ]

   (c) in no criminal or civil proceedings;   [ ]   [ ]

   (d) to confirm evidence given in criminal proceedings
   by any person under 16 years of age;   [ ]   [ ]

   (e) to ground any conviction otherwise based
   on confession evidence alone.   [ ]   [ ]

The rules of evidence allow for the exclusion of important evidence because there are problems with the way in which such evidence would have to be presented (eg because it would offend the hearsay rule[1]) or because a procedural requirement, such as the need for an alibi warning, has not been met. These procedures may operate particularly against the interests of an unrepresented party,[2] or those who obtain representation only at the last minute. Even where the rules of evidence mean that only part of a person's story would need editing/exclusion, this may paint a dramatically different picture from one that would appear if the courts operated a presumption of freedom of proof. For example, much of the context of a conversation – the communication episode of which it is part – may be lost.[3]

They also make psychologically dubious assumptions about the (un)reliability of certain categories of evidence, or categories of witnesses. For example, the English legal system has for many years operated rules requiring actual corroboration of children's evidence, and requiring the judge to issue corroboration warnings in respect of evidence from other suspect witnesses. Since 1991, these rules have been systematically reversed, for a variety of reasons.[4] For example, in the former case, because concerns about child abuse prompted researchers to question more closely the assumptions that had long been made about the reliability of children's testimony. To this extent legal truths are often socially and historically contingent, and may change with the system's changing perception (and reception) of external 'realities'.

Second, your presentation of a case can be affected by gaps in the factual information. For example, the defence may be unable to challenge prosecution forensic evidence, because the forensic material was all used up in the original tests, or because the integrity of that material has been destroyed by testing, or by the passage of time.[5] The court cannot refuse to come to a decision simply because the evidence has gaps in it. It must assess the issues by reference to the burden of proof, and decide whether there is sufficient evidence to discharge that burden. If there is not sufficient evidence, the court must find against the person carrying the burden.[6]

Third, evidence may be subject to a series of distorting influences which will affect the views of those receiving the evidence – eg selectivity exercised by the parties (as above); prejudgment or prejudice (see the fact management materials in Chapter 3); the quality of the advocacy itself, and by the sometimes partial conduct of the judge.[7] It is also worth noting that research in the United States suggests that there is a significant social dimension to the production of evidence. Cooney has attached the label 'the Matthew Effect' to this phenomenon, after the passage from St Matthew's Gospel: 'For unto everyone that hath shall be given, and he shall have abundance'.[8] Thus, it is suggested that high-status parties are more effective at obtaining high status advocates; they are therefore more likely to get the respected experts through their own and their advocates' networks; they will find it easier to get influential character witnesses. Indeed witnesses generally seem to be more willing to come forward to assist high status rather than low status associates, and so on.[9] These sorts of distortions will have an impact on the trial process.

It follows therefore that there is always a potential gap between truth and evidence.

Many of the problems go deeper than the evidential, however. As lawyers we tend to forget just how artificial and, indeed, alienating an environment the courtroom is. It is 'blind to the outside like an archive or a bunker, its reality is exclusively within'.[10] This helps create what Rock has termed a form of anomie – which he defines as 'social reality dissolving into meaninglessness'.[11] It is a discursive environment 'free of the conventional sensate world in which an audience could move about independently and probe and ask questions.'[12]

We shall continue to explore these contextual issues, and the techniques of advocacy, through a pair of case studies which are presented over the next few pages. You may find it useful to at least skim read them before you proceed to the next section of text.

1   The hearsay rule is intended to limit the use of 'second-hand' testimony. This is not as easy as it sounds. One particular consequence of the rule is that evidence in criminal proceedings must be produced from the most reliable source – ie the originator. Such evidence should be given as oral testimony. This means that, in theory, witness statements, confessions, etc are hearsay, but note the exceptions created to admit certain statements under the Criminal Justice Act 1988, ss 23–28. Confessions may be admitted, subject to the exclusionary rules in the Police and Criminal Evidence Act 1984, ss 76 & 78. In other contexts, be warned: sometimes the distinction between first-hand evidence and hearsay is extremely fine.

2   See eg the discussion in D McBarnet *Conviction: Law, the State and the Construction of Justice*, Macmillan, London & Basingstoke 1981, pp 127–8.

3   Cf the discussion of conversations and communication episodes in Chapter 5, above.

4   See the Law Commission Report No 202 *Corroboration of Evidence in Criminal Trials*, Cm 1620, HMSO, London 1991; the amendments to the law were brought in by the Criminal Justice Act 1991, s 52 (introducing s 33A, Criminal Justice Act 1988) and the Criminal Justice and Public Order Act 1994, ss 32 and 34. On the latter, see P Mirfield '"Corroboration" After the 1994 Act' [1995] *Criminal Law Review* 448.

5   On forensic issues generally see R Stockdale & C Walker 'Forensic Evidence' in C Walker & K Starmer (eds) *Justice in Error*, Blackstone Press, London 1993, p 75.

6   *Woolmington v DPP* [1935] AC 462; in civil cases, see eg *Rhesa Shipping Co SA v Edmunds* [1985] 2 All ER 712.

7   The classic adversary image of the judge as distant umpire is widely doubted, by criminal practitioners as well as academic lawyers. See eg the discussions in J Morison & P Leith *The Barrister's World*, Open University Press, Milton Keynes 1992, pp 149–50. There are a number of detailed analyses of individual cases: see eg James Wood on the summing-up by Bridge J (as he then was) in the original *Birmingham Six* trial in C Walker & K Starmer, op cit, pp 159–61; also M Fido & K Skinner *The Peasenhall Murder*, Alan Sutton, Stroud 1990 at pp 98–9 on the summing-up in the first *Gardiner* trial, discussed below. In some respects the change in civil procedure is even more dramatic, as judges are increasingly required to 'assert greater control over the preparation for and conduct of hearings than has hitherto been customary' – *Practice Direction (Civil Litigation: Case Management)* [1995] 1 WLR 262 (HC). See also C Glasser 'Civil Procedure and the Lawyers – The Adversary System and the Decline of the Orality Principle' (1993) 56 *Modern Law Review* 307; also Ipp J 'Judicial Intervention in the Trial Process' (1995) 69 *Australian Law Journal* 365. The increase in judicial intervention in civil cases has not, however, raised the same level of concern about judicial partiality as in criminal cases.

8   M Cooney 'Evidence as Partisanship' (1994) 28 *Law & Society Review* 833 at 850. (In fact, as Cooney notes, this label was coined by Robert Merton in his study of the process of recognition of scientific achievement – see 'The Matthew Effect in Science' (1968) 159 *Science* 56.

9   Ibid.

10 P Goodrich *Languages of Law*, Weidenfeld & Nicolson, London 1990, p 189.

11 *The Social World of an English Crown Court*, Clarendon Press, Oxford 1993, p 92.

12 Ibid, p 93.

Case studies

The first of the two studies, R v Bigg, is fictitious; we will use this as the primary vehicle for practising advocacy skills.The second case of William Gardiner is real and will be used for both practice and illustrative purposes.

Case study 1:   R v Bigg

On the following pages we reproduce the Statement under Caution and Proof of Evidence of the defendant, and the witness statements, taken at a police station after a supposed incident.

WESSEX CONSTABULARY

Station/Section: Gloucester Central   **Division:** C

Date: 21 February 199X

Statement of (name of witness): Rupert Brook

Age of witness: over 21

Occupation of witness: Retired

Address: 51, Long Lane, Little Wittering, Glos.

Tel no: 01272 56789

This statement, consisting of 1 page(s) signed by me, is true to the best of my knowledge and belief and I make it knowing that, if it is to be tendered in evidence, I shall be liable to prosecution if I have wilfully stated in it anything which I know to be false or do not believe to be true.

Dated the 21 day of February 199X

On the evening of 20th February I drove into Gloucester to meet some friends with whom I intended to see a show at the Playhouse. After the play we went for a drink to the Dog in the High Street and then on to one of my friends for coffee. He lives in one of the new sheltered homes off the bottom of Westgate Street. I stayed until nearly 12.30 am, and then started to walk back up Westgate Street, towards the Queens Road car park, where I had left my car. I stopped at the Wessex Provincial branch to get some money from the Cashline machine. I took out £30. As I turned to continue back up the road, three youths ran towards me. One pointed something at me. He said it was a gun and demanded the money. The shock made me feel dizzy. He grabbed the money and squirted water into my face. I ducked away and lost my balance. My glasses fell off and smashed. I reached out for some railings with my left hand. There must have been a sharp edge or something, because it cut my hand quite badly. I must have then just slid to the pavement. I am not sure where they went. I think all three ran off down a side street.

In a matter of moments a young woman came along and helped me up. Someone called an ambulance and the police. I was then taken to the Gloucester Royal Infirmary, where I received four stitches across the palm of my hand.

The lighting was quite good, but it all happened so quickly I did not get that good a look at them. They were all male, in their early twenties I would say. One about average height, the other shorter. The taller one had what I though was a gun. He was wearing a black leather jacket. They both had dark hair. The other one also had dark clothes, with a short coat which was zipped right up so I could not see his mouth and chin. I cannot be more precise than that. The third one remained in the background, I did not really get much of a look at him. I would guess he was about the same height as the lad with the water pistol.

Signed:

Witnessed:

WESSEX CONSTABULARY

Station/Section: Gloucester Central   **Division:** C

                                              Date: 21 February 199X

                                              Time: 02.20

Statement of: Francis John Forrest

Age of witness: 23

Occupation: unemployed

Address: 3, The Grove, Tivoli, Cheltenham.

This statement consisting of 1 page(s) each signed by me is true to the best of my knowledge and belief and I make it knowing that, if it is tendered in evidence, I shall be liable to prosecution if I have wilfully stated in it anything which I know to be false or do not believe to be true.

Dated the 21 **day of** February 199X

Signature

I was in the Coach and Horses on Eastgate Street in Gloucester on the night of 20 February. My girlfriend, Lisette Claymore was with me. Bobby Bigg came in and we had a few drinks together.

After the pub closed we went down the Purple Pussycat club, where we stayed till we got thrown out at about quarter to one in the morning. We had all had a lot to drink by then. I had brought my kid brother's water pistol along, intending to play a joke on Lise, but as Bobby had spent the night trying to get off with Lise I decided to make him look stupid. I had wrapped it in some plastic, so it wouldn't leak in my jacket. Halfway up Westgate Street I pulled it on Bobby. Covered in the plastic, he couldn't see it was fake. It scared the life out of him. He was really angry when he found out it was a water pistol.

About 200 yards further up Westgate Street there is a branch of the Wessex Provincial Bank. There was an old man getting some cash out of the dispenser. Bobby suggested we try and scare him. I though it would be a laugh and gave the gun to Bobby. We ran up to the man and Bobby pointed the gun at him. He said something like "Give us the money you old git, or else". I think Lise ran off down a side street about this time. The old guy looked really scared and started holding his chest and breathing funny. I thought he was having a heart attack. Bobby grabbed the cash from his hand sprayed water in his face and stuffed the cash and the gun in my hand. The man staggered against the railings, and fell forwards groaning. Bobby ran off down the same street as Lisette. I just panicked and headed back into the town centre. It was just my luck to run into the path of a police car at the top of Westgate Street.

I know what Bobby suggested was wrong and I went along with it, but I did not realise he intended to rob the old guy.

I was wearing a dark blue jacket and trousers over a red polo shirt and trainers. Bobby had black jeans, a white T shirt and a bomber jacket. I think that was also black. I am six foot tall. I would estimate I am about three inches taller than Bobby.

Signed:

Witnessed:

WESSEX CONSTABULARY

Station/Section: Gloucester Central   **Division:** C

                                                                        Date: 21 February 199X

Statement of (name of witness): Lisette Claymore

Age of witness: over 21

Occupation of witness: Catering Assistant

Address: 17 Popes Way, Gloucester

                                                                Tel no: none

This statement consisting of 1 page(s) signed by me is true to the best of my knowledge and belief and I make it knowing that, if it is to be tendered in evidence, I shall be liable to prosecution if I have wilfully stated in it anything which I know to be false or do not believe to be true.

Dated the 21 **day of** February 199X

I am 22 years old and work at the Belly Buster Fish Restaurant on the Bristol Road in Gloucester.

On the evening of 20 February after I finished my shift, I met up with my boyfriend Francis Forrest (Frankie) at the Coach and Horses on Eastgate Street. We were joined by a friend of ours, Bobby Bigg. We stayed in the pub until last orders and then went down to the Purple Pussycat club. We had a lot to drink there and were asked to leave sometime just after 12.30 am when the boys started getting a bit noisy.

After we left Frankie pulled this really stupid trick on Bobby with a water pistol wrapped in black plastic. It fooled Bobby, he thought it was a real gun, I don't know how, and he looked scared. Frankie laughed at him, and Bobby got angry, so I gave him a cuddle, which upset Frankie.

Further down Westgate Street Frankie suggested we pull the same stunt on a stranger. He had seen some old man getting cash from a cash dispenser. Bobby and I went along for the laugh. Once we realised Frankie was going to take his money we wanted nothing to do with it and ran off down a side road. We split up and I doubled back into town where I got a mini-cab from outside the Eastgate Centre to take me home. I got home at about 1.20 am. Bobby arrived about ten minutes later and we sat drinking and talking till about 3.00 am. I have not seen Frankie since the incident.

I was wearing a black blouson over a white T shirt and white cotton trousers.

Signed:

Witnessed:

WESSEX CONSTABULARY

Station/Section: Gloucester Central   **Division:** C

Date: 21 February 199X

Statement of (name of witness): Sukhjit Singh

Age of witness: 19 (d.o.b. 17.11.7Y)

Occupation of witness: Student

Address: 53 Old Cheltenham Road, Gloucester.

Tel no:

This statement consisting of 1 pages signed by me is true to the best of my knowledge and belief and I make it knowing that, if it is to be tendered in evidence, I shall be liable to prosecution if I have wilfully stated in it anything which I know to be false or do not believe to be true.

Dated the 21 day of February 199X

Earlier this morning, 21 February 199X, I was walking along Westgate Street with my brother-in-law, Surinder. We had been attending a party at my cousin's house and were heading into town to get the night bus back out to where we live.

We were walking up Westgate Street at about 12.55 am. I remember hearing one am strike a few moments later. Across the road and a little way ahead of us we saw there was some commotion. An elderly white man was being accosted by two or three people. I saw him fall over. I heard a woman's voice. It said "What's happening? I'm out of here." I think at that point the woman pushed past one of her friends and ran off down a nearby side road, to our left. The other two followed very quickly, one running back up Westgate towards the centre, the other down the same side road. Surinder realised what was happening very quickly. He said there was a payphone nearby and went to ring the police. I ran across the road to see if the old man was all right. A lady had already seen what was happening and was helping him to sit up. I helped her then waited for Surinder to return, and for the police.

The lighting is good on Westgate Street, but when it happened we must have been nearly 20 metres away, and it was over so quickly that I did not get that good a look at them. All three were white, and they all had short dark hair. The one I took to be a woman had slightly longer hair than the other two. She had a black jacket on and light trousers. The two men were both taller than her, both about average height, or a little taller perhaps. One had something in his hand, though I was unsure what it was. He was dressed in a black jacket and dark shirt. The other one also had a black coat on and dark trousers or jeans.

Signed:

Witnessed:

WESSEX CONSTABULARY

Station/Section: Gloucester Central   **Division:** C

Date: 21 February 199X

Statement of (name of witness): Rodney Smith

Age of witness: over 21

Occupation of witness: Detective Constable 209

Address: Gloucester Central Police Station.

Tel no:

This statement, consisting of 1 page(s) signed by me, is true to the best of my knowledge and belief and I make it knowing that, if it is to be tendered in evidence, I shall be liable to prosecution if I have wilfully stated in it anything which I know to be false or do not believe to be true.

Dated the 21 **day of** February **199X**

On the morning of Sunday 21 February 199X I was on duty at Gloucester Central Police Station. I was assigned as investigating officer in the case of a robbery and assault against Mr Rupert Brook. We had arrested two men in connection with the offence. I wished to interview one of these, Mr Robert Bigg, who had been left to sleep off the previous night's drinking in the cells. At about 7.20 am I went down to the cell with Sgt Adams, the custody officer, to see if Mr Bigg was ready to be interviewed. I went into his cell while Sgt Adams waited outside. Bigg opened his eyes as I walked in. He recognised me as I had dealt with him in connection with a previous offence. "Hello Smiffy, I though you'd be sniffing around," he said, "I've got in deep shit this time haven't I?" "Do you think so Bobby", I said. "Yeah" he replied, "I shouldn't have gone for the old man, knew it was a mistake." I then asked if he was ready to be interviewed. He said "O.K., but I want a mouthpiece. Get him here and piss off and let me sleep till he arrives." With this Bigg turned over and closed his eyes. I left him in his cell and told the custody officer of Bigg's statement and his request for a solicitor.

The duty solicitor arrived at 08.10. Biggs was interviewed at 08.30 and subsequently made a statement, marked 'RB1'.

Signed:

Witnessed:

RB1   **WESSEX CONSTABULARY**

Station/Section: Gloucester Central   **Division:** C

                                               Date: 21 February 199X

                                               Time: 09.15

Statement of: Robert Elvis Bigg

Age of witness: 21

Occupation: casual labourer

Address: 36 Princes Street, Gloucester.

STATEMENT UNDER CAUTION

I, Robert Elvis Bigg, wish to make a statement. I want someone to write down what I say. I have been told that I need not say anything unless I wish to do so and that whatever I say may be given in evidence.

Dated the 21 **day of** February **199X**

Signed

Witnessed

On the evening of 20 February I met with Francis (Frankie) Forrest and Lisette Claymore in the Coach and Horses public house on Eastgate Street, Gloucester. We drank there until 11 pm. We went from there to the Purple Pussycat club at the end of the High Street. We continued drinking in there and were asked to leave because the management thought we were getting too rowdy. This was about 12.40 pm. As we walked away, Frankie pulled something out of his pocket wrapped in a bit of black plastic. He said it was a gun and pointed it at me. When he pulled the trigger it squirted water in my face. He thought this was amazingly funny and suggested we try the same trick on a stranger. I did not think this was a good idea but as both Frankie and Lisette thought it would be a good laugh I went along with them. We ran up to a man outside the Wessex Provincial Bank in Westgate Street. Frankie pointed the gun at him and I took £30 off of him. The old bloke started groaning. I thought he was going to have a heart attack, then he fell and cut himself, I'm not sure where. Frankie swore, I started running and heard Lisette shout and follow me round the corner. Frankie did not follow me. Lise and me split up, and I walked back to her place, where I stayed drinking until about 3.00 am. I was arrested walking back to my own place

    I know we did wrong, but I didn't intend that old guy should get hurt. It wasn't even my idea to rob him — Frankie told me to take the money and like a fool I did.

Signed:

Witnessed:

I have read the above statement and I have been told that I can correct, alter or add anything I wish. This statement is true. I have made it of my own free will.

Signed:

Witnessed:

Proof of Evidence of Robert Bigg

ROBERT ELVIS BIGG of 36 Princes Street, Gloucester will state:

I have been charged with robbing and maliciously wounding a man called Rupert Brook in Westgate Street, Gloucester on or about 1.00 am on the 21 February 199X. To these charges I wish to plead not guilty. What happened was as follows.

On the evening of 20 February I met with my friends Francis (Frankie) Forrest and Lisette Claymore in the Coach and Horses public house on Eastgate Street, Gloucester. We drank there until 11 pm. We had had a lot to drink and were getting a bit drunk. I had consumed about six pints of lager. We decided to go to the Purple Pussycat club at the end of the High Street. We continued drinking in there and were asked to leave because the management thought we were getting too rowdy. This was about 12.40 pm. As we walked away, Frankie pulled something out of his pocket wrapped in a bit of black plastic, I think it was a piece of bin liner. He said it was a gun and pointed it at me. Frankie thinks he is a hard man. He is known to be involved with a gang in the town called the 'Cheltenham Ladies', so I would not have been surprised if he had a gun. I tried to play it cool, but I think Frankie must have seen I was scared. He laughed and said something about scaring me with his kid brother's water pistol, and squirted me in the face.

Frankie suggested we try the same trick on a stranger. I did not think this was a good idea but went along with them at first. Frankie ran up to a man outside the Wessex Provincial Bank in Westgate Street. When I saw he intended to rob the man I ducked off down a side street, pretending I needed to throw up. I did not tell Frankie I did not want to be involved because I did not want Frankie or Lisette to think I was scared. I shouted to Frankie that I was sick and was going home. Frankie swore, but did not follow me. I last saw him standing at the corner of Westgate Street. Lisette ran after me. She wasn't impressed with Frankie's joke either. She said she had had enough of Frankie and was going home. We split up, just in case the old man had seen us together. I walked back to Lisette's flat and we sat drinking until about 3.00 that morning, when I left to walk home. I was nearly at my place, when a police car pulled up from behind me. The policemen got out and asked me where I had been. I told them and they arrested me, on suspicion of being involved in a robbery they said. I cannot remember whether I was cautioned or not.

At the police station they told me they had caught Frankie after he had squirted some old bloke in the face with his water pistol and taken his money. They told me Frankie had admitted he was involved and had fingered me for it as well. I reckon he did it and then set me up, because he thought I'd had it away with Lisette. He has always been really jealous about her, even though she hasn't really got the hots for him. The best bit of all is that Lisette has told me that Frankie told the police he would co-operate if they kept her out of it.

I was still pretty drunk, but not so bad I didn't ask for a solicitor. The sergeant said they would have to wait for me to sober up before they interviewed me, but they would get a solicitor to me before then. I was put in a cell, where I fell asleep. I vaguely remember waking up when someone came to talk to me, but I felt sick and was too confused to really take in what was going on. I'm not sure who the bloke was. He wasn't in uniform, I know that.

At about 8.30 am I was woken up again. They had got me a duty solicitor. I told him my version of events and he said that the police had also told him that Frankie was saying that the robbery was my idea. I denied this. I was taken to the interview room. I still felt really rough. The solicitor advised me to answer questions, which I did. They said I had admitted the robbery in the cells that morning. I denied this, but they said I did, and they had Frankie's statement to support it, so I said a few things that seemed to shut them up. I just said them so I could get out. I felt sick, and I hate those places. I just wanted out, so I signed a statement under caution. After that I was charged and released on bail.

Case study 2: The case of William Gardiner[1]

In 1902–3 William Gardiner was tried for the murder of a young unmarried woman, Rose Harsent, who lived near his home in the Suffolk village of Peasenhall. The case was remarkable for the fact that Gardiner was actually tried twice, first in November 1902, then in January 1903. On neither occasion could the jury agree on its verdict. As majority verdicts were not acceptable at the time, Gardiner's case had to be set down for re-trial on each occasion. The case became of national interest even before the second trial, and it is probable that public sympathy for Gardiner was largely behind the authorities' decision to enter a nolle prosequi after the second trial, which mercifully spared him the ordeal of a third. No other person was ever tried for Rose's murder. William Gardiner died in 1941, at the age of 72, neither formally guilty nor formally innocent of the murder, and still overshadowed by it.

The facts of the case are quite complex, but can be best summarised as follows.

Gardiner was accused of murdering 23-year-old Rose Harsent at some time during the Saturday night/Sunday morning of 31 May–1 June 1902. Gardiner (aged 35) was a married man with six children. He was foreman carpenter at the local drill works and a prominent member of the Methodist congregation. His home in Peasenhall was some 200 yards from Providence House, where Rose Harsent lived and was employed as the servant of Mr and Mrs Crisp. Rose was friendly with both Gardiner and his wife. On the Saturday evening Gardiner had been seen outside his house from between 9.55 and 10.10 pm, chatting to a friend, Harry Burgess. Soon after 11.00 pm a heavy storm broke, which continued until around 1.30 am. At about 11.30 pm Mrs Gardiner went across the road to visit a friend, Mrs Dickinson, who had recently been widowed and was frightened by the storm. Her husband joined her after checking the children were all right – this was at some time between 11.30 and 12.00. They stayed with Mrs Dickinson until the storm abated and then went home and to bed at about 2.00 am. Mrs Gardiner was unable to sleep. After seeing to one of the children who had woken up, she went downstairs to get some brandy to help her sleep (at some time after 2.20 am). The brandy did not help and she was still awake when the Gardiners' twin girls woke about an hour later (the time is uncertain). She put one of the twins in with an older sister, and brought the other one back to her (and her husband's) bed. By about 5.00 am she had finally fallen asleep. Around 7.00 am a neighbour saw what appeared to be a larger than usual fire in the Gardiners' wash-house (where they normally boiled the kettle for their morning tea); he also saw Gardiner coming away from the wash-house half an hour later. Mrs

Gardiner got up at about 8.00 am.

Rose Harsent's movements are less well documented. Burgess saw a light in her attic bedroom on leaving Gardiner. A few minutes later, Rose said good-night to Mrs Crisp in the main hall of Providence House, as Mrs Crisp went upstairs to bed. Shortly after the storm broke, the Crisps went downstairs again to check that water was not coming into the house. Rose was not down-stairs at the time. They did not check the kitchen itself, which was built on to the west wall of the house, though, as she closed the door between kitchen and dining-room, Mrs Crisp noticed that the kitchen seemed unusually dark. The Crisps then went back to bed. Mrs Crisp was woken, she surmised, at some time between 1.00 and 2.00 am by a thud and a scream that seemed to come from inside the house. The storm was still raging over the village. She woke her husband (who was very deaf) and asked whether they should check on Rose. He thought that unnecessary, as Rose knew she could come into their bedroom if anything was wrong. They went back to sleep.

At 8.00 am the next morning, Rose's father, William Harsent, called round to Providence House to leave his daughter's clean linen for the week. He went round to the back of the house as usual, and noticed the conservatory door, which led to the kitchen, was open. He opened the kitchen door. The kitchen was darker than normal, as a black shawl had been pinned over the only win-dow. Rose lay on her back on the floor, with her feet pointing towards the outside door. Around her was a pool of blood that covered much of the floor in the small kitchen. There was a strong smell of paraffin and burnt flesh. Rose's night clothes were virtually burnt away; her right arm and the right side of her abdomen were charred. Harsent felt her arm; it was quite cold and he covered her body with a rug. He then told a neighbour what had happened and stayed with his daughter until the police and the doctor arrived (at around 8.30 am).

The scene that they discovered did not make the events any easier to recon-struct. The doctor estimated that Rose had been dead some four to six hours. She had died from having her throat cut. There were three wounds in her neck. The deepest had severed the left jugular vein and opened her windpipe – this alone would have proved fatal. A second wound ran from the angle of the right jaw up under the chin; this had missed major blood vessels but had also penetrated the windpipe. A stab wound also ran upwards from the junc-ture of the left collar bone and breast bone to the throat, where it joined the first, cutting, wound. There was a bruise on her right cheek and a number of cuts to her hands – one across the right forefinger, others to her left thumb and forefinger and the ball of the same thumb. Blood had spurted some 24 inches beyond her feet, and had also splashed the open door and steps to her bedroom, directly behind her head (as she lay). It was clear from the nature of her burns that these occurred after death. It also became apparent that Rose was pregnant – six months pregnant to be exact.

A variety of items surrounded the body. Rose's head lay on a copy of that Friday's *East Anglian Daily Times*. This was burnt at the edges only, and Rose's face and hair were unsinged. To the left of her head lay the candlestick she used to light herself to bed. This was upright and the candle had burned out. Between the candlestick and Rose's head was an oil lamp. This was unlit and unbroken, but had been taken apart; no paraffin had apparently been emptied from its well. Close to the candlestick were the pieces of a broken medicine bottle, which had contained paraffin. The neck of the bottle had rolled away from the body. The cork stopper was still in place, and there was a label around the neck which was covered in blood and paraffin. Only after it had been cleaned by Home Office experts could the inscription be read: 'Two or three teaspoonfuls' and 'Mrs Gardiner's chdn'. Among the fragments of the bottle were found a half-burnt match and a small piece of blue woollen fabric, which was never matched to any other items of clothing. A wooden shelf bracket to Rose's left, which supported a small wooden shelf on the wall next to the staircase door, had been broken, apparently by the door hitting it with some force. Despite all the blood no footprints appear to have been found at the scene. However, a set of impressions(not bloodstained) were seen by one witness at about 5.00 am that Sunday morning. Morris, a local gardener, saw a set of barred imprints on the wet road which seemed to lead from Gardiner's house to Providence House and back. Morris's statement was not made until a week after the murder, and the existence of the foot-prints was never corroborated.

When the police examined Rose's bedroom, it was clear that her bed had not been slept in. A number of letters were also found. One set, of love letters and indecent poems, were unsigned but later attributed to a young man (Fred Davis) in the village. There was another unsigned note, in a different hand, which read:

D R
I will try to see you tonight at 12 oclock at your Place if you Put a light in your window at 10 oclock for about 10 minutes then you can take it out again. dont have a light in your Room at 12 as I will come round to the back.

This was in a buff envelope which had been posted locally on the Saturday (31 May). Envelopes of the same kind were found in the Gardiners' home, but it was also established that the envelopes were of a common kind that were sold locally.

Two other letters were also of interest. These were signed by William Gardiner and had been sent to Rose a year previously. In them he referred to action he intended to take to clear their names after he and Rose had become linked in a village scandal. The scandal had arisen when Wright and Skinner, two younger men from Gardiner's works, claimed that they had seen Gardiner and Rose – separately – enter the village chapel one evening and that they had subsequently heard them making love there. This Gardiner vehemently denied, and he was cleared by an internal inquiry set up by the Methodist chapel. This did not stop village gossip from suggesting a relationship not only had existed, but was continuing. If true, this might well have given Gardiner a motive for murdering the now pregnant Rose. It was to be a matter of contention at the trials whether Gardiner was the author of the anonymous note which apparently set up Rose's last and fatal assignation.

If Rose's death was the result of a sexual assault, or some lovers' tryst that had gone wrong, was there any evidence that sexual activity had taken place before the murder? Interestingly, the issue appears only to have been raised at the second trial,[2] but the medical evidence on the point proved wholly inconclusive.

The only real evidence against Gardiner was his clasp knife which the Home Office analyst was able to show had recently been scraped clean of mammalian blood.[3] Gardiner's response was to say that he had recently used the knife to gut a rabbit. No bloodstained clothing or footwear was ever found and attributed to him.

So, Gardiner went to trial on the strength of this accumulation of circumstantial evidence. At both trials, his defence was led by a relatively young and inexperienced barrister, Earnest Wild.[4] The prosecution was led by Henry Fielding Dickens, a King's Counsel who was later elevated to the judiciary as Common Serjeant of the City of London.[5]

Having set the scene for our cases, we return to the practicalities of advocacy. We shall deal with these under three headings: Preparation, Speeches, and Examination. In each of these sections we have sought to recognise and distinguish between two related dimensions of competent advocacy. The first of these is a strategic dimension. All advocacy is involved in the development and advancement of a strategy for the case. The second dimension is the technical, in that your strategy is chiefly advanced by the use of practical techniques of presenting your case.

1   The case has spawned an extensive literature, including at least two novels. The main sources used here are W Henderson *The Trial of William Gardiner* (Notable British Trials series) Hodge, London 1934 (which relied heavily on the contemporary newspaper reports of the case) and M Fido & K Skinner *The Peasenhall Murder*, Alan Sutton, Stroud 1990, which is probably the most thorough of the modern studies.
2   This was not generally considered a fit subject for publication by the papers of the day, and only one of them, the *News of the World* noted, very obliquely, that Lawrence J raised the issue himself during the examination of Dr Richardson (who had conducted the postmortem). See Fido & Skinner, op cit, pp 114, 162.
3   Forensic science in 1902 could not distinguish human blood specifically in such circumstances.
4   Later Sir Earnest, and, from 1922, Recorder for the City of London.
5   He was also a son of the novelist Charles Dickens, a pedigree Wild made ironic use of more than once in the subsequent proceedings.

Preparation

Advocacy is the culmination of the litigation process. So, in a sense, everything the lawyer does in a contentious matter, from the moment of taking instructions, is preparation for advocacy, even though it is advocacy that may never happen. It is therefore important to be aware of how the advocate's role fits in with all the other stages and processes in litigation. This is perhaps why some lawyers would argue that the sum of a good litigator is greater than the individual parts. It is the capacity to bring it all together before the trial that really counts:

Litigation is a creative art form – you need tactical skill, a knowledge of factual background and a good level of academic knowledge. Attention to detail is important and the ability to move quickly and analyse material. You must be able to almost predict what will happen . . .[1]

As this suggests, much of the advocate's preparation is focused on developing an intimate knowledge of the details of the case: the facts alleged; the law; the evidence necessary to establish your claim, etc. In addition, there are a number of specific issues which you need to have considered. We will discuss these various points under three headings:

- Planning your case.
- Preparing your client.
- Preparing witnesses.

1 Solicitor cited by A Boon 'Assessing Competence to Conduct Civil Litigation: Key Tasks and Skills' in Boon, Mackie & Halpern *Skills for Legal Functions II: Representation and Advice*, Institute of Advanced Legal Studies, London 1992, p 23.

Planning your case

The importance of this goes without saying, and we have already discussed case preparation and management techniques at length in Chapter 3. So, by way of revision on some key techniques, do the following exercise.

Exercise 10.3   Gardiner: chronology and theory

Imagine you are counsel for Gardiner. Individually or in small groups:
(a)   Construct a chronology of the relevant events on the night of the murder.
(b)   Make a mind map of the issues as they appear to you from the summary of the case.[1]
(c)   Using your chronology and mind map, construct a theory of the case for the defence.

Here we will confine ourselves to developing a few additional points.

First, while it has become axiomatic to suggest that most first instance cases turn on issues of fact, you must not forget the law. One thing that has surprised us as teachers has been the readiness of (some) of our students to leap into court armed with a case that is built around often quite detailed and sophisticated factual argument . . . and not say a word about what needs to be proved by whom and to what degree. If you think back to our technique of five-level analysis, our starting point is –and has to be – the law. This should be reflected in case preparation and delivery. Cases where difficult points of law arise and need to be argued are a rarity, but this does not mean you should therefore overlook the need for research, nor should you underestimate the value of any authority which helps you construct a point of law. This is certainly true of civil work, as one of the barristers interviewed by Morison and Leith said:

If you have a point of law in your favour in the High Court, but even in the county court, it is very important . . . it will be listened to . . . You can win cases on legal points in the county court . . . despite the view that you sometimes hear.[2]

though it is perhaps rather less accurate for criminal trials where even more of the law in daily use is statute-based and cases tend to turn on factual or evidential rather than substantive issues.

Second, you should assess your evidential needs closely. The rules of evidence play a more significant part in the presentation of criminal than civil cases. The reasons for this are partly historical and partly a reflection of deliberate policy. The suggestion has been made on more than one occasion that the English law of evidence has always started from the general assumption that all witnesses are congenital liars! Since issues of fact in the more serious criminal cases are tried by a lay jury, it has been considered necessary to develop very detailed rules determining what evidence they may or may not take into account; these rules would almost certainly not have developed in this fashion had criminal trials been the responsibility of judges alone – contrast the greater freedom of proof which now exists in civil trials. The result is a system dependent upon a host of complex exclusionary rules. The law of evidence has, especially since the last century, been amended in a highly piecemeal and particularistic fashion, so that we have acquired thereby an even more complex list of exceptions to the exclusions.

An awareness of evidentiary needs is crucial at the preparatory stage. The defence must be aware of what evidence may be admitted to support their case, or indeed (so far as is possible) the admissibility of evidence that may go against your client's interests (eg a confession). This will obviously be critical in giving any detailed advice on ultimate liability, and hence on the plea. Evidentiary factors play a part in deciding what defence(s) you run, if any; and in making decisions regarding the mode of trial, etc. The prosecution particularly needs to consider whether there is sufficient evidence to support charges; whether to exercise their discretion not to prosecute, and whether there are grounds for multiple counts on the indictment. Both sides need to consider the need for, and availability of, sources of evidence, eg:

● availability of eye- and expert witnesses;
● whether witnesses can, or should, be compelled to testify;
● problems of hearsay in any documentary or oral evidence – which will mean statements may be inadmissible, or only admissible after editing.

You also need to consider procedural requirements, for example:

● for issue of proceedings and filing of documents;[3]
● for pre-trial exchange of witness statements,[4] etc;
● for issuing any appropriate notice to the opposing side, eg, in respect of an alibi defence,[5] or of intention to adduce hearsay evidence.[6]

If you are not personally responsible for taking these steps, you should satisfy yourself that the appropriate procedures have been followed.

Lastly, your organisational skills are also important. While we have considered techniques for problem-solving and developing your theory of the case, we have not talked much about basic information management. Many of the techniques are fairly obvious and self-explanatory, but worth thinking through nonetheless.

Your aim is to get into court in control of your information and therefore confident that you can access any information you are likely to need quickly and easily. The techniques do not require high-level skills, and you can get into the habit of using them quite quickly. One particular method, originally developed in America but now being used in the UK as well, is the 'trial notebook'.[7] This can be constructed out of one or more ring binders, which you can organise systematically into a number of sections. Most of you probably do something similar already, with your own coursework and study materials. The precise organising principles may vary somewhat between different methods, but the notebook should certainly contain:

- *A chronological summary of events* – this helps you to reconstruct the events as they happened. Key elements of the chronology may then be built into . . .
- *Your theory of the case* – this is best done in point form, though some advocates like to flesh it out to a full, narrative, history.
- *An analysis of the other side's case*, and their probable theory of the case.
- *A proof checklist.* This may be a two or three column list detailing (i) the points of law requiring proof and (ii) the relevant facts and the evidence proving those facts (these may be listed together, or in separate columns – it's up to you). For the defence, of course, this would involve itemising evidence in rebuttal, or evidence that supports an affirmative defence. This should be cross-referenced to . . .
- *The documents and exhibits*, which should be copied or recorded in a separate section.
- *Research notes*, if necessary, can be included on any complex points of law or on technical information required to understand any of the (expert) evidence.

1 You might find it interesting to compare your mind map with one Andy Boon constructs based on the facts of the Rouse case (discussed briefly below): see *Advocacy*, Cavendish, London 1993, pp 63–4 and 192.
2 J Morison & P Leith *The Barrister's World*, Open University Press, Milton Keynes 1992, p 108.
3 For example, CCR Ord 3, r 1 (issue of summons); Ord 6, r 1 (filing of medical reports).
4 Advance disclosure in criminal cases is becoming increasingly complex. Disclosure of prosecution statements has been the norm for some years, though the principles vary depending on the seriousness of the offence. Disclosure of defence statements is not a formal or mandatory requirement at present, though general defence disclosure was proposed by the *Royal Commission on Criminal Justice* (1993) and has been endorsed by a recent Home Office consultation paper (*Disclosure: A Consultation Document*, Cm 2864, 1995). More informal disclosures of defence positions, if not actual evidence, are a frequent consequence of pre-trial review procedures, and may become more generally required following the reforms to the right of silence. In respect of civil cases in the county court, see CCR Ord 20, r 12(A).
5 See Criminal Justice Act 1967, s 11.
6 Under the Civil Evidence Act 1968, s 8; see RSC Ord 38, rr 20–30/CCR Ord 20, rr 15–25 in civil cases. In criminal proceedings there is no corresponding duty to give notice, so that hearsay statements adduced under the principles in the Police and Criminal Evidence Act 1984, s 69 and the Criminal Justice Act 1988, ss 23–26 and Sch 2 are subject only to the normal requirements of advance disclosure.
7 See J McElhaney 'The Trial Notebook' (1980) 1 *Litigation* 1 (NB this reference is to an American journal, not the British practitioners' journal of the same name); Boon, op cit (1993).

Exercise 10.4   Bigg – a proof checklist

(a) *You are prosecuting Mr Bigg. Construct a proof checklist, on the assumption that he is to be tried on a charge of robbery.*
(b) *On the same assumption, now construct a proof checklist for the defence.*
(c) *Using the techniques you have practised in Exercise 10.2, develop a theory of the case either for the prosecution or defence.*

Preparing your client

> I was terrified up there. My legs were quaking.[1]

> I was in shock. It was unreal.[2]

These statements reflect what is a well known fact: that courts are often alien and unsettling territory for lay people. This is commonly put down to fear, and the inarticulateness of many who appear before the courts. But as both Carlen and McBarnet[3] have emphasised, this is an oversimplification. What most effectively silences the lay person is the trial process itself. This is not a problem unique to the criminal courts. The context could as easily be, for example, a debt or repossession action. Both Carlen and McBarnet's work focused on the silencing of the unrepresented defendant. We would argue that a represented person may also be effectively silenced by the trial process, in even more subtle ways. Worrall, for example, argues that the client becomes what she calls the 'dominated object of legal discourse':

> Solicitors do not talk about making assessments (as for example, do social workers, probation officers and doctors), they talk about 'taking instructions'. The implication is that they as servants articulate with confidence and competence in public that which the defendant has said haltingly and nervously in private. But what in fact happens is that a privileged discourse is constructed from the broken utterances of the powerless.[4]

Clark Cunningham offers a simple yet quite literal illustration of just such a silencing of a client.[5] As a law clinic supervisor he was involved with a client who had been charged with driving with excess alcohol.[6] The client spoke Spanish as a mother tongue, but very little English. The indications from the client were that he wanted to plead guilty, but translation problems generally made it difficult to advise and obtain instructions, even through an interpreter. The client's version of events also suggested that the police had administered the breathalyser test despite the fact that he had indicated that he did not speak English. This created an important issue for his lawyers. The police in this particular jurisdiction were required to obtain the suspect's consent to the test and to read a statement of rights to the suspect to ensure that any such consent was informed. Clearly, if the suspect could not understand English, and no attempt was made at translating his rights into Spanish, there could be no informed consent. Without that consent, the lawyers felt they had grounds for arguing the test results should be excluded from the hearing. Furthermore, the court file did not contain a police report, or the breathalyser test result. Cunningham takes up the story again on the day of the trial:

> We decided that our lack of necessary information made plea negotiations at the arraignment unwise. We therefore told our client, through the law student interpreter, that we recommended a plea of 'not guilty'. Our client said he did not understand and insisted that he was 'guilty'. At that point our case was called and we advised our client to 'stand mute', which he did. When we told the judge that our client was 'standing mute', he entered a plea of not guilty 'on behalf of' the defendant, as is customary . . .

Even though the client was silent, the judge, in effect, put words into his mouth: according to the record he 'pled' not guilty. The court (with our tacit connivance) 'made up' a defendant who took the proper adversarial position so that the case could proceed. In this sense, the defendant who 'appeared' in court was indeed only a 'representation', an image projected by the institutional needs of the judge and lawyers.[7]

Although the client's literal silence was converted into a figurative utterance, the client remained effectively silenced within the proceedings. His own version of his guilt or innocence was never heard.

We suggest that Worrall's argument rather overstates the case, by disregarding what it is actually possible for practitioners to achieve within the constraints of the existing system. Nevertheless we accept that 'silencing' happens, both literally (as Cunningham shows) and, more commonly, metaphorically, and it is an underlying theme to which we shall return again in this chapter. It is most certainly an issue at the preparatory phase. The question is: what can you do as a lawyer to try and prevent the silencing of your clients becoming what a number of legal theorists now term an act of (symbolic) violence against them?[8]

For the moment, we will try to answer that question in a very practical fashion.

1   Female witness, quoted by McBarnet in *Conviction: Law, the State and the Construction of Justice*, Macmillan, London & Basingstoke 1981, p 90.
2   Witness who was the accused's victim, cited by Rock in *The Social World of an English Crown Court*, Clarendon Press, Oxford 1993, p 128.
3   P Carlen *Magistrates' Justice*, Martin Robertson, Oxford 1976; D McBarnet, op cit.
4   A Worrall *Offending Women: Female Law Breakers and the Criminal Justice System*, Routledge, London 1990 at p 22.
5   'A Tale of Two Clients: Thinking About Law As Language' (1989) 87 *Michigan Law Review* 2459 at 2464–5.
6   For simplicity we have translated the American offence into its nearest English equivalent.
7   Op cit, p 2465. Note that similarly under English law, an accused who is 'mute of malice' will have a not guilty plea entered on their behalf – Criminal Law Act 1967, s 6(1).
8   See eg R Cover 'Foreword: Nomos and Narrative' (1983) 97 *Harvard Law Review* 4; cf also Gilligan's notion of violence and non-violence discussed in Chapter 4, above.

Exercise 10.5   A crusty in court

Your client, John, is a 22-year-old white male. He is charged with breach of the peace after getting caught up in a disturbance at a rally against a new Criminal Justice Bill, which proposes further restrictions on the movement of travellers. Your client is not a traveller: he is settled at home with his parents, who live in a very middle-class neighbourhood. He is sympathetic to the traveller lifestyle, however, and has a very 'crusty' appearance. The police have charged a group of eight individuals in total with offences arising out of the same event. Your client's version of events is that he and a friend were part of the demo, but were in fact leaving the scene because they could see things were turning nasty. He was arrested as they tried to push out of the side of the crowd and leave the area via a side street. They did not know the other people arrested (who were all travellers from outside the local area) and were not involved with them. Your client's friend, who dresses 'normally' was behind the group arrested, and did not get picked out by the police. Your client was not individually identified, but with the other seven was collectively identified as part of an aggressive crowd. He wants to plead not guilty.

Make a note of three or four practical matters of client preparation you need to address as the trial approaches.

Client preparation is an important part of the total process of trial preparation, and one where you must remember that your behaviour is clearly circumscribed by the Codes of Conduct which proscribe witness rehearsing. These rules are generally wide enough to encompass preparing both the client and any other witness.[1] Nevertheless, there are still a number of tasks you ought to complete before the hearing.

You must *confirm final instructions*. As the hearing approaches, your counselling role becomes more important. You must ensure you are covered by instructions from your client which are given in the light of clear advice from you about possible outcomes (eg the range of orders or awards the court might make) and the costs – or legal aid – implications of these various alternatives. This will be particularly important if (as quite often happens in civil cases) your client is not in court on the day.

In criminal cases, negotiating the plea with your client is often the most critical and, perhaps, most difficult preliminary task you have to perform. Defendants often do not receive legal advice until they see the duty solicitor in court. Even if they have received advice beforehand, they can change their plea right up to the last minute, with the result that discussions about the plea may continue until you are literally at the door of the court, or even in court. There is often considerable pressure placed on defendants, particularly in the magistrates' court, to accept the outcomes of plea- or charge-bargaining, not least because of procedural implications such as the need to adjourn for a special court, if a not guilty plea is entered. Consider the following example. This is taken from a real solicitor–client interview which took place in the interview room at a magistrates' court, on the day of the defendant's hearing.[2]

The defendant 'Janet' is a single parent accused of shoplifting with her boyfriend. She is charged with stealing the cassette tapes that were found in her boyfriend, Richard's, possession. She has also been charged with an assault on a police officer arising out of a scuffle in the police station cells. This happened after an officer took her cigarettes away when she complained that no one had heard her calling for a light. She has agreed to plead guilty to that offence. The theft case has been prosecuted as a 'joint enterprise' and there is evidence from a store detective and a shop assistant, alleging that Janet had put the tapes in Richard's bag. Janet denies this. Janet has previous convictions for petty theft, though none since the birth of her children. She states her intention to plead not guilty to the theft, and her solicitor ('Jane Gregson') is about to proceed on that basis, when she seems to change her mind, and starts to question her client again. We come in just after Janet has denied acting as look-out for Richard.

> S: I'll tell you what I think. I think you've been through the mill with this, partly because you've been frightened in the past and you feel you'll lose the children if you're sent to prison . . . My view is I

think you did know what was going on and you did help.

C: I didn't take part myself.

S: Did you put it in his bag?

C: I didn't.

S: I don't want to put you through the grief of a trial if you helped him . . . But you didn't walk off. You stayed with him. You're not a child . . . By staying with someone if they're doing something like that, it can be seen as encouragement. You could have walked out of the shop.

C: He'd have turned on me. I just stood away from him.

S: You should have got out of the shop . . . You see, if someone's with you when they're doing it and you stay there, that can be viewed as participating. I feel that's what happened and you're frightened to say that because of your fears. Am I right?

C: No . . . You see I had an idea but I didn't know for sure until we got out and he took the tapes out of the bag. I just told him to put them away.

S: Even telling him to put them away is actually participating. You should have said nothing . . .

You see, on the basis of what they're saying here, you'll be bound to be convicted anyway. But I think you'll be guilty because you stayed with him and assisted him. If you stay with anyone and assist in committing a crime, this means you're guilty.

C: But I didn't pinch anything.

S: Technically, I feel you're guilty, but I can present it to the court as if it's only a technical offence. Legally, if you assist someone by advising them before or after, you're guilty of taking part in crime. Technically you . . . So you will have to plead guilty to that. But it will be presented to the court as that. He's involved you in that against your will . . . *(Gregson moves towards the door)* . . . I wasn't happy representing you on your story before. Now I'm happy I'm at the bottom of it . . .[3]

1   See *LSG* 14.05; *CCB* 607.3.
2   The case is taken from M Travers *Persuading the client to plead guilty: an ethnographic examination of a routine morning's work in the magistrates' court*, Manchester Sociology Occasional Paper No 33, University of Manchester, Manchester 1992.
3   Ibid, pp 21–2.

Exercise 10.6   Jane's dilemma (1)

Working in pairs:

(a)   *In your view:*

(i)   *Does Janet comprehend why her solicitor is advising her to plead guilty?*

(ii)   *Why/why not?*

(iii)   *On the evidence you have, does Janet seem willing to participate in the redefinition of her 'innocence' as 'guilt'?*

(iv)   *Why/why not?*

(b)   *Do you feel that Jane (the solicitor) handled the question of Janet's plea appropriately in terms of:*
   (i)   *the law;*
   (ii)   *her responsibilities to her client;*
   (iii)   *her responsibilities to the court?*
   Give reasons for each of your answers.
(c)   *Now compare your answers with those of the other pairs in the group. Account for any differences you find.*

Any differences are likely to depend on whether you take a critical or pragmatic stance on what Jane should have achieved. Any practitioner's experience would tell them that Janet would be convicted on the evidence, even if she pleaded not guilty. It would also be clear that the offences would not justify a custodial sentence – Janet's greatest fear. In that context, it might be argued that Jane's strategy was to do the best she could for her client in the circumstances, which meant get it over and done with, without the stress of a full trial (and the possible loss of discount from the sentence for a guilty plea – though that would be marginal in a case like this). But could she have done more to take her client along with her, even allowing for the fact that the magistrates were sitting next door waiting for the case to begin? Was the way she handled the client heavily dependent on her exercise of superior knowledge and status – and hence power – over that client? Would you – could you – have handled it any differently? If so, how?

Exercise 10.7   Jane's dilemma (2)

Two volunteers should role-play Janet and Jane, to test out any alternative strategies that have emerged from the discussion.[1]

Another major issue is the question of *whether your client should testify*. This is an issue in both civil and criminal cases, though we will focus chiefly on the criminal side once again, addressing first the defence and then the prosecution perspective.

There are significant tactical implications to a defendant testifying, not the least being that the defendant who testifies leaves herself open to cross-examination on the issues, with generally no protection against self-incrimination. A defendant who testifies similarly may be cross-examined as to her bad character (if any), either if (i) she asserts her own good character, or (ii) attacks the character of a prosecution witness, or (iii) testifies against a co-accused.[2]

Equally there are compelling reasons why an accused should testify. In Kalven and Zeisel's classic study of the American jury trial, it was noted that less than a fifth of defendants relied on the presumption of innocence and did not testify.[3] Their study also assumed that, whatever judges may say about the presumption of innocence, it will be difficult to prevent juries from drawing adverse inferences from an accused's failure to give evidence.[4] Later mock jury research in the States appears to support that assumption as generally correct.[5] Further, in both civil and criminal cases, trying to prevent a defendant from testifying can also serve as a form of disempowerment that is inconsistent with the principles of participatory practice. Put simply, the opportunity to have a say can be of great significance to the way a person feels about their case, even if they lose.[6]

For the prosecution, the issue becomes: should the victim testify? The views of the victim of a crime are of some significance throughout the criminal process. The victim's support (or otherwise) for the action may be a factor in determining whether or not to prosecute in the first place.[7] The problem for the prosecution is often a simple one: without the victim's testimony, there would be no case. This creates difficulties which are widely recognised, though not necessarily widely acted upon.

First, the system itself remains generally unsympathetic to victims of crime. Despite counselling services and increased information on the prosecutorial process, victims can feel marginalised by the process. This is especially true of the trial, and a number of studies have independently shown that victims often feel unsupported by 'their'[8] lawyers at trial.[9] In the English context, victims' complaints include their lack of understanding of the process, and the general low level of interest shown by 'their' lawyers.[10]

Second, it is difficult to assess how much protection victims of crime can be given without destroying the due process of adversary trial and the rights of the accused. Sanders and Young assert:

> Our natural sympathy for victims of crime should not blind us to the fact that one of the objects of the system is to discover whether prosecution witnesses . . . are telling the truth or not. A system in which 'victims' were treated with kid gloves would be as indefensible as one which ritually humiliated them.[11]

Nevertheless, vulnerable witnesses can be assisted as much as possible to testify. Preparation is important, and you should assess whether the use of special procedures to help the victims of crime is appropriate – eg the use of documentary, video-link and videotaped testimony.[12] However, a victim cannot always be protected from cross-examination, and this has to be taken into account at the initial stages of any prosecution.

So, what would we suggest you should do to prepare your client (including, so far as possible, the victim)? Well, even though direct rehearsing is not allowed, there are four particular strategies available which would not seem to contravene the Codes of Conduct, and yet help prepare the client for the court.

First, build your case with the *co-operation* of your client. If both lawyer and client are committed to the theories and themes you wish to present, your client will feel more confident in the case and is, perhaps, less likely to do anything that will contradict the lines you intend pursuing.

The second of these is pure common sense. You should always send your client a copy of her *witness statement*, and get her to check it and let you know if there is anything she wishes to amend or reconsider. This will at least help refresh the client's memory of what she has said. Also, if anything is changed, you will be able to deal with it in advance, rather than be surprised in the hearing itself. Given the possible need for changes, it is best to do this a couple of weeks (rather than days) before the trial.

Third, you should outline the *basic trial procedure* to the client. Explain what will happen and how long it is likely to take; who the main functionaries are, and the basic order of events. If time allows, some of this can be done in the letter you send out confirming, or reminding her of, the date set down for trial but, regardless of this, you should always try to meet your client on the day and give her the chance to talk through any concerns.

Lastly, there seems to be no ethical difficulty in *role-playing* a client through testimony on facts different from those in their own case. This is not coaching them on their evidence, but it is getting them used to the style of examination and cross-examination that they are likely to face in court. It appears that a number of solicitors' firms have adopted this tactic on occasion.[13] It is certainly preferable to one American advocate's avowed tactic of the 'stress test' he applies to new clients:

> . . . I ask them to tell me everything they can about themselves and their case; then, using that information, I hit them with a barrage of insults and sarcasm.[14]

'Not surprisingly', Pannick adds, 'some break down, go home and never come back'.[15]

Creating the right impression may also have appeared, in some form or another, on your list. Your client's physical appearance may be an issue. You are probably aware of the fact that there are a number of 'image consultants' making a handsome living out of high profile (and high value) criminal defence work in the States – cases such as the O J Simpson murder trial – where they are employed to make witnesses and, if necessary, the defendant more presentable and, they would argue, more believable. To our knowledge, no one has yet tested the Legal Aid Board's views of an expenses claim for an image consultant in the UK, and we do not anticipate that English practice is in a hurry to follow this particular American trend. Nevertheless, English lawyers are certainly conscious that appearance could be an issue. Why?

The answer, of course, is stereotyping. Lay magistrates and juries in particular are thought to be judgmental and influenced by extraneous factors, such as appearance. This sort of ideology is supported by media images (think of the bigotry displayed by some of the jurors in the film *Twelve Angry Men*, for example), and certainly by advocates, in print, and otherwise.[16] But is this assumption accurate?

Research does suggest that factors such as ethnicity, mode of dress, and even gender may have some impact,[17] though it is debatable how far appearance factors have an independent effect, or whether they are only significant when taken in conjunction with other negative factors, such as a lack of linguistic skill or confidence,[18] or possibly because appearance is associated with powerful images of guilt – eg where an accused appears in handcuffs, or where the jury see an accused pleading guilty to another charge.[19] It is debatable whether any tribunal of fact will routinely allow a person's appearance to outweigh the impact of the evidence itself. However, in the end, most advocates will not take the chance.

So, you might well advise your clients to look neat, tidy and conventional (a particular issue in John's case), and encourage them to speak clearly and to the point. It is not going to do any harm to their case, though all this may not do much for their comfort or self-respect. Similarly, in John's case, you could warn him not to let any friends, who might want to disturb the proceedings by suitably anarchic comments or behaviour, come and give him their 'support'. In contrast, maybe you will encourage his parents along (good evidence of a supportive home environment) and any nice middle class character witnesses as well. And do not stop to ask what any of this has to do with the grander notions of justice that we are supposed to be concerned with!

1   In fact, we have deliberately distorted events slightly. Jane did not believe that Janet's final admission was the truth either. When challenged about whether she had put the tapes in the bag, Janet had tended to stress how the prosecution had got the description of Richard's bag wrong. This evasion left Jane suspecting, but unable to prove, that Janet had actively participated in the theft. Getting Janet to agree to this less culpable version was therefore easier than pursuing those doubts with her, and presented a less damaging 'truth' to the court. See M Travers *Persuading the client to plead guilty: an ethnographic examination of a routine morning's work in the magistrates' court*, Manchester Sociology Occasional Paper No 33, University of Manchester, Manchester 1992, pp 30–1.

2   These are the circumstances under s 1(f), Criminal Evidence Act 1898 in which an accused can lose the statutory protection of the 'shield' provided by s 1 of the same Act.

3   *The American Jury*, Little Brown, Boston 1966.

4   Ibid, p 144.

5   See eg the studies cited by D Shaffer 'The Defendant's Testimony' in S Kassin and L Wrightsman *The Psychology of Evidence and Trial Procedure*, Sage, Beverley Hills 1985, p 124 at pp 140–5.

6   Cf Cunningham's discussion of his second case, 'A Tale of Two Clients' (1989) 87 *Michigan Law Review* 2459, pp 2465–9; 2492.

7   See *Code for Crown Prosecutors*, January 1992 Edition, para 7(vii).

8   Strictly, of course, the prosecutor is not the victim's lawyer, and arguably this is part of the problem: the victim remains essentially unrepresented and largely invisible when she is not testifying.

9   See eg Rock in *The Social World of an English Crown Court*, Clarendon Press, Oxford 1993, pp 127–8, 305–6; also the comparative study by M Joutsen *The Role of the Victim of Crime in European Criminal Justice Systems*, Institute for Crime Prevention & Control, Helsinki 1987.

10 See ibid. What this certainly indicates is that prosecutors are very poor at explaining the effect of their ethical obligation not to discuss the case with the victim once she has been called. Prosecutors tend to take the safe course, which is to have no contact with the victim at this point, but the reason for this is not always explained to the victim in advance.

11 A Sanders & R Young *Criminal Justice*, Butterworths, London 1994, p 25.

12 See J McEwan 'Documentary Hearsay Evidence – Refuge for the Vulnerable Witness' [1989] *Criminal Law Review* 629.

13 A Sherr *Advocacy*, Blackstone Press, London 1993, p 42.

14 Roy Grutman & Bill Thomas *Lawyers and Thieves* (1990) cited in D Pannick *Advocates*, Oxford University Press, Oxford 1992, p 18.

15 Ibid.

16 See eg Clarence Darrow, cited by D Shaffer, op cit.

17 See eg W O'Barr *Linguistic Evidence: Language, power and strategy in the courtroom*, Academic Press, New York 1982; J Jackson 'Law's Truth, Lay Truth and Lawyer's Truth: The Representation of Evidence in Adversary Trials' (1992) III *Law and Critique* 29.

18 Cf M Myers 'Rule Departures and Making Law: Juries and their Verdicts, (1979) 13 *Law & Society Review* 781. We will return to the linguistic dimension in the next section.

19 See Jackson, op cit, p 48.

Evaluating and preparing witnesses

It is axiomatic to state that the quality of your case will turn largely on the quality of your witnesses. Indeed, Saks and Hastie[1] suggest that the nature and quality of evidence presented in the trial has greater impact on the fact finder than any other factor – including the composition of the jury.

Determining who you call is largely a matter for your own professional judgment – or luck. In many cases, you may have relatively little choice. You may need everyone you can get! But if you have a choice, what criteria do you use in exercising it? Witness evaluation is an important part of case preparation. You are looking, ideally for witnesses who will not just come up to proof, but will do so convincingly.

1   M Saks & R Hastie *Social Psychology in Court*, Van Nostrand Rheinhold, New York 1978.

Exercise 10.8   Superwitness

Imagine you were able to construct the ideal witness: what characteristics would that person have?

Make a list of no more than four or five things you would look for in a good witness.

We suggest you need to consider a number of factors which would influence the credibility of your witness:

● Will the witness answer questions immediately, without substantial delay or hesitancy?
● Will they answer questions directly, or will they 'beat about the bush'?
● Can they present their evidence chronologically? (This is difficult for most people to do spontaneously; it is also not that easy for you as the advocate to direct the chronology, especially in chief, when you cannot lead the witness.)

VERBAL BEHAVIOUR

Arguably, these factors all have one thing in common: the need for *narrative coherence* in court. The ability to tell a story well will often make or mar the 'quality' of testimony provided by witnesses. Chronology – a sense of the timing of events – is frequently important in this context. Times may well be at issue. For example, in the Gardiner case, part of Gardiner's defence rested on the alibi evidence provided by his wife and Mrs Dickinson for what, on the evidence, was the most likely time at which the murder was committed. In that sort of context, evidence of time of death, or of possible periods in which the accused's whereabouts could not be accounted for, will be critical, and a witness who has the ability to go through their evidence chronologically can greatly strengthen the case. Even where time is not at issue, a chronological delivery can increase the comprehensibility of a story.

But the problem goes beyond simple chronology. The practice in trials more generally favours those witnesses who are most capable of telling their story in the formal, relatively abstracted way expected in court. What do we mean by this?

First we would stress that legal discourse makes assumptions about what is the appropriate subject for legal argumentation. If someone fails to meet the expected criteria for a legal argument, we tend to ignore or silence their different voice. To illustrate this, we draw on the work of Conley and O'Barr, who distinguish between 'relational' and 'rule-oriented' discourse about law:

> Many litigants speak of their place in a network of social relations and emphasise the social context of their legal problems . . .

By contrast, the official discourse of the law is oriented to rules. This orientation is typical of all forms of official legal discourse, including both discourse among legal professionals and the talk that characterises the interaction of lawyers and judges with lay people. This dominant discourse of the law treats rules as transcending the social particulars of individual cases. It thus rejects the fundamental premise of the relational orientation . . .

The distribution of these orientations is not random, but is socially patterned. The discourse of relationships is the discourse of those who have not been socialised into the centres of power in our society. Gender, class and race are deeply entangled with the knowledge of and ability to use the rule-oriented discourse that is the official approach of the law. Thus, it is no surprise that the agenda of relational speakers is often at variance with the agenda of the law.

. . . the relational orientation and the powerless style are two components of a pattern of thinking and speaking that typifies those on the fringes of power.[1]

Let us illustrate this with an extract from one of Conley and O'Barr's small claims court cases. These are relatively informal tribunals yet, even here, the litigants who structure their arguments relationally are at a disadvantage. The case we will consider was brought against the parents of a minor who had borrowed a friend's car and then collided with the plaintiff's car. The judge clearly took the view that the parents' liability, as a matter of law, was beyond dispute, and that the only real issue was one of quantum. His discussion with the parents proceeds as follows:

Judge: Have you any questions as to the liability of parents for minors under ordinary circumstances?

Mr Floyd: Uh, in some cases because, uh, what chance do we have when he doesn't mind us, you know?

Judge: Well, sir, that's, that's nothing I can decide here today. There's a case has been filed . . . against two parents for the operation of a motor vehicle owned by the parents and in the possession of the minor, uh, son of the party. An accident arose and there was damage.

Mr Floyd: Well . . .

Judge: Basically the question is this, and I understand your concerns that the driver should pay, but that's, he's not a party to this and cannot be a party, uh, because of his age. He may have obligations to you. That's not before the court today. But are you concerned only with the dollar amount of what this is going to conclude to us?

Mrs Floyd: No. We're concerned with that also, but we don't feel that we're responsible. We feel that he should have to be responsible for it.

Judge: All right, well you're bypassing the question now. Are you saying that it, the accident was not the fault of your son?

Mrs Floyd: No, we're not saying that. We don't know whose fault it was.

Judge:	All right. We don't know. Then maybe that answers the next question, which is how this all got started. Uh, do you deny that it was your son's fault?
Mr Floyd:	Could be. His friend loaned him the car.
Judge:	Well, at the accident when this thing happened, are you admitting, let's phrase it that way, are you admitting that it was your son's fault?
Mr Floyd:	Yeah, I admit that.[2]

The parents' answers clearly show their different, relational, agenda. They are concerned with the rightness of their being held responsible for a son over whom they feel they have little control. They thus insist on raising a problem that is non-legal, which the judge feels he cannot address, let alone solve. Through their responses to the judge's questioning, they then display their incapacity to adapt their story to the judge's theory of the case. Similar problems will arise in formal trials.

Second, a number of studies point (albeit in different ways) to the conclusion that the court is a place where both some degree of standard language ideology[3] and certain narrative assumptions rule. For example, where witnesses use vocabulary incorrectly (malapropisms again), or try to overcorrect their speech styles, or where their narratives are fragmented by lots of short answers, or are full of qualification and hedging, their competence is likely to be underrated.[4] Counsel may even rely more powerfully and explicitly on standard language ideology to create inferences about a witness; the aim here is to pander to the view, to put it simplistically, that only 'bad people' know 'bad language'. Consider the following interchange. In this case the lawyer is cross-examining a woman who is jointly charged with possessing heroin with her daughter. She has just disclosed that her daughter has been in trouble with the police previously:

Counsel:	What kind of trouble?
Witness:	She was just found with some works in her pocket.
Counsel:	Works eh, now wher– where did you pick up the slang expression works?
Witness:	I've heard it used quite frequently.
Counsel:	What's meant by the term works?
Witness:	It means, uh, a needle.
Counsel:	A syringe?
Witness:	Yes, sir.
Counsel:	And cooker?
Witness:	Ye– I don' know about the cooker.
Counsel:	Pardon?
Witness:	I don't know about the cooker.[5]

The effect of this interchange is to show not just the witness's familiarity with the drug user's tools but also her familiarity with the slang ('works', 'cooker') used to describe them. The implication counsel is trying to plant in our minds is pretty obvious. People who are not involved in the drugs culture would not be familiar with such terms.

As Bennet and Feldman point out, when witnesses fail to meet the storytelling expectations of judge or juror:

the presumption is not that the speaker merely uses a different language code or structures accounts differently. The presumption is that the speaker's version of an incident is suspect.[6]

Would you expect witness credibility to be dependent solely on their *verbal* behaviours, or would you suspect that the process of building credibility is more complex than that? What else might play a part?

You will, of course, have made the connection with our earlier work on the communication process and recognised that credibility also turns on other factors.

NON-VERBAL BEHAVIOURS

O'Barr[7] describes actors in the courtroom (whether as witnesses or advocates) as being either powerful or powerless. His research suggests that the credibility of these actors is intrinsically connected to their style of delivery. NVC will often reinforce the signals that are sent out verbally. 'Limited' vocabulary, a hesitant speech style and a lack of audibility will combine to produce indications of powerlessness.

PHYSICAL APPEARANCE

As we noted in the context of client preparation, appearance factors may play a part in the evaluation of evidence. These same factors could also influence the way witnesses are perceived.

If necessary you may need to decide that a case cannot run simply because the evidence – as presented in court, rather than as presented on paper, or in conference – will not convince. This is difficult to assess. You cannot easily mimic the atmosphere of a courtroom to test how individuals will react, and sometimes it is the most unexpected witnesses who fail to come up to proof – 'I've known a bomb disposal officer faint in the witness box because he can defuse bombs but he couldn't give evidence.'[8] Really good witnesses are rare, so you are often trying to assess not so much whether witnesses are good, but whether they are not so bad as to make a real difference to your chances.

The principles governing witness preparation are essentially the same as those governing preparation of the client. Coaching is unethical, though in many criminal cases there will be insufficient time to undertake effective rehearsal, even if it was allowed.

1 J M Conley & W M O'Barr *Rules versus Relationships: The Ethnography of Legal Discourse*, University of Chicago Press, Chicago 1990, pp 172–3.
2 Ibid, pp 53–4.
3 See the discussion of this term in Chapter 5, above.
4 See generally W M O'Barr *Linguistic Evidence: Language, Power and Strategy in the Courtroom*, Academic Press, New York 1982.
5 Taken from P Drew 'Strategies in the Contest Between Lawyer and Witness in Cross-Examination' in J N Levi & A G Walker *Language in the Judicial Process*, Plenum Press, New York and London 1990, p 39 at p 52.
6 W Bennet & M Feldman *Reconstructing Reality in the Courtroom*, Tavistock, London and New York 1981, p 174. For a case study of where problems of linguistic register have actually led to perjury charges being brought against a witness, see R Shuy *Language Crimes*, Blackwell, Oxford & Cambridge, Ma 1993, pp 136–48.
7 Op cit.
8 Detective Constable at Wood Green Crown Court, London, quoted in P Rock *The Social World of an English Crown Court*, p 27.

Exercise 10.9   Bigg – witnesses

Look at the witness statements.

(a)   *Which witnesses would you intend to call for the prosecution. Why?*
(b)   *What additional information, if any, would you want to obtain from any of those witnesses?*
(c)   *Are there any additional witnesses you might need to seek out?*

Determining who you call is one of the most critical decisions. It can affect your case's credibility in a number of ways. First, as we have seen, you want to try and avoid calling poor quality witnesses, if you can. Second, despite the fact that corroboration as such is not strictly required in most contexts, the number of witnesses to the facts can influence the credibility of the story they support (or undermine).[1] If you have two or three witnesses supporting your version of events, against an accused offering an explanation that is inconsistent with your version of events, this will obviously strengthen your case and weaken the defence. This is something advocates should be quick to capitalise on by using confrontational techniques to challenge the other side's evidence. On the other hand, a parade of witnesses does not always strengthen your case. First, the court will certainly get suspicious of a string of friends and neighbours telling identical stories. Since most events which get into court do not take place in front of hordes of willing witnesses, too many witnesses can be as damaging as too few. Furthermore, since the credibility of each witness's story will affect the credibility of the whole, a story can be gradually undermined by exposing weaknesses and inconsistencies in and between different witnesses' versions of the events.

There are relatively few procedural rules which determine who you need to call but, obviously, you need to be aware of them. The main principles are as follows.

- As prosecutor, you are not strictly bound to call the victim or any other witness – either expert or to the facts. However, the prosecution should at least make available at court all witnesses from whom they have obtained a statement, even though their evidence may not support the prosecution case;[2] such witnesses may then be called and, even if not examined in chief, they may be cross-examined by the defence.
- The accused in a criminal case is a competent but not compellable witness for the defence. The decision is a difficult tactical one. The changes to the right of silence introduced by the Criminal Justice and Public Order Act 1994 may well force more defendants to testify as to why they exercised their right of silence in police custody, to try and prevent adverse inferences being drawn. Once a defendant testifies, she is, of course, available for cross-examination in the normal way.
- Despite the changes introduced by the 1994 Act, there are still a very few offences which require corroboration. The only summary offence in this category is speeding.

So, you have selected your witnesses: where do you go from here? As the day of the trial approaches, there are a number of additional practical steps you need to take (these are normally the responsibility of the solicitor managing the case):

- Warn witnesses of the trial date as early as possible.

- Obtain witness summonses for any witnesses you intend to call who you know or anticipate may be reluctant to appear voluntarily.
- Determine whether any witnesses will require 'conduct money' (ie expenses) to enable them to attend. Ensure professional fees have been agreed with any experts who are to appear.[3]
- Determine the order[4] in which your witnesses will be called, and give them an indication of when they are likely to be called.

We will return later in this chapter to the various final preparations required on the day of the trial.

Before we move on to consider the techniques of trial advocacy in detail, we need to establish an over-arching theme which provides a framework for understanding how advocacy skills are to be deployed.

1　See eg the discussion in McBarnet *Conviction: Law, the State and the Construction of Justice*, Macmillan, London & Basingstoke 1981, pp 93–4.
2　*R v Bryant* (1946) 31 Cr App R 223.
3　Outside of these exceptions, tendering any payment to a witness may be construed as a breach of the Code of Conduct, if it appears that payment is contingent on particular testimony being given – *LSG* 14.06.
4　See the section on examination in chief, below.

Speeches

Theme and method: advocacy as storytelling

In trial advocacy there are two specific modes of advocacy: what we call the *narrative* and *interrogatory* modes. The narrative mode refers to those points of a trial at which the advocate is free to make some form of speech – eg when opening or closing the case. The interrogatory mode operates at those points where the narrative is fractured into the classic question and answer style of examination or cross-examination. Any trial is likely to involve some use of both modes. Each mode requires often very different skills, but underpinning both there should be a common aim: *to tell your side's story*. We have already touched on the idea of the trial as a story or narrative at a number of points in this chapter. We now intend to develop this idea into a framework for the use of your advocacy skills.

THE STORY MODEL

The notion of a trial as a process of story reconstruction is by no means a novel idea. It builds on a variety of approaches which encompass the experimental, jurisprudential and experiential.[1] The strongest experimental support comes from the lengthy researches of Pennington and Hastie and their associates.[2]

Pennington and Hastie argue that jurors[3] use three techniques to construct trial stories. These they term 'story construction', 'learning verdict definitions' and 'making a decision'. In summary, the story model they propose suggests that juries construct stories from their available knowledge; they obtain instructions on the legally permissible verdict categories from the judge, and then reach a decision by matching their story to the best-fitting verdict category (see over page).

Pennington & Hastie's story model[4]

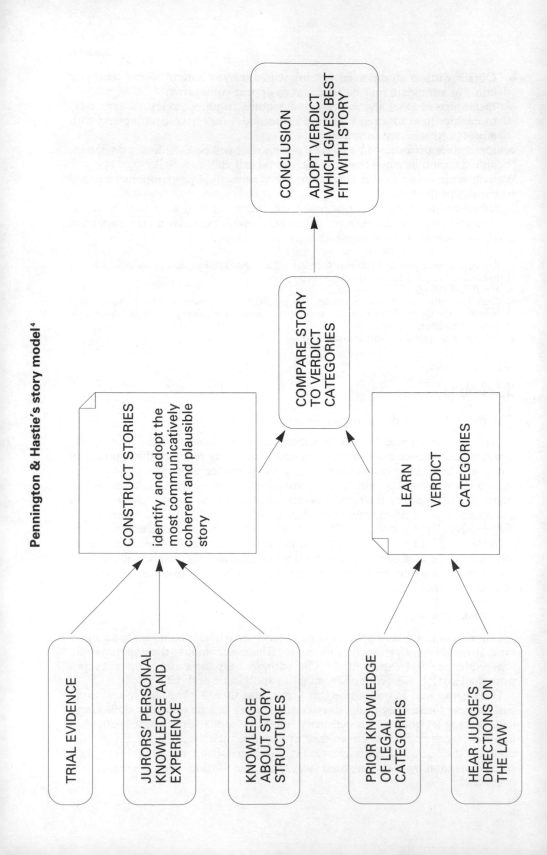

CONCLUSION

ADOPT VERDICT WHICH GIVES BEST FIT WITH STORY

COMPARE STORY TO VERDICT CATEGORIES

CONSTRUCT STORIES

identify and adopt the most communicatively coherent and plausible story

LEARN VERDICT CATEGORIES

TRIAL EVIDENCE

JURORS' PERSONAL KNOWLEDGE AND EXPERIENCE

KNOWLEDGE ABOUT STORY STRUCTURES

PRIOR KNOWLEDGE OF LEGAL CATEGORIES

HEAR JUDGE'S DIRECTIONS ON THE LAW

Story construction, Pennington and Hastie argue, determines the juror's decision. Trial stories are not constructed in a vacuum. Jurors bring 'outside' knowledge into the process, often inferentially, as a way of making sense of the evidence in court.[5] Such knowledge includes their understanding of ordinary practices in constructing discourse, and expectations about what makes a complete story; their knowledge of the world, perhaps of how people have behaved in similar situations, and so on. As trials normally involve the construction of two or more competing stories, individual jurors will tend to take the one which seems to them to be the most coherent as a communicative episode[6] and the most plausible as *their* story.

The *verdict definition* describes the legal information on the crime itself which the jury must absorb, chiefly from the judge's summing-up at the end of the trial. This is a difficult area for the jury. It often involves a relatively complex, one-off, learning task in which the jurors are expected to understand abstract information and then to apply it to a concrete situation. As Pennington and Hastie note, prior knowledge and experience will often interfere with this task, because a juror's exposure to the legal categories may be informed by media misrepresentations of the law.[7]

Making a decision involves matching the accepted story with the verdict definition or definitions (eg where alternative counts exist, such as wounding or wounding with intent). Although they recognise that this process of matching is also difficult, Pennington and Hastie point out that there is a cognitive link between the way in which we (all) represent human action as communication episodes and the way in which we (lawyers) describe the attributes of a crime.

Thus, as we have seen,[8] episodes have initiating *Events* which cause psychological *Responses* that are translated into *Actions* with particular *Consequences* (ERAC). Similarly, crimes generally arise in circumstances in which a person in a prescribed mental state commits an unlawful act. (We will try this matching exercise for ourselves later). This is not coincidental, but:

> a reflection of the fact that both stories and crimes are culturally determined generic descriptions of human action sequences.[9]

Moreover, Pennington and Hastie argue that the closer the fit between the episode schema and the verdict category, the greater the confidence the jurors will have in the rightness of their decision.[10]

1   Relevant studies include Bennet & Feldman *Reconstructing Reality in the Courtroom*, Tavistock, London and New York 1981; B Jackson *Law, Fact and Narrative Coherence* Deborah Charles, Roby 1988. Conley & O'Barr *Rules versus Relationships: The Ethnography of Legal Discourse*, University of Chicago Press, Chicago 1990; W Twining 'Lawyers Stories' in Twining *Rethinking Evidence*, Basil Blackwell, Oxford 1990.
2   Most of this work is summarised in N Pennington & R Hastie 'The story model for juror decision making' in Hastie (ed) *Inside the Juror: The Psychology of Juror Decision Making*, Cambridge University Press, Cambridge 1993, p 193.
3   Note that, strictly, their research and model apply only to jury decisions. Intuitively one suspects that other processes of lay adjudication are not, structurally, likely to be that dissimilar. The learning and matching of verdict categories to stories may be less problematic in the sense that the verdict categories are more familiar to, say, lay magistrates. This remains pure speculation, of course.
4   Adapted from Pennington & Hastie, op cit, p 193.
5   Ibid, pp 194–5.

6   Cf the discussion of communication episodes in Chapter 5.
7   Pennington & Hastie, op cit, p 200.
8   At p 136, above.
9   Pennington & Hastic, op cit, p 201.
10 Ibid.

Exercise 10.10   Let me tell you a story

(a)   *Prepare a brief story of no more than five minutes' duration on each of the fol-*
      lowing scenarios. Prepare your story in advance and commit it to memory, so
      that you can tell your story without reference to notes.
   (i)   *You have been on a day out with some friends. Relate the day's events*
          as you would to another friend who was not there.
   (ii)   *You are a trainee solicitor. Yesterday you were late for work for the third*
          time in two weeks. Your principal has called you in to her office and
          asked you to explain your continuing lateness.
(b)   *In small groups:*
   (i)   *present both stories (one presentation of each is adequate, but you can do*
          more if everyone wants a turn);
   (ii)   *reflect on the style of delivery and content, and particularly*
          –   *on whether each story involved all the ERAC elements;*
          –   *on the significance of context for the style of the story.*

With this model in mind, we can now begin to consider the specific courtroom skills of the advocate.

Opening and closing speeches

Opening and/or closing speeches in a case are the main, often the only,
opportunity that the advocate has to address the court at any length. There
are skills the advocate must use here which are therefore significantly different
from the skills used in examination or cross-examination. Opening and closing speeches also have particular formal functions which distinguish them
from other occasions when an advocate may be expected to deliver some form
of 'speech' (eg when arguing a point of law in a voir dire, or before an appellate court), though in other respects the latter situations have some similarities
in terms of the skills used.

   The formal requirements for opening and closing speeches differ between
civil and criminal cases and between different courts within each of those systems. It is therefore essential first to know whether you have the right to open
and/or close in a particular case, and then to decide whether to exercise that
right.

OPENING SPEECHES

A competent opening speech should achieve the following aims:
● It should introduce the advocates to the court.
● It should tell your story.
● It should address the court on the relevant law.

Do not think that the order indicated here needs to be followed absolutely slavishly – it does not, though we shall follow that order in our analysis of these stages.

Exercise 10.11   R v Bigg – the opening

We need two volunteers for this exercise, preferably from among those who have prepared a prosecution theory of the case in Exercise 10.4.

(a) *Re-read the case papers in R v Bigg. Prepare an opening speech for the prosecution. Try to commit as many of the facts as possible to memory, and minimise the need to refer to a written note.*

(b) *Those listening to the speeches should make notes on both content and style of the opening.*

(c) *Reflect on performance, and give feedback as usual.*

(d) *From this produce your own set of guidelines for an effective opening speech.*

We suggest the following points are of note. We will also use some additional exercises to break opening down into its component parts and thereby help you to build on the above reflection.

First, the prosecution/plaintiff should always introduce themselves and the advocate appearing for the other side. In so doing it is important to bear in mind the need to maintain (a) a style of introduction appropriate to your court and (b) the correct modes of address for your judge(s) and your opponent.[1]

Secondly, we have already said that the chief function of an advocate is to tell their client's story to the court. In court, your story should be as brief as the facts allow; it should be plausible, and presented in language that is clear. Do not forget your basic oral communication skills: use eye contact, body language etc to your advantage. Consider also who you have to persuade. How does that affect your sense of audience and the style of what you have to say? Try the following exercise.

---

1   The formalities are outlined in most of the advocacy guides – see eg Boon *Advocacy*, Cavendish, London 1993, pp 33–4.

Exercise 10.12   The road map[1]

Divide into pairs. In each pair one person should be designated the 'guide', the other the 'driver'. The 'driver' must select a road journey that is known to both participants. The 'guide' has one minute to describe the route. The 'driver' should then judge how well the 'guide' has performed the task.

After the first run-through 'driver' and 'guide' should exchange roles and repeat the exercise with a different start and finish point.

It is important we do not forget the purpose of an opening (or closing) speech. It is to provide the advocate with an opportunity to present that story in a coherent narrative form. This is invaluable. In telling your story in an opening speech, however, you should not just set out to present 'the facts' as you see them; you should aim to:

- summarise your version of what has happened;
- identify the issues between the parties;[2]
- outline what your witnesses will say.

By so doing you are telling the tribunal of fact precisely what you are setting out to do and how you will do it. As in Exercise 10.12, the opening speech enables you to identify your route via the key landmarks along the way. In Pennington and Hastie's terms it provides you with an opportunity to establish 'goodness-of-fit' of your story with the verdict category you seek. But, it is worth noting that there is a line of psychological research[3] which also suggests that if you misjudge the theme you pursue, so that there is a serious lack of fit between some parts of your story and the evidence, it is this mismatch that may be remembered better than the parts that fit.

While this warning is quite important, it is probably impossible wholly to guard against inconsistency. If things were that clear cut, there would be little need for a trial in the first place. But the fit should be as good as you can make it. Favourable explanations for such inconsistencies as arise will need to be provided in the course of the trial. Whether you should address such inconsistencies in your own opening is rather more debatable. What do you think are the pros and cons?

It might be useful to consider a real example here. Look how, in the second Gardiner trial, Wild sought to explain away the medicine bottle (of paraffin), which he seems to have regarded as the most critical piece of evidence against his client:

> But for [the bottle] Gardiner would never have been accused in this case. But the police in Peasenhall had got the bottle, and they said to themselves: 'Gardiner did this murder, and he has left his card. Out of consideration for us, in order not to tax our brains too heavily, Gardiner has considerately brought a labelled bottle with his name on it – and, of course, he did the murder.' If this were not a murder case, it would make us laugh . . .
>
> In all probability the bottle was on that shelf which was broken, because you remember the shelf was standing above the side of the door and the bottle fell down, and the pieces were found just on the left of the girl's head. It would be exactly where they would be found if they fell off the shelf. The very fact of this paraffin falling in the scuffle that must have ensued made the [murderer] suddenly think: 'I will try to burn the body.' So he at once went to get the paraffin out of the lamp, and in his hurry neglected to hide the bottle.[4]

What do you think of this extract? What is there about it that works for you? Is there anything that does not fit?

Lastly, you should always address the court on the law. In a criminal case before a jury the prosecution must explain the nature of the offence and the burden and standard of proof and also indicate the division of functions between judge and jury. Whether the defence wishes to go over this territory again is for the defence to decide. If the prosecutor has been wholly scrupulous and fair, it may be unnecessary to dwell on the same issues at length. However, it is usual to stress points such as the presumption of innocence together with any major procedural points affecting the prosecution case, eg the dangers (in a case such as Gardiner's) of convicting on circumstantial evidence.

In a civil case, the plaintiff's lawyer should open by stating the obvious – what the case is about, eg: 'May it please your Honour, this is a claim for damages for breach of contract'. This is really a standard ritualistic opening, but it is an easy way of getting started. It leads you into summarising the facts and reading through the pleadings (or giving the judge the opportunity to read through them). You should then briefly refer to any rule of law relevant to your case, and state why, on the law and facts, the plaintiff should succeed.

The defence may open as a matter of course before the High Court, but need not do so. In county court procedure, the practice tends to vary, but neither plaintiff nor defendant has an absolute entitlement to a second speech, so the common practice is for plaintiff to open and defence to close.

CLOSING SPEECHES

The closing speech is the one aspect of the (criminal) trial which gives the advocate the occasional opportunity to indulge in Perry Mason fantasies! Most advocates regard the closing speech as potentially critical.[5] It gives both sides the opportunity to try and make a last impression on the bench or jury. The closing speech should contain the following:

● a reminder of your themes/theories;
● a recapitulation of the evidence;
● some reiteration of the relevant law;
● reference to burdens/standards of proof.

Again this is not in any given order of tasks. In closing, it is often best (certainly for the defence) to stress first the onus on the jury, and then to consider the evidence. Once again, the best advice is to go for quality, not quantity. Keep it short and to the point. In recapping the evidence, try to follow the order in which it was presented and concentrate on the evidence critical to your themes/theories. In the closing speech concentrate on the evidence which best supports your case. In the first Gardiner trial, for example, Wild did this by stressing three key points in his client's favour:

> The first was – struggle and moving of the body, yet no sign of blood or paraffin on the clothes, boots or shoes of the accused man; the second, the agreement of independent explanations given by both husband and wife to the police before they had the opportunity of consulting; the third, that piece of cloth on the bottle, which was undoubtedly hacked in some way from the clothes of the murderer, but which was certainly not hacked from any clothes that the prisoner possessed.[6]

It is debatable whether some of its impact would have been lost on the jury as much else of Wild's speech was taken up with defensive work (some, perhaps, not wholly necessary) on his own evidence and some rather risky theorising, as we shall see in a moment.

If there is admissible evidence which damages your case, deal with it if you can by challenging its weight or interpretation. Try to make your challenge as reasoned and as objective as possible – do not be seen simply to dismiss it out of hand. If you have to make limited concessions, do so, and make it clear that this is what you are doing: it will make you seem reasonable. It should also heighten the impact of your challenge of other aspects of the evidence. There are two particular techniques that are widely used to challenge the opponent's case.

First, advocates often say that the best advice is always to concentrate on an opponent's weakest points – the principle of concentration of fire. This applies to cross-examination, to arguments about legal principles, and certainly to the closing speech. As we noted a moment ago, possibly the weakness of Wild as an advocate was his tendency to extemporise theories to explain away the prosecution case. One example of this was his attempt to divert attention by showing someone else had committed the killing. Possibly a reasonable tactic, where the evidence supports it. But Wild had little reliable positive evidence to lay the blame elsewhere. When it came to the closing speeches, Dickens was able to dent Wild's case by taking up his suggestion and seeming to sink it, almost without trace:

> What conditions must be fulfilled in order to make the unknown man fit in with the circumstances of the case? He must have been the man who wrote the letter 'A' [the assignation note], who, according to the defence, wrote in a handwriting extraordinarily like the prisoner at the bar;[7] who on that night wore indiarubber shoes and walked to and fro between the prisoner's house and Providence House; a man who had a knife similar to the kind of knife found in the possession of the prisoner; who was curiously brought into connection with a medicine bottle bearing the words, 'Mrs Gardiner's children'; who got hold of those buff envelopes in order to write that letter making the assignation; who had the same reason to get rid of the woman as we have been able to prove the prisoner had; who must have been on the look-out for the light in the window at ten o'clock, in the way that the prisoner was; he must have been a man of such position that it was imperative for him to conceal his shame, as we say the prisoner's position was. It is my painful duty to point out these facts. Are all these coincidences? Is it probable that this unknown man who committed the murder must fulfil all the conditions which in every case point to the prisoner at the bar?[8]

What makes this an impressive piece of argument? Does it really matter that it had been countered in many particulars by defence evidence?

Second, it is often better if you can contradict evidence in an innocent rather than hostile fashion, for example, by finding a plausible explanation that a witness was mistaken rather than suggesting they were lying. This Evans terms the practice of 'showing the jury the way home'.[9]

In assessing how much you need to say in a closing speech, you should rely heavily on your powers of observation. All through the trial you need to observe closely the reactions of participants: when is the judge writing (especially in examination/cross-examination)? When do jurors take notes/look bored/fidget/pay close attention? Use these elements to assess how aspects of the case have been received, and use that information to inform your approach to your closing speech. You should also use it generally for more pragmatic purposes – to gauge a jury's understanding of your points, your speed of delivery, etc.

We have so far provided a basic structure for opening and closing speeches and addressed some of the specific tactics that apply to each. However, there are also a number of common threads that are worth exploring before we move on to consider interrogatory techniques.

TECHNIQUES COMMON TO OPENING AND CLOSING

First we wish to stress again that the ultimate purpose of a speech is to persuade. This engages the *rhetorical* dimension of advocacy. The great advocates of history are the orators who possess the ability to persuade by both the force of their arguments and their use of language. The grand style of rhetorical advocacy, personified in the great Victorian and Edwardian barristers like Marshall Hall, has passed out of fashion. But effective use of language and style has not. While it cannot wholly overcome poor logic and even less, poor preparation, it can help to sway the jury in your favour. Your syntax, the careful use of pace, metaphor, repetition and the adoption of powerful imagery can all increase the rhetorical effect of your speech. Consider, for example, the next exercise.

1 Adapted from Sherr *Advocacy*, Blackstone Press, London 1993, p 74.
2 This may be of less significance in a defence opening, if the territory has been covered objectively enough by the prosecution.
3 See eg R Hastie 'Memory for behavioral information that confirms or contradicts a personality impression' in R Hastie, T Ostrom, E Ebbesen, R Wyer, D Hamilton & D Carlston (eds) *Person Memory: the Cognitive Basis of Social Perception*, Lawrence J Erlbaum, Hillsdale, NJ 1980, p 155.
4 Quoted in Fido & Skinner *The Peasenhall Murder*, Alan Sutton, Stroud 1990, p 118
5 Whether this intuitive view is wholly supportable on psychological grounds is doubtful – the complexity of the trial process as a whole makes it harder to predict in general which phase, if any, has the greatest potential impact on the tribunal of fact – see the discussion by E Allan Lind and Gina Ke 'Opening and Closing Statements' in Kassin and Wrightsman *The Psychology of Evidence and Trial Procedure*, Sage, Beverley Hills 1985, p 229 at pp 242–3.
6 Fido & Skinner, op cit, p 94. Counsel for the defence was never really able to explain these points away convincingly.
7 The dispute over handwriting was highly problematic at both trials. Forensic graphology was in its infancy. The prosecution had called one of very few 'professional' experts in the field, who had found few similarities between the note and Gardiner's handwriting, and indeed was contradictory in his own evidence. Though he did conclude that the authors of a letter written by Gardiner and the assignation note were the same, it was not a strong performance. See Fido & Skinner, op cit, pp 83–4. The amateurs engaged by the defence fared even worse, with one suggesting that the writer of the assignation note was actually trying to imitate Gardiner's hand – hence Dickens's comment in this passage!
8 Ibid, p 95.
9 K Evans *Advocacy at the Bar: A Beginner's Guide*, Blackstone Press, London 1983, p 76.

Exercise 10.13   Done to death?

Assess the impact each of the following statements has as a plea against the imposition of the death penalty. What is it about them that is effective or ineffective?[1]

REFLECTIONS ON THE GUILLOTINE

Albert Camus

Instead of saying, 'If you kill someone you will pay for it on the scaffold', would it not be more politic – if we are interested in setting an example –

to say instead: 'If you kill someone, you will be thrown into prison for months or even years, torn between an impossible despair and a constantly renewed fear, until one morning we will sneak into your cell, having taken off our shoes in order to surprise you in your sleep, which has at last overcome you after the night's anguish. We will throw ourselves upon you, tie your wrists behind your back, and with a pair of scissors cut away your shirt collar and your hair, if it should be in the way. Because we are perfectionists we will lash your arms together with a strap so that your body will be arched to offer unhampered access to the back of your neck. Then we will carry you, one man holding you up under each arm, your feet dragging behind you, down the long corridors, until, under the night sky, one of the executioners will at last take hold of the back of your trousers and throw you down on a board, another will make sure your head is in the lunette, and a third one will drop, from a height of two metres twenty centimetres, a blade weighing sixty kilograms that will slice through your neck like a razor.'

FURMAN V GEORGIA
(1972) 408 US 238, 405

BLACKMAN J: Cases such as these provide for me an excruciating agony of the spirit. I yield to no one in the depth of my distaste, antipathy, and, indeed, abhorrence for the death penalty, with all its aspects of physical distress and fear and of moral judgment exercised by finite minds. That distaste is buttressed by a belief that capital punishment serves no useful purpose that can be demonstrated. For me, it violates childhood's training and life's experiences, and is not compatible with the philosophical convictions I have been able to develop. It is antagonistic to any sense of 'reverence for life' . . .

It is comforting to relax in the thoughts – perhaps the rationalisations – that this is the compassionate decision for a maturing society; that this is the moral and the 'right' thing to do; that thereby we convince ourselves that we are moving down the road toward human decency; that we value life even though that life has taken another or others or has grievously scarred another or others and their families; and that we are less barbaric than we were in 1879, or in 1890, or in 1910, or in 1947, or in 1958, or in 1963, or a year ago, in 1971, when *Wilkerson, Kemmler, Weems, Francis, Trop, Rudolph* and *McGautha* were respectively decided.

The focus on rhetoric emphasises the extent to which lawyers need to influence the tribunal of fact, to use the psychological jargon, affectively (meaning through their feelings and emotions) as well as cognitively. Boon stresses the importance of using issues of fact as 'psychological anchors'[2] to achieve this end. 'Psychological anchors' are points of fact that are so significant the jury will not only remember them, but may use them to organise and make sense of the conflicting stories in the trial. Boon takes as an example of the use of an anchor, the opening speech of Sir Norman Birkett in his prosecution of Alfred Rouse for murder.[3] The passage opens with the report of a conversation between Rouse and two strangers he passed on the road shortly after setting fire to the car:

. . . one of them said 'What is the blaze up there?' pointing to a glare up the lane, and then, having gone 15 or 20 yards beyond the men, the accused said these very remarkable words: 'It looks as if someone is having a bonfire up there'. Members of the jury, you will hear what was found up that lane. You will hear the accused's part in it, and you will bear in mind at every stage of this case the fact that, right at the outset, when the accused met these two young men, he passed without a word. No appeal for help! No call for assistance! Nothing. And then 'it looks as though someone is having a bonfire up there'. You will hear what he called a bonfire was the burning of his own car; and that there was the body of that unknown man being steadily burned beyond all recognition. The significance of the remark 'It looks as though someone is having a bonfire up there' cannot be over-emphasised in view of the fact that 400 yards away there was that terrible fire. The car had shortly before been drawn up by the side of the road by the prisoner himself; he had shut off the engine and put on the brake . . . and yet, at that moment, his observation to these two young men was 'It looks as if someone has had a bonfire' . . .[4]

What is it in this speech that makes the psychological anchor so effective?

Second, we suggest that *focus* is also essential. In a jury trial, it is the jury that you have to persuade. You ignore your jury at your peril – particularly at the opening and final stages. Focus on the jury: you want to make eye contact and to observe their reactions, though not to the extent that you are entering into an individual staring match, or constantly shifting your gaze to one or other of twelve pairs of eyes – try this and you will probably end up appearing nervous, shifty, cross-eyed or some permutation of the three! Talk to the jury, not to the judge, or some point on the floor, or half way up the wall. Try to make them feel that they are your exclusive audience, and that they want to hear what you have to say.

Third, you should use your speeches to try to establish and maintain an organising *frame* that helps give coherence to your story. That frame may be technical, causal or chronological: each has its own particular uses. For example, a technical frame is one which adopts some technical organising principle – based upon a scientific or legal concept that is central to the case. It will often serve in cases, especially civil cases before a professional judge, where you can afford to organise your factual information around the legally relevant categories, such as duty, breach, and damage. A causal frame seeks to describe circumstances according to some recognisable behavioural explanation – eg where the defence might try to argue that the situation was such that the accused acted under extreme provocation. A chronological frame is one that is commonly adopted. In this you establish an order of events that makes sense of what happened. The advantage of a chronological approach for new advocates is that it will usually fit easily with any theory of the case you wish to pursue. Both causal and chronological explanations fit particularly neatly with conventional story structures.

Whichever type of frame you adopt, there are two things you need to be aware of. First, you are, to an extent, prioritising one aspect of the communication episode that is your story. This is fine, so long as you recognise that the frame forms part of a wider story which the tribunal of fact needs to understand. To take the chronological example, it is one thing to stress what happened and when, but the court will often need to understand how and why as well. The frame is only an organising principle, not an end in itself. Second, for much the same reason, it needs to connect logically to your theory of the case.

1   Both passages are taken from J White *The Legal Imagination*, Little Brown, Boston 1973, pp 131–2; 137–9.
2   Boon *Advocacy*, Cavendish, London 1993, pp 75–6.
3   Rouse was convicted of killing a man to whom he had given a lift in his car. It transpired that he had strangled the man and then set fire to the car in an attempt to destroy the body sufficiently to prevent its identification. His aim thereby was to fake his own death, so that he could disappear with his mistress. Rouse confessed after the trial, and was executed in March 1931. His victim was never identified. The text of the trial has been republished in the Penguin *Famous Trials* series.
4   Cited in Boon, op cit (1993) p 76.

Exercise 10.14   Closing Bigg

This is an individual exercise.

(a)   *Based on the documentary evidence, and your notes of an opponent's opening speech (Exercise 10.11), prepare and deliver a closing speech for the defence of Mr Bigg.*
(b)   *Feedback is given in the usual way.*
(c)   *Remember to make a note for your learning diary of your experiences and feedback. Use these to construct your own guidelines on opening and closing speeches.*
(d)   *Compare your guidelines with other members of your group or 'firm'; discuss and revise as necessary.*

Summary

WHEN OPENING:
–   INTRODUCE THE ADVOCATES.
–   ESTABLISH YOUR FACTUAL THEORY AND THEMES.
–   IDENTIFY WHAT YOUR WITNESSES WILL SAY.
–   DON'T FORGET TO EXPLAIN THE LEGAL ISSUES AND BURDEN/STANDARD OF PROOF.
–   REMEMBER THE POWER OF RHETORIC.

WHEN CLOSING:
–   IDENTIFY WHAT HAS TO BE PROVED AND BY WHOM.
–   REITERATE THEORY/THEMES.
–   SHOW THE LINKS BETWEEN LAW AND EVIDENCE.
–   IDENTIFY WEAKNESSES IN OPPONENT'S CASE.
–   TELL THE TRIER OF FACT WHAT YOU WANT.
–   REMEMBER THE POWER OF RHETORIC.

Examining witnesses

The skills required for the examination of witnesses differ substantially from those used in other forms of advocacy. There are also significant stylistic and tactical differences between the different forms of examination. Accordingly, we have divided this section of the chapter into three parts, to consider examination in chief, cross-examination and re-examination respectively.

Examination in chief

Surprising though it may sound, examining your own witness is probably the most difficult of the advocacy skills to develop. Why might that be?

We think it is difficult for three reasons:

- You are seeking to present a witness's story in a non-narrative form.
- You are constrained in the type of questions you may ask.
- At the same time, you are attempting to protect that testimony from effective cross-examination.

Let us now look at how these difficulties arise, and how they are best dealt with.

We have already said that the structure of the examination is interrogatory. That is, it works by the process of question and answer, thus:

Exercise 10.15   Twenty questions?

Read the following extract from a fictitious examination in chief:

Q: Mrs Smith, can you please tell the court where you were on the evening of 3rd February 1995? *(This question assumes that, broadly speaking, the time and date are not in dispute)*.

A: I was at home.

Q: Did you stay at home all evening, or did you go out?

A: Well, I went out once, to get some cigarettes.

Q: Can you recall what time that was?

A: It must have been about 8 o'clock.

Q: And did anything in particular happen while you were out?

A: Yes, it was just before I got to the newsagent's on the corner. I saw this young couple arguing.

Q: Can you tell the court more precisely what you saw?

A: Well, they were really having a go at each other, shouting and screaming . . .

Consider the following questions.

(a)   What type of questions is the advocate using here?

(b)   What effects does this form of question and answer process have on the narrative? Note down three or four points before you continue reading.

Although this is a simple illustration, you have probably come up with a number of both positive and negative aspects to the process. We have noted some of our own ideas below.

On the positive side, it has a number of practical advantages. The use of clear, focused, questions gives you, the advocate, substantial control over the direction in which the testimony is going by making sure you just get small chunks of very specific information. It helps make your witnesses cross-examination proof by limiting the risk of them introducing inconsistencies in their evidence. Such questions should also help make the information clear to the jury. However, it thus puts the onus on you to maintain narrative coherence.

On the negative side, it potentially makes the storytelling process far more drawn out than in everyday talk – it can easily take half a dozen questions to establish who the witness is, and what their connection with events is – before you actually get into the details of the story. Listening to evidence elicited in this way can become very tedious for judge or jury. As we have seen, it can serve to fragment the narrative and may present the witness as 'powerless'.[1] This might appear to create difficulties for all sides in the criminal process, but research in fact suggests it creates a particular bias against defence witnesses, often precisely because of their lack of courtroom experience:

> . . . we were struck by the fact that a whole lineup of witnesses for certain defendants produced testimony that was hard to reconstruct in story form, while prosecution witnesses (particularly police officers and experts) delivered accounts that fit easily into coherent stories.[2]

A neat example of the effect courtroom experience can have is offered by the cross-examination of Wright in the second Gardiner trial. Wright had been seriously embarrassed by Wild's cross-examination of his version of the chapel incident in the first trial. However, he was rather more ready the second time around, and even won one exchange against his sharp-tongued cross-examiner:

Wild:	Did you leave out [in the magistrates' court] about hearing Rose Harsent say 'Oh, oh!' and hearing the rustling noise?
Wright:	Yes, I left that out.
Wild:	Why?
Wright:	Because it did not come into my mind; there was a long time between.
Wild:	But there is a longer time between [then and] now?
Wright:	I have been over it since.
Wild:	Oh! Who have you been over it with?
Wright:	I have with you.[3]

So, how do we limit the fragmentation and anomie caused by interrogatory advocacy? Think about this and then try the next exercise.

1   See p 337, above.
2   Bennet & Feldman *Reconstructing Reality in the Courtroom*, Tavistock, London and New York 1981, p 174. This overlooks the extent to which victim-witnesses may themselves often be subject to the same disadvantages – cf the case analysis in Rock *The Social World of an English Crown Court*, Clarendon Press, Oxford 1993, pp 95–129, especially at pp 127–9.
3   See Fido & Skinner *The Peasenhall Murder*, Alan Sutton, Stroud 1990, p 106.

Exercise 10.16   R v Wainwright

Garry Wainwright has been charged with assault occasioning actual bodily harm to Terry Kline. Wainwright has claimed he acted in self-defence. In the Appendix is a witness statement from an eyewitness to the incident, Jenny Lee, who has been called as a witness for the prosecution.

Select a pair of volunteers: one to act as advocate, the other to act as witness. They should both take some time to familiarise themselves with the witness statement and prepare for the examination (10 minutes should suffice). The rest of the group should pretend to be the jury. Jurors should not look at the witness statement.

Tasks:
- *Student A: examine Jenny in chief;*
- *Student B: answer questions put by counsel;*
- *Group: take notes.*

So how easy or difficult did you find that? In our experience, most student advocates find it rather easier than expected. In some respects, it should not be that difficult, as the statement is short and reasonably chronological in its order. But is that intuition right?

Exercise 10.17   You, the jury

Now, ask at least two members of the jury to repeat the evidence they have heard.

(a)   Did they get the date and time the events took place?
(b)   Did they get an identification of the accused?
(c)   Are they clear that, on Jenny's evidence, it was not Terry's fault?
(d)   What was the advocate's organising frame?
(e)   What do they think was the advocate's theory of the case?

So, let's use the Wainwright case to reflect more generally on the examination in chief.

First, in preparing the case, get a clear sense of how each witness's testimony relates to the whole story you are trying to tell. Part of the difficulty in the Wainwright exercise is that there is not a complete case history to provide that context. It is a bit like going into court when you have not had time to go through all the case papers.

Second, it is critical, if you can, to maintain 'story order'[1] – ie a sequence of testimony that matches the temporal or causal sequence of the events (which you have already emphasised by your choice of frame in opening, or will emphasise in closing). Pennington and Hastie indicate that significant differences between story and witness order make it far harder for the jury to construct the story for themselves.[2] As we have noted, there are few procedural constraints on witness order, so it should normally be possible to set up the appropriate witness order for yourself.[3]

1   N Pennington & R Hastie 'The story model for juror decision making' in Hastie (ed) *Inside the Juror: The Psychology of Juror Decision Making*, Cambridge University Press, Cambridge 1993, p 210.
2   Ibid, pp 210–12.
3   Note, however, that if an accused testifies, she must do so before any other witnesses to the facts, unless the court in its discretion decides otherwise – Police & Criminal Evidence Act 1984, s 79. The parties in civil cases normally testify first also, but this is customary rather than required by law.

Exercise 10.18   Witnesses against Bigg

You are counsel for the prosecution in R v Bigg. You have already decided who you will call.

(a)   What order will you call them in?
(b)   Why?

Next, you need to think about the way you phrase your questions. Closed questioning gives you a lot of control and direction, but it reduces the witness's freedom. In some situations, the last thing you will want to do is give the witness freedom, but in others it is more effective to let the jury hear the story in the witness's words, with little interruption from you. The use of open questions (ie of the 'what happened next?'/'what did you do then?' variety) will certainly help. If your witness is a good story teller, do not interrupt the flow. The jury will find the witness's story far more memorable if it is not consistently interrupted. But, do remember that a great deal of your tactics will depend on your perception of the witness's quality. If you are uncertain about how your witness will come across, of what she will say, or of your own ability to redirect a narrative that has gone off in the wrong direction, then keep the witness under close control. On balance, the best examinations are generally those which use a mixture of questioning styles. Try using a technique like the funnel or 'T' technique[1] in your questioning in court.

You can also use the style and direction of questioning to help sustain your storyline. Two particular techniques are useful here: these are the use of *transitional questions* and of *points of reference*.

A transitional question is a means of moving a witness from one topic to another. It is permissible, though not necessary, to signal that change by some kind of short statement, such as 'I would like to turn now to the circumstances of your meeting with Mr Jones'. You can also use such statements to help highlight the key issues in the testimony.

Points of reference can be helpful in adding emphasis or detail to the testimony. It is a method of including in a further question reference to a fact already stated by the witness. Thus:

Q: Did the defendant have anything in his possession?
A: Yes, he was holding a gun.
Q: Can you describe the gun that he was holding?

emphasises the importance of the gun and gives the witness the cue to provide more detailed testimony about the weapon.

Lastly (within the context of each examination) you should also think about the order of the questions you ask. How did you start the examination of

Jenny Lee? What did you allow the jury to find out about her as a person? Did you establish her connection to the victim? It is a good idea for a number of reasons to start with the testimony that is most familiar to the witness, and least contentious. This usually means you start by asking about *them* rather than the incident. It helps get your witnesses used to testifying. For example, if you are examining a witness about an accident at work you might begin by asking them about the job they do, how long they have been employed etc, before getting into the details of the accident. Most judges and opposing counsel understand the need to build up the witness in this way, and will not usually challenge the relevance of such early questions, provided you keep the process brief, and reasonably relevant. These contextual questions can also help 'personalise' your witness and make them and their evidence more memorable, perhaps even more believable.

It makes sense to rough out a plan of your questions, based on each witness's proof of evidence. This helps you keep track of the issues and, so long as the proofs have been ordered chronologically, it helps you sustain the chronology too. However, even with a plan of the examination, witnesses can wander off course. How do you bring them back? The answer lies in your ability to link the issues coherently, so as to move the witness from where she is now to where you want her to be. Try it with the next exercise.

1 See Chapter 6, above.

Exercise 10.19   The gestatory period of the African elephant[1]

Divide the group into pairs – one advocate and one witness. The witness must think of a topic as far away from the gestatory period of the African elephant as possible. Tell your advocate what the subject is.

The advocate must begin the examination by asking this question: 'Do you know what is the gestatory period of the African elephant?' Using the witness's answer, the advocate must link in the next question and following questions until the advocate can get to a question on the witness's chosen topic.

One reason why linking can be difficult in trial contexts is that you are normally not allowed to lead your own witness. So all of you who got through Exercise 10.16 by leading Jenny through her evidence should consider yourselves disbarred!

It is not always easy to spot, never mind avoid, leading questions. Leading questions are those which are phrased so as to assume facts which are yet to be proven, so that, as Evans puts it, 'the facts come from the advocate and not from the witness'.[2] For example, a question phrased: 'Did you see Smith driving down the road?' would be a leading question if it had not been established already by that witness that Smith was present at the time and place referred to, and that he was driving, rather than walking, riding a unicycle or any other form of transport. Try and work the next one out for yourselves.

1 From Sherr *Advocacy*, Blackstone Press, London 1993, p 87.
2 K Evans *Advocacy at the Bar: A Beginner's Guide*, Blackstone Press, London 1983, p 126.

Exercise 10.20   You lead and I'll follow

Read the following extract. Which question(s) if any are leading and in what circumstances?

> *Note: Assume the following exchange takes place in the examination in chief of a witness to the facts who will testify that he saw the accused punch the victim in a pub brawl. We come in just after the witness has identified himself . . .*

Q: Mr Birks, please tell the court your occupation.
A: I'm a barman.
Q: And where do you work?
A: At the Frog and Frigate in Dilchester High Street.
Q: Have you ever seen the accused before?
A: Yes, I know him.
Q: How do you know him?
A: Because he is a regular at the Frog and Frigate.
Q: Did you see the accused on the evening of 12 April 199X?
A: Yes.
Q: In the Frog and Frigate?
A: That's right.
Q: Did anything happen in the pub that night?
A: Yeah, there was a punch-up.

Leading a witness leaves you open to challenge by your opponent, and to rebuke by the judge.[1] In either case it can damage your witness's credibility by giving the impression that you cannot trust the witness to tell her own story.

A useful guide to avoiding leading questions is what Murphy and Barnard term the 'two-for-one rule'.[2] They point out that most leading questions fail because the advocate is trying to be too specific. You should try asking two questions instead of one. If you take a step back, and ask a more general or open question first (eg, 'what happened?', 'where did you go?', 'what did you do then?') you can use that to lead into the specifics. Try this on the text in Exercise 10.20.

The best practice is to avoid leading the witness whenever possible. However, there are times when leading is permissible, and sometimes necessary.

It is permissible to lead on facts which are not in issue. This is a right which should be used judiciously, as it is easy to get into the habit of leading the witness. It is vital to keep in mind the boundaries of what is or is not in dispute when framing leading questions. For example, in Exercise 10.15, if it is not disputed that the defendant was in the pub, the question 'In the Frog and Frigate?' is unobjectionable. If the accused claims misidentification, the question would be leading.

You can lead in situations where you have obtained the agreement of the other side. This tends to happen only where the evidence is not in dispute, or at least not really crucial, or where the distress caused to the witness by giving testimony in the ordinary way would be so counter-productive that the other side are happy to agree.[3] If you get agreement to lead, you should tell the judge of this before you begin the examination.

If a witness is hostile,[4] you are entitled to lead that witness. In effect the rules allow you, within certain parameters, to cross-examine a witness you have called who proves hostile. You can only treat a witness as hostile with the leave of the judge.

Sometimes it will be worth taking the risk and deliberately leading the witness on a particular point, especially if failure to lead may mean that your witness does not come up to proof on a key part of her testimony. An objection from the other side will be of limited use at this stage. The question has been asked, and even if you are required to rephrase it, it has served its purpose: the witness had been reminded of the critical event.

1   Evidence obtained in chief by leading questions carries little evidential weight – *Moor v Moor* [1954] 1 WLR 927.
2   P Murphy & D Barnard *Evidence & Advocacy*, 4th Edition, Blackstone Press, London 1994, p 143.
3   In the second Gardiner trial, for example, Dickens and Wild agreed that Dickens could lead Rose's father through his testimony, to save him the distress of having to describe in his own words, for the fourth time, how he found his murdered daughter.
4   See Criminal Procedure Act 1865, s 3; Civil Evidence Act 1968, s 3(1). A witness is hostile if they testify against your interests through malice or bad faith, see *R v Prefas & Pryce* (1988) 86 Cr App R 111.

Exercise 10.21   There are more questions than answers . . .

Assume the following is the transcript of an examination by the prosecutor (P) in an assault case where accused and complainant are husband and wife. The witness is a neighbour. P is seeking to establish where she was when the events happened, and the fact that she heard the husband threaten his wife at a time consistent with the latter's complaint.

Consider:
(a)   The nature of each question asked – what sort of question is it?
(b)   How effective is each question at carrying the story along?
(c)   Are there other questions you might want to ask, or questions you would ask differently?

Q: May it please your Honour, I call Mrs Sally Sings.
     (Witness enters and takes the oath.)
Q: Please give the court your full name and address.
A: Sally Margaret Sings, and I live at Flat 143, Bevan Tower, Summerhayes Lane, Bristol.
Q: So you are a resident of the same flats as the defendant and his wife?
A: Yes, they live just opposite me.
Q: Have you lived there long?
A: About six years.
Q: And have you got to know Mr and Mrs Jackson in that time?
A: Oh yes, they moved in shortly after me, and Janice and me, well, neither of us work, so we've got to know each other pretty well.
Q: Would you say that you know the defendant, Mr Jackson, well?
A: Mike? Not really well; he doesn't much like me going across to their flat. He says Jan and me spend too much time gossiping.
Q: I see. Let me now turn to the real issue here. Do you recall anything particular happening on the evening of June 15th, 1995?

A: Yes, there was a fight between Mike and Janice.

Q: How do you know this?

A: I heard them.

Q: How did you come to hear them?

A: I had just got back from Tesco's with my shopping. I put the bags down outside my door while I got the keys from my handbag. I could hear them shouting at each other through the wall. You can hear a mouse sneeze through those walls, they're that thin. Anyway, I could hear him really shouting at Jan, going mad he was – then she screamed . . .

Q: Could you hear anything that was said?

A: A lot, I reckon, there was certainly enough f–ing and blinding.

Q: Could you hear what Mr Jackson said?

A: Yes. I heard him say something like 'I'll get you for that, you bitch'.

Q: You are quite sure that was what he said?

A: Yes.

Q: So you have no doubt that it was the defendant who attacked Mrs Jackson?

A: No, none.

Q: What happened after that?

A: That was when she screamed. And I got my keys, ran into the flat and phoned the police.

Q: And then?

A: Well, after I put the phone down, I just sat and waited for a bit. I hardly dared go out. I heard their door slam after a minute or two. I went out into the corridor. I couldn't hear anything from their flat. I knocked on the door. Jan came to the door, and said 'Who is it?' I said it was me, and she opened the door. She was in a bad way. She had a bloody nose – I think it was broken – and she had been crying. I think I said something like 'Oh Jan', and we both had a bit of a weep, then the police arrived.

Q: Thank you, Mrs Sings. Please wait there.

Summary

WHEN EXAMINING IN CHIEF:
–   NEVER LEAD, UNLESS YOU REALLY HAVE TO.
–   PLAN THOROUGHLY, BOTH FRAME AND QUESTIONS.
–   MAKE THE LINKS TO YOUR THEORY AS EXPLICIT AS YOU CAN.
–   KEEP TO STORY ORDER.

Cross-examination

Imagine you are representing Mike Jackson in court. You now have the chance to cross-examine Mrs Sings. Your client maintains that his wife started the argument, and struck him two or three times. He will testify that her injury was caused unintentionally when he slammed the bedroom door shut, just as his wife launched herself at him. The Jackson's next-door neighbour will testify that he heard a door slam just before Mrs Jackson screamed. Mr Jackson has a low opinion of Mrs Sings, whom he regards as a busybody. As he puts it, 'Jan tells her all sorts, which she then spreads around her mates in the flats – all sorts of rubbish about us. I had it out with her once – was none too polite about it. She's had it in for me ever since.'

Exercise 10.22   The worm turns?

You have two minutes in which to decide:
(a)   Do you cross-examine Mrs Sings at all? Why/why not?
(b)   If you do, what will you want to achieve by that cross-examination?

This exercise is intended to establish two very basic points. One, that you should not assume that you need to cross-examine every witness the other side presents, and, two, that you need to identify quickly, but carefully, your aims in cross-examining.

So, first, how do you decide whether or not to cross-examine? It is likely that several factors will influence your decision.

You need to consider how close to the 'truth' of the events the witness's testimony is. You might assess this by virtue of the evidence's consistency or inconsistency with other testimony in your possession, or by its internal coherence, and its vividness – ie the depth and detail of the description.[1] If the evidence scores highly on such criteria there may be little to gain from cross-examination. A cross-examination which merely reinforces the other side's case clearly does you little good.

Equally, you may feel that not to cross-examine the witness (especially if this is the only witness you do not intend to cross-examine) will itself have a damaging effect on your case. Arguably, you will be seen by the jury to be giving absolute credence to that testimony, or in some way avoiding a confrontation with the witness or her evidence. Moreover, if there is a direct conflict between your client's version of events and this witness's, you have some responsibility to your client to put the case, even if this means you end up with a string of denials. In such a situation, it is advisable to keep the cross-examination low key, and you should not try too hard to test the witness.

Assessing which is the right decision is terribly hard. It is one aspect of advocacy where, trite though it sounds, experience really does tell.

If you decide to cross-examine, you need to have a clear idea of what you want to achieve. Any cross-examination has two basic aims:

- To advance your own case.
- To undermine the case for the opposition.

These aims can be achieved by a number of tactics, some of which can serve both ends.

TRY TO OBTAIN FAVOURABLE TESTIMONY

Do not make the mistake of assuming that a witness called by the other side is inevitably hostile towards your case. Most witnesses can be led into giving testimony that will support your case in some detail or other.

In seeking favourable testimony an obvious approach is to look for possible points of consensus – eg on a point of identification evidence, will this witness support your client's contention about the lighting conditions/distance apart at the time of the sighting/length of the sighting, etc? Such an admission may provide valuable corroboration.

Equally, you may try to obtain favourable testimony by other means. Consider, for example, Sir Edward Carson's cross-examination of Oscar Wilde,[2] which is often thought of as a copybook example. Carson's defence was one of justification, which had the effect of putting Wilde's character in issue. Carson therefore set out, first, to build a picture of Wilde as an immoral person before adducing direct evidence of his homosexuality.[3] In the following extract, Wilde is being cross-examined on the significance of his novel, *A Portrait of Dorian Gray*. Carson began by reading a short extract from the book:

Carson:	'There is no such thing as a moral or immoral book. Books are well written or badly written.' That expresses your view?
Wilde:	My view on art, yes.
Carson:	Then I take it, no matter how immoral a book may be, if it is well written, it is, in your opinion, a good book?
Wilde:	Yes, if it were well written so as to produce a sense of beauty, which is the highest sense of which a human being can be capable. If it were badly written, it would produce a sense of disgust.
Carson:	Then a well-written book putting forward perverted moral views may be a good book?
Wilde:	No work of art ever puts forward views. Views belong to people who are not artists.
Carson:	A perverted novel might be a good book?
Wilde:	I don't know what you mean by a 'perverted' novel.
Carson:	Then I will suggest *Dorian Gray* is open to the interpretation of being such a novel?
Wilde:	That could only be to brutes and illiterates. The views of philistines on art are unaccountable . . .
Carson:	The majority of persons come under your definition of Philistines and illiterates?
Wilde:	I have found wonderful exceptions.
Carson:	Do you think the majority of people live up to the position you are giving us?
Wilde:	I am afraid they are not cultivated enough.
Carson:	Not cultivated enough to draw the distinction between a good book and a bad book?
Wilde:	Certainly not.
Carson:	The affection and love of the artist of *Dorian Gray* might lead an ordinary individual to believe that it might have a certain tendency?
Wilde:	I have no knowledge of the views of ordinary individuals.
Carson:	You did not prevent the ordinary individual from buying your book?

Wilde: I have never discouraged him![4]

What devices does Carson use to get Wilde to damn himself by his testimony?

ALWAYS BE SEEN TO 'PUT YOUR CASE'

In cross-examination you should put to the witness every fact disputed by your client to which that witness is competent to speak. This is called putting your case. It is a vital part of any good cross-examination and is a central means of advancing your theory of the case. In its simplest form, putting your case can involve questioning by confrontation – lawyers will actually use a ritualised form of question to signal this, thus: 'I put it to you that (X happened)'. But putting your case is also achieved by a number of more subtle means.

In the Gardiner trials, for example, Wild recognised that the time of the murder was at issue. The key witness here was Mrs Crisp, who heard Rose's scream in the night. Mrs Crisp had clearly been uncertain about the time when she testified, both before the Coroner at the inquest, and before the magistrates. The prosecution theory of the case was undoubtedly weak on this point. They did not challenge Gardiner's alibi and thus, implicitly, left it to the jury to determine whether Gardiner could have committed the killing after leaving Mrs Dickinson's, and before going to bed at about 2.00 am. Wild's cross-examination of Mrs Crisp pressed home the advantage. He obtained two vital admissions: first, that it could have been after midnight when she and Mr Crisp first came downstairs; second, that the storm was still raging when she heard Rose scream. This placed the time of the murder squarely within the period for which Gardiner had an alibi.

INSINUATION

Questioning by insinuation is an important means of putting your case to the witness. It is a technique in which you present your theory of the case as a counterpoint to the theory which opposing counsel had initially tried to establish through the same witness. The effect of insinuating cross-examination is to give force and momentum to your version of the facts. Wild used insinuation against Wright in the second Gardiner trial, to suggest malice against Gardiner as a motive behind his evidence:

Wild: Were you found fault with in your work?
Wright: No; not by Mr Smyth.
Wild: Mr Gardiner?
Wright: No, I don't think I was.
Wild: You don't know one way or the other?
Wright: I feel perfectly sure.
Wild: You feel a little surer as you go on?
(*Laughter*)[5]

What impact does Wild's questioning have, do you think? How does he achieve that effect?

Various techniques of insinuation can be used. Accusations are routinely made against opponent's witnesses, and these are most effective because they are treated as routine. The advocate can, by tone of voice and choice of phrase, signal to the jury that a witness's mendacity is to be expected. It is not a subject for histrionics, but, rather, so self-evident as to require no especial comment:

> Accusations would be slipped in and proved by fiat: in one ordinary instance, a defence counsel asked a police officer, 'Having been abusive to him, did you . . .' as if the abusiveness itself was not in doubt.[6]

Witnesses' partiality is similarly to be signalled by phrase and tone – 'According to your version of events'; 'yet you insist that . . .' and so on. In its most powerful form insinuation can operate by the use of false leads[7] and what the American literature calls 'tag questions' – where the question is presented in the form 'You did x, didn't you'. Thus, instead of saying: 'Did you see the accused?' you could ask: 'You saw the accused, didn't you?'. Research suggests that, where people are under pressure, tag questions are more likely to receive a positive response than less loaded questions.[8]

It is not usually necessary to put the same challenges to cumulative witnesses, unless you anticipate getting inconsistent responses, or particularly wish to emphasise some aspect of your case to the jury.

LOOK FOR WAYS TO DISCREDIT THE WITNESS'S TESTIMONY

This is probably the most common form of cross-examination. It does not mean that you are challenging every witness and proclaiming them to be liars. The tactic of saying to a witness 'I put it to you that you are lying' is risky. You may use this technique to plant doubts about the veracity of the witness, but as it is most likely to get the response 'No I'm not', you need to be reasonably sure that your jury are going to be more persuaded by your accusation than the witness's denial. Unless you have a previous inconsistent statement which you intend to prove, you are stuck with that answer![9] Discrediting may involve either attacking the witness's recollection itself, or the character of that witness more generally.

As a first step you should concentrate on inconsistencies or points where, from proofs of evidence, or from their performance in chief, you suspect the witness's recollection may be unreliable. There are a number of techniques that can work here. *Probing* questions – that ask Who? What? When? Why? or How? – are pretty much the stock in trade of cross-examination. They can be used in an attempt either to get more detail out of a witness, or to handle evasion or prevarication by the witness, or simply to get the admission 'I don't remember' or 'I am not really sure', which is well worth having. Loftus & Goodman cite a simple example of how this operates:

> Q: . . . and . . . you rolled down the window of your car . . .
> A: [It] was rolled down.
> Q: . . . [it] was a warm evening?
> A: Yeah
> Q: . . . 'bout how warm was it? [Do you] remember?
> A: No, I don't.
> Q: Seventies? Eighties?
> A: I don't remember![10]

Arguably, the witness in this situation is caught in a trap by the lawyer's questions about the temperature. If she finally answers, eg, 'seventies' she risks being seen as inconsistent. But, by continuing to say she does not know she may lose credibility, or be perceived as hedging, especially if such responses become commonplace. Having said that the extent to which her credibility is, or is not, damaged may well depend on the evidential importance of the issue on which she hedges.[11]

CONFRONTATION

Confronting the witness can also work well, if the evidence allows it. This may be done directly by, eg, confronting the witness with a document which contradicts her evidence, or by a tag question on some aspect of the testimony. In the right context, it hardly matters if your question receives a denial. The point is that the momentum and style of questioning carries its own impression of the 'truth'. Often, confrontation may be achieved by building up to a trap by a process of insinuation, possibly by encouraging the witness to embellish evidence by fabricating some detail which she thinks she should have known. This technique indicates clearly the importance of your thinking about what a witness should or should not know about an event.

Attacking the character of a witness is risky. Attacks on the character of a prosecution witness leave the defence open to the prosecutor adducing evidence of the accused's bad character (if any). Unless character is at issue, or the defence has already lost its 'shield' protecting the character of the accused,[12] attacks on the character of an accused by the prosecutor are a serious breach of procedure and would normally warrant a re-trial. If character is 'fair game', then use it. Cross-examination on character can leave a very powerful impression.

In pursuing these strategies, you need to think carefully about the style of questioning you adopt. As a general guide, you should:[13]
- rely heavily on closed and leading questions;
- prevent the witness from qualifying her answers in a way that limits the impact of your question;[14]
- adopt a fairly fast pace of questioning, which can force the witness into hurrying her evidence;
- never misquote the witness's evidence in chief – this will do your credibility no good;
- listen carefully to the answers you get – be prepared to change your line of questioning, or to ask supplementary questions where necessary;
- resist the temptation to ask one question too many – only television advocates always get to deliver the one question that totally demolishes the witness.

Style of delivery is another factor. As a rule, ask your questions politely and confidently. In certain circumstances, do you think there is any place for lawyers to display anger in a trial? We certainly get used to media images of counsel haranguing a reluctant witness. Is that appropriate behaviour, do you think?

1   Whether or not such vivid descriptions are true, they tend to be seen as convincing – a view shared by advocacy texts and psychologists – see eg E Loftus & J Goodman 'Questioning

Witnesses' in Kassin & Wrightsman (eds) *The Psychology of Evidence and Trial Procedure*, Sage, Beverley Hills 1985, pp 265–6; M Stone *Proof of Fact in Criminal Trials*, W Green & Son, Edinburgh 1984, pp 181–5.

2   This is taken from Wilde's action against Lord Queensberry in 1895, for the alleged criminal libel of calling Wilde a 'sodomite'.

3   The direct evidence was never adduced in this trial; the threat was sufficient for Wilde, on legal advice, to withdraw the action. It did come out in the later prosecutions of Wilde himself for indecency.

4   Adapted from H Montgomery Hyde (ed) *Famous Trials 7: Oscar Wilde*, Penguin Books, Harmondsworth 1962, pp 109–10.

5   M Fido & K Skinner *The Peasenhall Murder*, Alan Sutton, Stroud 1990, p 105.

6   Op cit, p 61.

7   For example, where you might ask, 'Could you describe the colour of the defendant's coat?' knowing full well the defendant was not wearing one at the time. Unless the witness spots the trap and answers accordingly, you have got them – even the answer 'No' is potentially damaging to a question of this sort.

8   E Loftus 'Language and memories in the judicial system' in R Shuy & A Shnukal (eds) *Language Use and the Uses of Language*, Georgetown University Press, Washington 1980, p 257.

9   For an example of this kind of cross-examination in action, see Rock *The Social World of an English Crown Court*, Clarendon Press, Oxford 1993, pp 104–8.

10   E Loftus & J Goodman, op cit, at p 275.

11   Ibid, pp 275–6.

12   See Criminal Evidence Act 1898, s 1(f) and Murphy & Barnard *Evidence & Advocacy*, 4th Edition, Blackstone Press, London 1994, pp 93–100.

13   Many of these points are repeated as folk wisdom in the advocacy manuals: however, there is a certain amount of psychological support as well – see Loftus & Goodman, op cit.

14   This is best achieved by a focused style of questioning, rather than asking the witness, in true movie style, to 'please confine yourself to answering my question', which can come across as discourteous.

Exercise 10.23   Anger

For this exercise, follow your tutor's instructions.

Generally, haranguing a witness may lose you the support of judge and/or jury, and the court is no place for 'genuine' anger to be displayed by the lawyers involved. This does not mean that some simulated anger cannot be directed at the situation or even a particular witness. As one practitioner explains:

> The amount of acting you do is almost directly proportional to how much is required. A lot of cases are very laid-back and there is no acting involved at all. A fraud case, for example, which is just document after document. Apart from some humour, to keep the thing alive, there is no acting. But if you have police officers who are accused of lying or civilians who are accused of lying or bad conduct, an element of artificial heat is generated by counsel in parts of cross-examination. Not all of it. But those parts that it's important to emphasise or to express the rage of your client's case. But its simulated rage, or ought to be.[1]

The principle most commonly expressed is, reserve such tactics for those few witnesses who deserve it. If a witness is obviously messing you about, you can go into the attack and still seem a perfectly reasonable character. If you have an aggressive witness, stay calm: the last thing you want is for cross-examination to degenerate into a slanging match.

1   From Rock, op cit, p 56.

Summary

ALWAYS START BY ASKING, WHY CROSS-EXAMINE?
WHEN CROSS-EXAMINING:
− KEEP IN CONTROL OF THE WITNESS.
− ALWAYS PUT YOUR CASE.
− LOOK FOR POINTS OF AGREEMENT WITH YOUR CASE.
− FOCUS ON THEIR WEAKEST POINT.
− KEEP CALM.
− RESIST THE ONE QUESTION TOO MANY.

Exercise 10.24   Driven to distraction?[1]

This exercise may be run in pairs or as a demonstration. Each performance requires one lawyer and one witness (Forsythe). The basic facts are as follows, though 'Forsythe' may need to be prepared to invent some explanations for the testimony given in chief:

James/Jane Forsythe is being prosecuted on a charge of dangerous driving. S/he has given sworn evidence that s/he has been driving for 10 years and has never had a conviction. In fact s/he has held a licence for eight years (s/he is 26 years old) and has had convictions in 1989, 1990 and 1991, all in the Oakleigh Magistrates' Court, for speeding, driving with excess alcohol and driving without due consideration for other road users.

(a)   Cross-examine Mr/Ms Forsythe.
(b)   Feedback as usual.

1   Adapted from Leo Cussen Institute 'Introduction to advocacy' in N Gold, K Mackie & W Twining *Learning Lawyers' Skills*, Butterworths, London & Edinburgh 1989, p 255 at p 301.

Re-examination

The skills involved in re-examination are not very different from those involved in examining in chief. For that reason we will deal with this phase of the trial very briefly.

The purpose of re-examination is to give the advocate an opportunity to repair damage caused in cross-examination. The basic principle to remember about re-examining is: don't do it unless you have to! At its worst re-examination is merely a damage limitation exercise, and will be seen as such. It can be better not to admit that the damage has been done in the first place!

Evans[1] suggests that re-examination should only be undertaken with at least one of three aims in mind:

CLARIFICATION & CLEARING UP

Cross-examination may only have elicited a partial answer. Often it will have got the answer the cross-examiner wants, but not the explanation that you want. Re-examination, therefore, can be used to clarify the standpoint or position of your witness, or to try and clear up any muddled testimony created by the cross-examination.

CRUCIFIXION

This term (Evans's, not ours) describes the very rare situation where the re-examining advocate has knowledge of a piece of testimony (arising out of facts already before the court) that did not emerge either in chief or under cross-examination. Now is the chance to deliver it as the coup de grâce.

TAKING ADVANTAGE OF THE OPEN DOOR

This is rather more common. It describes the situation where, typically, the cross-examiner has inadvertently raised inadmissible evidence, or evidence of character. This evidence thus becomes available to the opponent to raise at re-examination. If you have substantial evidence of good character on your side, this can sometimes be tantamount to being given the verdict on a plate.

So far as tactics are concerned:
● You should not seek to raise fresh evidence by re-examination.[2]
● You should not lead the witness.
● You should keep it short and to the point.

1 *Advocacy at the Bar: A Beginner's Guide*, Blackstone Press, London 1983, pp 169–73.
2 *Prince v Samo* (1838) 7 A & E 627.

Conclusion: advocacy, ethics and adversarialism

In the title of this chapter we suggested that through advocacy we enter the deepest and murkiest area of the legal swamp. We hope that you can now begin to see why we made that suggestion.

At anything above the most basic level, advocacy becomes a highly complex activity, dependent upon your ability to use a matrix of practical skills and technical knowledge. The capacities to think on your feet and to learn quickly from mistakes are central to the art of the advocate.

But advocacy is not just about technical artistry. The courtroom is an important site for both relational and ethical problems. The participatory principles of practice can be difficult to sustain. Clients are easily silenced (as we have seen in this chapter), often by good intentions, such as the desire to protect their legal interests[1]: perhaps sometimes by the simple desire to win the case. Themes and theories may thus be constructed around the client, rather than with her.[2] The adversarialism of the court can also bring into stark relief the ethical problems surrounding 'hired gun' approaches to lawyering.[3] In particular, adversary ethics do not easily admit to the demands of community which are stressed in the revisionist versions of ethics currently being debated (largely) outside the law schools: at least in England, that is. It is these dimensions which also serve to create a 'swampy' environment, and one which ultimately you must learn to negotiate by yourselves.

1   Cf Cunningham 'A Tale of Two Clients' (1989) 87 *Michigan Law Review* 2459.
2   Cf L E White 'Goldberg v Kelly on the Paradox of Lawyering for the Poor' (1990) 56 *Brooklyn Law Review* 861.
3   Cf Chapter 5, above.

Exercise 10.25   Concepts

The procedure for learning these concepts is as follows:

1. *Divide into pairs.*
2. *Each pair is to:*
    (a) define each concept, noting the page(s) on which it is discussed, and under-taking any additional research that is necessary; then
    (b) make sure that you both understand the meaning of each concept.
3. *Combine into groups of four. Compare the answers of the two pairs. If there is disagreement, look up the concept and clarify it. Make sure you are all agreed on the definition and understand it.*

anomie	*corroboration*
freedom of proof	*Matthew effect*
powerful/powerless speech	*proof checklist*
psychological anchor	*putting the case*
rhetoric	*relational discourse*
rule-oriented discourse	*silencing*
story construction	*tag questions*
transitional questions	*verdict definition*
voir dire	

Exercise 10.26   Review questions

1. *Review your experience of advocacy so far. What aspects do you most need to improve? Identify the steps you will take to make those improvements.*
2. *In this chapter we have tried to do two things. We have attempted to present advocacy as it is in the reality of an adversary system, and we have also tried to offer a number of insights that are consistent with the participatory approach to lawyering that has informed the rest of this book. Do you consider:*
    (a) that there is a contradiction between the zealous advocacy traditionally implicit in the adversary system and a client-centred approach to lawyering? If so, why; if not, why not?
    (b) If there is a contradiction, how might you resolve it?

Appendix: Additional documentation for skills exercises

Index to appendix

The Appendix contains additional documentation for the following exercises:

Chapter 2

Exercise 2.1

There are three people working in the office. Two are non-smokers, the third, Paul, smokes about 30 cigarettes a day. The office is small and poorly ventilated. Opening the window makes the office very cold most of the year round.

The two non-smokers have come to you to complain about the third person smoking in the office. They find it unbearable and want something done about it. The company will not go to the expense of installing an extractor fan, and in fact it has recently become company policy to ban smoking in all the buildings. The ban is to become effective in the next six months. The three workers cannot be separated, because they work very closely as a team. In any case, there is very little alternative space available.

You have decided to have a word with Paul to see what can be done.

You are one of three people working in your office. The other two don't smoke. (Roger gave up smoking six months ago, and Maxine has never smoked.) You have smoked 30 a day for years, and have no intention of stopping.

Your office is small and poorly ventilated. Opening the window makes the room very cold most of the year round.

The company's new policy on smoking has made you very angry indeed. You've smoked for many years, and consider this recent ruling to be an infringement of your rights. They won't stop you smoking; if necessary you will spend all day in the toilet.

You sometimes get the feeling that Roger and Maxine dislike your habit, but they haven't actually said anything to you. Anyway, they've put up with it now for so long, they can hardly expect you to change.

You have been told that your boss, Jane/John, wants to have a word with you.

Exercise 2.2

INSTRUCTIONS FOR THE LAWYER – JO(E) EVANS

You have just completed the second year of your law degree. You are working for a firm of solicitors during your summer holidays. For most of the time you are working in the conveyancing department, which consists of a solicitor, Mary Carmichael, and an articled clerk, Jasvir.

Today Mary and Jasvir are at the local university on a conveyancing update course. They will be away from the office all day. It is 3.00 pm. You are sitting in the office checking through some Enquiries Before Contract documents. The telephone rings. It is the firm's receptionist. She says:

'There is a Mr/Ms Cross in the office wanting to see Ms Carmichael immediately.' She adds ominously: 'I think you'd better come down.' The name doesn't ring a bell, and you can't lay your hands on a case file. You go down to the reception area to meet the client with no information, having decided to ask politely how you can help.

INSTRUCTIONS FOR THE CLIENT – MR/MS CROSS

You and your husband/wife are due to complete on a new house in two days time, but have been given no information about how and where the completion is to take place. Ms Carmichael, your solicitor, has told you that she would give you this information a good week before it happens. You have heard nothing, and have phoned the firm seven times but haven't managed to speak to Ms Carmichael, or Jasvir, her articled clerk. You are extremely worried. You don't know what to do about booking a removal firm, or whether to start packing. The buyer of your house is threatening to pull out.

You have decided to go down to the solicitor's office and find out what is going on. By the time you get there you have worked yourself up into a rage. This is made worse when the receptionist tells you neither Ms Carmichael nor Jasvir are available.

The receptionist phones Ms Carmichael's office, and tells you there is someone there, a Mr/Ms Evans, who might be able to help you. She asks Mr/Ms Evans to come down to reception to see you.

By the time you meet Mr/Ms Evans, you are beside yourself with rage, so much so that you shout abuse at him/her and don't allow him/her to get a word in edgeways. Eventually you calm down sufficiently to start to tell the lawyer what you are so upset about. However, your explanation is fairly incoherent, because you are still so angry. You say you will not leave the office until this lawyer (you've been too upset to take in the name) tells you exactly what's going on.

Chapter 3

Exercise 3.8

NOTE A

You are the head of a medical unit responsible for the vaccination programme in a major city. The city is in the grip of an Asian flu epidemic. There is also a shortage of appropriate vaccine.

Your team have compiled a report on the epidemic and the options open to you. The report estimates that 600 people in the city's population are in the highest risk (of mortality) category.

The report offers two programme options affecting the high risk group:
(a) Under the first, 200 people can definitely be saved.
(b) Under the second, there is a one-in-three probability of saving 600 people, but a two-in-three probability that no one will be saved.
Which option do you choose?

NOTE B

You are the head of a medical unit responsible for the vaccination programme in a major city. The city is in the grip of an Asian flu epidemic. There is also a shortage of appropriate vaccine.

Your team have compiled a report on the epidemic and the options open to you. The report estimates that 600 people in the city's population are in the highest risk (of mortality) category.

The report offers two programme options affecting the high risk group:
(a) Under the first, 400 people will definitely die.
(b) Under the second, there is a two-in-three probability that 600 people will die, but a one-in-three probability that no one will die.
Which option do you choose?

Chapter 5

Exercise 5.10

[Materials adapted from Johnson & Johnson *Joining Together: Group Theory and Group Skills*, Prentice-Hall, Englewood Cliffs, NJ 1991, pp 125–6.]

The materials which follow comprise the text of the story to be read out by the co-ordinator. Copies should be available for each of the observers. The parts in italics are the details which observers should check off in accordance with the score sheet printed below the story.

THE STORY

A *farmer* in *western Kansas* put a *tin roof on his barn*. Then a *small tornado blew* the roof off and when the farmer found it *two counties away*, it was *twisted and mangled* beyond repair.

A *friend* advised him that the *Ford Motor Company* would pay him *a good price* for the scrap tin, and the farmer decided he would *ship the roof* up to the company to see *how much he could get for it*. He crated it up in a *very big wooden box* and sent it off to *Dearborn, Michigan*, marking it plainly with his *return address* so that the Ford Company would know where to *send the cheque*.

Twelve weeks passed, and the farmer didn't hear from the Ford Company. Finally, he was just on the *verge of writing to them* to find out what was the matter, *when he received a letter* from them. It said, 'We don't know *what hit your car*, mister, but we'll have it fixed for you by the *fifteenth of next month*.'

SCORE SHEET

Person	Number of details correct	Number of details incorrect	Number of details left out	Maximum number of details
1				20
2				20
3				20
4				20
5				20

Chapter 6

Exercise 6.4/6.9

ROLEPLAY 1

You are Peter/Petra Williamson; you are a licensed taxi driver in Northavon.

Three weeks ago you were involved in a collision between your taxi and a van owned and run by Bristol City Council. You are very hesitant to talk about the accident itself, but as a result your taxi was written off, and you received relatively minor injuries to your legs. These are healing well but still causing discomfort at the site of some stitches and from bruising caused by the accident.

You are presently in receipt of incapacity benefit as you have been declared medically unfit to work; you think the doctor is likely to declare you fit within the next couple of weeks. You are self-employed, and the taxi has been your sole source of income. You are extremely worried. Your insurance company has not yet paid up because, it says, it is still investigating the circumstances of the accident. You are concerned that the Council may try to avoid liability because the van was, at the time, being used by its driver to move furniture to his new house, without the knowledge or authority of his employers.

You want to know the quickest way of getting some money for a replacement vehicle, and don't really care if it comes from your insurers, the Council, or the van driver. Ultimately, you would hope that if your insurers pay up, they would be able to recover the costs from elsewhere, as you don't want to see your premium go 'through the roof'.

If the lawyer questions you directly about the accident:
- The accident occurred when the van turned into your path from a side street. You braked hard, but did not have time to stop, and skidded into the rear corner of the van. You think that the driver could not have looked in your direction.
- Only if you are asked directly about the speed you were travelling should you admit that you were actually doing 45 mph in a 30 mph zone. If you are further pressed, you might admit that the accident happened as it was starting to get dusk. The day was rather overcast, and you were about to put your lights on, but had not yet done so. You drive a black cab.

ROLEPLAY 2

You may use your own name/details or adopt an appropriate identity. You have come to see a solicitor about problems you have been having with a neighbour. You moved into your present house with your wife and a young child about four years ago. Since then you have had another child, who is now about eighteen months old.

The property is mid-terrace, and everything was fine until a young man named Peter Brown moved into the house next door just over a year ago. He seems to lead a very active social life, and has held four long and noisy parties

375

since moving in. You have complained to him about these and, in fact, he has not held a party in the last couple of months. You think this may be because you threatened to inform the local Environmental Health Officer after the last one.

Your other main cause of complaint concerns parking on your street. Peter has a car of his own, and frequently has friends visiting in the evening, as well as a regular girlfriend who often stays overnight or at weekends (you could indicate some disapproval of this, if you wish!); all of these people tend to leave cars parked on your street. This has meant that, particularly as you work shifts, you find it nearly impossible to park in front of your own house. This you feel is highly inconsiderate given the fact that you have a young family to transport around the place. You have also spoken to Peter about this, on numerous occasions, but he has become increasingly unco-operative in his attitude to you.

Things came to a head last Friday morning. As you were about to go into work, you saw that someone had used a sharp implement of some sort to make a long, deep, scratch along the side of your new car. You were convinced that it was Peter, as you had had a lengthy argument with him about the parking situation the night before. You phoned the police, who came round to see the damage. You told them of your suspicions, but the officer seemed to think that there was little they could do in the circumstances, without further evidence. You are annoyed at this because you do not feel that your views were taken sufficiently seriously by the officer.

On Sunday evening you returned home late from a skittles match at a pub in a nearby village. You found Peter's car parked in your space. You parked across the road and, in a fit of temper, took a monkey wrench from the toolbox in your car boot, and smashed the offside rear passenger window of his car. You were startled by the noise it made, and quickly ran indoors. However, you must have been seen by somebody, as the police arrived and asked you various questions. You admitted that you had smashed the window, and have been informed that you are likely to be charged with criminal damage.

You feel rather ashamed at what you have done, but also angry that Peter has 'got away with it' while you have been caught. You want advice about the criminal charge, but also would like to know if there is some legitimate grounds for complaint about Peter's 'harassment' of you and your family. In fact, what you are really after is some means of getting even with him.

ROLEPLAY 3

[This is an amended version of a roleplay developed by Mary Holmes & Judith Maxwell: see 'Communication Skills for Lawyers: A Teaching Programme' in Gold, Mackie & Twining *Learning Lawyers' Skills*, Butterworths, London 1988, pp 40–1.]

You can be either yourself or adopt an appropriate identity.

You are an undergraduate reading English at University. You live in Bristol, with your parents. You do not receive a maintenance grant, but get an allowance from your parents, which you supplement with part-time work.

Three nights ago you were working behind the bar in one of the local night-clubs. At about 1.30 am there was a police raid in search of drugs; you believe that the police had been tipped off that one of the bar staff dealt in drugs at the club. You are not aware of anyone who is a regular dealer, but you think that one or two of the bar staff use 'soft' drugs and possibly pass stuff onto friends who come into the club. All the staff were interviewed and were searched. You do not recall being asked to consent to the search. Nothing was found on your person. You were then asked to identify your jacket which had been hanging in the room behind the bar. When you had done so, the police asked you to go down to the station to answer some questions. Not wishing to appear difficult, you agreed.

At the station you were taken into an interview room and informed that a packet of pills – amphetamines – had been found in your jacket pocket. You denied any knowledge of this and said that someone must have planted them to avoid being caught in possession when the police raided the club. You don't think that you were believed, as you were interrogated for the next couple of hours. Before releasing you on police bail they offered not to press charges if you gave then the name of your pusher. You do not have a definite name from the club, and do not know what to do.

Only give the following information if directly asked (use your discretion in assessing how much you say without prompting):

– You have been arrested once before in similar circumstances where you were found in possession of four 'tabs' of 'acid' (LSD). You were charged and convicted of that offence. One of the policemen on this raid recognised you from interviewing you in connection with that earlier event. You still use drugs occasionally, but did not have any on the night you were arrested. You get your own supplies from a close friend at University and have no desire to get him into trouble.

– Your parents were extremely angry when you were convicted last time and threatened to cut off your allowance and throw you out of the house. You take both those threats seriously.

Exercise 6.8

BRIEF 1

You have to find out what your partner in this exercise did last weekend. Your aim is to get as much information as you can. You have five minutes to complete the task.

All your questions *must* begin with one of the following words:

How . . .

What . . .

When . . .

Where . . .

Why . . .

BRIEF 2

You have to find out what your partner in this exercise did last weekend. Your aim is to get as much information as you can. You have five minutes to complete the task.

All your questions *must* begin with one or other of the following words:

Are . . .

Can/Could . . .

Did . . .

Is . . .

Will/Would . . .

OBSERVER BRIEF

Your task is to watch the interaction between the participants. Do not ask questions during the exercise, and do not feed back to the participants in advance of the group discussion.

In observing the participants, listen to the questions that are being used, but also try and pay attention to any non-verbal clues that betray how the participants feel during the exercise.

Be prepared to feed back to the group on the following:
  (i)   Who got the most information?
  (ii) Why did they get more information than the other?
  (iii) Who had to work the hardest for information?
  (iv) Did anyone get frustrated? Why?

Exercise 6.12

[This is adapted from David Cruickshank and Andrew Pirie 'Counselling' in Gold, Mackie & Twining *Learning Lawyers' Skills*, Butterworths, London 1988, p 97.]

CONFIDENTIAL CLIENT INSTRUCTIONS

The purpose of this meeting is for the lawyer to help you decide what to do about the car. Try to get as much information from the lawyer as possible with respect to any solutions that are proposed – including some analysis of risk if possible. Remember that you are a lay person and should assess the clarity of the lawyer's advice accordingly.

In deciding the options open to you, you should be guided by the facts as stated in the text. However, during the first few minutes of the session, you should also raise one or two of the following points (the choice is yours):

(i)   Tell the lawyer that you have had enough and want to sue your friend immediately because you are not prepared to be kept waiting to get *your* property back. You do not particularly care what it will cost to make your point.

(ii) Tell the lawyer that this friend is, in fact, a former lover; that you lent him/her the car on an open-ended basis during your 'affair', and that you suspect s/he is simply keeping the car out of spite at you for break-ing off the relationship. You are somewhat embarrassed to have got into this mess, and would rather it was not made public.

(iii) Tell the lawyer you have had enough of this whole business and just want the lawyer to get on and do what s/he thinks is best.

(iv) Tell the lawyer you are so angry with your friend, that you have talked through the possibility with another friend of arranging that the car is vandalised one night, so that you can then sue the former and 'get even' that way.

(v)   Ask the lawyer for an immediate estimate as to the likely cost of any course of action which s/he proposes.

Exercise 6.13

LAWYER INSTRUCTIONS

You will be told your client's name before the interview commences.

Your client is 45 years old, married with four children. The client runs a small publishing company, employing twelve people, eight men and four women. S/he has got to cut costs, and this means four staff have got to be made redundant. Three have agreed to take early retirement. Your client has selected the fourth, Tania, ostensibly on the basis that she is the newest employee. However, your client has also admitted that Tania has become a bit of a trouble-maker, and this influenced his/her decision.

When told of the decision Tania threatened to bring proceedings against your client for unfair dismissal and sex discrimination.

The client wants you to help him/her decide how to resolve the problem.

CONFIDENTIAL CLIENT INSTRUCTIONS

You can use your own name or adopt an appropriate identity.

You are 45 years old, married with four children. You run a small publishing company, which produces textbooks on legal skills and practice matters. You employ twelve people, eight men and four women. You promote a friendly working atmosphere and look on all your staff as 'family'. You have never had problems with an employee before and so the company has a good employment relations record. To preserve this 'family' atmosphere, you don't allow your staff to be trade union members.

Because of the recession and heavy competition in the publishing market, you are having to cut costs, and this means four staff have got to be made redundant. Three have agreed to take early retirement, provided you come up with a reasonable package. This is no problem: you are prepared to negotiate a deal with them. Your problem concerns the fourth person you have in mind for redundancy.

Tania, your newest employee, has been working with you for eight months. She is 24 years old, and a single parent with a two-year-old daughter. Her work has always been satisfactory, though she has had quite a lot of time off: because of problems with child-minding, so she says. She leaves the child with her mother most days, but her mother is not always reliable and Tania sometimes has to make other arrangements at very short notice. Tania hasn't quite fitted in with the other staff, and does not respond positively to the co-operative working atmosphere in the company. In fact you regard her as a bit of a trouble-maker. She spreads rumours about other staff, and is a disruptive influence. This is why you have selected her for redundancy.

When you called Tania in to your office to tell her, she threatened to sue you for unfair dismissal and sex discrimination.

You want your lawyer to help you decide how best to handle the situation.

If you are asked, there isn't another employee that you would be willing to make redundant; Tania is the obvious choice. In your view, she is also the fairest choice, on a 'last in, first out' basis.

DO NOT REVEAL UNLESS PRESSED:

1. You do not pay your staff enough for them to afford child care, nor will you allow Tania to work hours that are more suited to her needs, although she has asked you to be flexible on several occasions.

2. The 'rumours about other staff' actually concern you. Tania alleges you took her to the pub one evening after work and propositioned her. Also, that you brush up against her, put your arm round her, cuddle her, etc, whenever you get the chance. Admit that you often go to the pub with staff, and that you have taken Tania there, but make weak excuses about the other allegations.

Chapter 8

Exercise 8.13

Conditions for Telephone Service

There are explanations of some of the words used in these conditions in paragraph 19 and in our Price List.

The Service we promise to provide

1   What the Service is

The Service we (BT) will supply to you (our customer) is the ability to make and receive a Call. The Service does not include any phones or other equipment that we may supply to you under a separate agreement. In providing the Service, we promise to use the reasonable skill and care of a competent telecommunications service provider.

2   Things we may have to do

2.1   We may have to do some things that could affect the Service. These things are listed in paragraph 2.2. If we have to interrupt the Service we will restore it as quickly as we can.

2.2   Occasionally we may have to:

a   Change the code or phone number or the technical specification of the Service for operational reasons;

b   interrupt the Service for operational reasons or because of an emergency;

c   give you instructions that we believe are necessary for health or safety, or for the quality of the Service that we supply to you or to our other customers.

3   Phone number

The phone number for the Service and all rights in that number belong to us. You cannot sell it or agree to transfer it to anyone else and must not try to do so.

4   The Phone Book and Directory Enquiries

4.1   We will put your name, address and the phone number for the Service in The Phone Book for your area and make your phone number available from our Director Enquiries Service, as soon as we can.

However, we will not do so if you ask us not to.

4.2   If you want a special entry in The Phone Book you must let us know. Where we agree to a special entry you must pay an extra charge and sign a separate agreement for that entry.

5   When we will provide the Service

We will provide you with the Service by the date we agree with you. If we do not, you may be able to claim compensation under our Customer Service Guarantee, unless we fail for a reason covered by paragraph 10.

6   Repairing faults

6.1   We cannot guarantee that the Service will never be faulty. However, if we do not put right a failure of the Service within the time limits set out in our Customer Service Guarantee, you may be able to claim compensation under that Guarantee, unless we fail for a reason covered by paragraph 10.

6.2   We will work on any fault that is reported to us according to the repair service we have agreed to provide you. These repair services are explained in our Price List.

6.3   When we agree to work on a fault outside the hours covered by the repair service that we provide to you, you must pay us the extra charge set out in our Price List.

6.4   If you tell us there is a fault in the Service and we find either that there is not or that someone at your premises has caused the fault, we may charge you for any work we have done to try to find the fault or to repair it. Our charges for this are set out in our Price List.

What you agree to do

7   Paying our charges for the Service

7.1   **Charges**

a   You must pay the charges for the Service as set out in our Price List. This applies whether you use the Service or someone else does. We can change the charges as explained at paragraph 13.2.

b   If someone makes a Call without your knowledge, from our side of the main telephone socket, you will not have to pay for the Call, unless we prove that you could have taken reasonable steps to prevent the Call being made.

7.2   Rental

You must pay us rental from the day we supply the Service. We will usually ask you to pay the rental in advance. The rental will depend on how we classify your line. The classifications are explained in our Price List. If we supply you with temporary Service, you may have to pay the rental in advance for the whole period that you want the Service.

7.3   Calculating the Call charges

We will calculate the charges for Calls using the details recorded at our telephone exchange.

7.4   Bills

We will send you your first bill shortly after we provide the Service. We will send you further bills about every 3 months, but we may send you a bill at any time. We will send bills to the address you ask us to.

7.5   Payments in advance and deposits

a   We may ask you for a payment before one is normally due. This will not be more than the connection charge and rental for the Minimum Period of Service.

b   We may ask for a deposit at any time, as security for payment of your bills. Our procedures for deposits are published in our main offices.

7.6   When you must pay

You must pay all charges and rental as soon as you receive your bill, and deposits when we ask for them.

8   Your other responsibilities

8.1   Connecting and using your equipment with our network

a   You may only connect phones, extension wiring, sockets or other equipment to our network using a main telephone socket that we have fitted and maintain, unless we agree otherwise. We may end any such agreement after giving you reasonable notice.

b   Equipment must only be used with our network in a way that meets the relevant standards and your licence. If your equipment does not meet those standards or your licence, you must immediately disconnect it, or allow us to do so at your expense. If you ask us to test your equipment to make sure that it meets those standards or your licence, you must pay us the charge set out in our Price List.

8.2   Supplying a place and electricity for our equipment

We will have to place equipment on your premises to provide you with the Service. For residential customers this will normally be just a main telephone socket. You must provide a suitable place and conditions for our equipment. If we have to supply equipment that needs a continuous mains electricity supply and connection points, you must provide them where we need them at your own expense.

8.3   Preparing your premises

You must prepare your premises before we arrive according to any instructions that we give you. When our work is completed, you will also be responsible for putting items back and for doing any necessary re-decorating.

8.4   Entry to your premises

a   If our engineers have to enter your premises you must let them do so as long as they show their BT Identity Card. We will meet your reasonable requirements about the safety of people on your premises and you must do the same for us.

b   If we need someone else's permission to cross or put our equipment on their premises, you must get that agreement for us and make any necessary arrangements.

8.5   Damage

Nobody must tamper with our equipment that is on your premises. If anyone does and there is any damage to or loss of our equipment, you must pay the charge in our Price List for any necessary repair or replacement.

8.6   Misuse of the service

Nobody must use the Service:

a   to make offensive, indecent, menacing, nuisance or hoax Calls;

b   fraudulently or in connection with a criminal offence;

and you must make sure that this does not happen. The action we can take if this happens is explained at paragraph 11.1 and 11.2.

8.7 Indemnity

You must indemnify us against all claims that anyone other than you threatens or makes against us because of the way the Service is used or because the Service is faulty or cannot be used.

If things go wrong

9 If we break this agreement

9.1 We accept liability for being late in providing the Service, or repairing a failure of the Service, or for failing to keep an appointment, unless for a reason covered by paragraph 10. However, our liability is limited as set out in the Customer Service Guarantee and in this paragraph 9.

9.2 We accept liability if you are injured or die as a result of our negligence. We do not limit that liability and paragraphs 9.3 and 9.4 do not apply to that liability.

9.3 Unless the Customer Service Guarantee says otherwise, we have no liability under this agreement or for our negligence or otherwise:

a   for a failure in provision of the Service or the Service itself; or

b   for any indirect loss, loss of business, revenue, profit, or savings you expected to make, wasted expense, financial loss or data being lost or harmed.

9.4 Any liability we have of any sort, (including any liability because of our negligence), is limited to £1 million for any one event or any series of related events, and in any 12 month period to £2 million in total.

9.5 Each part of this agreement that excludes or limits our liability operates separately. If any part is disallowed or is not effective, the other parts will continue to apply.

10 Matters beyond our reasonable control

If we cannot do what we have promised in this agreement because of something beyond our reasonable control such as lightning, flood, or exceptionally severe weather, fire or explosion, civil disorder, war, or military operations, national or local emergency, anything done by government or other competent authority or industrial disputes of any kind (including those involving our employees), we will not be liable for this. However, we will refund a day's rental to you for any day, or part day, that there is a failure of the Service because of something beyond our reasonable control.

11 If you break this agreement

11.1 In addition to anything else we can do, we can suspend the Service or end the agreement (or both) at any time without telling you if:

a   you break this agreement or any other agreement you have with us for telephone, telex or private service;

b   we believe that the Service is being used in a way forbidden by paragraph 8.6. This applies even if you do not know that the Calls are being made or the Service is being used in such a way;

c   bankruptcy or insolvency proceedings are brought against you, or if you do not make any payment under a judgment of a Court on time, or, you make an arrangement with your creditors, or a receiver or administrator is appointed over any of your assets, or you go into liquidation.

11.2 If we suspend the Service, we will not provide it again until you do what you have agreed, or satisfy us that you will do so in future or that the Service will not be used in a way that is forbidden by paragraph 8.6.

11.3 If you miss a payment, we will not suspend the Service or end the agreement until 28 days after the payment was due. However if we suspend the Service and you miss another payment during the 12 months after we provide the Service again, we may then suspend the Service or end the agreement (or both) 14 days after the payment was due.

11.4 If we suspend the Service because you break this agreement, the agreement will still continue. You must pay us rental until we end the agreement by giving notice under paragraph 11.1 or you or we end the agreement by giving notice under paragraph 16.1.

12 Arbitration

If we cannot resolve any dispute with you, you can refer the dispute to the Chartered Institute of Arbitrators under our simple procedure. This does not apply to disputes that involve more than £5,000 or a complicated issue of law. Details of how to refer a dispute to arbitration are set out in our Code of Practice for Consumers.

Changing and ending the agreement

13 Changing the agreement

13.1 In general
If you ask us to make any change to the Service we may ask you to confirm your request in writing. If we agree to a change, this agreement will be changed when we confirm the change to you in writing.

13.2 Conditions
We can change the conditions of this agreement including our charges at any time. We will publish any change in our main offices at least 2 weeks before it takes place and we will inform you with your next bill if there has been a change to our liability.

14 Transferring the agreement

You cannot transfer or try to transfer this agreement or any part of it to anyone else.

15 Cancelling the Service before it is provided

You may cancel the Service or any part at any time before we have provided it. You must pay us for any work we have done and money we have spent in getting ready to provide the Service.

16 Ending the agreement after the Service is provided

16.1 This agreement, or the supply of the Service, can be ended by:

a   1 month's notice from us to you; or

b   7 days' notice from you to us.

16.2 If we give you notice, you must pay rental up to the end of that notice. If you give us notice, you must pay rental until 7 days from the date we receive your notice, or until the end of the notice if that is later.

16.3 If you give us notice that ends during the Minimum Period of Service, you must pay us an amount equal to the rental for the rest of the Minimum Period. We will work this out using the rental that is current when this agreement ends.

16.4 If you have paid any rental for a period after the end of the agreement, we will either repay it or put it towards any money you owe us.

16.5 You must pay all charges for the Service until the date on which we stop providing the Service to you.

16.6 We can end this agreement at any time without telling you, if paragraph 11.1 applies.

The other things we need to tell you

17 How to give notice

Any notice given under this agreement must be delivered by hand or sent by telex or prepaid post as follows:

a   to us at the address shown on the Telephone Service Agreement form or on your last bill, or at any other address we give you;

b   to you at the address you have asked us to send bills to.

18 Other documents

18.1 These conditions, the documents referred to in them, the Customer Service Guarantee and the Telephone Service Agreement form set out the whole agreement between you and us for the Service.

18.2 Our Price List contains explanations, definitions, notes and conditions which form part of this agreement. You can see a copy of our Price List or obtain copies of the relevant pages at any of our main offices.

19 Explanations of certain words

"Call"
means a signal, message or communication which is silent, spoken or visual on each line that we agree to provide to you under this agreement.

"Customer Service Guarantee"
The details of this appear on the back of the Telephone Service Agreement Form.

"your equipment"
means equipment that is not part of our network and which you use or intend to use with the Service.

"failure of the Service"
means the continuous total loss of the ability to make or receive Calls or the continuous total loss of a related service.

"your licence"
means the Licence (granted under Section 7 of the Telecommunications Act 1984), that authorises you to run your telecommunications network.

Appendix

"your line"
means a connection to our network.

"main telephone socket"
means the point where your equipment is connected to our network which is called the Network Termination Point in your licence.

"Minimum Period of Service"
means the first 12 months of the Service or the period set out in our Price List.

"our network"
means BT's public switched telecommunications network.

"your premises"
means the place where the Service is or will be provided.

"relevant standards"
means the standards designated under section 22 of the Telecommunications Act 1984.

"the Service"
means the Service explained in paragraph 1 and includes any related services listed in our Price List that we agree to provide to you under this agreement.

"we and us"
means British Telecommunications plc (BT).

"working day"
means Monday to Friday not including Public Holidays.

"you"
means the customer we make this agreement with. It includes a person who we reasonably believe is acting with the customer's authority or knowledge.

Chapter 9

Exercise 9.4

NEGOTIATION PROFILES

CASE 1

Pam and Wilf

Pam Butler is 53 years old. She was married once and has three children who all live and work abroad. Pam works for the Gripeton Health Care Trust as a health visitor.

About ten years ago Pam inherited 9 Woodbridge Way under her mother's will. She lets the property out as three small flats. 9a is let to Wilf Ryan, a student at Gripeton University. He has lived there for three years. 9b is let to Mr and Mrs Glover, an elderly couple. They have rented the flat for 15 years. James Nott, a bank manager, has recently taken the tenancy on 9c. He stays there during the week and returns to his house in the country every weekend.

Pam makes a point of being on good terms with her tenants. She gets problems sorted out quickly and keeps the flats in good repair. She has never had a serious complaint from any of her tenants and often pops in for a cup of tea or a glass of wine with Wilf or the Glovers.

During the last year Pam has started to get back trouble. She has seen a specialist several times, but no clear diagnosis has been made. She has been told to rest as much as possible. Her GP prescribes her pain killers, but these make her dizzy. She gets some relief from acupuncture once a week, but the treatment is expensive, and she is not sure she can afford to continue with it much longer.

Pam is worried that she is taking too much time off work because of her back, and she is afraid she may have to think of giving up her job if it doesn't improve in the next six months or so. She doesn't know how she will manage financially if she has to do this, because she has no other sources of income apart from her salary and rent from Woodbridge Way.

Wilf and Pam

Wilf Ryan is 22 years old and is studying English at Gripeton University. He is taking his final exams in two months' time. He is expected to get a first class degree.

Wilf gets a grant from his local authority, topped up by his parents. He has rented 9a Woodbridge Way at a reasonable rent for the last three years. He gets on well with Pam Butler, his landlady, and she often calls round for a drink and a chat. He is very friendly with the tenants of the other flats.

Lately, Wilf has got into debt. He has a part time job working in a wine bar four nights a week, but hasn't been able to make ends meet since his girlfriend, Maria, lost her job. For the last seven months he has been helping to support her financially while she searches for work. Wilf's parents have lent him £1,000 to pay some bills but they can't afford to lend him any more. Wilf hasn't told them how big the debt is (he currently owes about £2,500), or that he is helping to support Maria. His parents don't like Maria very much.

Wilf is naturally under a great deal of pressure, and has asked Pam to let him stay in the flat until his exams are over. She told him she would think it over, but that she is pretty desperate for money. Wilf is so worried that he is finding it increasingly difficult to concentrate on his revision. He was hoping to enrol on a journalism course next academic year, but instead has agreed to take a full-time job in a Gripeton betting shop as soon as he has finished his exams.

CASE 2

Frances and her Employer

Frances Jackson recently graduated with a first class degree from Cambridge University. She was offered several posts and decided to accept one with a well-known firm in the City of London. Rajeev, her partner, was quite upset when she decided to accept the job. They had been living together for three years in Cambridge. Rajeev has a steady job and was not prepared to give it up to go and live in London. Also, living with someone who he thought was turning into a 'hard-nosed career woman' did not appeal to him. Their arguments became more and more heated. They decided to split up. Frances moved to London.

When she found she was pregnant, Frances wasted no time in making up her mind what to do. She told her employer immediately that she wanted to keep the job and the baby, and she asked if the firm would give her three months' unpaid leave while she had the baby.

Frances was surprised and very upset when her employer terminated her contract. Although she had only been with the firm for a short time, she knew she was highly thought of, and that her work could not be faulted. She had been led to believe, at the job interview and since, that she had an excellent future ahead of her with the firm. She feels humiliated at 'such shoddy and hypocritical treatment', especially in the light of what she has already given up to pursue her career.

The Employer and Frances

The partners of Midge, Wasp and Hornett were delighted when Frances accepted their job offer. In fact, they were so impressed with her at the interview that they raised the already generous salary by 10% in an attempt to persuade her to accept the job.

However, they were all deeply shocked when she told them she was pregnant. At their meeting next day the shock turned to anger and disappointment. One partner said: 'She's so young. How could she do such a stupid thing? Why isn't she on the pill?'

'She's really let us down,' said another. 'Nobody has had the nerve to do this to us before, after only a couple of months. It's quite unacceptable. We'd have been spared all this trouble if we'd appointed that young man Brian instead.'

'You have to commit yourself body and soul if you want to work here, especially at first,' they told Frances. 'After you've finished training and have got a few years behind you, that's the time to think about starting a family. We're sorry, but we're going to have to let you go. We're prepared to give you two months' salary in lieu of notice if you want to leave now.'

The partners are anxious that the matter does not reflect badly on the firm's reputation. They have already been contacted by William Wobbegong, a reporter with the *Financial World*, and asked to comment on allegations of discrimination.

CASE 3

Bob and Carol Powell

Bob is 35 years old. He has an interesting and well-paid job and is often away from home. He would be happier if he weren't away so much, but his boss has told him that working abroad is essential if he wants promotion in the next couple of years. At least if he were promoted, he would then be based near home.

When he was home, Bob was often too tired to help much around the house or with the children. He suggested to Carol on several occasions that they employ a live-in nanny, so that he and Carol could get out more, or even go away together for a weekend now and then. She would also get more time to indulge her painting hobby. However, Carol never seemed keen to have someone else living with them, and said she would rather they did things together as a family.

Bob and Carol hadn't been out together for several months. In the evenings Bob would usually fall asleep in front of the TV. Carol would go out with friends quite often. Their sex life had been virtually non-existent for the past two years.

Bob thought their marriage was going through a bad patch, but that things would improve when he got his promotion and could be home more. In the ten years of their marriage he has never slept with anyone else or even been tempted to do so. However, since he split up with Carol, he has been spending a lot of time with a work colleague, Joanne. Joanne has recently been through a painful divorce and has been very supportive. Bob now finds he is becoming attracted to her.

When Bob found out about Carol's affair he felt disgusted, humiliated and embarrassed because the 'other man' was another woman. Everyone in the village was gossiping about it. The children are very unhappy away from their mother, and this distresses Bob, but he won't let them see her as long as she continues this affair. He has employed a nanny to look after the children when he is away.

Carol and Bob

Carol felt frustrated and miserable for the last six years of the marriage. She felt stuck at home. Bob was too wrapped up in his work and the prospect of promotion to devote much time to the family. Since she had the children, she has had no chance to pursue her career as an artist, and although she had discussed this with Bob over and over again, he never took the idea of her having a career seriously.

Carol was offered several teaching jobs over the last few years, but always considered teaching a waste of her talent. She hopes that when the financial arrangements are made after the divorce she will be able to afford to move into the city and become involved in the exhibition scene once more.

Carol never wanted to employ someone to look after the children because she thought Bob would come home even less often if the burden of child care was lifted from her. She was sure he often had affairs with other women whilst away from home, and was afraid that one day he would stop coming home altogether. She never talked to him about these fears, because he never seemed interested in talking. She felt sure he no longer loved her, because he rarely seemed interested in sex these days.

Carol got involved with Rachel at first because she was bored. She never intended things to go as far as moving in with her. In fact their affair is over, and both of them want Carol to move out as soon as possible. Most of Carol's friends think she has behaved so badly to Bob that they are not talking to her. She could go and stay with her parents, but they live 50 miles away, and Carol wants to stay as near the children as possible in case Bob changes his mind and lets her see them.

Carol would like to try again with Bob, but is prepared to accept that he is too hurt to take her back. More importantly, she wants the children back. She has heard from Marilyn, a friend of Bob's nanny, that her eight-year-old son has been having nightmares since she left home. According to Marilyn, the nanny thinks all the children should be back with their mother as soon as possible.

CASE 4

Randall, Cliff and the Chairman

Randall Dolph is the darling of the media. He is always ready to talk to the press and his numerous emotional entanglements with high-profile women fill the gossip columns. He has been captain of Melton FC for the last two years, a year after his transfer from Gripeton Wanderers. This season Melton was promoted to the Premier League and is now third in the League table. It is generally accepted in the game that the team's recent success is in large measure due to Randall's exceptional talent as a midfielder and his ability to inspire his team-mates. Randall is very popular with everybody – except Nobby Chandler, the Club Chairman.

Nobody at the club can understand why Nobby is so hostile to his successful captain, so they put it down to Randall's tendency to shoot his mouth off without much forethought in the tabloid press. However, Randall knows it is racism. He hasn't said anything to anyone about it, even Cliff, his best friend. He either ignores Nobby whenever they meet, or provokes him into an argument. These arguments often end as heated exchanges in which Randall's aim is to expose Nobby's lack of knowledge about the game.

At the time, Randall wasn't sorry that his remark got reported, but now he regrets it. However, he could not bear the humiliation of having to make a grovelling public apology to someone he despises so much. He has told Cliff he would rather transfer to another club than do that. In fact this is the last thing he would ever want to do.

Cliff, Randall and the Chairman

Cliff Ferguson has managed Melton for the last two years. When he came from Gripeton Wanderers he brought Randall Dolph with him, and the two are close friends.

Cliff can't put his finger on why Randall and the Club Chairman not only don't get on, but seem to go out of their way to upset each other. Nobby Chandler, the Chairman, is usually friendly and sociable with everyone, but is hostile and sarcastic with Randall. Cliff thinks Nobby must be jealous of Randall. He has tried to discuss it with Randall, but he won't talk about it.

Cliff has enjoyed a good relationship with his Chairman until now. Nobby has been happy to leave Cliff in charge and has not interfered in any management decisions. This is the first time he has given Cliff an instruction.

Cliff is at a loss to know what to do. He feels completely out of his depth in this dispute. He has tried to reason with Nobby, but to no avail. Randall absolutely refuses to apologise to Nobby and has threatened to leave the club.

The Chairman, Cliff and Randall

Nobby Chandler has achieved his life's ambition – to own a Premier League football club. He achieved it five years ago when he bought Melton FC. During the five years he has put millions into the club and has seen it change from an ordinary first division team to a well-drilled machine full of talent and imaginative, attacking football. It is his money that has achieved this.

When he appointed Cliff as manager, it was a stroke of genius. Cliff has turned the side round, and it is now challenging for top honours. He had reluctantly agreed to Cliff's wish to bring in Randall, in spite of Randall's reputation. Randall had also been a success, up to a point. You couldn't fault his football, but he was a bit of a loose cannon with the press. This latest, personal attack couldn't be allowed to go by without some retaliation. Some things are more important than football.

It has also been obvious for some time that some of the older, back-room staff at the club don't like having a black man as team captain. It seems to go against the traditions of the club, somehow. Nobby sympathises with this view.

This last outburst was the final straw. It would be in everybody's best interests to get rid of Dolph, cup final or no cup final. He would command a top price, so they could replace him with another top signing. The fans would kick up for a while, but they'd soon come round with a new signing to get behind.

As for this ludicrous strike, the players would soon come round when they realised how much money they were going to lose by their refusal to play. Not only that, but with Dolph gone, the captaincy would be up for grabs.

CASE 5

John and Maxine

John Rose is a 28-year-old building surveyor. He has recently accepted a job in Sydney, Australia, where he will be earning a good deal more than his present £26,000 a year. He is due to start the job in two months' time.

John was on his way to work on 20 May 1994 when he was knocked off his bike by Maxine Krantz. His left kneecap was fractured; it was set in plaster, and John had to have six weeks off work, during which time he received Statutory Sick Pay. The leg continues to be stiff, and John still attends a fracture clinic. He also hit his head in the accident, and suffers with severe headaches every now and then. He never had headaches before the accident.

John's bike was also damaged in the accident, and cost £55 to repair. His damaged clothes and shoes would probably cost about £70 to replace.

John used to cycle to work most days, and is quite sure that the accident was Ms Krantz's fault. She was driving too fast to stop, and so pulled out to overtake him in a street lined with parked cars where there was not enough room to pass.

You estimate John could claim general damages in the region of £7,000–£10,000, plus special damages for loss of past earnings and property damage.

John is a bit worried that he might run into Ms Krantz socially. She is a property developer and an important client of his partner, Rita Stern. Rita is the managing partner of a small firm of architects which has been given a large amount of work by Maxine Krantz. Ms Krantz doesn't know of the connection, but John is afraid he might meet her at one of the social events put on by Rita's firm for its major clients.

Maxine and John

Maxine Krantz is a 43-year-old property developer. On 20 May 1994 she was involved in an accident with a cyclist, John Rose. She was on her way to an important meeting and was anxious not to be late. She drove slowly behind Mr Rose for some metres, not able to overtake because the street was lined on both sides with parked vehicles. She noticed he was riding erratically, wobbling all over the road. Then she saw a large space on the left which would give her room to overtake. Mr Rose rode into the space, but as she began to pass him, he pulled out in front of her, so that she could not avoid hitting him.

She panicked at this point and so didn't stop to check whether the cyclist was hurt. She did see one or two people in the street, and saw one woman run over to Mr Rose. She therefore assumed he would be looked after and taken to hospital if necessary.

Maxine has heard from Mr Rose's solicitors that he is making a claim against her for compensation in the region of £13,500, £10,000 of which is general damages. She does not intend to pay him anything as she is convinced the accident was his fault.

Your firm has been instructed by Maxine's insurance company to deal with the matter on their behalf.

Chapter 10

Exercise 10.16

You are Jenny Lee. You are to be called as a prosecution witness against Wainwright. You are an articulate young woman, but rather quiet, and nervous about testifying.

Your testimony should be based on the following proof of evidence, though you may need to ad lib as well.

STATEMENT OF JENNY LEE

My name is Jenny Lee. I attend the University of Mercia, where I am on the final year of a Business Studies degree. I am 20 years old. On Saturday xx February 199X, I went out with some friends to the Bierkeller in Newtown. There were four of us in total including my boyfriend David Simms, Maria da Costa, and Terry Kline: they are also on the same course as me at the University. It was David's birthday and we were planning a bit of a celebration. We arrived at the Bierkeller at about 7.00 pm and stayed there until closing time. We all had rather too much to drink, and were a bit loud. Terry tends to get belligerent – a bit mouthy – when he has had a few. He does it just to wind people up.

Terry was supposed to be driving us home after the bar closed, but he was too drunk, so we decided to try and find a taxi, as the last bus to our end of town had already gone. We waited for ages at the taxi rank. There were a lot of other people wanting taxis, and there did not seem to be many around that night. We were near the back of the queue, and Terry was getting really impatient.

It must have been well gone midnight when our turn finally came. We all got into the cab, and it drove off. Just after we set off, Terry started generally fooling around – telling some really blue jokes, and then singing loudly. Dave started to join in, when the taxi pulled into the kerb. We were near Sixways, so still more than a mile from home. The driver got out, opened the rear door of the cab and told Terry and David to get out. I can't remember exactly what he said, something about bloody students getting drunk and throwing up in his cab. He said he would take Maria and me home, but not the boys. Terry got pretty angry at this and started shouting at the driver. Terry is tall (about six foot), quite heavily built, and can look pretty nasty when he is angry, though he would never hurt anyone. The taxi driver was nearly as tall and did not act as if he was going to be intimidated. The driver started shouting back and told the boys to 'piss off'. He turned to get back into the car, and I think Terry must have gone to grab him, I do not think he tried to hit the driver – even when he is drunk I do not think he would have turned violent. The driver turned round quickly and punched Terry right in the face. It happened really fast, but I am sure it was only the one punch. Terry just dropped like a stone. I was standing on the pavement at the time and could see what happened really clearly. David and I were trying to help Terry up. He was dazed, and his nose was in a mess, there was blood all over the place.

While we were trying to sort Terry out, Maria must have got out the taxi, because the driver just drove off. David went off and found a phone box and called for an ambulance. When it arrived we went with Terry to the hospital, and then, after he had been patched up, we got another taxi home. We all share a house in Southville, about three and a half miles from the city centre. Maria had got the taxi driver's licence number. Having talked to Terry the next day, we agreed that we ought to contact the police, which we did. We went to Southville police station where the police took statements from all of us. That is really all I can tell you.

Index